WOMEN TODAY:
A MULTIDISCIPLINARY
APPROACH
TO WOMEN'S STUDIES

WOMEN TODAY: A MULTIDISCIPLINARY APPROACH TO WOMEN'S STUDIES

Mary Anne Baker
Catherine White Berheide
Fay Ross Greckel
Linda Carstarphen Gugin
Indiana University Southeast

Marcia J. Lipetz
American Judicature Society

Marcia Texler Segal
Indiana University Southeast

BROOKS/COLE PUBLISHING COMPANY
Monterey, California

A Division of Wadsworth, Inc.

Printed in the United States of America

10 9 8 7 6 5 4 3 2 1

Library of Congress Cataloging in Publication Data

Main entry under title:

Women today.

    Bibliographies at ends of sections.
    Includes index.
      1. Women's studies—United States—Addresses, essays, lectures.   2. Feminism—United States —Addresses, essays, lectures.   I. Baker, Mary Anne.
HQ1181.U5W62   301.41'2'0973   79-11834
ISBN 0-8185-0341-6

Acquisition Editor: *Todd Lueders*
Manuscript Editor: *Margaret C. Tropp*
Production Editor: *Marilu Uland*
Interior Design: *Ruth Scott*
Cover Design: *Susan Moffett Matthias*
Typesetting: *Graphic Typesetting Service, Los Angeles, California*

PREFACE

This multidisciplinary text focuses primarily on women in the United States within the last 20 to 30 years. It is designed to be used as a basic text for courses on women's studies at any level. We have tried to guide the reader to instances where the literature of each discipline bears on the others, and we have tried to place both our society and our time in historical and cultural context. Students, with the help of their instructors, may wish to integrate more fully the findings of the several disciplines on particular topics such as working women, participation of women in the political process, or implications of research on sex roles for educational policy. In addition, students and instructors may want to consider the range of situations and issues to which the information can be applied.

We have been aided by a number of people in developing this book. In particular, we wish to thank Linda Albright for all her help, Todd Lueders and Bonnie Fitzwater for their help and encouragement throughout, Sandra Hack for typing the complete manuscript, Indiana University for financial support, Carol Stevens for her editorial assistance, and the students who have read and commented on the manuscript. We are grateful to Elizabeth Almquist of North Texas State University, Roslyn Feldberg of Boston University, Suzanne Kurth of the University of Tennessee, Barbara Pope of the University of Oregon, Nancy Porter of Portland State University, Molly Rosenhan of Stanford University, and Juanita Williams of the University of Southern Florida, all of whom reviewed the manuscript. In addition, we wish to thank Joyce Ebling, Virginia Minshall, Kathleen Quinkert, Janet Rorapaugh, Colleen Sheehan, Anne Thomas, and Nancy Totten.

Mary Anne Baker
Catherine White Berheide
Fay Ross Greckel
Linda Carstarphen Gugin
Marcia J. Lipetz
Marcia Texler Segal

CONTENTS

INTRODUCTION

There is no spectacle on earth more appealing than that of a beautiful woman in the act of cooking dinner for someone she loves.[1]

Maybe it'll sound silly to you, but I still belong to the Business and Professional Women's Club here. When I get dressed up to go to one of their meetings, it's the only time I feel like a whole individual. I'm not somebody's wife, or somebody's mother. I'm just Karen. I suppose that's why I liked working, too. When I'd be there, I could just be who I am—I mean who I am inside me not just all those other things.[2]

Years ago, my mother was in the office while I was giving some directives to one of my male managers. When I finished, Mom apologized to him. She said: "Don't pay any attention to Dotty. She was always bossy!"[3]

If you had an investment in a bank, you wouldn't want the president of your bank making a loan under these raging hormonal influences at that particular period. . . . There are physical and psychological inhibitants that limit a female's potential. . . . All things being equal, I would still rather have had a male J.F.K. make the Cuban missile crisis decisions than a female of similar age who could possibly be subject to the curious mental aberrations of that age group.[4]

    These comments reflect different individuals' perspectives on the roles and behavior of women. They are points of view with which everyone is familiar. How accurately do these points of view portray women? Are the opinions expressed well founded? In fact, what do we really know about women? An objective of this book is to answer questions such as these.

    To more fully understand the objectives of the book, we need to consider how it developed. This study about women is the product of a cooperative effort by six social scientists representing four separate disciplines—psychology, sociology, economics, and political science. The idea for the book developed out of an interdisciplinary seminar on women initiated several years ago when issues about women were becoming prominent in social, political, and economic circles, as well as in academia. Those issues have in-

---

   [1] From *The Web and the Rock*, by Thomas Wolfe. New York: Harper and Brothers, 1939.
   [2] An American housewife, quoted in *Worlds of Pain: Life in the Working Class Family*, by Lillian Breslow Rubin. New York: Basic Books, 1976.
   [3] A female executive, quoted in "When Men Have Women Bosses," by Letty Cottin Pogrebin. *Ladies' Home Journal*, May 1977, p. 24.
   [4] Dr. Edgar Berman, quoted in "Role of Women Sparks Debate by Congresswoman and Doctor," by Christopher Lydon. *The New York Times*, July 26, 1970, p. 35.

creased in prominence, and that seminar has now become the introductory course in a program leading to a certificate in Women's Studies.

When we began teaching the seminar, we felt that no text satisfied our particular needs, as defined by the course objectives and the nature of the students enrolled in the course. Our solution was to prepare a text that met these needs. Specifically, we wanted a text that brought together in a single source information widely dispersed in scholarly papers and publications and that presented this information in a form easily understandable to the nonprofessional. In addition, we wanted to integrate the information in such a way as to overcome the narrowness of perspective that is inevitable with a single-discipline approach, without attempting to cover all relevant scholarly disciplines. Focusing on four social science disciplines, we wanted to compare findings from each discipline to see what additional insight might be gained about women.

Thus, we will be examining behavior from the perspectives of four different social sciences: political science, economics, sociology, and psychology. As social scientists, we study human behavior. We formalize the study of human activity in order to make general statements about how people behave and why. To accomplish this goal, we systematically gather information about how people act in particular situations. Each section of the book presents the perspective of a particular social science. Some aspects of behavior—child rearing, for example—are discussed in most or all of the chapters. But the reader will find that, even when the same topic appears, each discipline treats the subject differently. That is because every social science looks at human behavior from a somewhat different perspective. And while there is some overlapping of topics, no one discipline covers all of the areas of female behavior in which we are interested. The total range of human behavior is too varied and complex for any one social science to encompass it all.

The book starts with an overview of the American women's movements. This opening section is concerned with the 19th- and 20th-century women's movements from a sociological perspective. The authors draw upon social movement theory to analyze the various organizations and activities associated with these movements. This analysis introduces the reader to a broad range of issues relating to women—issues that are pertinent to the information provided in the subsequent chapters of the book.

Psychology and sociology, the social sciences represented in the next two sections, are concerned with women in a rather general context. Psychologists study behavior in close relation to mental processes. Their interest in mental aspects of behavior is evident from the subjects they study: human personality; the ability to learn and to remember; how the senses, such as hearing and sight, react to the outside world; and the development of human beings, from infancy to adulthood. Section 2 examines some of the same areas of behavior as do later sections, but it emphasizes the physiological influences on behavior. For example, it explains how the physiological development of females may contribute to their higher verbal ability.

Sociologists study women's behavior in groups, ranging from small informal groups, such as couples, to large structured ones, such as the PTA. Section 3 discusses the roles women play in a society, such as mother, employee, or politician. Furthermore, it focuses on such important social processes as sex-role socialization, through which girls learn what behaviors are appropriate for females. Many variables common to economics and political science (age, marital status, and the like) are used by sociologists as well.

Economics and political science focus on specific ranges of human behavior—namely, how people provide for their material wants and needs and how people achieve and use political power. Section 4 is concerned with women's economic roles and their status in the home and in the labor market. In analyzing women's economic experience, economists examine such topics as the supply of and demand for female employees, the wages earned by men and women, and the economic contribution of homemakers.

Section 5 deals with women's behavior as voters, as members of political parties, as officeholders, and as government employees. In analyzing and explaining this behavior, political scientists consider such influences as a woman's age, race, marital status, the presence of children, her education, work experience, and the political influence of her parents or husband. Political scientists have found, for example, that women with jobs are more likely to vote and to believe that they have some political power than women who are full-time homemakers.

In the Conclusion, we will tie together elements common to all the disciplines in such a way as to foster a broader understanding of women's behavior. Drawing upon the findings presented in the various sections, we will assess their implications for the status and roles of women in our society.

This book focuses on the behavior of women and on the various factors influencing this behavior. The purpose is to provide the reader with a concrete body of knowledge, not to project a particular point of view. We do not wish to dictate any answers to questions that remain open, nor to integrate all the material into a single point of view, whether scientific or political. The current state of each of our disciplines precludes scientific integration in terms of one general theory, and our own heterogeneity as well as that of our audience precludes integration around any political theory.

SECTION
ONE

WOMEN'S
SOCIAL
MOVEMENTS

Marcia J. Lipetz and Catherine White Berheide

The status of women in this society has been unequal to the status of men for centuries. Indeed in 1776 Abigail Adams wrote her husband expressing her concern about the position of women under the new government.

> . . . in the new Code of Laws . . . I desire you would Remember the Laidies, and be more generous and favourable to them than your ancestors. Do not put such unlimited power into the hands of the Husbands. Remember all Men would be tyrants if they could. If perticuliar care and attention is not paid to the Laidies we are determined to foment a Rebelion, and will not hold ourselves bound by any Laws in which we have no voice, or Representation [Adams, 1776/1973, pp. 10–11].

At two points in the history of the United States, concern with the unequal status of women has gone beyond individual interest and become a collective effort. The first time was the woman's rights movement of the 19th century. The second is the women's liberation movement still in progress today. This section will explore the structure and development of each of these movements.

Historical Origins

Before beginning that exploration, we need to examine briefly the changing position of women in the United States to see why these movements arose when they did. From the time America was first colonized until the Industrial Revolution, both men and women worked at home. The United States was an agricultural country, a country of small family farms. "There was a rough division between men's and women's work: the men were responsible for most of the work in the fields; the women, for looking after the infants who arrived in rapid succession, and for work that could be done in and around the home" (Easton, 1976, p. 389). Women made cloth, clothes, household items, and food. They took care of gardens and farm animals. Furthermore, women and children worked in the fields alongside the men when needed. The work women did on a farm was as essential to the family's survival as the work their husbands did. Although their legal rights were restricted in a patriarchal society that gave men authority over women, women had some power because of the economic importance of their labor (Wertheimer, 1977).

Then the Industrial Revolution began in the late 18th century. From that point until the beginning of the 20th century, the United States developed into a nation of employees, rather than small independent farmers. The men went off to work in factories instead of in the fields. The women stayed home and did the work they had always done (except for single women or poor married women, who had to supplement their husbands' income either by working in the factories or by performing jobs, such as spinning or taking in laundry, by which they could earn money at home). Women's work in the home became less critical as factories began to produce clothing, food items, and other household goods. The money that men earned became more important for purchasing products

Section opening photo: A 19th century suffragist parade. (Photo courtesy of Culver Pictures, Inc.)

women had previously provided. Thus, the Industrial Revolution decreased the status of women by making them more dependent economically on their husbands and by making their husbands less dependent economically on them.

In a country founded on equalitarian principles, the inequalities women faced in a patriarchal society triggered the woman's rights movement in the 19th century. Legal rights were necessary if women were to fight increased male domination (Easton, 1976). Thus, awareness of inequities and a sense of relative deprivation helped set the stage for the woman's rights movement.

The woman's rights movement declined after it won the vote for women in 1920. However, social trends such as increasing industrialization and the declining birth rate continued. These trends ultimately led to a renewed interest in the status of women. Women had fewer children. They were freed from the necessity of remaining near young children because safe alternatives to breast feeding had been developed (Huber, 1976). Compulsory public education meant that older children were no longer at home during the day. Thus, child rearing ceased to occupy such a large part of women's time.

Many women reentered the labor force as soon as their youngest child reached school age. In the early part of the 20th century, the typical employed woman was young and single. After the 1950s, the typical employed woman was married, older, and had children. Since the early 1900s, there has been a great increase in the demand for clerical and sales workers (Oppenheimer, 1970); married women have been pulled into the labor force to meet this demand for workers. These low-level white-collar occupations in which so many women are employed offer low pay, low prestige, little power, and little opportunity for promotion. For women to work outside the home is now a common and accepted occurrence. And yet, the job rewards women receive are much less than those men receive, despite the fact that, on the average, women have as much education as men have.

Many women have come to recognize these economic inequalities. Others have noticed the strain created while trying to live up to the traditional mother/housewife role and hold a job at the same time. These problems are relevant now to a majority of women—even those who are not currently in the labor force. Thus during the politically active 1960s, when other types of inequality were being challenged, the women's liberation movement was born.

The two chapters that follow will analyze the two American social movements concerned with the status and rights of women in our society from the sociological perspective of social movement theory. This analysis must be preceded by a brief introduction to that theory.

Social Movement Theory

Some social groups are oriented to social change. A social movement is one such group. A *social movement* can be defined as collective action directed toward promoting or resisting change in society. The women's liberation, or feminist, movement is a social movement; as such, it shares certain basic elements of social movements in general.

Social movements cannot be viewed as stable, well-structured, well-organized groups. They typically change membership, leadership, and goals as they persist over time. Any study of a social movement must identify the social conditions that promote the emergence and growth of the movement, trace changes in the movement over time, and identify personal or social changes that may be related to the movement.

Facilitating conditions—that is, general cultural conditions—can promote the emergence of a social movement. Certain members of society must recognize a problem situation that they feel will not be corrected through existing structures or institutions. For example, those dissatisfied with organized religions may form a new religion to address unmet spiritual needs. Those dissatisfied with the Democratic or Republican parties may form another political party.

Facilitating conditions must be supplemented by conditions or actions that call attention to dissatisfaction. These *activating conditions* may take the form of collective behavior. *Collective behavior* is defined as relatively unstructured behavior on the part of large numbers of people—that is, behavior that may be spontaneous, atypical, and unpredictable. The Watts riots may be seen as an activating condition for the Black civil rights movement. Demonstrations and riots serve as attention-getters and force members of society to recognize that a problem situation may exist.

Not all activating conditions take the form of collective behavior. A particular individual or preexisting group may activate a social movement. Many religious movements have begun through the efforts of one person. The crucifixion of Jesus may be seen as the activating condition for the social movement that became Christianity.

Once a social movement becomes an identifiable entity, the social scientist investigates what the movement hopes to accomplish and what tactics are used. Other aspects of a social movement, such as ideology, movement organizations, and members, are also studied.

Units of Analysis for Each Social Movement

Goals.   The goal of any social movement is to change some aspect of society or to maintain an aspect of society when change is threatened. Exactly what is to be changed or preserved is set forth by movement members. Many goals become public knowledge and may take rather general form. The most general public goal of the civil rights movement, for example, was equality for Blacks. General public goals frequently call for new attitudes in society.

Other goals, however, may not be explicitly stated for some reason. They may be too threatening to the public or may subject the movement to ridicule if widely publicized. Many people present at the first woman's rights convention in Seneca Falls, New York, for example, were afraid that demanding the vote for women would endanger the entire movement (Kraditor, 1968).

Specific goals also are often outlined by social movements. Definite legal changes, changes in textbooks, and more press coverage often appear as specific goals.

Ideology. Social movements usually generate many statements outlining their goals. These statements of goals form the bulk of the ideology of a social movement. Ideologies are belief sets or world views that justify the interests of those holding the beliefs or views. Ideologies frequently point to specific historical events or cultural patterns that have created the problems being attacked by the movement.

Ideologies may include vivid pictures of what society will be like if the movement's goals are achieved or are defeated. The movement members create a "heaven or hell" image of the consequences of success or failure. Documents such as *The Feminine Mystique* (Friedan, 1963) and the *Communist Manifesto* have contributed to the ideologies of their respective social movements.

Tactics. A movement's tactics are the activities it undertakes to achieve its goals, recruit new members, and maintain its membership. Tactics must differ according to the goals of each movement and the degree of access each movement has to existing structures that can generate change. In order to achieve their goals, social movements may use a wide variety of tactics, ranging from letter-writing campaigns to sit-ins or even violence, to bring about change.

Movement Organizations. Within large social movements, a variety of distinct groups tend to form. Each group believes in the general goals of the movement but attempts to achieve those goals in a unique way. The philosophies of the various groups may differ in emphasis, priorities, and tactics. Such movement organizations may work together or may go totally separate ways if there are intergroup conflicts. Members of one group may form a second group because of differences within the original group. Such groups as Planned Parenthood and Zero Population Growth are part of the birth-control movement and yet are distinct groups.

Members. Membership in a particular social movement does not necessarily take the form of belonging to specific groups. While some members may join specific movement organizations, others may do little more than agree with the general goals of the movement. The movement organization itself usually determines how formal membership requirements are. Social movement theory concentrates on the motives individuals have for allying themselves with social movements. Some people join a social movement because of a sense of relative deprivation—a feeling that they are not receiving a fair share of resources.

Careers of Social Movements

As social movements emerge in society, they go through several stages until goals are reached or it becomes obvious that the goals cannot be reached. The early days of a social movement are characterized by episodes of collective behavior and statements of general goals.

As a movement grows, goals are stated more explicitly. Movement organizations begin to form. More members join. Goals may change from idealistic to realistic. The movement may concentrate on what it can do rather than on what it would like to do. Some movement organizations may resist becoming more conservative. They may continue to pursue radical goals. Other groups may die out as coalitions are formed.

Successes or failures of a movement can be fully evaluated only in retrospect. Some statements or activities may gain or lose importance as the movement continues through time. Because the current women's movement has not run its full course, the following analysis using social movement theory may need revision in the near future.

THE FIGHT FOR WOMEN'S RIGHTS BEGINS

CHAPTER

1

There have been two important social movements in the history of the United States that have attempted to change the traditional social and legal roles of women. Movement authors consistently use specific titles to differentiate between these two social movements. The 19th-century movement is referred to as the *woman* movement, the woman's rights movement, social feminism, or suffrage. The modern movement is called the *women's* movement, women's liberation, or feminism. These titular distinctions have been adopted in this chapter and the next.

The Career of the 19th-Century Woman's Rights Movement

The 90-year career of the "woman movement" culminated in 1920 with the ratification of the 19th Amendment to the U.S. Constitution, which guaranteed women the right to vote. However, this singular achievement did not accomplish all of the goals of the woman's rights movement. As in most social movements, the goals of the 19th-century feminists changed significantly as the movement persisted through time and became focused on a single issue—the vote.

Although there were feminist theorists in the 18th century, including Mary Wollstonecraft and Judith Sargent Murray, they were more committed to analysis than action (Rossi, 1973). In contrast, political action was emphasized by the woman movement that began in the 1830s. The chief facilitating condition for its emergence was discussion of the abolition of slavery. Some women interested in the issue began to speak out publicly. They joined antislavery groups. Since such leadership and public speaking by respectable women was extremely unconventional, it was angrily denounced by such groups as the Massachusetts Congregationalist Clergy:

> The appropriate duties and influence of woman are clearly stated in the New Testament. . . .
> The power of woman is her dependence. . . . But when she assumes the place and tone of a

man as a public reformer . . . she yields the power which God has given her for protection, and her character becomes unnatural [Pastoral Letter of the Massachusetts Congregationalist Clergy, 1837/1968, p. 51].

Women such as Sarah and Angelina Grimké responded to these attacks by speaking about discrimination against women as well as abolition. During the 1830s and 1840s, many of the women who became leaders of the woman movement—including Susan B. Anthony, Antoinette Brown, and Lucy Stone—learned organizational and political skills in the temperance, moral reform, and abolition movements (Rossi, 1973).

The chief activating condition for the emergence of a movement concerned with the women's issue was the treatment of American female delegates to the World Anti-Slavery Convention held in London in 1840. Even though the women attended the convention as elected delegates of various American antislavery groups, they were allowed neither to be seated on the floor of the convention nor to address the other delegates. Elizabeth Cady Stanton and Lucretia Mott, two originators of the woman movement, met at this convention (Salper, 1972b).

These women returned to the United States and continued their work on abolition. They also attempted to speak for needed legislative reforms concerning women's property and family rights. Mott and Stanton recognized the need for a public meeting devoted solely to the "woman issue," and on July 14, 1848, they announced in the Seneca County (New York) *Courier* a "Woman's Rights Convention," to be held July 19–20 in Seneca Falls, New York. Some 300 men and women met and adopted a Declaration of Sentiments, outlining the original goals of the developing woman movement.

The Declaration of Sentiments was modeled after the Declaration of Independence. It attacked men for repeated injuries and the government for restrictive laws. It specifically denoted those wrongs done by man to woman, including the following:

> He has never permitted her to exercise her unalienable right to elective franchise.
> He has compelled her to submit to laws, in the formation of which she has no voice. . . .
> He has taken from her all right in property, even to the wages she earns.
> He has so framed the laws of divorce, as to what shall be the proper causes, and in case of separation, to whom the guardianship of the children shall be given, as to be wholly regardless of the happiness of women—the law, in all cases, going upon the false supposition of the supremacy of man, and giving all power into his hands. . . .
> He has monopolized nearly all the profitable employments. . . .
> He has denied her facilities for obtaining a thorough education, all colleges being closed against her.
> He has created a false public sentiment by giving to the world a different code of morals for men and women, by which moral delinquencies which exclude woman from society are not only tolerated but deemed of little account in man [Seneca Falls Convention, 1848/1968, pp. 184–186].

Twelve resolutions were adopted at Seneca Falls to remedy the injuries inflicted on woman.

These original goals of social feminism were expressed in other woman's rights conventions held in parts of the East and the Midwest in the 1840s and 1850s. One such convention in Salem, Ohio, refused to seat or recognize men as valid participants in the convention. Women's journals such as *The Lily* and *Women's Advocate* emerged after women at conventions expressed a distrust of the national press. Some women focused attention on what they considered to be restrictive women's clothing by wearing "bloomers," a loose-fitting pant-type garment (Flexner, 1959).

Public political activities focusing on women's issues virtually stopped during the Civil War. After passage of the 13th Amendment to the U.S. Constitution, abolishing slavery, attention was turned to a proposed 14th Amendment, which would extend civil rights to newly freed persons. The second section of the 14th Amendment penalized states for denying the right to vote to males—but not for denying the vote to females. This was the first time that a sex distinction appeared in the U.S. Constitution. Women activists argued against the reference to sex but were unsuccessful. Women also argued unsuccessfully that the 15th Amendment, which prohibited denying suffrage because of race, should also prohibit denying suffrage because of sex (O'Neill, 1969). Although women could vote in several states, they had no federal guarantee of suffrage.

By 1869, female activists throughout the United States agreed that the right to vote was a necessary prerequisite for other desired female rights. The American Woman Suffrage Association, formed in 1869, became the first movement organization to focus solely on the issue of suffrage. The second major group, the National Woman Suffrage Association, formed in 1890 under the leadership of Susan B. Anthony and Elizabeth Cady Stanton, continued to be concerned with all of the original goals stated in the 1848 Declaration of Sentiments. Thus, the distinction between suffragists and social feminists began.

Beginning in the 1840s, the issue of temperance was embraced by some female activists. Women, they argued, were not protected from ill treatment by husbands acting under the influence of alcohol. They felt that temperance was one method to gain such protection. Because women were not allowed equal participation in male temperance groups, female groups such as the Women's Christian Temperance Union were formed after the Civil War.

By 1890, the woman movement had become concentrated on one issue, suffrage. As noted previously, movements tend to focus on a specific goal and become more conservative in demands and approach as different kinds of people join movement organizations. Several of the original activists left the struggle for suffrage in order to work toward the other goals of social feminism, which by 1890 were disregarded by the mainstream of the movement. Elizabeth Cady Stanton, for example, concentrated on the subordination of women perpetuated through organized religion. Stanton wrote *The Woman's Bible*, a reinterpretation of the Bible showing sexual equality rather than male dominance (Flexner, 1959).

As some female activists left the movement after it became the suffrage movement, other groups of women allied themselves with the suffragists, or "suffragettes," as they were called. A large number of charitable and voluntary groups had emerged among middle- and upper-class women during the latter part of the 19th century. Many members of the newly formed Junior League, the General Federation of Women's Clubs, and the National Consumers League, among others, joined the move to guarantee women the constitutional right to vote (Salper, 1972b). While these women acted as a conservative force in the movement, other younger new members allied themselves with a radical wing of the movement.

A new set of members, tactics, and nonsuffragist allies contributed to the ratification of the 19th, or Anthony, Amendment on August 26, 1920. In focusing solely on suffrage, the woman movement had experienced goal displacement—a process by which a single goal, gaining the right to vote, overrode the initial objectives of social feminism (Ash, 1972).

Goals and Ideology of the Woman's Rights Movement

Some of the goals of the woman movement have already been identified in the discussion of the career of the movement. The recognized national goals changed from the broad concerns of the social feminists to the narrow goal of the suffragists—the right to vote.

The 1848 Declaration of Sentiments, discussed earlier, served as the chief ideological statement of the social feminists. In contrast to the suffragists, who focused on the vote, social feminists were concerned with the larger issues of social justice for women and the poor. The goals of social feminists, who sought broad social change, included divorce rights, custody of children during separation or divorce, control over inherited property, increased educational and professional opportunities, and the right to vote. These goals were pursued in the individual states, with some success, long after most groups selected suffrage as the primary focus because it was a symbol of the power women were denied outside the home. Many suffragists felt that with the vote women would automatically gain social equality.

By 1880, when woman suffrage attracted the most attention and became the top priority of the movement, a variety of ideological themes surfaced. Perhaps most prevalent was the nature-versus-nurture controversy. Antisuffragists felt that women were, by nature, unequal to men and, therefore, not suited for responsibilities of state. Women belonged in the home. The suffragists countered the traditional argument by stating that socialization patterns placed women into the homemaking role. Cultural change could allow women full participation as citizens, which was their natural right (Kraditor, 1965).

The opening phrases of the Declaration of Sentiments of 1848 epitomize the natural-right argument used to support the suffragist viewpoint.

When, in the course of human events, it becomes necessary for one portion of the family of man to assume among the people of the earth a position different from that which they have hitherto occupied, but one to which the laws of nature and of nature's God entitle them, a decent respect to the opinions of mankind requires that they should declare the causes that impel them to such a course.

We hold these truths to be self-evident: that all men and women are created equal; that they are endowed by their Creator with certain inalienable rights; that among these are life, liberty, and the pursuit of happiness [Seneca Falls Convention, 1848/1968, p. 184].

By the turn of the century, suffragists were concentrating on suffrage as expediency rather than suffrage as a natural right. The expediency argument stated that the vote would allow women to get things done. Various reform groups were urged to support suffrage in order to allow women to vote for the causes supported by those groups, such as child-labor laws and prohibition.

Not all of the goals supported by members of the woman movement were solely concerned with women. There were many alliances between social feminists and other social movements. Social feminists supported the efforts of labor unions; many were active in the cause of temperance; others supported the Progressives' interest in social welfare and Margaret Sanger's growing movement for birth control (Banner, 1974). The woman movement organizations worked with nonmovement organizations such as the Junior League and the Women's Christian Temperance Union to achieve specific goals.

Movement Organizations

As is the case in many social movements, a variety of distinct groups existed within the woman movement. Originally, all social feminists were primarily abolitionists. The formation of social-feminist groups came about after the controversy over the wording of the proposed 14th Amendment to the U.S. Constitution.

The 14th Amendment was designed to extend civil rights to newly freed persons, but it specifically limited that right to males. One faction of abolitionists—social feminists, led by Susan B. Anthony and Elizabeth Cady Stanton—argued that the amendment should be defeated because of its inherent sex discrimination. They formed the National Woman Suffrage Association in 1869. In the same year, others such as Lucy Stone and Henry Ward Beecher formed the American Woman Suffrage Association. They argued that it was better to guarantee the vote to male ex-slaves than to no ex-slaves at all.

These first two movement organizations differed more over the 14th Amendment than over other issues. The two groups shared similar goals and tactics. They concentrated on changing the laws of individual states through legislative pressure, support from male voters, educational meetings, and petition drives. In fact, the similarities led to merger in 1890, when suffrage became the primary goal. The newly merged organization became known as the National American Woman Suffrage Association (NAWSA).

The NAWSA, which continued as the primary movement organization until 1914, was relatively conservative. It assumed that suffrage was an issue best decided by the individual states. A group of younger suffragists headed by Alice Paul disagreed with this states-rights approach. They broke away from the NAWSA in 1914 to form the Congressional Union for Women's Suffrage (CU). The CU, which later spawned the Woman's Party, was more militant in its approach to suffrage. Its members focused on the U.S. Congress, rather than on the individual states. CU members picketed the White House, an unheard-of activity for women. CU also revived organizational interest in social-feminist issues such as divorce and equal pay and fought for new feminist concerns such as birth control (Kraditor, 1965).

Few woman movement groups were organized on a local level. Decisions were made at the national organizational level and then pursued in the various states (Banner, 1974). Suffragists thus dealt with a single national structure, rather than state and local chapters—a structure that contributed greatly to the unification of goals within the movement.

Membership and Leadership

The abolitionists who were first involved in social feminism were primarily White, upper-middle-class women. Most were married. Many were raised in atmospheres that encouraged education for women in a time when women were largely uneducated. Most had been employed at some time during their lives. Many came from Protestant backgrounds (Kraditor, 1965).

The early leadership of the woman movement reflected this set of characteristics, as the following biographical sketches of Sarah and Angelina Grimké, Elizabeth Cady Stanton, and Susan B. Anthony show.

Sarah and Angelina Grimké, daughters of a wealthy South Carolina family, were born in 1792 and 1805, respectively. They were both educated in such traditionally male topics as science and mathematics. The sisters moved to Philadelphia, where they became Quakers, and wrote and spoke in favor of abolition. The criticism they evoked from Congregational ministers has already been cited. Angelina married Theodore Weld, a minister who was involved in abolition, temperance, and religious revivalism; Sarah lived with her sister and brother-in-law. By 1837, Sarah was preaching women's equality. Her work influenced early movement leaders, including Lucretia Mott and Elizabeth Cady Stanton (Nies, 1977).

Elizabeth Cady Stanton was born in Johnstown, New York, in 1815. Her father was an attorney, and she grew up hearing about the problems women faced because of the existing laws concerning marriage and divorce. Like the Grimké sisters, she was taught mathematics, the classics, and the unfeminine sport of horseback-riding. She married the abolitionist Henry Stanton in 1840 and attended the World Anti-Slavery Convention with him the same year—as one of the delegates who was not allowed to participate. Along with Lucretia Mott, Stanton was a convener of the Seneca Falls convention in 1848; in 1890, she was elected the first president of the National American Woman Suffrage

Figure 1-1. Elizabeth Cady Stanton was the first president of the National American Woman Suffrage Association. (Photo © by The Courier-Journal and Louisville Times Co.)

Association. Stanton wrote *The Woman's Bible*, a commentary on the status of women in the Bible (Nies, 1977).

Susan B. Anthony was born in 1820 in Adams, Massachusetts. Her father was involved in the issue of temperance. Anthony was educated to be a teacher, but as a teacher and headmaster of a school, she found that she was paid less than her male colleagues. This job discrimination, coupled with the discrimination she faced at temperance meetings, led her in 1853 to the Third National Woman's Rights Convention, where she was elected secretary. She organized volunteers to collect signatures on petitions concerning equal earnings, custody of children after divorce, and suffrage. She concentrated primarily on the New York state legislature as a source of reform. Anthony was also involved in helping working women—cigar makers, printers, and typesetters—to organize into labor unions (Hahn, 1974).

By the beginning of the 20th century, a new generation of women became involved in the suffrage issue. These women were similar to their predecessors in that they were generally married to supportive spouses, had been raised in homes where their individuality was encouraged, and had rejected the traditional feminine roles. These newer members, however, were young women in their 20s. Many of the original social feminists had remained active from the Civil War through the turn of the century. They were approaching old age by the time suffrage became the chief concern. The new members added a new perspective in part by contacting working-class women. They introduced new tactics, such as picketing and hunger strikes, and attempted to sustain interest in many of the original social-feminist concerns (Sochen, 1973).

Alice Paul, the founder of the National Woman's Party, was born in Moorestown, New Jersey, in 1885. Raised in a Quaker home, she continued her education through a Ph.D. and three law degrees. Her studies took her to England, where she became involved in militant suffrage activity. On her return to the United States in 1910, she continued her militant tactics. Active in the Congressional Union, which spawned the Woman's Party, Paul engaged in picketing and hunger strikes for the cause of suffrage. When woman suffrage became a reality, Alice Paul and the Woman's Party decided that the newly introduced Equal Rights Amendment had to become the new goal of feminists (Sochen, 1973).

Thus, the early members and leaders of the movement were from the same social groups and shared similar ideas. The following discussion of tactics will point out how increased diversity in membership provided by the new, younger, more militant suffragists was partly responsible for the successes of the early feminists.

Tactics

The tactics employed by the early social feminists grew out of their experiences in the abolition movement. Using the acceptable means of the times, social feminists called conventions of their own and sent representatives to state legislatures and political conventions. After 1868, the social feminists concentrated on legislative petition drives in individual states. The relatively small numbers of women who traveled throughout their states were extremely successful in their efforts to reach the public, especially considering conditions of the time and the status of women (Kraditor, 1965).

After suffrage became the chief concern, the most innovative tactic was the use of the suffrage parade. Although parades had previously been used for celebrations or to demonstrate group solidarity, the suffragists were the first protest group in America to use the parade as a political demonstration (Banner, 1974).

With the formation of the Congressional Union in 1914, new tactics emerged. Dissatisfied with the focus on state legislatures, members of the CU concentrated on two approaches. First, they became actively involved in party politics, campaigning against the Democratic Party in 1916 because it failed to support a strong plank on suffrage. While the NAWSA discouraged involvement in party politics as too risky, CU members saw it as the only way to exert power. Elected officials were seen as most vulnerable on issues during election campaigns.

The second tactic employed by the Congressional Union—which by 1916 had become the Woman's Party—also focused attention on the federal level. CU members began an around-the-clock picketing of the White House in 1917. The demonstrators were arrested on orders of President Wilson, put in jail, and force-fed when they refused to eat. After they were released from jail, the District of Columbia Court of Appeals ruled that their arrests had not been valid (O'Neill, 1969).

The tactics employed during the various stages of the movement reflected the membership. As new members introduced new tactics, success became more of a possibility. Opposition groups recognized these changes and responded accordingly.

Opposition

As is the case with any controversial social movement, those opposed to the goals of the social feminists/suffragists organized into opposition groups. These groups, frequently led by prominent women, used three basic arguments to combat proposed changes in the status of women. As Banner (1974) has pointed out, these arguments were based primarily on religious beliefs and sought to maintain the social status quo.

The first approach used by the opposition was to appeal to tradition and divine intent: women were *naturally* intended to be mothers; participation in civic affairs by women was not natural. Because of their roles as mothers, went the second argument, women were too weak and delicate to stand the rigors of full citizenship. Biology was thus destiny. The third argument combined biology and natural determinism by stating that women had been given a definite role in life—that of maintaining the family. If the family, rather than the individual, was the primary unit of society, then each family member had to accomplish certain tasks. The duty of the male head of the family was to relate to the rest of the world through work and civic participation. The female's duty was to relate internally to the family, to care for the home and children. Each of these three approaches relied on traditional beliefs (Kraditor, 1965).

While members of the opposition initially belonged to a series of splinter groups, changes among suffragists demanded changes in the opposition. In 1911, opposition groups united to form the National Association Opposed to the Further Extension of Suffrage to Women. Because suffrage had become the chief goal of the movement, the opposition united against suffrage. The liquor industry was involved in the opposition because of the rising interest in temperance. The liquor lobby joined the political machines, other types of businessmen, Southern Democrats, and the Catholic Church to create a diverse opposition force (Flexner, 1959).

The opposition was only partially successful. Although it delayed the ultimate passage of suffrage, it did not prevent it. The opposition did lessen support for social-feminist concerns by diverting much of the movement's energy toward the single goal of suffrage. Thus, the opposition helped ensure the decline of the movement after 1920.

Successes and Failures of the Woman's Rights Movement

The ultimate success of a social movement must be measured by the ways in which that movement affected society. Social feminism and suffrage did achieve some measure of success at the state and national levels. Those successes were not without complications, however.

The ultimate success of the movement was a national guarantee of the right to vote for women. What is often forgotten is that this national suffrage occurred some 30 years after individual states started granting female suffrage. The women of Wyoming could vote when that territory became a state in 1890. Colorado followed in 1893, Utah and Idaho in 1896. The Anthony Amendment in 1920 extended this right to women in all the states.

The fight for the right to vote was a long and hard one. Although the movement began before the Civil War, women were not enfranchised until after World War I. In the estimation of many men, women proved themselves worthy of the right to vote by keeping the country going while the men were overseas fighting. It is difficult to judge whether gaining suffrage would have taken even longer had World War I not occurred.

Other successes of the social movement are often forgotten, perhaps because they seem less dramatic than the right to vote. In the long run, however, these changes may be as important as suffrage. For example, participation in the political arena became acceptable for women. In fact, Jeanette Rankin of Montana became the first female member of the House of Representatives in 1917—three years before final ratification of the 19th Amendment.

This legitimation of female political participation brought other important results. Women were partially successful at the state level in changing some laws concerning divorce, property and inheritance rights, and custody of children after divorce or separation. Other social changes resulted from the combined efforts of social feminists and members of other social movements. For example, social feminists and Progressives together were instrumental in achieving the passage of protective legislation for working women. Because of the conditions in the factories at the turn of the century, many groups called for restrictions on working hours and other working conditions, and such laws were passed in many states. Today, these same laws are under attack by feminists who claim that protective legislation hinders women's economic progress.

Social feminists were also involved in other social movements. Many supported Margaret Sanger in her attempts to make birth control methods available to women.

Others were active in the temperance movement and were successful in calling for Prohibition.

The efforts of social feminists and suffragists did not all end in success. Passage of new laws did not ensure enforcement of those laws. Attitudes toward temperance are well known. Nor were states particularly rigorous in their enforcement of protective legislation in factories. Many working women were hesitant to obey restrictions on the number of hours they worked, for fear of losing their jobs.

Social movement theory predicts that a social movement may simply end when it accomplishes its goal; at the same time, other groups may posit new goals to ensure continuation of the movement. Both of these things, in fact, did happen after 1920. The suffrage movement clearly ended. The National American Woman Suffrage Association disbanded upon completion of its primary goal, but many of its members joined the League of Women Voters to continue some form of political involvement. At the same time, the more radical social-feminist arm of the movement, the Woman's Party, changed its goal. It adopted the Equal Rights Amendment, first introduced in 1923, as its primary thrust. The Woman's Party also continued to be active in other areas of reform.

Most important for the origins of the feminist movement of the 1960s, however, was the failure of social feminists to sustain large-scale interest in their activities or any large, influential national organization. New groups with new goals emerged in the 1960s and began trying to achieve many of the things that their predecessors had not. The early movement also failed to alter significantly the traditional image and role of women. The earliest social feminists pointed out these problems in their attacks on the treatment of women in the law and in the churches. Although there was some interest in social-feminist issues after 1920, a major new movement did not develop until the 1960s.

Forty Years: 1920–1960

Although the suffrage movement had ended, interest in issues of concern to women did not end with the passage of the Anthony Amendment. During the 1920s, suffragists splintered into four diverse groups, each pursuing some of the general goals that had been sought before suffrage became the primary goal.

The largest group of veterans of the suffrage movement carried on the tradition of social feminism. They continued to urge legislatures to change state laws that discriminated against women, and they pressed for increased educational opportunities for women. The League of Women Voters—the largest organization pursuing social-feminist goals—was, in effect, the successor of the National American Woman Suffrage Association.

The second category to which suffragists turned after 1920 was the peace movement. Arguing that war-making was a male pursuit, many women joined the Women's International League for Peace and Freedom. WILPF was instrumental in getting national governments to organize and attend disarmament and peace conferences after World War I.

A third group of suffragists, considering their professional activities to be of primary importance, turned to organizations such as the National Federation of Business and Professional Women's Clubs. These women concentrated on enhancing professional opportunities for women.

The fourth concern of suffragists after 1920 was carried on by members of the more radical wing of the suffrage movement. The National Woman's Party, with Alice Paul still involved, continued its activities well after 1920. It set as its primary goal passage of the newly introduced Equal Rights Amendment.

The efforts of ex-suffragists during the 1920s were not particularly well received. Many Americans felt that, because women had won the vote, they needed no other reforms. Antifeminism was strong. Yet young women were involved in increasing the social acceptability of freedom and independence for women, particularly with respect to sexuality. The flappers of this decade—by cutting their hair, smoking in public, and changing their dress—defied social conventions that had previously limited women's behavior. Furthermore, as Rossi (1973) points out, several feminist books were published in the 1920s, including Suzanne LaFollette's *Concerning Women* and Virginia Woolf's *A Room of One's Own*.

With the Depression of the 1930s, the need for social reforms became more obvious. Many employers took advantage of the state of the economy to fire married women in order to employ men, arguing that men needed to work far more than women because men had families to support. This argument ignored the fact that many women, especially during the Depression, were the sole supporters of their families. Thus, the economic position of many women worsened during this period.

The League of Women Voters was one of the chief supporters of the Social Security Act of 1935. Other groups urged improved public education, and a larger proportion of women than ever before in fact received higher education. During this period, according to Friedan (1963), women fought for the rights of workers, Blacks, and the victims of fascism.

Franklin D. Roosevelt included a concern for women in his presidential activities, partly at the urging of his wife, Eleanor Roosevelt. He appointed many women to advisory positions, including Frances Perkins as Secretary of Labor—the first woman to hold a Cabinet position. His legislative programs, however, did not reflect a particular interest in women.

World War II opened many new employment opportunities to women. Because of the shortage of male workers, women gained entrance to previously all-male occupations. The government itself quadrupled the number of women it employed and established child-care centers for children of female employees. Many states suspended laws that specified restrictions and protections for female employees (Banner, 1974).

It was assumed that women would be willing to return to homemaking roles after World War II. This was not the case. A 1944 Women's Bureau survey indicated that 80% of working women did *not* want to stop working. Some employers fired women in order to reemploy veterans. During the 1940s and 1950s, older married women, including those with children, joined the work force in ever-increasing numbers, despite attempts to persuade them to return to the home. However, they were displaced from the production jobs they had held during the war into more traditionally female occupations, particularly clerical and sales work.

There was some overt feminist activity during the 1950s. The Equal Rights Amendment was first introduced in 1923 by Representative Daniel Anthony (Susan B. Anthony's nephew) and has been introduced every year since 1923. The Amendment passed the Senate in 1950 and again in 1953, but successful lobbying by the Committee to Defeat the Unequal Rights Amendment, a coalition of 43 national groups, prevented its passage in the House of Representatives. Meanwhile, some states enacted equal-pay legislation (Komisar, 1971).

Despite social gains between 1920 and 1960, there was no organized social movement that had women's rights as its primary concern. Instead, there were separate organizations for different types of women, such as the American Association of University Women and the National Council of Catholic Women. Women were involved in various social-welfare concerns, including Margaret Sanger's birth control movement. Simone de Beauvoir's *The Second Sex* (1952) has been characterized in retrospect as "the product of the transitional period between the old and the new feminism" (Rossi, 1973, p. 674). However, it was Betty Friedan's *The Feminine Mystique* (1963), rather than *The Second Sex*, that helped stir American women to renewed political activity on their own behalf.

CHAPTER
2

THE FIGHT CONTINUES

Facilitating Conditions of the Women's Movement, 1961–1964

The new feminist movement, termed the women's movement or women's liberation movement, emerged in the middle 1960s. Several things occurred in the early 1960s that facilitated this emergence. These took the form of presidential actions, the passage of new laws by the U.S. Congress, and the appearance of two pieces of literature speaking to the issue of sexual inequality.

On December 14, 1961, President John F. Kennedy issued an Executive Order calling for the creation of a Presidential Commission on the Status of Women. The charge to the Commission was to examine barriers that prevented women from enjoying their full citizenship rights. Hole and Levine (1971) suggest that the President created the Commission to repay female campaign workers and to gather facts to be used *against* the proposed Equal Rights Amendment to the U.S. Constitution, an amendment that had been introduced every year since 1923.

The recommendations of the Commission covered a wide spectrum of issues but did *not* include passage of the Equal Rights Amendment. The Commission believed that women were covered adequately by the 5th Amendment, guaranteeing due process of law, and the 14th Amendment, guaranteeing equal protection under the law. However, the Commission did state that women needed equal employment opportunities. Furthermore, they pointed to the need for improved day-care centers for children of employed women and increased tax exemptions for working women.

The Commission urged the creation of two groups: the Interdepartmental Committee on the Status of Women and the Citizen's Advisory Council on the Status of Women. The Interdepartmental Committee was made up of Cabinet members and heads of governmental departments concerned with women's affairs. The Citizen's Advisory Council, composed of 20 private citizens, became the more active of the two groups. The Citizen's

Council recommended banning sex-segregated job advertising and eliminating other forms of sex discrimination related to employment (Freeman, 1975).

The creation of the Commission was as important as its actual recommendations. Its existence led indirectly to the formation of one branch of the women's movement. Following the lead of the federal government, commissions on women were created in every state by 1967 (Komisar, 1971). The impetus for the beginning of the National Organization for Women (NOW) came at a national meeting of members of these commissions in 1966.

President Kennedy was involved in at least one other women's issue. In 1963 he signed the Equal Pay Act, which guaranteed federal employees equal pay for equal work. The Act was amended in 1972 to include administrative, executive, and professional positions.

The Johnson Administration recommended passage of a Civil Rights Act in 1964 to prohibit discrimination on the basis of race, color, religion, and national origin in employment, public accommodations, and housing. The word "sex" was added to Title VII, the section dealing with employment by private employers, employment agencies, unions, and state and local governments. The introduction of the word "sex" by Democratic Congressman Howard Smith of Virginia was, in fact, an attempt to undermine the entire Act. For this reason, some liberal supporters of the Act voted against the Smith Amendment. Nonetheless, both the Amendment and the Act passed in 1964. By Executive Order 11375, President Johnson banned sex discrimination in employment within the federal government and by employers with federal contracts (Freeman, 1975).

While these executive and legislative changes provided an atmosphere of legal equality, legal changes were not the only facilitating conditions for the emergence of the women's movement in the 1960s. At least two written works served as an added impetus to the beginning of the movement.

In 1963, Betty Friedan published her landmark book, *The Feminine Mystique*. The book must be seen as the first widely read 20th-century American work suggesting that American women were not allowed to reach their full human potential because of social restrictions. During the post-World War II era in the United States, the "feminine mystique" urged women to leave industry and return to their "rightful" places in the home. Friedan suggested that the "housewife" role expanded to fill the time available. She argued that the dissatisfaction women felt as housewives could not be cured by Freudian psychoanalysis, helping them adjust to their "proper" role. Instead, she proposed changes in society that would allow women greater opportunities to use their talents outside the home, especially in the labor market. Friedan recommended changed patterns of socialization for children; increased educational opportunities for women, including home-study courses, summer courses, and courses to develop hobbies and special talents; and increased child-care facilities. Her book also contains strong criticism of sexism in sociology, Freudian psychology, and American advertising.

A second publication, which appeared in 1964 in *Daedalus*, was an essay entitled "Equality between the Sexes: An Immodest Proposal" by sociologist Alice S. Rossi.

Although Rossi's work is strikingly similar to *The Feminine Mystique,* it could not have drawn on Friedan's ideas because of the publication dates. Her article received little attention outside academic circles. Its importance lies in the fact that the condition of women was drawing attention in diverse areas. Rossi stated that sex-role differences result from patterns of child rearing. If women were to be social equals of men, three factors had to change: (1) adequate child care had to be available; (2) residential patterns had to change so that women could have access to schools and industry, or schools and industry had to relocate to the suburbs; and (3) women had to *want* to participate equally in society. Similar points have since been made countless times in writings concerning the status of women (see, for example, Berheide, Berk, & Berk, 1976).

Activating Conditions, 1964–1968

To characterize the modern women's movement as a unified, unidirectional movement with a distinct set of goals and tactics would be a mistake. Most observers of the women's movement separate it into two or more categories. Firestone (1970) divided the women's liberation movement into the radical feminists and two types of reform feminists—the conservatives, such as NOW, and the politicos, whose primary loyalty is to the New Left. Similarly, Polk (1972) felt that women who find justification for the liberation of women within a socialist political framework should be seen as a third branch. Thus, some observers of the women's movement have made a distinction between Marxist and non-Marxist feminists.

In contrast, both Hole and Levine (1971) and Carden (1974) identified only two branches within the movement: (1) those members and groups interested in *women's rights,* who concentrate on changing laws, employment policies, and schools; and (2) those focusing on *women's liberation,* who want changes in socialization patterns, attitudes toward women, and images women have of themselves. Freeman (1975) has criticized such categorization on the grounds that the goals of women's rights or reform groups are not really so different from those of women's liberation or radical groups. As she astutely points out, both women's liberation organizations and women's rights groups are active in the political arena, and both are involved in service projects such as rape counseling and medical self-help centers.

As a result, Freeman prefers to distinguish between an older branch consisting of groups such as NOW and a younger one made up of many small local groups doing a wide variety of activities. "Structure and style rather than ideology more accurately differentiate the two branches, and even here there has been much borrowing on both sides. In general the older branch has used the traditional forms of political action while the younger branch has been experimental" (Freeman, 1975, p. 57). Since *women's rights* and *women's liberation* are the most commonly accepted terms used to describe these branches, it is more convenient to use *women's rights* to refer to the older branch containing formally structured groups engaged in traditional political activity and *women's liberation* to refer to the younger branch of less structured and more experimental groups.

Situations that activated the formation of groups, as well as the groups themselves, reflect this split in the movement.

The origins of the women's liberation segment of the women's movement have been traced to reactions of small groups of women active in the Black civil rights movement in 1964 and in certain organizations of the New Left in 1965. In 1964, Ruby Doris Robinson, one of the co-founders of the Student Nonviolent Coordinating Committee (SNCC) spoke to an SNCC conference and protested the inferior status given women in SNCC. Robinson was verbally abused as a result of her comments. The attitude of some SNCC men was expressed by Stokely Carmichael: "The only position for women in SNCC is prone" (Seese, 1970, p. 176).

Some Black and White women in the newer civil rights groups began to examine their roles in movement organizations. The women were expected to perform secretarial duties as well as cook and clean, jobs male activists rarely did. Women did participate in political activities of the civil rights groups but faced problems in those projects. For example, in the South, female members of SNCC worked with children and the elderly in community centers and freedom schools, while their male counterparts engaged in the primary task of voter registration. Such discrepancies were further complicated when women in the male-dominated groups such as SNCC and CORE noted that some Southern women did community organizing on their own and were able to rise in the hierarchy of groups such as the Mississippi Freedom Democratic Party (Seese, 1970).

What is significant about expressed discontent in civil rights groups is not that these discussions led directly to the formation of women's groups. To the contrary, there is no evidence showing the emergence of any group because of sex-related controversies in SNCC. What is significant is that a small number of women began questioning the roles delegated to women in social movement organizations. Like its 19th-century predecessor, the modern women's movement had some roots in a concern for the rights of Blacks.

Some women in New Left organizations encountered attitudes similar to those experienced by women in SNCC. They found themselves performing secretarial roles and being excluded from leadership positions. At a 1965 Students for a Democratic Society (SDS) national convention, women who attempted to discuss women's issues were verbally abused. Some of those women presented a plank supporting women's liberation to the same convention in 1966 and were asked to leave the speaker's platform. At the 1967 National Conference for a New Politics (NCNP) in Chicago, women presented a female civil rights plank. The plank was replaced by a "women for peace" plank through maneuvering on the floor of the convention. The significance of the 1967 NCNP conflict was the realization among some New Left women that their loyalties were to women's liberation rather than to the New Left (Hole & Levine, 1971). The New Left women began defining their primary loyalties and asking themselves whether a socialist revolution could occur without a revolution in the treatment of women (Koedt, 1973). Marlene Dixon (1971) expressed the dilemma:

> Women had learned from 1964 to 1968 that to fight for or even to sympathize with women's liberation was to pay a terrible price: what little credit a woman might have earned in one of the Left organizations was wiped out in a storm of contempt and personal abuse [p. 55].

Members of the New Left started to form the first "women's liberation" groups—groups oriented to sweeping social changes. A "woman's caucus" emerged within the Students for a Democratic Society. After the NCNP convention, Jo Freeman helped form Chicago's Women's Radical Action Project. Shulamith Firestone, who had participated in the Chicago women's liberation groups, went to New York and began to organize Radical Women, the first New York group (Ware, 1970).

The emergence of the "women's rights" segment of the women's movement occurred in very different circumstances. New Leftists were not directly involved. Rather, the founders of the first women's rights group, the National Organization for Women, were participants in the third national Conference of Commissions on the Status of Women, state commissions formed in response to Kennedy's Presidential Commission on the Status of Women.

Freeman (1973) notes that the men and women appointed to serve on the commissions on women generally were politically active. State commissions had documented the legal and economic problems of women. Some commission members hoped to improve these conditions. On June 30, 1966, a number of participants in the conference urged passage of a resolution calling for enforcement of Title VII of the 1964 Civil Rights Act, the section dealing with nondiscrimination in employment on the basis of sex. The majority refused to pass the resolution.

Disturbed by inactivity on the part of the conference, a group of men and women, Betty Friedan included, called for a national conference to organize a group to deal with women's legal rights. On October 29–30, 1966, some 300 men and women met in Washington, D.C., and formed the National Organization for Women (Freeman, 1973). Officers and a board of directors were elected, bylaws were adopted, and a statement of purpose was issued. The goal of NOW was to "take action to bring women into full participation in the mainstream of American society *now*" (National Organization for Women, 1971, p. 193).

NOW had a membership different from groups formed out of the New Left. The first board of directors included seven professors, four government officials, five labor union officials, and four business executives. Betty Friedan was the first president. The decision to use legal tactics and to have a formal structure in part separated NOW from other types of movement organizations (Carden, 1974). Those differences will be treated more fully in the discussion of various women's movement groups.

The emergence of various movement organizations may mark the beginning of the women's movement. However, two public events of 1968 brought the movement to the attention of the general public.

In January 1968, a coalition of women's peace groups sponsored the Jeanette Rankin Brigade, a Washington, D.C., demonstration. Of the 4000–5000 participants, almost 500 women sponsored a torchlight parade in Arlington National Cemetery to distribute the New York Radical Women's pamphlet entitled "The Burial of Traditional Womanhood." The pamphlet called for women to become aware of their own oppression in society. The demonstration has been seen as the first public action by radical women who were defining themselves primarily as feminists rather than as members of the New Left (Hole & Levine, 1971).

Figure 2-1. *Betty Friedan, one of the founders of the feminist movement, became the first president of NOW. (Photo © 1975 by The Courier-Journal and Louisville Times Co.)*

The second public action received an enormous amount of publicity, not because of the action itself but because it occurred at the Miss America Pageant in Atlantic City, New Jersey, on September 7, 1968. The demonstration took the form of street theater, as women from New York, Washington, D.C., New Jersey, and Florida made a "freedom trash can" one of the centers of attention. Women deposited "symbols of male oppression"—curlers, high-heeled shoes, traditional women's magazines, girdles, and bras—into the garbage. The image of the "bra burners" originated at the Miss America Pageant, even though no bras were burned. Because the demonstration was covered so widely by the national press, the women's movement became a nationally recognized fact in 1968 (Hole & Levine, 1971).

To say that a women's movement emerged or became a fact is not to understand the component parts of the movement itself. A social movement is more complex than just its history. The following sections of this chapter will discuss those component parts— members, leaders, groups, goals, ideology, and tactics. This discussion must not be seen as an analysis of a movement that has run its course. The current movement is little more than a decade old, and there are no signs to indicate that its career has run full course.

Goals and Ideology of the Women's Movement

It would be impossible to present a complete statement of ideas expressed within the framework of the women's movement. Members of the women's movement do not all agree on the basic issues, a set of goals, nor an ideological orientation. However, there is one overriding goal that unites the current women's movement: equality and freedom for women. The women's rights branch tends to adopt a more traditional definition of equality and freedom than the women's liberation branch. Women's rights groups seek equal opportunities for women. As Cassell (1977) has noted, "in this definition it is not hierarchy (including individual differences) but *discrimination* that is to be banned" (p. 165). Rather than abolish power relations, this branch wants women to have their fair share of power. Thus, it works for women's civil rights, particularly in the legal and economic spheres. Women's rights groups tend to address specific social and legal problems of women in society. They concentrate on concrete issues that can be dealt with in a short-range political-action framework.

Women's liberation groups also embrace the concept of equal rights, but they move beyond this definition of equality to one involving the destruction of traditional sex roles, power inequities, and prestige distinctions. They seek to alter female and male identities, human relationships, the family, and society. Thus, this branch is frequently involved in social experimentation as it tries to develop alternative structures and roles for women (and men). Within this branch, there are groups that use the ideology of the New Left or radical movements to analyze women's issues. They view women as an oppressed class and economically exploited. Men, the patriarchal family, and capitalism are seen as the causes of women's oppression. Thus, they, too, call for a radical transformation of society.

Despite this difference in the approach to equality, there is a common core of ideology within the women's movement. Feminists agree that women face sexism, oppression, and discrimination. They also agree that social change that would increase alternatives for both sexes is necessary to free women from oppression and sexist practices. Members of the movement want to win for women free and equal participation in all aspects of society. Women must not be restricted in terms of opportunities or activities. Movement organizations and theorists call for the removal of legal and social barriers that they believe prevent women from enjoying the full rights of personhood and citizenship. Members of both branches also agree on particular issues, such as gaining legal rights and political power for women, eliminating economic and employment discrimination, giving women control over their own bodies, and changing sex-role socialization. These goals are reminiscent of the goals of the earlier social feminists. In short, although they often disagree on tactics for achieving goals and the explanations for the causes of specific problems, both branches agree on a general direction for the feminist movement.

Ideology and Goals within the Women's Rights Branch

Those involved in women's rights organizations (for example, NOW, Federally Employed Women) have concentrated on specific areas of society where change can occur through existing legal or institutional channels. Laws, books, media coverage, and institutional treatment of women have been attacked. Specific recommendations for change have been made. The need for changes tends to be justified with factual information, such as employment statistics and outdated laws. Women's liberationists have dealt with many of the same issues. However, the liberation-oriented ideology tends to define most problems in radical political and philosophical terms. It attributes most issues to a patriarchal society with its tradition of male domination.

The following is a summary of six goals of women's rightists.

1. *Passage of the Equal Rights Amendment (ERA)*. The Equal Rights Amendment simply states: "Equality of rights under the law shall not be abridged by the United States or by any state on account of sex." The ERA was passed by Congress on March 27, 1972. Needing the ratification of 38 states to become law, the ERA had been ratified by 35 as of 1978. In October of 1978 Congress passed an extension to the deadline for passage of the ERA. The ERA now must be ratified by June 30, 1982.

2. *The Availability of Quality Child Care*. Two of the first statements calling for a change in the traditional role of women denoted child care as a pressing need for women. Both Friedan and Rossi pointed out that, because women assume primary responsibility for child care, they are denied the opportunity to engage in roles other than home-making unless alternate arrangements can be made for the care of children. (See also Chapter 8.)

3. *Life-Style Options: Marriage, Motherhood, Work*. Modern feminists support a woman's right to choose her own life-style rather than have to follow a particular set of roles required of all women—namely, motherhood and marriage. Feminists argue that women must be free to choose whether or not to marry, to have children or remain childless, and to work as employees, volunteers, or homemakers.

4. *Abortion*. Many feminists have been concerned with the goal of ensuring women access to safe, legal abortions. Feminists have called for the repeal of all abortion laws. They argue that abortion is a medical procedure and that the need for any medical procedure must be determined by a patient and a physician, not by the state. With the January 22, 1973, Supreme Court decision in *Roe* v. *Wade* and *Doe* v. *Bolton*, abortion became legal during the first two trimesters of a pregnancy. Because of this legal victory and the antiabortion movements that developed in its wake, the goal now is to protect the

court decision against suggested constitutional amendments that would prohibit abortion. Feminists are currently fighting to reinstate government funding of abortions for poor women.

5. *Sex-Role Stereotyping in Educational Materials.* If the overriding goal of the women's movement is to guarantee women full social and legal rights, feminists argue, then male and female children must be taught equality in early life. Feminists have noted the need for change in media images of women and in sex-role stereotypes presented in educational materials. If children learn that they must grow up to fulfill specific roles, they will be prepared to fill only those roles.

6. *Equal Employment.* Since its inception, the women's movement has considered the equitable treatment of women in employment one of its primary goals. Feminists have worked to end discrimination against women in hiring, promotion, and pay. They have pushed to expand job opportunities for women through vocational training, career counseling, and affirmative action programs. They have attacked the sex segregation of the job market by encouraging women to enter traditionally male occupations and by successfully challenging sex-segregated want ads.

Ideology and Goals within the Women's Liberation Branch

When women's liberation groups demand radical forms of social change, the women's rights groups such as NOW appear conservative by comparison. To the general public, many of the goals of the women's rights branch appear reasonable and legitimate when contrasted with the more radical goals of the other groups. Freeman (1975) has characterized the women's liberation branch as the ideological vanguard of the women's movement. "Here, new issues and interpretations are first raised and legitimated. . . . What began as a debate within the radical underground feminist media eventually emerges as a NOW resolution" (pp. 98–99). NOW changed its positions on consciousness raising and lesbianism after both had received extensive support from women's liberation groups. Similarly, the Women's Equity Action League reversed its stance on abortion in 1972. Indeed, the phrase "women's liberation" was first used by the more radical groups. Only after it became an accepted label for the current women's movement did women's rights groups begin to use it.

Whereas several of the specific goals of the women's rights segment are easily identifiable, some of the goals of the women's liberationists appear to be neither so specific nor so easily identifiable. There is a large body of ideology justifying certain goals as well as social change in general. For example, Kate Millet (1973) characterizes the "struggle" for equality as resulting from male domination in all societal institutions. Socialist women use the works of Marx, Engels, Lenin, and Marcuse as the theoretical bases of their analyses of the position of women more frequently than do other liberationists (see, for example, Rowbotham, 1973).

Social movement theory suggests that the ideology of a movement specifies goals and justifies the need for reaching the implicit or explicit goals. The ideology also gives a heaven-or-hell version of the world—what the world will be like if the movement succeeds, as opposed to what it is like without the movement. Many ideological statements describe present or past society—the negative side. Gloria Steinem (1972) proposes a positive vision of the future if the movement succeeds:

> Women don't want to exchange places with men. . . . But we do want to change the economic system to one more based on merit. In Women's Lib Utopia, there will be free access to good jobs—and decent pay for the bad ones. . . . Men will have to give up ruling-class privileges, but in return they will no longer be the only ones to support the family, get drafted, bear the strain of power and responsibility. . . . What will exist is a variety of alternative life-styles. . . . In other words, the most radical goal of the movement is egalitarianism. If Women's Lib wins, perhaps we all do [pp. 184–188].

Movement Organizations

During the feminist movement's early years, the most common type of group was the "consciousness-raising" (CR) or "rap" group. These groups are still found within both branches of the movement, although they began in the women's liberation branch. Consciousness raising is oriented to changing the perceptions of individuals, and the CR group allows its members to share common and yet personal experiences. The members then realize that certain discriminatory things happen to them because they are *women*, not because of individual traits (Freeman, 1972). Thus, the members learn that "the personal is political"—that is, they see the social basis of their private, seemingly individual problems. In this way, private troubles are linked to public issues concerning the structure of society. Since women become aware of inequality through CR groups, the groups have been seen as prerequisites for action. They have been labeled "the heart of the movement" (Polk, 1972, p. 323).

Consciousness-raising groups, typically composed of 6 to 12 members, can take advantage of a variety of guidelines prepared by such groups as NOW and the New York Radical Feminists. Guidelines have suggested three stages in the development of a CR group. First, the group should organize itself out of a prior organizational or friendship network. Second, it begins topical discussions about family, childhood and adolescence, men, marriage, or women, in order to allow each member to share her experiences and ideas. A "feminist consciousness" should emerge when group members realize that many women share similar experiences. Once consciousness has been raised, group members are advised to reach the third stage by developing specific projects such as setting up workshops, organizing a child-care center, or challenging laws that seem discriminatory ("Consciousness Raising," 1973).

In her study of the women's movement, Carden (1974) found that the CR groups in her sample lasted an average of 9 months. Members did reconceptualize their lives in terms of feminist ideology. Some groups attempted to set concrete goals for action. Most, however, disintegrated, and the members ceased active participation in the movement.

Researchers and movement authors have dealt with the failure of consciousness-raising groups to evolve into groups with goals for action. Jo Freeman, writing under the name Joreen (1973), called for the formation of groups with specific goals. Payne (1973) described the need to concentrate on "specific projects with tangible results" (p. 284). Kontopoulos (1972) cited the need for more structure or organization within CR groups.

Although members of both branches of the movement participate in CR groups, different types of organizations are also found in each branch. The women's rights branch consists primarily of national and formally structured hierarchical organizations with elected leaders, official policymaking bodies, dues for membership, and written policy statements. In contrast, virtually no women's liberation group has a nationwide focus or membership. The liberationists have tried to evolve a structureless pattern of organization (Freeman, 1972).

This concept of structurelessness exerts great influence in the women's liberation branch. Power and decision making are shared by all members of a group, regardless of the individual's interests or abilities. This desire for structurelessness is a reaction against what is seen as a male pattern of organization, giving more power and prestige to some people than to others. Because there is no definable power structure, groups seem to lack unity of direction as well as clear-cut goals. This uncertainty surrounding goals has been seen as a major problem of the movement. Although "structurelessness" implies a total lack of structure, Jo Freeman, writing under the name Joreen (1973), has suggested that there is an informal structure in all groups. Cassell (1977) found that friends who were very active made up the informal structure of the ideologically structureless women's liberation group she studied. Structurelessness may be demonstrated more successfully in consciousness-raising groups than in movement organizations. (For a discussion of these types of issues in women's organizations, see Chapter 14.)

The following is a brief description of six women's groups—three within the women's rights sector and three that focus on liberation.

Women's Rights Groups

National Organization for Women (NOW). The emergence of NOW in 1966 was described at length in an earlier section of this chapter. It is the oldest women's movement organization now in existence and is estimated to have approximately 590 local chapters. NOW has been regarded by some as a relatively conservative movement organization because it has focused on achieving changes through existing mechanisms such as legislatures and courts and changes in the policies of specific industries. NOW's first activity, a demonstration against *The New York Times'* policy of segregating all want ads by sex, was ultimately successful. NOW's present priorities are ratification of the Equal Rights Amendment, use of the federal Equal Employment Opportunity Commission to enforce nondiscrimination in employment on the basis of sex, modification of the media images of women, and modification of school textbooks that have been termed "sexist" (Gager, 1974).

Women's Equity Action League (WEAL).   The Women's Equity Action League emerged in 1967 when a group of NOW members felt that NOW's approach was too militant. WEAL, which has some state and local affiliates, has concentrated primarily on legal and educational inequities. It has brought charges of sex discrimination against colleges and universities, local governments, and financial institutions. WEAL uses the tactics of lobbying, lawsuits, and studies, avoiding confrontation and demonstrations.

National Women's Political Caucus (NWPC).   The National Women's Political Caucus was formed in 1971 by several members of NOW and other women interested in getting women involved in the political process. With 500 to 700 local chapters, NWPC has focused its activities on reforming the major political parties to include more women in the political process, encouraging women to run for public office (including financial support for selected female candidates), and lobbying for legislation on child care, health reforms, welfare, and the Equal Rights Amendment (Gager, 1974).

Women's Liberation Groups

The emergence of new groups from existing groups has been seen in the three movement organizations described above. Liberation groups have followed a similar pattern, as members differ over ideology and tactics and leave to form a new organization. For example, Salper (1972a) points out that in 1968 the first New York group, the New York Radical Women, split into three groups: Redstockings, WITCH (Women's International Terrorist Conspiracy from Hell), and a third group which dissolved shortly.

New York Radical Feminists (NYRF).   New York Radical Feminists was formed in 1969 by dissatisfied members of Redstockings, which in turn had grown out of the original New York Radical Women, and of the Feminists, which had split off from NOW. Thus, it is a third-generation organization. NYRF was originally composed of a number of loosely connected brigades or organizational units. Each brigade was to engage in consciousness raising and merge into a coalition to take action. This form has been modified because it was seen as too structured. The ideology of NYRF stresses the need for changes in both women *and* men. It places the blame for sexism on oppressive relationships, not on capitalism, which some liberationist groups see as the enemy. NYRF still exists as a series of individual brigades.

Chicago Women's Liberation Union (CWLU).   Formed in December 1969, the Chicago Women's Liberation Union has a socialist-feminist orientation. The CWLU "required all members to agree with a statement that they would 'struggle against racism, imperialism, and capitalism and dedicate ourselves to developing consciousness of their effect on women'" (Freeman, 1975, p. 108f). From the late summer of 1970 until June 1971, the Socialist Worker's Party and its youth affiliate, the Young Socialist Alliance, attempted to take over the CWLU. Ultimately, SWP/YSA was excluded from the CWLU. In 1975 the CWLU offered "such services as a Rape Crisis Line, a Legal Clinic, Direct

Action for Rights in Employment, Women's Health Work Services, and a Liberation School for Women" (Grimstad & Rennie, 1975, p. 238).

The Boston Women's Health Book Collective.   At a women's conference in Boston in 1969, a group of women took part in a discussion session on women and their bodies. Afterwards, some women decided to continue the discussion and formed a group. After sharing medical experiences, they began to do research about women's health issues. Next, they taught a course. Ultimately, they wrote *Our Bodies, Ourselves* (1973). The Boston Women's Health Book Collective, then, is an example of a group that was able to move beyond sharing experiences to action. *The New Woman's Survival Sourcebook* (Grimstad & Rennie, 1975) describes many other women's groups engaged in projects ranging from health care to feminist theater and women's centers.

Leadership within the Women's Movement

The women's movement as a whole is unique because it has developed a distinct antileadership philosophy. Fundamental to this philosophy is the idea that all women must participate equally in the movement. Stambler (1970) contends that leaders would usurp power from members and would point organizations or the movement itself in directions chosen by the leaders. Hole and Levine (1971) quote a woman who suggests that leaders are avoided in order to prevent co-optation by other groups and to prevent a "gap" in the structure if the leader becomes inactive. Carden (1974) states that some groups allow limited leadership for purposes of coordination and communication, but major decisions come from the group, not from individuals. Women's rights groups rely on grass-roots participation for major decisions. Consciousness-raising groups are structureless and, therefore, leaderless.

In line with this philosophy on leadership is the movement's lack of recognition of spokespersons—designated individuals capable of speaking for the movement. Although numerous individuals appear in the media, deliver speeches, or write articles and books articulating movement ideas, they are seen by other members as expressing their own personal thoughts rather than speaking for the movement. Ideological statements are seen by movement members as representing only the particular interpretation or feeling of the author or authors. Movement members stress the importance of personal statements in the belief that each individual's concept is valid. "Any expression of 'expert' authority, such as an explanation of how to organize a demonstration, can be interpreted as an elitist put-down of the other women and is frequently attacked on that basis" (Carden, 1974, p. 91).

The absence of official spokespersons has created some problems for the media, as Jo Freeman (1973) explains:

> While it has consciously not chosen spokespeople, the movement has thrown up many women who have caught the public eye for varying reasons. These women represent no

particular group or established opinion; they know this and usually say so. But because there are no official spokespeople nor any decision-making body the press can query when it wants to know the movement's position on a subject, these women are perceived as the spokespeople. Thus, whether they want to or not, whether the movement likes it or not, women of public note are put in the role of spokespeople by default [p. 292].

Thus, certain women are labeled as "stars" by the media. But these "stars" are selected by the media, not by members of the movement.

Although the movement espouses this principle, it is not carried out entirely. Leadership functions of group coordination and communication are accomplished by specific individuals or by everyone in the group on a rotation basis. Some movement organizations elect coordinators or facilitators. Those filling organizational roles are often designated by the media as leaders and, therefore, receive more attention. Individuals such as authors Betty Friedan and Kate Millet, journalist Gloria Steinem, and politicians Bella Abzug and Shirley Chisholm have performed a variety of leadership tasks in the movement. These movement "stars" may be functional in clarifying issues and attracting new members. At the same time, they may be dysfunctional because they perpetuate traditional leadership concepts.

The antileadership philosophy of the women's movement seems to be more a goal to strive for than a situation that exists in reality. Although some groups may not recognize official leaders, and those spotlighted by the media clearly state that they are speaking for themselves, there seems to be no indication that many movement members support or are even aware of this antileadership principle. Radical groups may be exceptions. Large movement organizations, particularly women's rights groups, do have mechanisms such as national elections to ensure the performance of leadership tasks.

Membership in the Women's Movement

There are no card-carrying members of the women's movement. Women may belong to a particular movement organization. Most groups have no requirements for membership other than general agreement with goals. Many organizations collect some dues. Dues are frequently waived if a member feels that she is unable to pay. In general, if an individual feels that she is a movement member, whether she belongs to a group or not, she is counted as a member of the women's movement. Although Carden (1974) has estimated that 90,000 individuals belong to some type of women's movement group, it is impossible even to estimate the number of individuals who consider themselves to be members of the movement.

In a national study of 718 women, Ball-Rokeach (1976) found that 11% had favorable attitudes toward sexual equality and had actually participated in organizations or activities working for sexual equality. Another 51% of the women had favorable attitudes, even though they did not indicate any active participation. Similarly, Welch (1975) found that women who expressed opposition to women's liberation nonetheless agreed with an average of 10 out of 17 goals of the women's movement. She concluded that those who are against "women's liberation" are not necessarily opposed to any given issue that the movement has raised; in fact, they probably are supportive of most of them. It would appear that many women have been frightened by the notion of "women's liberation" and will profess not to believe in it, yet are supportive of what the movement stands for, in a large part [p. 226].

Thus, there seems to be considerable support for the women's movement and its goals among women who are not active participants in the movement.

Various authors have suggested categories of individuals into which movement members fit. Altbach (1971) has suggested that campus groups and White middle-class homemakers form the constituency of the movement. Campus groups include students and faculty members who have felt sexual discrimination or who may anticipate it in future careers. They may be using the movement to solve professional problems of discrimination, or they may want to improve society generally.

Dixon (1972) has suggested that three categories of women form the constituency of the movement and that each is initially interested in one major issue of the women's movement. Working-class women have joined over economic issues; middle-class women have joined in order to overcome their limited roles as mothers and homemakers; students have become aware of the sexual exploitation of women and have defined the movement as a means of fighting it.

Carden (1974) found that women in the women's rights segment were generally in their late 20s or early 30s and usually married. Those in women's liberation groups were younger, in their 20s, and a greater number were divorced. All of the women were found to be cosmopolitan, very highly educated (college, graduate, or professional degree), oriented to professional careers, and not deeply committed to institutionalized religion. Most members had been encouraged by a role model to "be an individual" or to "be successful."

Other research lends support to Carden's. Freeman (1975) noted that the median age of women's rightists was higher than that of women's liberationists. Daniels (1979) indicated that WEAL consisted mainly of professional women. Bernard (1971) concluded that movement women tended to be young, White, and middle class. A survey by *Ms.* magazine of its subscribers in 1973 discovered that "supporting feminists, at least those that subscribe to *Ms.*, appear to be highly educated, employed, and earning considerably less than their husbands" (Freeman, 1975, p. 37). Welch (1975) found that younger, more highly educated, liberal women, who did not attend church regularly and who were not homemakers, were more likely to express support for women's issues and the women's movement in general.

Members of the working class have been seen as potential members by both Carden and Dixon. In a 1972 case study of two working-class women active in the movement, Lipetz found that these women were active because of personal problems of economic discrimination and that they deactivated when the problem was solved. Carden (1974) has suggested that socialization patterns encourage women in the working class to be satisfied with traditional social roles. Therefore, they are less likely to be concerned with the issue of social inequality. Working-class women are drawn to the movement by economic matters; they are interested in job discrimination, not general social inequality. In March 1974, the Coalition of Labor Union Women was formed. Its goal is to promote equality for working women on the job, in the unions, and in politics. CLUW is also committed to organizing employed women who are not already in unions (Wertheimer, 1977).

The theory of relative deprivation can be applied to members of the women's movement. According to this theory, discontent is produced when an individual feels she will not be permitted to reach a goal in society that that individual feels she can reach or has a right to reach (Morrison, 1973). In the case of some movement members, role models and high educational attainment have created rising expectations in terms of success in society. If a woman is not allowed to reach her own goals, either because of discrimination in employment or because of traditional role expectations for women (wife and mother), the resulting frustration may lead to alliance with the women's movement.

On the surface, modern movement members seem to be as homogeneous a group as 19th-century movement supporters—White, middle class, and so forth. However, many movement members do not fit this stereotype, including lesbians and Black women. The lesbian issue has created dissension among several women's movement organizations.

In 1968, lesbians were first recognized as members of the movement by the Feminists in New York. Other groups were more hesitant to accept lesbians as members or to deal with the issue of lesbianism as a concern of the movement. Betty Friedan referred to the lesbian issue as the "lavender menace" or the "lavender herring" of the movement, fearing that all women in the movement would be labeled as lesbians. This labeling, thought Friedan, could damage the movement's public acceptance.

A feminist group called Radicalesbians, formed in 1970, participated in a variety of demonstrations. Lesbians were accepted by some groups and rejected by others. In 1970, *Time* magazine attacked the credibility of movement theorist Kate Millet (Abbott & Love, 1973) by publicizing her admitted bisexuality, a fact that emerged during a demonstration for child care and abortion in New York. Friedan called on Millet to drop the issue of homosexuality because of this "bad" publicity. Other movement "stars," including Gloria Steinem, Florynce Kennedy, and Ti-Grace Atkinson, showed support for Millet's personal rights of sexual preference by denouncing the *Time* article. They encouraged her to disregard media attacks on her credibility.

NOW, the group that opposed dealing with the lesbian issue, voted in the fall of 1971 to accept lesbianism as a valid life-style and to support lesbians legally and morally. The issues that concern lesbians include the right to marry, divorce, and have custody of or adopt children. Lesbians want the freedom to declare their sexual preference publicly without being subjected to employment, residential, and other forms of discrimination.

Lesbian feminists have stated that homosexuality is considered deviant because society is oriented to male domination of women. If society did not rigidly define sex roles and "appropriate" behavior, lesbianism would not be an issue. The Radicalesbians (1973) believe that women should define themselves in terms of women and not as subordinates to men.

Black women have not identified themselves with the women's movement in as large numbers as might be desired. This may stem from the fact that historically in our society Black women have been more independent than White women. "Unable to depend on the black man for the economic necessities or for protection, they did not acquire the habit of subordination to masculine authority" (Ware, 1973, p. 82; see also Chapter 8). Williams (1972) has suggested that Black women could become more interested in the women's movement if the movement concentrated on issues of concern to Blacks, such as welfare, employment, working conditions, poverty, and child care. Williams also points out that some Black women see the women's movement as anti-male, and some Blacks fear that a division between Black women and Black men could undermine any successes of the Black civil rights movement.

Perhaps involvement in the civil rights movement has militated against membership in the women's movement. If the primary identification of a Black woman is that of race rather than sex, the civil rights movement may be defined as more relevant to Black women than the women's liberation movement.

Several Black women's groups do exist. Groups such as the National Council of Negro Women have supported the Equal Rights Amendment, even though their primary focus is on racial problems. One Black women's movement organization did emerge in 1973. The National Black Feminist Organization was organized to encourage Black women to participate fully in society and to "assume positions of leadership and honor in the black community" (Gager, 1974, p. 428). With such groups as the National Black Feminist Organization and the Coalition of Labor Union Women, the women's movement is no longer composed solely of White middle-class women.

Tactics

The diversity of goals of the women's movement has been discussed in detail in a previous section of this chapter. The tactics that have been employed in seeking to accomplish these goals reflect this diversity. In addition, women's rights and women's liberation segments have frequently used different tactics to reach a similar goal.

Consciousness-raising groups have been discussed as a type of movement organization. CR itself must be viewed as a primary tactic of the movement, and women will become aware of problems faced by all women through CR. The use of consciousness raising as a tactic seems to be more widely accepted in the women's movement than it has been in other social movements.

Whereas consciousness raising focuses on movement members, other tactics have been used to attempt to achieve movement goals within the context of American society as a whole. These have ranged from litigation and legislation to teaching women basic techniques of self-defense.

Radical women in the liberation branch of the movement have employed "zap" actions—surprise demonstrations at business offices or public meetings—to express complaints about the operation of the business concerned and to demand changes in the organization's policies. Many of these zap actions have been directed at mass-media corporations. In 1970, the Women's Liberation Front of San Francisco invaded a CBS stockholders' meeting. The group accused the network of denigrating women in its programming and in commercials aired by the network. The same group also distributed "sexist" articles printed by the *San Francisco Chronicle* inside the newspaper's offices, urging officials to improve coverage of women (Hole & Levine, 1971). A group called Media Women zapped the *Ladies' Home Journal* in 1970 to protest that magazine's refusal to give coverage to nontraditional women's issues. The women were condemned by the editors for interrupting phone calls and smoking the editor's cigars, not for protesting the magazine's policies (Bird, 1973), and the magazine allowed the women to publish a supplement to the August 1970 issue to deal with women's liberation (Hole & Levine, 1971).

Litigation has been a primary tactic of women's rights groups. They bring test cases to court that challenge existing laws or attempt to force compliance with existing laws. Individuals and groups have frequently used Title VII of the 1964 Civil Rights Act to challenge discriminatory employment policies of large corporations. *The New York Times* stopped segregating its want ads by sex because of pending action. Colgate-Palmolive was forced to abandon weight-lifting restrictions placed on female employees, thus opening higher paying jobs to women. Both *Newsweek* and *Time* lost sex-discrimination suits filed by female employees. The Supreme Court ruled in *Phillips* v. *Martin-Marietta* in 1971 that companies could not refuse to hire women with small children unless the same policy applied to men with small children (Komisar, 1971). Recent criminal and civil court decisions have affected issues such as employment benefits for women, rape, and abortion. Some of these decisions have benefited women; others have worked to their detriment.

Legislative activities have been a major thrust of many movement women. Seeing laws as a source of discrimination as well as a way to end discrimination, women have run for public office and lobbied Congress and state legislatures with varying degrees of success. Women gave personal testimony during the New York State Assembly's abortion hearings in 1970, a tactic that Bird (1973) credits as "one of the most effective . . . in getting the New York State abortion law liberalized" (p. 538). Women in every state have urged their state legislatures to ratify the Equal Rights Amendment to the U.S. Constitution.

Several states have gone well beyond ratification of the ERA. For example, noting that many of Kentucky's state laws were discriminatory, the governor, movement women, Kentucky's Commission on Women, the Legislative Research Commission, and several members of the General Assembly prepared a legislative program to change more than 125 laws that discriminated against women. Insurance rates, credit applications, parental consent, and membership on state commissions were among the areas affected. The entire legislative package was passed by the General Assembly in 1974.

Feminists have adopted a wide variety of other tactics to reach other goals. Some have turned to karate and judo lessons for self-protection. Some have opened counseling centers for rape victims. Others have conducted classes in topics as different as women's history and auto mechanics. Self-help health clinics and women's centers have emerged in many cities (Grimstad & Rennie, 1975).

Feminists may also select a variety of tactics to accomplish the same major goal. In seeking to change the media images of women, for example, some groups have staged zap actions. Others have filed suit against media corporations. Still others have developed guidelines for dealing with the media in interview situations to ensure accuracy in news or feature stories. Those guidelines include: (1) speaking only to female journalists; (2) insisting that two or more group members participate in the interview; (3) taping the interview themselves; and (4) exercising final editorial control over the story. Some feminist groups have chosen to boycott the press entirely (Ware, 1970).

The tactics selected to reach any particular goal depend on the nature of the problem and the type of group planning the action. Women's rights groups have most frequently used legislation and litigation. Women's liberationists have depended more on demonstrations and zap actions. Individuals in both women's rights and women's liberation groups use consciousness raising, self-help classes, and counseling centers. Cassell's (1977) evaluation of the choice of tactics is that "women's liberation goes to the 'root cause' of the problem and calls for a radical transformation of values, relationships, and institutions; women's rights groups attack symptoms, seeking palliative and redressive measures to raise the status of women" (p. 183). Because the liberationists are challenging the traditional structure of society, successes are more difficult to attain. Women's rightists are chipping away at identifiable problems women face. Most feminists today recognize the importance of both the women's liberation and women's rights approach to equality. As one feminist said about NOW, "they are freeing us to get on with the work we feel is ultimately revolutionary. Thank the Goddess for NOW!" (Grimstad & Rennie, 1975, p. 229).

Opposition

Whenever social change is proposed, opposing groups are likely to arise. Opposition to any social movement may take a variety of forms. An organized countermovement may emerge, as may ideologies challenging the movement ideology. Specific groups acting in opposition to movement organizations may attempt to offset any gains made by the social movement (Killian, 1973). Opposition to the women's movement consists of counter-ideologies and a number of groups that encourage the maintenance of traditional femininity or oppose specific goals of the women's movement.

Midge Decter has been cited as one of the most formidable intellectual adversaries of the women's movement. In *The New Chastity* (1972), Decter discusses four major areas of concern: housework, sex, the role of the wife, and childbearing. Her principal conclusions are:

1. Women should recognize their own freedoms—they are free to work or to choose to remain in the home.
2. The sexual revolution has been more of a victory for men than for women because women can no longer use sexual favors to gain attention.

3. Marriage allows women to gain further freedoms and to share their destinies with a person of choice.
4. Motherhood allows a woman to do the one thing that only she can do—create and bear a new individual.

Esther Vilar, author of *The Manipulated Man*, has also articulated an antimovement ideology. Vilar states (Dreyfus, 1973) that men are actually victims of a world created to suit women's wishes. Women are parasites because they may choose to be totally dependent on men by staying home.

In addition, the books *Total Woman* and *Fascinating Womanhood* and the courses based on them are part of the backlash against the women's movement. They urge women to follow the traditional feminine role and be submissive to their husbands. Happiness of Womanhood offers charm-school-type courses to help women develop skills in being feminine. Women are encouraged to treat men like kings in order to be treated like queens.

A variety of organizations that see the women's movement as a threat to the traditional women's role have emerged. Some express antifeminist philosophies. Others help women become more "feminine." Carden (1974) found that members of the antifeminist groups are typically middle- and lower-middle-class housewives and mothers between the ages of 30 and 40. Most antifeminists are political, and in some cases religious, conservatives who oppose government intervention in any area of life (except in the area of abortion rights). Therefore, they resent attempts to legislate equality between the sexes.

The most active political countermovements have been organized to undo the gains the women's movement has made in the area of abortion and to block progress toward another key goal, the ERA. Right-to-life organizations are actively opposed to abortions and especially to the use of public tax funds to pay for them. The Stop ERA Committee, a group opposed to the ratification of the Equal Rights Amendment, has been involved in the defeat of the amendment in most of the states that have not yet ratified it. The group has been most successful in southern and central states. Phyllis Schlafly, a speechwriter for conservative Republican presidential candidate Barry Goldwater in 1964, is the group's organizer and chief spokesperson.

Schlafly (1973) argues that the Equal Rights Amendment would "deprive women of the legal rights, benefits, and exemptions they now possess" (p. 18). State legislatures may change undesirable laws, but the ERA, she believes, would change many laws that some women consider beneficial to them. Schlafly supports (1) laws that require husbands to support their wives; (2) the practice of awarding custody of children to the wife during a divorce; and (3) legislation protecting women from various working conditions such as overtime and night hours. Unfortunately for her, however, the courts are already taking these "privileges" away from women, even without the ERA.

While a significant number of individuals are personally opposed to or indifferent toward the women's movement, those actively involved in opposing it seem to be organized around specific issues. Those groups and individuals that oppose the goals of the women's movement seem to favor maintenance of the status quo or changes that either would not affect the traditional concepts of masculinity and femininity or would reestablish old patterns.

In discussing opposition to the women's movement, it is important to remember that those who have a stake in the status quo have reason to oppose the changes the movement proposes. Powerful groups have benefited from sexism. These groups (including government, corporate, and union leaders) are being asked to give up those benefits and share their power. Men, in general, stand to lose their privileges, such as not having to do housework or compete with women for jobs. It is no wonder, then, that various institutions—from national corporations to organized labor and the National Collegiate Athletic Association—with investments in sexual inequality are on opposite sides of issues from women's groups. Their opposition can sometimes be seen when women's issues are debated in a public forum such as a state legislature.

Successes and Failures of the Women's Movement

The significance of social movements . . . lies not in their careers but in their consequences for the larger society and its culture. Unless a social movement results in significant social change, it becomes merely an interesting sidelight to history, a curiosity [Killian, 1973, p. 47].

A number of changes have occurred in American society since the women's movement emerged as a viable social movement. The movement has not been the only cause of legal and social change affecting women; however, some association between the movement and such changes does exist. In some areas, specifically employment, legal changes have not created major economic gains for women as a whole. In others, such as media coverage of women's areas, change has been significant. Major social change can occur with institutionalization and public acceptance of movement goals. The extent of social change can be measured only at some point in the future after the women's movement has run its course.

The following areas of concern and the accompanying statistics document some of the changes related to the women's movement:

1. *Equal Employment Legislation.* A number of federal laws protect women against sex discrimination in work. The first major piece of legislation restricting sex discrimination was the Equal Pay Act of 1963, which required equal pay in situations where men and women did substantially equal work. This law was followed a year later by Title VII of the Civil Rights Act of 1964, which declared it illegal for employers or unions to discriminate on the basis of race, color, national origin, religion, or sex. The Civil Rights Act protects women against employment discrimination by private employers, state and local government employers, employment agencies, and labor unions.

Two executive orders and a congressional statute prohibit discrimination by federal agencies. Equal Employment Opportunity Commission guidelines allow the EEOC to investigate all sex-discrimination complaints and order conciliation, take the case to district court, or refer the case to the Attorney General.

Many women also receive some protection from the 1967 Age Discrimination in Employment Act, which forbids discrimination against employees or job applicants aged 40 to 65, and from the recent amendments to Title IX of the Education Act, forbidding sex discrimination in educational institutions.

The primary intention of these laws was to provide equal treatment of employees (or students). Executive Order 11246, issued by President Johnson in 1965, went a step further. This order, with its later amendments, required federal contractors (generally businesses and institutions of higher education) to develop affirmative action programs. Under these programs, the contractor must compare its own employment of women and minorities with their availability within the labor market. If such a comparison indicates that the contractor is "underutilizing" women or minorities, the employer must then make special efforts to recruit and hire qualified members of the underutilized group. Affirmative action programs also include provisions for equal pay and for upward mobility, and various other aspects with a more positive, expansive thrust than the term "equal opportunity" generally suggests.

It is a little early to tell how effective these laws and executive orders have been. The question is a controversial one, with complaints voiced on all sides. Opponents of affirmative action protest that the government programs result in expensive paperwork, reverse discrimination, and a lowering of employment standards. Advocates of women's rights protest that the programs have produced token responses rather than substantive gains for women. Both sides can point to numerous examples to support their claims.

Although the overall picture is not yet clear, working women have made some definite gains. Starting salaries for men and women are more nearly equal. The merging of help-wanted advertising into a single, nonsexist listing and the federal government's campaign to remove sex designations from job titles represent small but significant steps toward reduced sex-typing of jobs. Doors that were long closed to women have begun to open—for example, in coal mines, police stations, and fire departments. And many employers, large and small, have had to make provisions for the advancement of female employees or, where wage discrimination has been found, to pay large sums for back wages. These are encouraging beginnings, and it is likely that women will continue to find improvements in employment conditions. However, the rate at which the new strides will be taken remains uncertain.

2. *Media Coverage.* Media coverage of women involved in the women's movement has increased significantly. In 1966–1967, the *Reader's Guide to Periodical Literature* listed 15 articles about movement activity. In 1969–1970, the same publication listed over 200 articles of feminist concern (Carden, 1974).

3. *Feminist Media.* In 1975, *The New Woman's Survival Sourcebook* listed 170 feminist publications (Grimstad & Rennie, 1975).

4. *Women's Studies in Colleges.* In 1975, 112 programs in women's studies and 4658 women's studies courses were offered by colleges and universities (Grimstad & Rennie, 1975).

5. *Women's Centers.* Many women's centers have been established. Some handle only one specific problem, such as abortion, birth control, rape, or battered wives, while others tackle any problem a woman faces.

Not all of the social changes related to the women's movement can be quantified. Rape, child care, and legalized abortion have emerged as national issues during the career of the movement. And the statement "I'm for equal pay, but I'm not a women's libber" is familiar. The women's movement has become a part of American society.

It is difficult to cite specific failures of the women's movement. Ultimate success or failure can be assessed only through the objectivity of retrospective analysis. However, it is possible to point out some areas that are problematic to the movement in the late 1970s.

Some people may not have been attracted to the movement because it has not succeeded in clarifying its goals to the general public. There is considerable confusion surrounding the Equal Rights Amendment, and the movement has been unsuccessful in defusing misunderstandings about its goals. In 1968, the movement was faced with the media label of "bra burners"—a label that was generally accepted by the public as fact. Despite numerous tries in a variety of circumstances, movement members have not been able to shed the original image.

Although the women's movement has achieved legislative victories with regard to equality in employment, credit, insurance, and other areas, that legislative success has not been a major source of social change. In many instances, the laws are simply not enforced. Some institutions set up affirmative action offices and go through the motions of legal compliance without actually changing policies. Others hire "token" females to meet expected guidelines, thus following the letter but not the spirit of the law. Many organizations are forced into compliance through lawsuits, while others comply willingly. In too many instances, the goals of equality have yet to be achieved.

Conclusion

There are both similarities and differences between the woman's rights movement of the 19th century and the women's movement of today. Both movements generated many goals. A legislative goal, suffrage, became the primary goal of the earlier woman's rights movement; ratification of the Equal Rights Amendment is a central goal today. The more conservative organizations in both movements supported these legal changes, while the more radical elements of both concentrated on more widespread social changes.

Other similarities are equally striking. Both had early connections with the rights of Blacks. Both introduced new tactics—parades and consciousness raising, respectively. Both had splits between radicals and conservatives. Both were concerned with issues surrounding reproduction—birth control and abortion. And both had to deal with unfortunate media labels—"bloomer girls" and "bra burners." In sum, both social movements concentrated on the position of women in relation to education, health, family, politics, and employment.

The second women's movement was able to build on the gains of the first one. At the beginning of the woman movement, women had few, if any, political or legal rights. The current feminist movement has been able to use the political and legal rights won by the earlier movement to push for further progress in the status of women. Today, women are spending more years in school and in the labor force and fewer years in childbearing and child rearing. The increase in female labor force participation and the ability to control fertility have challenged the traditional unequal division of labor between the sexes. The social inequalities women still face, in both their role as homemakers and their role as paid employees, are being addressed by the feminist movement.

One difference between the two social movements involves the development of mass media and modern transportation. Word of an emerging concern with women took years to spread and develop in the 1840s. In the 1960s, it was only a matter of months between the time dissatisfaction was expressed and a meeting was called by Betty Friedan. The media provide instant news coverage today. When media coverage is inadequate, feminists today use their own newsletters or begin telephone communication for fast action. In sum, modern feminists have been able to accomplish more in less time.

Another difference between the two is the opposite direction in which efforts have been exerted with regard to protective legislation on working conditions. Early social feminists (except for the Woman's Party) joined Progressives in getting women and children covered by some protective laws. Hours of work were shortened, and working conditions were improved. Modern feminists contend that present working conditions are vastly different from those of the past. They observe that the remnants of those laws have hurt women more than they have helped them. With federal legislation and union contracts regulating hours, wages, and working conditions, old laws have restricted rather than protected many women (as the Woman's Party foresaw). Again, this difference is due to changes in society.

One final difference between the two movements involves their respective members. The women who were active in the early movement were quite homogeneous and made few attempts to diversify until after 1900. The women's liberation movement has a little more diversity by race and social class, but both members and opponents of the movement have expressed concern over the relative lack of heterogeneity in the membership. The woman movement had its male supporters, but changing the roles of men was never a central issue. In the modern movement, men have been excluded from membership in some groups. But the modern movement *is* concerned with freeing men from the debilitating effects of the traditional male sex role. Feminists want to change the male role so as to include housework and child-care responsibilities. Men have gained child-custody rights. Some protective legislation, such as guaranteed rest periods, has been extended to cover men.

A men's liberation movement and male consciousness-raising groups have been one outgrowth of the women's movement. Today, increasing numbers of men are questioning their traditional sex role and looking at the limitations they face as a result of sex-role socialization and societal expectations (Pleck & Sawyer, 1974). According to Farrell (1974), sharing breadwinning as well as housework and child-care obligations with women will free men to be less job oriented and to pursue other interests. Broadening the male sex role would allow men to be more emotional and nurturing (Balswick & Peek, 1975). A crucial component of men's liberation is for men to learn not to exploit or dominate women (Nichols, 1975). Thus the men's and women's liberation movements have complementary goals.

The future of the modern feminist movement is difficult to predict with certainty. Social movement theory is useful in making some predictions. The movement can be expected to continue to diversify its membership. As more people become affiliated with it, goals will change and become more conservative. In reaction to a conservative force, a new radical arm may emerge. It is possible then that new and more radical groups could develop within the movement.

Once the movement completed its successful all-out drive to extend the deadline for passage of the ERA from March 1979 to June 1982, it redirected its efforts toward ratifying the ERA. If ERA becomes the chief goal and ratification is achieved, the movement will be forced to reevaluate itself to determine new directions. Some groups may disband with the victory rather than find new directions. If the ERA is not ratified, a new legislative push in that direction seems likely.

The modern movement must continue in its efforts to win the confidence of society. Its members are beginning to achieve leadership roles in society. The movement must come to grips with its problem of leadership: either it must accept its own philosophy of leaderlessness, or it must begin to develop its own leaders. Today, many women in leadership roles are denounced or criticized for acting "unsisterly" precisely because they are effective in those roles.

Most important for the future of sex roles in our society, the modern movement must learn from the failures of its predecessor. Feminists must somehow encourage movement organizations to change goals and still remain active. And the movement must force implementation of all new legislative gains. Unenforced laws are useless. The status and rights of women will change only if American society becomes committed to that change.

If the modern feminists can achieve continuity, growth, and implementation, the goals of the women's movement will have been achieved. If those goals remain uncertain or if interest in sex roles wanes, American society can expect yet a third social movement in the future concerned with the status and rights of women.

Points to Ponder

The following selections present three different points of view concerning the fight for women's rights. The first dates from the suffrage movement and argues for equality for women; the second represents a contemporary antifeminist perspective on women's position in society; the third dates from the current women's movement and takes a radical feminist stance.

Another writer asserts that the tyranny of man over woman has its roots, after all, in his nobler feelings; his love, his chivalry, and his desire to protect woman. But wherever the roots may be traced, the results at this hour are equally disastrous to woman. Her best interests and happiness do not seem to have been consulted in the arrangements made for her protection. She has been bought and sold, caressed and crucified at the will and pleasure of her master. . . . It is often asserted that as woman has always been man's slave—subject—inferior—dependent, under all forms of government and religion, slavery must be her normal condition. This might have some weight had not the vast majority of men also been enslaved for centuries . . . who, in the progress of civilization, have reached complete equality ["History of Woman Suffrage," 1973, pp. 458–459].

The theoretical model that conceives of male success in attaining positions of status, authority, and leadership as *oppression* of the female is incorrect. . . . The fact that women lose out in these competitions . . . is an inevitable byproduct of the reality of the male's aggression advantage and not the cause, purpose, or primary function of it. . . . Whether the losers in such competitions are . . . women is important only in that—because so few women succeed in these competitions—the society will attach different expectations to men and women (making it more difficult for the exceptional, aggressive, woman to attain such positions even when her aggression is equal to that of the average man). . . . To call that which is inevitable "oppression" would seem to confuse more than clarify and, if one feels that male dominance is "oppressive," this model offers an illusory hope of change where there is no possibility of change [Goldberg, 1978, pp. 97–98].

Humanity has begun to outgrow nature: we can no longer justify the maintenance of a discriminatory sex class system on grounds of its origins in Nature. . . . The problem becomes political . . . when one realizes that, though man is increasingly capable of freeing himself from the biological conditions that created his tyranny over women and children, he has little reason to want to give this tyranny up. . . . To assure the elimination of sexual classes requires the revolt of the underclass (women) and the seizure of control of *reproduction:* not only the full restoration to women of ownership of their own bodies, but also their (temporary) seizure of control of human fertility. . . . So the end goal of feminist revolution must be, unlike that of the first feminist movement, not just the elimination of male *privilege* but of the sex *distinction* itself: genital differences between human beings would no longer matter culturally [Firestone, 1970, pp. 10–11].

References

Sources of particular interest to the reader are marked with an asterisk.

Abbott, S., & Love, B. *Sappho was a right-on woman.* Briarcliff Manor, N.Y.: Stein & Day, 1973.
Adams, A. Remember the ladies (1776). In A. Rossi (Ed.), *The feminist papers.* New York: Bantam Books, 1973.
Altbach, E. H. (Ed.). *From feminism to liberation.* Cambridge, Mass.: Schenkman, 1971.
Ash, R. *Social movements in America.* Chicago: Markham, 1972.
Ball-Rokeach, S. J. Receptivity to sexual equality. *Pacific Sociological Review*, 1976, *19*, 519–540.
Balswick, J. O., & Peek, C. W. The inexpressive male: A tragedy of American society. In J. W. Petras (Ed.), *Sex: male/gender: masculine.* Port Washington, N.Y.: Alfred Publishing, 1975.
*Banner, L. W. *Women in modern America: A brief history.* New York: Harcourt Brace Jovanovich, 1974.
Berheide, C. W., Berk, S. F., & Berk, R. A. Household work in the suburbs: The job and its participants. *Pacific Sociological Review*, 1976, *19*, 491–517.
Bernard, J. *Women and the public interest.* Chicago: Aldine-Atherton, 1971.
Bird, C. A new kind of woman. In R. Evans (Ed.), *Social movements: A reader and source book.* Chicago: Rand McNally, 1973.
Boston Women's Health Book Collective. *Our bodies, ourselves: A book by and for women.* New York: Simon & Schuster, 1973.
*Carden, M. L. *The new feminist movement.* New York: Russell Sage Foundation, 1974.
Cassell, J. *A group called women: Sisterhood and symbolism in the feminist movement.* New York: David McKay, 1977.
Consciousness raising. In A. Koedt, E. Levine, & A. Rapone (Eds.), *Radical feminism.* New York: Quadrangle, 1973.
Daniels, A. K. WEAL: The growth of a feminist organization. In B. Cummings (Ed.), *On the road to power: Women's struggle for equality.* Metuchen, N. J.: Scarecrow Press, 1979.
*de Beauvoir, S. *The second sex.* New York: Bantam, 1952.
Decter, M. *The new chastity.* New York: Berkeley Publishing, 1972.
Dixon, M. Where are we going? In E. H. Altbach (Ed.), *From feminism to liberation.* Cambridge, Mass.: Schenkman, 1971.
Dixon, M. Why women's liberation? In W. Martin (Ed.), *The American sisterhood.* New York: Harper & Row, 1972.
Dreyfus, C. Women are the creators of male chauvinism. *Mademoiselle*, February 1973, pp. 122–123; 170–172.
Easton, B. Industrialization and femininity: A case study of nineteenth century New England. *Social Problems*, 1976, *23*, 389–401.
Farrell, W. *The liberated man.* New York: Random House, 1974.
Firestone, S. *The dialectic of sex: The case for feminist revolution.* New York: Bantam, 1970.
Flexner, E. *Century of struggle: The woman's rights movement in the United States.* Cambridge, Mass.: Belknap Press, 1959.

Freeman, J. Structure and strategy in the women's liberation movement. *The Urban and Social Change Review*, 1972, 5, 73–74.

Freeman, J. The origins of the women's liberation movement. In J. Huber (Ed.), *Changing women in a changing society*. Chicago: University of Chicago Press, 1973.

*Freeman, J. *The politics of women's liberation*. New York: David McKay, 1975.

Friedan, B. *The feminine mystique*. New York: Dell, 1963.

Gager, N. (Ed.). *Women's rights almanac 1974*. Bethesda, Md.: Elizabeth Cady Stanton Publishing, 1974.

Goldberg, S. The inevitability of patriarchy. In A. M. Jagger & P. R. Struhl (Eds.), *Feminist frameworks*. New York: McGraw-Hill, 1978.

Grimstad, K., & Rennie, S. (Eds.). *The new woman's survival sourcebook*. New York: Knopf, 1975.

Hahn, E. *Once upon a pedestal*. New York: Mentor, 1974.

History of woman suffrage. In A. Rossi (Ed.), *The feminist papers*. New York: Bantam, 1973.

*Hole, J., & Levine, E. *Rebirth of feminism*. New York: Quadrangle, 1971.

Huber, J. Toward a socio-technological theory of the women's movement. *Social Problems*, 1976, 23, 371–388.

Joreen. The tyranny of structurelessness. In A. Koedt, E. Levine, & A. Rapone (Eds.), *Radical feminism*. New York: Quadrangle, 1973.

Killian, L. Social movements: A review of the field. In R. Evans (Ed.), *Social movements: A reader and source book*. Chicago: Rand McNally, 1973.

Koedt, A. Women and the radical movement. In A. Koedt, E. Levine, & A. Rapone (Eds.), *Radical feminism*. New York: Quadrangle, 1973.

Komisar, L. *The new feminism*. New York: Franklin Watts, 1971.

Kontopoulos, K. M. Women's liberation as a social movement. In C. Safilios-Rothschild (Ed.), *Toward a sociology of women*. Lexington, Mass.: Xerox College Publishing, 1972.

*Kraditor, A. S. *The ideas of the woman suffrage movement 1890–1920*. New York: Anchor, 1965.

Kraditor, A. S. (Ed.). *Up from the pedestal: Selected writings in the history of American feminism*. Chicago: Quadrangle, 1968.

Lipetz, M. J. Sociologists and working class women. Paper presented to the North Central Sociological Association, June 1972.

Millet, K. Sexual politics: A manifesto for revolution. In A. Koedt, E. Levine, & A. Rapone (Eds.), *Radical feminism*. New York: Quadrangle, 1973.

Morrison, D. E. Some notes toward a theory on relative deprivation, social movements, and social change. In R. Evans (Ed.), *Social movements: A reader and source book*. Chicago: Rand McNally, 1973.

National Organization for Women. Statement of purpose. In C. F. Epstein & W. J. Goode (Eds.), *The other half: Roads to women's equality*. Englewood Cliffs, N. J.: Prentice-Hall, 1971.

Nichols, J. *Men's liberation: A new definition of masculinity*. New York: Penguin, 1975.

Nies, J. *Seven women: Portraits from the American radical tradition*. New York: Viking Press, 1977.

O'Neill, W. L. *The woman movement: Feminism in the United States and England*. New York: Barnes & Noble, 1969.

Oppenheimer, V. K. *The female labor force in the United States*. Population Monograph Series, No. 5. Berkeley: University of California Press, 1970.

Pastoral Letter of the Massachusetts Congregationalist Clergy (1837). In A. S. Kraditor (Ed.), *Up from the pedestal: Selected writings in the history of American feminism*. Chicago: Quadrangle, 1968.

Payne, C. W. Consciousness raising: A dead end? In A. Koedt, E. Levine, & A. Rapone (Eds.), *Radical feminism*. New York: Quadrangle, 1973.

Pleck, J. H., & Sawyer, J. (Eds). *Men and masculinity*. Englewood Cliffs, N.J.: Prentice-Hall, 1974.

Polk, B. B. Women's liberation: Movement for equality. In C. Safilios-Rothschild (Ed.), *Toward a sociology of women*. Lexington, Mass.: Xerox College Publishing, 1972.

Radicalesbians. The woman-identified woman. In A. Koedt, E. Levine, & A. Rapone (Eds.), *Radical feminism*. New York: Quadrangle, 1973.

Rossi, A. Equality between the sexes: An immodest proposal. *Daedalus*, 1964, 93(2), 607–652.

Rossi, A. Equality between the sexes: An immodest proposal. In R. J. Lifton (Ed.), *The woman in America*. Boston: Beacon Press, 1964.

*Rossi, A. (Ed.). *The feminist papers: From Adams to de Beauvoir*. New York: Bantam, 1973.

Rowbotham, S. *Woman's consciousness, man's world*. Baltimore: Penguin, 1973.

Salper, R. The development of the American women's liberation movement, 1967–1971. In R. Salper (Ed.), *Female liberation: History and current politics*. New York: Knopf, 1972. (a)

Salper, R. Introduction. In R. Salper (Ed.), *Female liberation: History and current politics*. New York: Knopf, 1972. (b)

Seneca Falls Convention. Declaration of sentiments and resolutions (1848). In A. S. Kraditor (Ed.), *Up from the pedestal: Selected writings in the history of American feminism*. Chicago: Quadrangle, 1968.

Schlafly, P. ERA: Loss of protection . . . *Trial Magazine*, November/December 1973, pp. 18–22.

Seese, L. You've come a long way, baby—Women in the movement. In J. Cooke, C. Bunch-Weeks, & R. Morgan (Eds.), *The new women*. Greenwich, Conn.: Fawcett, 1970.

Sochen, J. *Movers and shakers*. New York: Quadrangle/New York Times, 1973.

Stambler, S. (Ed.). *Women's liberation—Blueprint for the future*. New York: Ace, 1970.

Steinem, G. What it would be like if women win. In W. Martin (Ed.), *The American sisterhood*. New York: Harper & Row, 1972.

Ware, C. *Woman power: The movement for women's liberation*. New York: Tower Publications, 1970.

Ware, C. Black feminism. In A. Koedt, E. Levine, & A. Rapone (Eds.), *Radical feminism*. New York: Quadrangle, 1973.

Welch, S. Support among women for the issues of the women's movement. *Sociological Quarterly*, 1975, *16*, 216–227.

Wertheimer, B. M. *We were there: The story of working women in America*. New York: Pantheon, 1977.

Williams, M. Why women's liberation is important to black women. In W. Martin (Ed.), *The American sisterhood*. New York: Harper & Row, 1972.

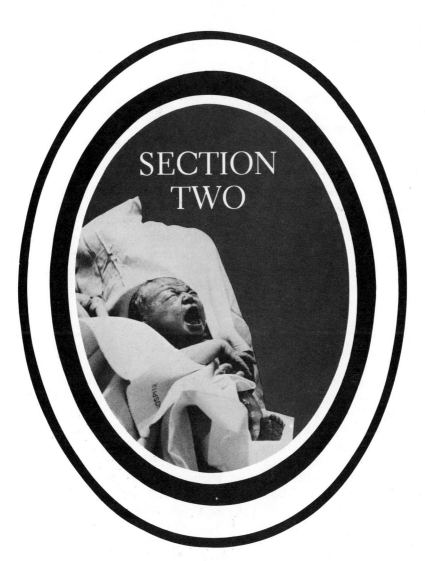

SECTION
TWO

HOW
ARE WE
BORN
DIFFERENT?

Mary Anne Baker

We know that the rights and roles of women are changing. In later sections of this book, we will examine the different roles and options society makes available to females, as well as specific aspects of women's behavior in the economic and political world. All of these areas depend heavily on behavior learned in the process of growing up in a particular culture.

Before we begin these discussions, however, we need to consider the biological bases for differences in behavior. Many people accept the idea that some people are born more intelligent than others. It seems that some people are "born athletes," while others are "all thumbs." In general, there is wide acceptance that there are biologically based differences in some kinds of behavior. Are there biological bases for differences in male/ female behavior? To this broad question, the answer must be yes. Obviously, each sex plays a different role in reproductive behavior. The question of interest to us here, however, is whether there are unlearned sex differences that contribute to observed differences between boys and girls, men and women, in such areas as learning, seeing, and growing.

Until recently, the role of unlearned sex differences in such areas have been largely ignored. Now the idea of studying behavior in a "biosocial context," as Williams (1977) calls it, has begun to come of age. That is to say, both the biological and the social contributions are being considered. In this section, we will consider the role of the unlearned contribution to developmental differences (Chapter 3), differences in the ability to see or hear (Chapter 4), learning differences (Chapter 5), and the role of physiological factors in personality (Chapter 6). The material reported in each of these chapters is based on the work of experimental psychologists.

A great deal of research has been carried out to compare men and women in a number of aspects of behavior that are important to what we do and become. For example, Matina Horner (1970) has suggested that women learn a fear of success: we often back away from promotions and other chances for advancement. (For a discussion of these findings, see Williams, 1977, pp. 184–186.) Research of this type is of interest to many psychologists who study women and is reported in a number of books and articles (for example, Unger & Denmark, 1978; Tavris & Offir, 1977; Williams, 1977; Bardwick, 1971; Sherman, 1971). We will not review these data here but will focus instead on those data most relevant to answering the question "Are we born different?"

Before considering these findings, we need to understand what kind of data psychologists gather. While the specific kinds of data will vary depending on the topic of the study, psychologists try to make precise measurements related to the behavior of interest—if possible, numerical or quantitative measurements. For example, in the study of growth, we look at bone development and age of puberty. In sensory studies, we measure how loud something needs to be in order to be heard. In learning studies, we

Section opening photo: No one denies that there are differences between males and females at birth, but what are these differences and how do they affect us? (Photo by The Courier Journal and Louisville Times Co.)

consider the number of times a subject must see a list of words to repeat it without error. And in the area of personality, we use the test scores of individuals.

We also need to ask who the subjects are. Most psychologists live in North America or England, and for the most part the data reported have been gathered from human subjects in those locations. When subjects from other locations have been used, their country of origin will be noted.

In addition, psychologists use animals as subjects. In the following four chapters, animal studies will be reported on occasion. Why include animal studies when many people feel that they cannot be very useful in understanding human behavior? The answer is that we can obtain very important information from animals that we cannot get from human subjects. In terms of the data presented here, the study of animals permits experimenters to control and vary factors that could not be considered easily—or, in some cases, not at all—in human subjects. For example, a series of studies on sweetness preferences is reported in the section on the sense of taste (Chapter 4). In these studies, the amount of sweetened or unsweetened water consumed was measured for male and female rats after they had been operated on to control the production of sex hormones. It would have been impossible ethically to use human subjects in a similar manner. Also, animal studies are used because the human life span is so long. To consider sweetness preferences of adult human subjects whose previous experience with sugar was known exactly would require watching the person for at least 20 years.

Despite the practical advantages of animal studies, as Bleier (1976) points out, the effort is at best questionable if the findings cannot be applied to the understanding of human behavior. Research with different animals indicates that there are certain ways in which different animals are similar. One area of similarity is in the functioning of the nervous and hormonal systems. The same kind of brain center that controls the drinking of water in rats appears to control liquid intake in humans; therefore, in this area, data from rat subjects can be applied to human subjects. Thus, animal studies are included where they are relevant and helpful.

In the next four chapters, some of the actual data regarding unlearned contributions to observed sex differences will be considered, along with various explanations for the meaning and importance of these findings.

GROWING UP FEMALE; GROWING UP MALE

CHAPTER 3

The first area of psychology we will consider is that of human development. The subject matter of human development covers a very wide range of information. Traditionally, developmental psychology has included such diverse areas as genetics, prenatal development, physical growth and nutrition, intelligence, language development, personality development, and social interaction. Thus, developmental psychology touches on many other areas of psychology. Its distinguishing feature is its emphasis on the role and effect of changes that occur in the individual during the aging process.

In this chapter, we will consider data on the contribution to observed sex differences of the unlearned aspects of each area of development.

Sex Differences in Conception Ratios and Birth Rates

Are the same number of males and females born? Despite the biological probability that half of all sperm cells should contain Y chromosomes (producing male offspring) and half X chromosomes (producing female offspring), evidence indicates that more males are born than females. The exact ratio varies from sample to sample as different factors are controlled, but in each case the male births outnumber the female births. For example, Rubin (1967) found that during 1964, among Caucasian Americans, there were 105 male births for each 100 female births; among non-White Americans, he found 102 males for each 100 females. Other factors such as age of parents, birth order, and season of the year have been found to affect birth ratios (see Table 3-1).

The ratio of male to female conceptions is not so easy to determine as the ratio of births, because the actual conceptions cannot be counted. One can attempt to estimate the conception ratio, however, by considering the ratio of the sexes at birth and the sex ratio of prenatal deaths. Most studies find a greater number of male than female prenatal

Table 3-1.   Sex Ratio by Live-Birth Order and Race for the United States, 1964

Order of Birth	White Males per 100 Females	Non-White Males per 100 Females
1	106.2	103.8
2	105.2	101.6
3	105.3	104.2
4	104.7	102.8
5	103.6	101.8
6	103.3	101.4
7	102.9	101.3
8 and over	104.4	99.1
Total	105.2	102.1

From "The Sex Ratio at Birth," by E. Rubin, *American Statistician*, 1967, 21, 45–48. Copyright 1967 by the American Statistical Association. Reprinted by permission.

deaths (M. Ounsted, 1972, pp. 177–202; Williams, 1977, pp. 119–120)—thus implying an even higher rate of male to female conceptions.

Of what importance are these differences? They indicate that from the very earliest stages of development biological differences are found when people are classified according to sex. A more important question is whether these differences indicate other, more significant differences that could affect the individual in important ways. It appears from data presented in later sections that this may be the case. Consideration of the pattern of prenatal development points out some of these differences.

Prenatal Development

Although both sexes begin with the union of a sperm and an ovum, their prenatal development is not identical. Physiological differentiation according to sex begins early and is the product of several factors that operate at different points during the prenatal period. The sex of the fetus is also an important influence on many aspects of the total development of the organism (J. D. Wilson, 1978).

Before discussing these data, it is important to note that the sex of an individual is not totally determined by the X and Y chromosomes present at conception. For example, the presence of a Y chromosome in a newly conceived organism does not ensure that the child will be a boy. A number of prenatal variables can contribute to the child's being born with external female sex organs or a mixture of both male and female sex organs. The fetus contains structures for developing both the vagina and ovaries of the female and the penis and testes of the male. Although control of the development of these structures is not fully understood, A. Jost (1953) has demonstrated that the male sex hormones (androgens) are necessary for the development of the penis and testes in the genetically male

organism (that is, a fetus with a Y chromosome). The fetus will develop female characteristics if the male hormones are not present at a critical period.

On the basis of these and other findings, it is often said that organisms are basically
female unless differentiated as male. It is likely that this is true because all fetuses are
exposed to female sex hormones present in the mother's blood and in the placenta.
Although the fetus is not exposed directly to everything in the mother's blood, we know
that hormones do cross. Since we do not have the situation in which sex hormones are
absent in prenatal development, we do not know if fetuses are basically female unless
differentiated as males or if the female hormones present cause them to differentiate as
females (J. D. Wilson, 1978; Bleier, 1976).

Although it is not inevitable that the individual will be the same sex as the genetic
(chromosome) determination, in the vast majority of cases the observed sex of the individual is consistent with the chromosome content. For the most part, then, differences
between males and females begin with conception. The X and Y chromosomes, carriers
of genetic information, differ substantially in size. The X chromosome (female-
producing) is considerably larger than the Y chromosome (male-producing) and, therefore, contains more genes. Thus, the female begins life with more genetic material. The
role and significance of these extra genes have not been determined for the most part. One
current hypothesis is that, because they have less genetic material, males are less resistant
to many types of trauma, both prenatally and in later life.[1]

The chromosomal differences begin early to affect the developmental patterns of
males and females. By the 16th day after conception, differences within individual cells
have developed. During the 6th week, the gonads—internal sex organs—begin to differentiate. An originally neutral gonad develops one section (the medulla) into testes if the
individual has a Y chromosome and develops another section (the cortex) into ovaries if
the individual has only X chromosomes. The timing of the onset of these developments is
not the same. The female differentiation begins around the 6th week after conception; the
differentiation of the testes does not occur until about the 12th week.

There must be many differences occurring in brain development during the prenatal period. The little research that has been done in this area indicates that some centers
in the brain operate differently in males than in females. The hypothalamus, an organ
near the center of the brain, controls the production of many of the hormones present in
any individual. Studies have shown that hormones produced during the prenatal period
by the testes or ovaries influence the hypothalamus to develop in such a manner that it
will control either male or female adult hormone production. In the female, this center
controls the cyclical variation in hormone production associated with the menstrual cycle,
while in the male it controls a rather even production of hormones (Money & Ehrhardt,
1972, p. 56).[2]

[1]For a discussion of the theory of inheritance of intelligence through the X chromosome, see Wittig,
1976.

[2]For a discussion of problems with research and interpretation of information in this area, see Bleier,
1976. Although her conclusions may be overstated, she raises some important questions.

In an attempt to explain the observed differences between males and females in rates of development, Christopher Ounsted and David Taylor (1972) have hypothesized that the Y chromosome affects the growth rate of the individual. They suggest that the Y chromosome, while not carrying much genetic information itself, slows down the rate at which genetic information coded in the other genes is used by the male organism. They suggest as an analogy that males and females can be seen as "the occupants of two cars proceeding up the same highway at different speeds, pausing for different periods, who will finish some distance apart and have different experiences on the journey" (p. 246). The Y chromosome simply makes for a different developmental experience.

Many types of evidence are relevant to an assessment of this hypothesis. For example, the hypothesis is supported by the later prenatal development of the male sex organs. Throughout this chapter, we will find evidence from many areas of research that the male develops more slowly than the female. Whether the Y chromosome controls any of these differences cannot be determined from the data presented here. As Ounsted and Taylor point out, differences in the rate of development definitely occur, and their hypothesis is a possible explanation of these differences.

Sex differences are evident in nearly all areas of child development. It is almost certain that an important contributing factor to these observed sex differences is the difference in the rate of development of the two sexes. These differences can be seen in several areas of development after birth: physical growth, intelligence, language learning, personality, and social interaction. Although no one of these areas is independent of the others, separating the areas for the purpose of reviewing the findings helps to bring some order to a very complex problem.

Physical Growth

From everyday experience, it might appear simple to measure growth; however, because there are so many aspects of growth, there can be no single "right" way. Growth has been measured by height and weight, use of carbohydrates and fats (Beal, 1961), and bone development (Acheson, 1966). Sex differences have been found for all three of these measures. In most cases, the rate of female development is found to be faster than that of males, although, in absolute terms, males are usually taller and weigh more.

Leona Bayer and Nancy Bayley (1959) reported that the average weight at birth for males was 8.4 pounds (3800 grams), compared to 7.5 pounds (3400 grams) for females; the average height at birth for males was 19.8 inches (50 cm), compared to 19.3 inches (49 cm) for females. These differences at birth forecast the fact that males will be taller and weigh more throughout life. (It should be noted that the subjects in the Bayer and Bayley, 1959, study were American and predominantly Caucasian.)

If, however, the height and weight at birth are considered as percentages of mature height and weight achieved, females on the average have achieved 30.9% of their adult

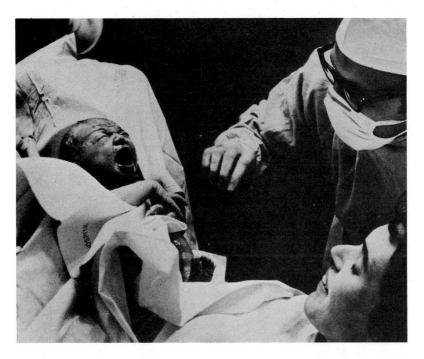

Figure 3-1. At birth, girls are smaller than boys, on the average, but they have attained a higher percentage of their adult height. (Photo © by The Courier Journal and Louisville Times Co.)

height at birth, compared to 28.6% for males (see Table 3-2). Throughout the entire growth period, sex differences in percentage of mature height achieved show females to be closer to their adult height than males. However, in actual height males are taller. For example, at 5 years of age, females have attained 66.2% of their mature height, while males have attained only 61.8%; but the average height of 5-year-old girls is 43.1 inches (105 cm), while the average height is 43.7 inches (112 cm) for 5-year-old boys (see Table 3-2).

There are also differences in age of mature growth—that is, the average age at which full growth is attained. Females, on the average, attain their full height at 17.0 years of age, while males do not reach their full height until 18.5 years of age. The mean height for females is 65.3 inches (168 cm) at maturity, while for males it is 70.9 inches (181 cm) (Bayer & Bayley, 1959).

Do different measures of growth lead to the same conclusion about sex differences in rate of growth? Evidence presented by A. B. Nicholson and C. Hanley (1953) indicates that they do. They gathered data on age of reaching maximum growth, skeletal development, percentage of mature height, and age of walking. The results indicated that age of

Table 3-2.   Sex Differences in Rate of Growth

	Girls			Boys	
Age (Years)	Average Height (Inches)	Average Percentage of Mature Height Achieved	Age (Years)	Average Height (Inches)	Average Percentage of Mature Height Achieved
Birth	19.3	30.9	Birth	19.8	28.6
1.0	29.1	44.7	1.0	30.7	42.2
2.0	34.4	52.8	2.0	34.6	49.5
3.0	37.5	57.0	3.0	38.0	53.8
4.0	40.6	61.6	4.0	40.8	58.0
5.0	43.1	66.2	5.0	43.7	61.8
6.0	45.9	79.3	6.0	45.8	65.2
7.0	48.1	74.0	7.0	48.7	69.0
8.0	50.4	77.5	8.0	50.9	72.0
9.0	52.7	80.7	9.0	53.1	75.0
10.0	55.1	84.4	10.0	55.3	78.0
11.0	57.5	88.4	11.0	57.5	81.1
12.0	60.7	92.9	12.0	59.1	84.2
13.0	63.0	96.5	13.0	61.4	87.3
14.0	64.2	98.3	14.0	64.6	91.5
15.0	64.8	99.1	15.0	68.1	96.1
16.0	65.2	99.6	16.0	70.1	98.3
17.0	65.3	100.0	17.0	70.5	99.3
			18.0	70.9	99.8
			18.5		100.0
			19.0		

Adapted from "Growth Curves of Height and Weight by Age for Boys and Girls, Scaled according to Physical Maturity," by N. Bayley, *Journal of Pediatrics*, 1956, 48, 187–194. Copyright 1956 by the C. V. Mosby Company. Reprinted by permission.

reaching mature height, skeletal development, and percentage of mature height all consistently lead to the same conclusion: females experience a faster rate of growth than males.

Age of walking was found to have little relationship with any of the other measures. In everyday experience, age of walking is often seen as an important indicator of the development of a child. However, because many cultural and nutritional factors can change the actual age at which walking occurs, it does not serve well as an indicator of development (Nicholson & Hanley, 1953).

All parts of the individual are developing, not just the body, but the parts do not all develop at the same rate. For example, Bayley (1956) found that rate of intellectual development was not correlated with height or bone development. The study of intelligence, which we take up next, is one indirect way of studying the development of the nervous system in the child because intellectual functioning is limited by the level of development of the nerve centers of the brain.

Intelligence

Although we associate a single number, the IQ score, with intelligence, there are many components involved in the concept of intelligence as it is commonly used. There are two long-accepted subdivisions of intelligence—verbal and performance. Verbal-intelligence scores are based, for the most part, on reading and vocabulary skills. Performance-intelligence scores are based on tasks such as puzzle solving and cancelation of certain numbers or shapes in a series. The single intelligence-test score can be seen as an average of the scores on the verbal and performance sections of the test. Often an individual obtains similar scores on both sections of the test; in that case, the single score measures the performance on both test sections fairly accurately. It is not uncommon, however, for an individual to obtain quite different verbal and performance scores. The average score, in this situation, does not give an accurate picture of either score. Therefore, one must look beyond the level of the single score to approach an accurate understanding of intelligence. Nevertheless, before we turn to examine intelligence in greater detail, let us consider briefly the findings on sex differences in overall scores.

Studies of overall scores on many standardized intelligence tests do not generally find sex differences (Maccoby & Jacklin, 1974, p. 65) because many of the tests have been deliberately constructed so that sex differences in the overall score do not occur when given to large groups of individuals. (See Hutt, 1972, p. 88, and Maccoby & Jacklin, 1974, p. 68, for a fuller discussion of particular tests, and compare with Garai & Scheinfeld, 1968, p. 196.) When the tests were being developed, questions that resulted in different scores for males and females were dropped from the test.

For our purposes, the most productive approach to studying intelligence comes from considering three parts of intelligence, often called intellectual abilities. These parts are not the same as the two sections of the IQ tests, even though one of the names is the same. The three areas are verbal, mathematical, and spatial skills.

Each of these areas is studied separately because it is thought that each can develop somewhat independently of the others. Verbal skills are related to size of vocabulary, as well as reading and talking ability. Mathematical skills are related to the ability to do simple arithmetic, as well as more complex logic. Spatial skills are measured by the ability to solve geometric problems and use maps. Sex differences at some point in development have been reported for each of these three intellectual areas.

Although it is widely believed that females outperform males on verbal tasks in general, the present evidence does not support such a broad generalization. According to Garai and Scheinfeld (1968), research findings indicate that females show superiority in some areas, and males show superiority in others. Studies have found that females possess greater verbal fluency than males from infancy on, and that females begin speaking at an earlier age because of earlier maturation of speech organs and level of articulation. The superior verbal fluency of females was not found to be the product of a larger vocabulary or better verbal comprehension. In a study of verbal reasoning requiring the drawing of deductive conclusions, high school boys were superior to girls, other factors being held equal.

After reviewing many studies based on many types of data, Maccoby and Jacklin conclude that there are three phases in verbal development. In the first stage, before 3 years of age, earlier studies showed superiority for females at this age, whereas more recent studies tend to show no differences. In the second stage, beginning at about age 3, the boys catch up, if they were ever behind, and in most population groups the two sexes perform very similarly until adolescence. A third phase of differentiation occurs at adolescence, with females outscoring males throughout the high school and college years.

Studies of mathematical skills ordinarily show no significant differences during the preschool, elementary, and junior high school years. During the high school years, however, males often are found to outscore females on tests of mathematical ability, even when both sexes had taken the same number of math courses (Garai & Scheinfeld, 1968, pp. 200–201; Maccoby & Jacklin, 1974, pp. 85–89).

The occurrence of sex differences in mathematical ability at approximately the same age as the beginning of puberty could suggest a physiological or hormonal contribution to these differences. While such a contribution should not be automatically ruled out, the very important and substantial social changes that occur at this period must be given first consideration as explanations for these differences. Dating and adult male/female relationships begin to develop at this time. A discussion of the nature and impact of these changing sex roles is found in Chapter 8. At this point, let us simply point out that the stereotype of females being poor in mathematics and the idea that males select females for dates could unconsciously influence sex differences in mathematical performance. Although this seems to be a logical explanation, it has not really been tested. Researchers have not yet gathered the necessary data on either the physiological or the socialized aspects.

Many studies show male superiority in tasks requiring the perception, judgment, and manipulation of spatial relationships (Buffery & Gray, 1972). Maccoby and Jacklin conclude that few recent studies report sex differences until adolescence, while A. W. H. Buffery and J. A. Gray conclude that male superiority begins during the preschool years and continues throughout development. These differences in conclusions about spatial ability may be due to differences in definitions about what data ought to be included in assessing spatial skills.[3]

An interesting explanation of the differences in spatial and verbal skills has been offered by Buffery and Gray (1972). They hypothesize that the timing of the development of the dominance of control by one half of the brain is in large measure responsible for the difference in spatial and language development.

Before looking at their hypothesis, we need to present some information about the structure of the brain. The largest part of the human brain, the *cerebrum*, is composed of two halves, called *hemispheres*, which are responsible for controlling our thinking and our higher mental functioning in general. The two halves of the brain look like mirror images

---

[3] Sherman (1978) provides an interesting discussion of sex differences in spatial skills. She suggests that spatial differences may affect behavior on other tasks that have been interpreted as differences in personality and social relationships.

on casual examination. Detailed examination, however, reveals certain physical differences. Studies of the control of specific kinds of behavior indicate that only one hemisphere is involved in some aspects of behavior. On other specific tasks, one side of the brain acts faster than the other side in controlling behavior. The side that acts faster is known as the *dominant* hemisphere. Many people believe that we are born with neither side dominant and that dominance develops during the preschool years.

Buffery and Gray suggest that, when the left half—where the center for the control of language is located in most people—becomes dominant, language abilities will appear but that spatial ability develops when neither half is dominant. Studies of spatial development suggest that spatial material is handled by the right, or nondominant, hemisphere (Knox & Kimura, 1970). Therefore, optimal development in both language ability and spatial ability is not possible. Research findings support the hypothesis that dominance develops later in the male, thereby physiologically predisposing him to having better spatial ability, and earlier in the female, thereby predisposing her to having better verbal skills.

In sum, it seems reasonable to say that many specific studies of intelligence show sex differences but that the data do not support any clear overall superiority for either sex. On overall intelligence scores, the importance of any observed differences is diminished by the fact that many tests were developed with the specific intent of minimizing sex differences. Studies of intellectual abilities, rather than intelligence-test scores, have found sex differences for some aspects of verbal, numerical, and spatial ability. The reason for these observed differences is not easily determined. Learned behavior regarding the proper roles for males and females undoubtedly contributes to the differences. Are there any unlearned bases for the differences? We do not know for sure, but sex differences in the development of brain dominance may play a role.

Intellectual abilities are influenced by many factors in the child's development. Language skills, for example, contribute both to the general ability to answer test questions and to specific scores on verbal intelligence. Language development is also important to the overall development of the child in many ways not related to intelligence. Let us now consider information about language development and possible sex differences in this important area.

Language Development

Language development begins in infancy with coos and other sounds. From this general beginning, infants soon develop the ability to generate sounds, called *phonemes*, that are the parts of adult language. Then they develop the ability to say words and, after a couple of years, to say simple sentences. From then on, they develop the capacity to produce sentences that are more and more like those of the adults. Let us consider each of these stages of language development in turn.

Sounds

Infants begin making sounds by about the age of 2 months. Out of the total range of possible sounds, only a limited group of sounds is used in any given language. Many, but not all, studies of phoneme production have found sex differences during the first year.

O. C. Irwin and H. P. Chen (1946) found that during the first year females utter a slightly greater variety of sounds, on the average, than do males. These small differences were not found to be statistically significant. In a review of the relevant literature, D. McCarthy (1954) found that many studies showed these small but nonsignificant differences. Maccoby and Jacklin (1974) report that more recent studies, using small groups of subjects, do not find consistent sex differences.

It is hard to say what importance should be attached to these differences. A variety of sounds must be available to the infant before it can utter words, so it is possible that more rapid development of even a slightly larger range of sounds can contribute to more rapid development of later stages of language development. Data do not exist to provide definite answers at this point.

First Words

Although individual sounds are the units from which words are developed, a child is generally considered to have begun talking only when he or she says identifiable words.

Although it may seem so on the surface, identifying the first word spoken by a child is not simple. The definition of what constitutes the first word varies among investigators, from a vaguely stated certerion, "the child commenced to talk" (Mead, 1913), to a highly precise definition, "the conscious association of a word or sound with an object for the purpose of communication" (Abt, Adler, & Bartelme, 1929). With such variation in criteria, it is not surprising that reports vary widely on the average age at which the first word occurs. In a review of studies using children without speech defects as subjects, the average age of occurrence of the first word was reported by F. L. Darley and H. Winitz (1961) to vary from 4 to 60 months of age. In all of these studies, in which separate data are reported for males and females, females were found to speak the first word at a slightly earlier age. For example, using children of college students, Mead (1913) found an average age of 16.5 months for males and 15.5 months for females. M. E. Morley (1957), whose sample comprised every tenth child born in Newcastle-upon-Tyne, England, found an average age of 12.0 months for boys and 11.4 months for girls.

What can be said about the source of the differences that have been observed? There are certainly both unlearned and learned components contributing to them. Physically, females develop more rapidly; as a part of this more rapid development, their speech organs and control centers in the brain develop more rapidly than do those of males. We begin, then, with an unlearned difference, but learned factors have an impact as well.

Studies of parent/child verbal interaction, even with very young infants, have found differences that could contribute to learned sex differences. H. A. Moss (1967) found that mothers of first-born children consistently showed differences in talking that were affected by the sex of the child. The sounds of female children were repeated by the mother more than those made by the males. These findings were consistent for 1 month and 3 months of age, although the differences were significant only at 3 months.

These differences in the mothers' behavior were found despite the fact that male and female infants showed about the same amount of talking at both ages. The mothers, therefore, were reinforcing females more, even though there were no observed sex differences in the behavior of the infants.

In a study of father/child verbal interaction, F. Rebelsky and C. Hanks (1971) also found that between 2 and 4 weeks of age fathers talked more to female than to male infants. This pattern was reversed by 3 months of age, when fathers talked more to male than to female infants. The Moss study showed that mothers talked more to females at this age than they did to males. Since in our present American culture, fathers generally spend much less time with children, especially infants, than do mothers, the impact of the father on learned behavior is much less than that of the mother. The effect of verbal interaction between adults and children on the child's verbal behavior in later years still needs to be studied.

First Word and Intelligence

The age at which the first word is uttered is often considered a measure of intelligence. Whether or not this factor does indeed measure intelligence is a question often raised by parents. Studies indicate that severely retarded children speak the first word much later than do children with average or above-average intelligence scores, but within the normal range of intelligence, age of first word has not been found to be an important predictor of intelligence.

It appears from the data of T. Moore (1967) that, at 18 months of age, speech quotient—a general measure of language development—is a good predictor of intelligence-test scores for girls, but not for boys. At age 3 years, Moore found that language is still a good predictor of intelligence for girls, but less so for boys.

Sentences

Another important stage in language development is speaking in sentences. Several studies generally show that females develop these skills earlier. Girls were found to produce longer and more complex sentences (Bennett, Seashore, & Wesman, 1959) from 18 months on and to make fewer grammatical mistakes (Smith, 1935). The superior ability shown by females in these areas is not related to size of vocabulary, because boys were found to have larger vocabularies than girls (Levinson, 1960; and studies cited by Maccoby & Jacklin, 1974, pp. 75–85, who discuss limitations on the generalizability of these findings).

Studies of the development of the ability to speak in sentences seem to provide less insight into the sources of observed differences in the performance of males and females than the previous areas considered. We really have no evidence by which to assess the importance and origin of such differences as have been found.

Overall, in the area of language development, evidence indicates that unlearned differences do exist, especially at the age at which talking begins. These differences interact with the learned differences that come with socialization. (For a fuller discussion of the cultural contribution in socialization, see Chapter 7.)

Personality and Social Interaction

As we move to a consideration of personality and interaction between people, we are in areas of behavior that are highly influenced by learning. Some of the important social factors influencing the development of sex differences in these areas are discussed in Chapter 7, in the context of sex-role socialization. What we wish to consider here is whether or not there is any evidence of physiological bases for observed sex differences in the developing personality and in social interaction. Before discussing the possibility of physiological influences in these areas, we need to consider where relevant sex differences have been found.

In their very broad review of the literature on sex differences, Maccoby and Jacklin (1974) conclude that there is evidence that boys and girls differ on several measures of temperament, social relationships, and power relationships.

In the area of temperament, as measured by activity level, studies have shown a tendency for boys to be more active than girls, at certain ages and under certain conditions (Maccoby & Jacklin, 1974, p. 177). Although some studies find no sex differences, those that do find sex differences report boys to be more active. Moreover, the activity level of boys increases when they are with other boys, whereas girls do not usually show an increase in activity level in the presence of other girls. As Maccoby and Jacklin point out, this distinction helps to explain some of the differences between results obtained in various studies.

Studies of social behavior in children reveal other types of sex differences. Boys have a greater number of friends than do girls. Boys are also more influenced by peer values and more often use peers as sources of interesting activities (Maccoby & Jacklin, 1974. p. 211).

Studies of power relationships have shown, to no one's surprise, that boys exhibit more aggressive and dominance-seeking behavior than girls. Boys engage in more rough-and-tumble play and more physical assaults. Boys have been found to be more aggressive in many situations at various ages (Maccoby & Jacklin, 1974, pp. 230–233). It is possible that the aggression level in boys is related to the higher activity levels reported previously.

> We saw . . . that boys were likely to be more active than girls in precisely those situations where aggression may also be observed—namely, during play with other boys. It seems quite possible, then, that aggression and activity may be linked in boys in much the way that parents believe it is, although whether intense activity arises from the arousal of aggressive impulses or vice versa, we do not know [Maccoby & Jacklin, 1974, p. 229].

Aggression is also related to dominance behavior in boys. Studies indicate a greater tendency among males to attempt to dominate one another. In childhood, aggression plays an important role in determining dominance within groups of boys. Since, in most play situations, boys play with boys and girls play with girls, there is little evidence on whether boys attempt to dominate girls (Maccoby & Jacklin, 1974, p. 274).

To summarize, studies have found higher activity levels in boys and a tendency to have larger peer groups, and these have greater influence on them than peers do on girls. Boys have been found to be more aggressive and to strive more for dominance in groups of males than females do in groups of females.

Is there any evidence for proposing a physiological contribution to any of these observed differences? The answer is that for some of this behavior there is evidence of a physiological contribution, whereas for other behavior there is no relevant evidence available.

For the origin of differences in the size of peer groups, no evidence exists as to whether or not there is a physiological contribution. Since peer-group interaction does not begin until the child is at least 2 or 3 years of age, there is ample opportunity for learning to affect this behavior. To date, no studies have been made on which we can base any specific conclusions.

The other areas—activity level, aggression, and dominance—tend to form a cluster of activities. The existence of a physiological contribution to these behaviors is very likely. High levels of activity and aggression occur together in boys' behavior, and aggression functions as the means by which a dominance role is established. Particularly high levels of activity and aggression occur in boys who hold dominant positions within boys' play groups.

There seems to be a physiological component of this behavior. Studies have shown a relationship between levels of male sex hormone, testosterone, and aggression in animals (Quandagno, Briscoe, & Quandagno, 1977). J. A. Gray (1971), in a study of aggressive behavior in mammals, has shown that levels of aggression decreased when levels of testosterone were decreased in castrated male rats and that aggression increased again when testosterone was injected into the castrated males. Injection of testosterone had no effect on females, and the level of the female sex hormone, estrogen, did not appear to affect aggressive behavior. Gray proposes that testosterone facilitates the development of aggression in a male animal, but that hormones do not affect aggression in a female animal.

Since testosterone is broken down into a form of estrogen, a question of interest is whether the male sex hormone is really different from the female. In a current review of the literature in this area, J. D. Wilson (1978) suggests that the total level of testosterone and the resulting estrogen is different in males. That difference alone may be sufficient to explain how the biochemically similar hormones contribute to sex differences.

For the cluster of behavior that includes activity level, aggression, and dominance, then, there is rather strong evidence to support the hypothesis that these behaviors are in part physiologically controlled. The importance of this physiological contribution is potentially very great. Even though social position in adult groups is not usually dependent on physical aggression, the roles that one adopts in childhood have great influence throughout life. (See Chapter 7 for a discussion of the effect of early learning patterns on later behavior.) The role relationships that are developed among boys are greatly affected by levels of aggression, and levels of aggression are evidently affected by levels of male sex hormones. Thus, male sex-hormone levels can have a significant effect on an important component of adult social behavior.

To accept the important contribution made by physiological components is not to discount the role of learning in the development of aggression, dominance, and activity level. Clearly, socialization affects these behaviors, but the effect builds upon the un-learned component. The two factors may well interact to produce the differences in male/female behavior that are commonly observed.

Summary

Growing up female is not the same as growing up male. Approximately 105 boys are born for each 100 girls. The conception ratio probably favors boys even more. At each age, male deaths outnumber female deaths; this pattern begins prenatally.

The male-offspring-producing Y chromosome is not so large as the female-offspring-producing X chromosome. The rate of development, as measured in several ways, is different from soon after conception until maturity. The female offspring develops more rapidly, as measured by percent of mature height and weight, rate of bone develop-ment, and age of growth maturity.

Intelligence-test scores do not usually show sex differences because the tests were designed to minimize sex differences. Studies of three intellectual abilities—verbal, mathematical, and spatial—often show sex differences. Females appear to develop some verbal skills earlier than males. Differences in mathematical scores begin to occur at junior or senior high school level. At this point, social pressure to follow sex-stereotyped behavior patterns is great. It is likely, therefore, that social pressure for boys to take courses in math and for girls not to take them contributes to the observed differences. Males generally show greater skill at spatial tasks. Although there are many contributing factors, Buffery and Gray propose that differences in the rate of development of dominance of the cerebral hemisphere can contribute to these differences.

In the development of personality and social interaction, people often think that boys are more aggressive and girls more affected by their friends. Data indicate that boys are more active and, in many situations, more aggressive than girls. But it is also the boys who have larger, more hierarchically organized peer groups. These groups seem to have more influence than the smaller, more loosely organized groups of girls. Data from several sources indicate that there may be hormonal and other physiological characteris-tics that contribute to these differences.

Overall, the evidence for unlearned contributions to development is extremely strong. The sum of the effects of these differences is not so clear. It may be that some of the differences are subsequently reinforced and exaggerated by learned differences. The physiological differences taken alone may be small; unmagnified, they could well be unimportant. But in combination with what we learn to expect as proper behavior for men and women, they become important. Thus, the differences we observe in adult behavior are built upon physiological differences that begin very early.

We turn now to consider the evidence concerning sex differences in sensory functioning. This area gives us important insights into the extent of physiologically determined sex differences because the functioning of our senses is much less likely to be influenced by socialization than are personality and interaction between people.

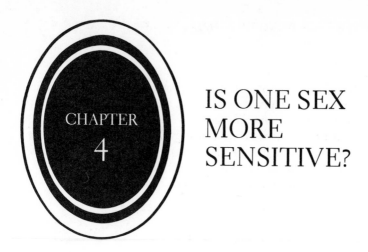

IS ONE SEX MORE SENSITIVE?

The study of sensation is essentially the study of our contact with and organization of the external world. Information from the outside world comes through our senses: eyes, ears, tongue, nose, and skin. What we know about the world beyond our bodies is limited by what our senses are capable of experiencing. There are things we cannot experience. The "silent" dog whistle, for example, emits sounds that are within the range of the dog's ears but not ours. Sensation is the study of these limits.

Research in the area of sensation is divided into several subareas, based on the sense organ through which the stimulation is received. The senses include vision, hearing, smell, taste, touch, temperature, pain, balance, and deep-muscle sensation. Research about sex differences in sensation, however, has been limited for the most part to the senses of hearing, vision, temperature, taste, and smell. It is these differences that will be considered here.

Hearing

Of the many areas of study within the field of hearing, only one will be considered in detail here. *Presbycusis* is the study of how the ability to hear soft sounds changes with age. It is commonly observed that, as a person gets older, his/her ability to hear decreases. The study of presbycusis is a technical study of these changes. Sex differences are an integral part of this study because hearing-ability changes are different for males and females.

In a 10-year study of age and sex differences in pure-tone thresholds for subjects between 18 and 65 years of age in University Park, Pennsylvania, J. F. Corso (1963) found that males show greater hearing losses than do females, and their losses begin to occur at least 5 years earlier than those of females.

Figure 4-1 shows the curves from Corso's data at 4000 cycles per second (cps). Males between 60 and 65 years of age require much more intense sounds than do 18-year-old males. The 65-year-old must have the sound increased by 35 decibels (units of

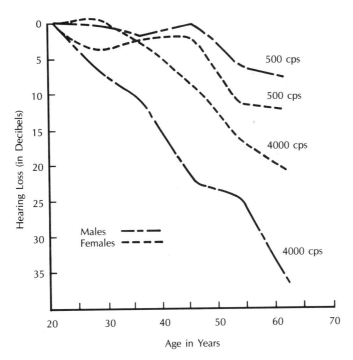

Figure 4-1. Comparison of hearing loss for males and females at 500 cps and 4000 cps. The curves for each sex are computed as mean hearing loss relative to the original threshold sound-pressure-level values for 18-year-old to 24-year-old subjects of the respective sex. From "Age and Sex Differences in Pure-Tone Thresholds: Survey of Hearing Levels from 18 to 65 Years," by J. F. Corso, Archives of Otolaryngology, *1963, 77, 385–405. Copyright 1963. Reprinted by permission.*

sound intensity) in order to hear what the 18-year-old hears. Females aged 60 to 65 need an increase of only 17 decibels. The sex difference in hearing loss is great. If the curves for 4000 cps are compared for the period between ages 30 and 40, it can be seen that, although hearing loss occurs in both sexes, hearing deteriorates faster in males than in females.

Why does this sex difference occur? It is commonly suggested (as in Glorig and Nixon, 1960) that the greater hearing loss for males is caused by greater exposure to gunshots and noisy factories (both situations have been demonstrated to cause hearing loss). There does not appear to be an experimental test of this explanation, but some data suggest it is not correct. Corso found that, when he compared a sample of nonnoise-exposed males to a sample of females from the general population, the males still showed a greater hearing loss than the females did. This evidence suggests that male hearing loss is not caused by gunshots and noisy factories alone and that other factors should be considered to explain sex differences in hearing.

Studies such as Corso's have looked at changes in hearing over the years. In a study of hearing thresholds during the menstrual cycle, Baker and Weiler (1977) found changes that seem to parallel changes in the level of female sex hormones—progesterone and estrogens. They tested a group of women once a week for several weeks and found that in the second half of the menstrual cycle, when the levels of these hormones are high, the sensitivity of their hearing improved. They also tested a group of women who were taking birth-control pills. Birth-control pills contain large doses of female sex hormones; therefore, these women had high hormone levels during most of the monthly cycle. (They drop only at the time they stop taking the pills to start the menstrual flow.) These women consistently showed good hearing sensitivity. Thus, when hormone levels were high, all women showed greater sensitivity than when hormone levels were lower.

Although it is not possible to point with certainty to any one explanation for sex differences in hearing, there is little reason to think these differences are learned as part of our sex-role socialization. Let us consider sex differences in other areas of sensation to see if there is further evidence of a physiological contribution.

Vision

The sense of vision is considered by many to be the most important sense to people in their everyday functioning. In part because of this belief, a vast amount of research on vision has been done. Little of this work, however, has included sex as a variable. As one researcher commented to me, "I always considered an eyeball to be an eyeball, whoever it belonged to." Given the differences in hearing for males and females, this assumption regarding vision would seem to be worthy of reexamination. Studies of acuity (the clarity with which we see) suggest that sex differences also exist here.

In a review of studies of the occurrence of nearsightedness and farsightedness in children, M. J. Hirsch (1952) found sex differences compounded with age differences. In a summary of these findings, Hirsch (1963) concluded: "Almost all studies of the refraction of children show a difference between boys and girls. Both groups have similar changes over time but these tend to occur two or three years earlier among girls than among boys" (p. 150). Specifically, girls were found to peak in nearsightedness during the period between ages 10 and 13, whereas boys were found to peak between ages 13 and 16. The earlier peaking for females parallels the accelerated maturation rate of females discussed in the section on growth in the previous chapter.

Indirect influences about visual acuity can be drawn from a study by M. Alpern (1967) of the proportion of people in Tecumseh, Michigan (population 9500), who wear glasses. At each age tested, from 6 to 70 years, a higher percentage of females wore glasses than did males. By age 45 for females and 55 for males, 93% of the population wore glasses.

Neither of these studies was designed to look for origins of the observed differences. However, a study by M. Diamond, A. L. Diamond, and M. Mast (1972) considered the relationship of visual acuity to variation in sex-hormone levels in females. It was found

Figure 4-2. The sensory capacities of these four generations of females differ because of the differences in their ages. However, a similar group of males would exhibit even greater sensory differences. (Photo courtesy of the University of Louisville, from the Canfield and Shook Collection.)

that women who had normal menstrual cycles showed increased visual acuity at the beginning of menstruation and during the following one to two weeks. The level of acuity then returned to the levels consistently shown by males and by females taking oral contraceptives. Apparently, the hormone patterns that occur during the first half of the menstrual cycle, which are different from those found during the second half of the cycle and different from those of the females taking oral contraceptives, are related to the females' increased ability to see light. These findings parallel those for hearing thresholds reported by Baker and Weiler (1977).

Again for vision, we find sex differences in areas where learned differences should be minimal. We also find an indication that these differences are related to the very hormones that are important in determining the sex of an individual. If it is clearly established that sex differences in sensation are related to variation in female sex-hormone levels, then we will have evidence of unlearned sex differences that are determined when the sex of the individual is determined. Such differences could underlie and interact with learned differences that develop from social interaction in our culture.

Skin Senses

The skin senses are usually considered to include touch, pain, and temperature. The study of touch involves the analysis of our ability to experience something in contact with our skin. The study of pain attempts to identify when we feel pain and what causes it. The study of temperature involves measuring our ability to identify an increase or decrease in a warm or cold stimulus exposed to the skin. Although each of these areas of study is concerned with a different type of stimulus, all three involve sensations that occur in the skin.

We will consider here only one of the skin senses—temperature. Sex differences have been found in thresholds for change in temperature, as well as in the temperature at which subjects feel comfortable. We always experience some sense of warmth or cold; we are never without some sense of temperature. Therefore, any study of a threshold for temperature must consider changes from an existing temperature.

In a study of these thresholds, D. R. Kenshalo (1970) found that females can detect a cool stimulus more readily than can males. He further found that the threshold for females varies during the menstrual cycle. During the second half of the menstrual cycle, the threshold is lower than for the first half (.6° C as compared to 1.2° C).

In a study of the range of temperatures considered comfortable by seated subjects, F. H. Rohles (1970) found that, although both sexes felt comfortable in a wide range of temperatures (62° F to 98° F, or 17° C to 37° C), males felt warmer than females did during the first hour they were exposed to any particular temperature. Men adapted to the temperature of the room in about 1.5 hours, whereas women adapted much faster. As a result, he concluded:

> if the flight of a commercial airliner lasts approximately one hour, the male passengers will probably be significantly warmer than the women passengers. However, if the flights are longer, the men will adapt downward so as to obtain the same thermal sensation as the women. In contrast, if the temperature is such that the men will be comfortable during the first hour, the women will probably be cooler than comfortable—a fact that might account for the often observed practice in women of keeping on their coats in churches and other buildings that are occupied for short periods of time [p. 21].

The findings about sex differences in temperature sensitivity fall into the same pattern as the findings about hearing and vision. That is to say, sex differences have been found, and, although the data are very limited in scope, there is some indication that some of these differences are related to the activity of sex hormones.

Taste

As with the other senses, some studies of taste thresholds have found sex differences among human subjects. In addition, a series of studies with animal subjects has shown a clear relationship between levels of female sex hormones and preference for sweetened water (Zucker, 1969; Wade & Zucker, 1969).

In the few human studies of taste thresholds where sex of the subject has been considered, some differences have been found. R. M. Pangborn (1959) found that, on the average, females have lower identification thresholds for sweetness than do males. Sweetness is one of only four different flavors we are capable of tasting; the others are saltiness, sourness, and bitterness. The other flavors we think we taste are really smells.

In a more comprehensive study of all four flavors, Meiselman and Dzendolet (1967) found that 34% of the females were able to recognize all four flavors, whereas only 16% of the males met this criterion.

An origin of differences such as these was suggested by the work of Hansen and Langer (1935), who found that women are less aware of salty tastes during pregnancy than at other times. This finding suggests that changes in taste threshold are associated with changes in female sex hormones that occur during pregnancy.

A clear relationship between sex hormones and taste preference for sweet substances has been demonstrated in animals. E. S. Valenstein, V. C. Cox, and J. W. Kakolewski (1967) found that both male and female rats chose sweetened water when given a choice between distilled and mildly sweetened water. When given a choice between mildly sweetened and highly sweetened water, both males and females chose the very sweet water at first, but after 3 days the males switched to the mildly sweetened water. Females continued to prefer the very sweet water. The females showed a continuing preference for very sweet taste experiences.

In studies of the relationship between hormones and preferences for sweets, Zucker (1969) and Wade and Zucker (1969) varied the amount of female sex hormones (estrogen and progesterone) and male sex hormones (androgens) available to both male and female rats. Male rats that had been castrated and female rats that had been spayed were used as subjects because spaying and castrating reduced the production of sex hormones. Controlled levels of estrogen and progesterone were then given to the subjects. It was concluded that estrogen in the presence of progesterone controls the sweetened-water preference: females given estrogen and progesterone drank more sweetened water than did any other animals.

Although, in general, the effects of hormones are the same in rats and in humans, we still need direct tests of human subjects. We do not have those tests, but we do have common reports from women who have cravings for specific foods, especially sweets, just prior to menstruation, a period of rapidly changing hormone levels. Thus, for yet another sense, there is a strong suggestion that sex-hormone levels affect sensory thresholds and preferences.

Summary

In senses of hearing, vision, temperature, and taste, sex differences have been found. Males lose their hearing more rapidly than do females. Girls become nearsighted at different ages than do boys, and more women than men wear glasses at each age. Women have lower thresholds for cold than do men; they also adapt more quickly to a room temperature. Females show lower thresholds for tasting sweet, salt, bitter, and sour.

There is a strong suggestion that at least some of these sex differences are related to effects of the sex hormones. In each of these senses, changes in threshold have been shown to occur with variation in female sex-hormone levels. Baker and Weiler (1977) found changes in hearing threshold within the menstrual cycle. Diamond, Diamond, and Mast (1972) found parallel differences in vision threshold, and Kenshalo (1970) found similar variations in the threshold for cold. Finally, Zucker (1969) and Wade and Zucker (1969), using rats as subjects, found that changing sex-hormone levels affected preference for sweetened water.

Findings from the various senses offer a unique opportunity to consider the role of unlearned factors. Sensation is one of the few areas of human activity in which sex stereotypes do not generally exist and where there is little awareness of the functioning as it occurs. Although the data are limited, results from studies in all the senses point to sex differences that are related to differences in sex-hormone levels. Differences in the very mechanisms by which we acquire sensory information affect the way we receive that information. Thus, unlearned factors affect our ability to interact with the external world—and it is through our contact with the external world that we acquire all of the learned parts of our behavior.

Because of the sensory differences, the same message may not be received by males and females, even when the same message is being sent. These unlearned differences in sensation must have an influence on all other differences between people. With regard to the present study, it would follow that these differences in male and female sensory functioning have some effect on the learned differences considered throughout this book. In the next chapter, we will consider the role of sex differences in learning.

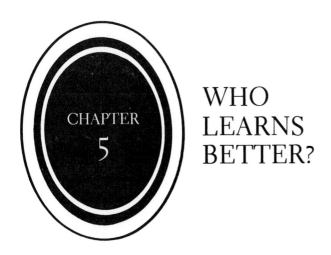

WHO LEARNS BETTER?

CHAPTER 5

Learning can be seen as the next step in the sequence of handling incoming sensory data. The stimulus first causes activity in the central nervous system and is experienced as a sensation. This process deals mainly with currently present information. When this information is stored so that it is available for future use, learning comes into play. We cannot measure learning directly; that is, we do not have access to what is stored in the brain. Instead, we must study behavior that we assume to be controlled, in large part, by the brain and what is stored there.

Interpreting sex differences in learning is complicated by the finding that the sex of the experimenter affects the results. The sex of the experimenter—of which the subject is almost inevitably aware—has been shown to have differential effects on male and female subjects in several types of learning, including classical conditioning (Gold, 1969), instrumental conditioning (Gardner & Kaufman, 1968), verbal learning (Littig & Waddell, 1967), and social reinforcement (Paletz, 1970). In most of these studies, it was found that the performance of female subjects is improved by the presence of male experimenters.

The results of studies in all areas of learning in which sex differences are found should be interpreted in light of this effect, since the experimenter is most often male. We do not have a neutral condition in which the experimenter is neither male nor female, so a direct test of sex differences without the confounding effect of the sex of the experimenter cannot be made. The only alternative that comes to mind is for computers to give written instructions to the subject—and even then, subjects might assign a gender to the computer.

The study of learning has traditionally been divided into several categories, according to the situation in which the learning takes place. For example, one speaks of maze learning when the subject is asked to learn in a maze. Of the many areas of learning, we will consider only those areas in which sex differences have been found—maze learning, motor-skill learning, verbal learning, probability learning, and problem solving.

The first two areas require little or no verbal interaction and can be investigated using human or nonhuman subjects; the last three require some form of verbal communication and involve human subjects almost exclusively. These two broad types of learning—nonverbal and verbal—will be considered in turn.

Figure 5-1. Almost any activity can be a learning experience for children. The kinds of toys they are given, for example, can teach children what expectations society has for them. (Photo by Jim Pinckney.)

Learning Not Requiring Language

Maze Learning

In maze learning, the subject is expected to solve a maze in order to reach a goal. Typically, the goal and the path to it cannot be seen by the subject. There are blind alleys in the maze, with barriers that stop the subject when a blind alley is chosen; the subject must return and choose another route to reach the goal. For human subjects, the mazes are often drawn on paper and the path is traced with a pencil. For animal subjects, the mazes are generally elevated boards or paths with high sides that keep the animal in the maze and stop the animal from seeing the goal before it is reached.

Sex differences in maze performance in rats have been long established. Males have been found to learn the task more rapidly than females (Tyron, 1931; Sheldon, 1969). Experimental tests have employed many different breeds of rats in various types of mazes, with findings that are consistently the same: males are superior at maze learning.

Few studies of sex differences in human maze performance exist, but studies such as that by J. Kunce, L. S. Rankin, and E. Clement (1967) have also found human males to be superior. In this study, Alaskan natives with varying levels of education were tested on maze performance. It was found that males at all educational levels consistently showed better scores.

Although learning in human subjects is almost certainly affected by learned expectations about male and female performance, the results of animal studies suggest the possibility of an unlearned component as well. There is little or no reason to suspect that rats have learned culturally stereotyped sex-role behavior. Even though the brain complexity is different, we have reason to believe that findings from animal studies are useful in understanding some human performance. Thus, there is a need to consider more fully the possible role of unlearned differences in maze learning in humans.

Motor-Skill Learning

The study of motor-skill learning involves measuring the acquisition of the muscle coordination necessary to carry out a task. A common measure employs the rotary-pursuit apparatus. The subject is instructed to keep a metal rod in contact with a small metal circle located near the edge of a larger revolving circle that resembles the turntable of a record player. Studies have found males to be superior at this task. M. Geblewiczowa (1969) found that males were better at the beginning of the test and continued to perform better than females over 3 days of testing. C. E. Noble (1970) has reported that males maintain an average of 7.8% better performance.

Another method of measuring motor skill is the mirror-tracing device. The task is to trace a figure, often a star, while looking only in a mirror. In this task, K. Kumari (1970) has found that females make fewer errors than do males.

The results of these two types of motor-skill tasks seem contradictory. A full explanation cannot be offered until the underlying mechanisms involved in the tasks are better understood. But a logical assessment of the two tasks suggests that these opposite results are not in direct conflict with each other. Each task, though falling within the general area of motor-skill learning, requires a different kind of skill. The rotary-pursuit apparatus requires that the subject follow the lead of the moving target with a steady hand. The mirror-tracing apparatus requires that the subject control his or her muscles to move in the reverse direction of the image seen. The two tasks, then, require different specific skills.

These specific differences may not prove to be important, but the differences on these motor-skill learning tasks point out another constraint that needs to be considered in interpreting findings: the results of a group of experimental findings cannot be considered as a whole unless we are confident that the tasks employed in the experiments require the same skills of the subjects. Thus, we may not be able to draw conclusions about whole areas because the individual tasks may not require the same skills. We need to consider individual findings in assessing the importance of and origins of sex differences, rather than simply summing up the number of studies in an area that present similar results.

Learning with the Use of Language

The use of language on the part of the experimenter and the subject is required in the areas of verbal learning, probability learning, and problem solving. In verbal learning, subjects learn and recall words or groups of words. In probability learning, subjects are asked to predict which of two or more events will occur in the next trial. In problem solving, subjects must derive for themselves a relationship between complex parts of a problem. By far the greatest amount of work on sex differences has been done in the area of verbal learning.

Verbal Learning

Many different experimental relationships (paradigms) have been developed for the study of verbal learning. We will discuss only those experimental situations in which sex differences have been studied. Those areas include paired-associate learning, intentional and incidental learning, and recall of meaningful material. We will describe these experimental conditions as we discuss the research findings in each area.

Paired-Associate Learning. In paired-associate learning, the subject sees or hears pairs of words or words and pictures. The objective is for the subject to respond with the second item in the pair when the first item is presented.

Studies have found generally that females are superior to males in paired-associate learning. Using pairs consisting of a physical object or the name of a physical object and a three-letter syllable, J. W. Reich and R. A. Alexander (1970) found that adult females learned to associate the pairs more quickly than did adult males in seven out of eight experimental conditions. Using concrete and abstract words and forms, R. F. Klein, G. A. Hale, L. K. Miller, and H. W. Stevenson (1967) found that the mean number of correct responses for concrete forms and for concrete words was significantly higher for girls than for boys. (Concrete words or forms are those that have a specific object or shape associated with them, such as a dog or a flag.) In paired-associate learning, then, studies have shown that females generally outperform males.

Incidental and Intentional Learning. In a learning situation in which incidental and intentional learning are studied, subjects are instructed to learn a list of words—the intentional-learning phase. There also exists some other information in the word list; for example, the words are printed in different colors. Any learning of the information that the subject was not instructed to learn is considered incidental because there were no specific instructions to learn it. Studies by D. L. Meinke (1969) and C. H. Ernest and A. Paivio (1971) have found that females recall more of the information they are instructed to learn (the intentional learning), and they also recall more of the incidental information. Thus, in this area of verbal learning, we again find experimental evidence supporting better performance by female subjects.

Meaningful Material. In studies of the recall of meaningful material—material consisting of typical prose passages—several types of measures of learning have been used, including the total number of words recalled, the total number of words identical to those in the given passage, the number of concepts recalled, and the number of word sequences. In a study using the text of a short story, W. B. Todd and C. C. Kessler (1973) found that females showed higher levels of recall on all four of the measures, and three of the four differences were statistically significant.

From the information available, we cannot tell whether these findings are biased. In a study of school children, C. Braun (1967) found that words related to a subject of interest to one sex were recalled more frequently by that sex. This suggests the need for caution in interpreting any finding about sex difference in the recall of meaningful material. Because the recall of meaningful material depends on the content of the material and the interest of the subjects in the material, one cannot interpret the findings of Todd and Kessler or any other study without knowing whether the passages used were likely to interest females more than males—or vice versa.

Summary. The results of these studies indicate that, on the whole, females appear to perform better than males on verbal-learning tasks. Findings, such as those of Todd and Kessler, that might be affected by individual interests, however, suggest the need for great caution in assessing the validity and significance of observed sex differences in verbal-learning tests.

Probability Learning

We now turn to probability learning, a quite different kind of learning situation. In this type of learning, the subject is presented with a series of choices and is asked to predict which of the two or more events will occur the next time (trial). For example, the subject could be asked to predict whether a penny would come up heads or tails on the next flip. In most experiments, the alternatives do not occur with equal frequency or probability.

Since there is no way to be correct on every occurrence, the subject must pick a strategy that seems best. There are many different approaches that a subject can take to this problem. While we cannot say with certainty which approach the subject has chosen, it has been found that male subjects come closer than females to picking a given alternative (for example, heads) at the frequency at which it occurs in the actual experimental situation (Pecan & Schvaneveldt, 1970). That is, if heads occur 80% of the time and tails 20% of the time, males come closer than females to matching the 80:20 ratio in predicting the outcome.

It has been hypothesized that subjects with prior knowledge about probability tend to adopt the probability-matching strategy (Kroll, 1968). The observed sex differences may well be accounted for simply by the often-observed fact that males take more advanced classes in mathematics and, therefore, are more likely to have greater knowledge about probability. If this hypothesis is correct, the findings of sex differences in probability learning are not explained by any general sex difference, learned or unlearned, but rather by a specific factor related to this particular type of learning.

Problem Solving

In problem-solving tasks, the subject is asked to find an answer to a question or problem. Various types of problems are used, including finding a way to attach a burning candle to the wall using a given selection of objects, or finding the smallest number of links in a chain that must be cut in order to give away the chain one link at a time. Perhaps the most similar problems experienced by most of us are the "written problems" found in many school math textbooks.

An extensive series of experiments studying sex differences in problem solving and the variables that affect these differences has been conducted by N. R. F. Maier and others. Generally, it has been found that males perform better on these problem-solving tasks, such as the chain problem, than do females (Hoffman & Maier, 1978). Several factors have been found to influence the differences in male and female scores. Using female experimenters improves the scores of females under standard motivation conditions. In addition, it has been found that males perform better on all types of problems, but females score relatively better on problems that require the subject to use information not presented explicitly in the instructions for the problem (Maier & Casselman, 1970).

Summary and Explanation

Sex differences have been demonstrated in maze learning, motor-skill learning, paired-associates, incidental and intentional learning, and problem solving. However, interpretation of the studies and confidence in the findings are complicated by indications that several experimental factors influence the results. A number of studies have shown that the sex of the experimenter differentially affects the performance of male and female subjects. In addition, interest in the content of verbal material has been shown to affect the performance of subjects, and it has been further shown that males and females are typically interested in different material.

Studies that have found sex differences in specific types of learning have not, for the most part, considered the sources of these differences. Moreover, the data do not point to a common basis for the observed differences. Based on a review of findings about sex differences in learning, however, D. M. Broverman, E. L. Klaiber, Y. Kobayashi, and W. Vogel (1968) have offered a physiological hypothesis to explain sex differences in certain forms of learning, including all of those considered here.

Broverman et al. summarize the findings about sex differences as follows: "Females surpass males on simple, overlearned, perceptual-motor tasks, males excel on more complex tasks requiring an inhibition of immediate responses to obvious stimulus attributes in favor of responses to less obvious stimulus attributes" (p. 23). More specifically, they conclude that females are superior to males in tasks that (1) are based on past experience rather than new problem solving; (2) depend on fine motor coordination, such as typing; and (3) involve little complex thinking, such as color naming. Males are superior to females in tasks that (1) require inhibition or delay of the response to a stimulus (that is, males wait until responses other than the most obvious have been considered); (2) involve complex thinking rather than an automatic response; and (3) involve solving normal problems.

The data presented in the present chapter do not correspond completely with these conclusions. In the area of fine motor control, for example, we have seen that males perform better on one fine-motor-skill task (rotary-pursuit apparatus), whereas females show better performance on another (mirror tracing). It seems that Broverman et al. have oversimplified the findings.

But let us look further into their explanation. It is their hypothesis that sex differences in learning reflect differences in the functioning of the male and female nervous systems. Several different chemicals operate within the nervous system. Broverman et al. hypothesize that sex differences in learning occur because the male nervous system is controlled by one chemical, and the female nervous system by another.

To fully understand the types of experimental findings cited to support this hypothesis, we would need to deal with details of the functioning nervous system that are beyond the scope of this book. Suffice to say that, in support of their hypothesis, they cite a large number of diverse studies that have investigated sex differences in nervous-system functioning. The data indicate to their satisfaction that the male and the female nervous systems react differently to many types of experimental manipulation in a way consistent with their hypothesis.

In an evaluation of the Broverman hypothesis, Mary Brown Parlee (1972) points out a number of errors in the assumptions underlying the hypothesis. According to Maccoby and Jacklin (1974), moreover, their review of the literature does not support many of the conclusions about sex differences presented by Broverman and associates. In general, despite their detailed analysis of the hypothesis regarding the origins of sex differences in learning, the data do not support their conclusions. As of now, the value of this hypothesis is largely heuristic: it may lead to further study of the physiological contribution to learning.

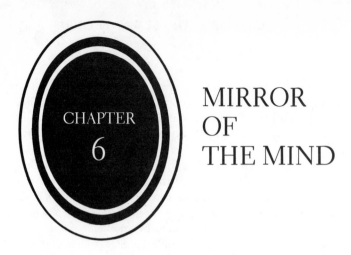

MIRROR
OF
THE MIND

CHAPTER
6

In the minds of many people—including some psychologists—personality is synonymous with psychology. To this way of thinking, the study of personality is all there is to psychology, or at least most of what is important is covered by it. As we hope the reader has come to understand and appreciate by now, there are other approaches to defining the subject matter of psychology, including looking for unlearned components in behavior. It is this viewpoint that we are taking in this analysis of personality, although we recognize that many other psychologists approach the same subject by considering almost exclusively the learned aspects.

Historically, much of the study of personality has developed on the assumption that personality is learned. The most influential works have been theories of personality such as that of Sigmund Freud (1856–1939). Freud's theory developed out of his work in Vienna with patients, many of whom were women (Cohen, 1969). The theory developed from a clinical setting, where individuals are treated for existing personality problems, rather than from data gathered in an experimental laboratory. As his theory is not central to our discussion here, and a good summary would take many pages, the reader who is unfamiliar with Freudian theory is encouraged to look at the personality-theory section of an introductory psychology textbook, or at a summary such as Cohen's (1969).

Since Freudian theory was developed in a clinical setting, it is not surprising that much of the work on sex differences in personality has been clinical in nature. J. A. Sherman's *On the Psychology of Women* (1971) is still the best review of the findings from this area of research. Using a Freudian framework, she considers the findings on sex differences from a number of areas.

The intent of the present chapter is different. We want to see whether research has uncovered any sex-related unlearned influences on personality. Unlike the other areas of psychology we have considered, much of the research focusing on the physiological bases of personality is concerned with changes in the personality of females over time, rather than with comparisons of male and female personalities. We will limit our consideration here to research about personality changes associated with changes in sex-hormone levels in women. These changes occur in two time frames. First, changes in the level of the female sex hormones, estrogen and progesterone, occur during the menstrual cycle; second, the levels of sex hormones vary during the life cycle. We will consider the changes associated with the life cycle first.

Hormones in the Life Cycle

Important changes in hormone levels occur at puberty, when adult levels of hormones begin to appear; during pregnancy, when a different pattern and higher levels of certain hormones exist; and at menopause, when levels of some hormones drop markedly. Little substantial research appears to have been done on personality changes associated with pregnancy and puberty, but work has been done on changes associated with menopause.

Studies show that many physical and personality changes occur with menopause. Menopause is often accompanied both by physical symptoms, such as hot flashes, headaches, dizzy spells, breast pains, and poundings of the heart, and by psychological symptoms, including depression, irritability, crying spells, and inability to concentrate (Bardwick, 1971, p. 37).

It has been found that the production of estrogens in menstruating women is about six times as great as in menopausal women (Wilson & Wilson, 1963). This drop in estrogens at menopause has been accepted by many gynecologists as the major factor in the observed physiological changes. To reduce the symptoms associated with menopause, estrogens are often prescribed. M. Goldberg (1959) found that treatment with estrogens relieved the symptoms and created a feeling of well-being in women. When some women received estrogens and others received a placebo (a "fake" medicine designed to have no physiological effect), H. I. Kantor, C. M. Michael, S. H. Boulas, H. Shore, and H. W. Ludvigson (1966) found a significant improvement in the estrogen-treated group.

An explanation for the joint occurrence of the decrease in estrogens and increase in physiological and psychological complaints has been offered by R. Greenblatt (1955), who has suggested that part of the nervous system is dependent on estrogens for balance. The swift decline in estrogens that accompanies menopause disrupts the balance, and this imbalance is then reflected in the physiological and psychological complaints. If this hypothesis is correct, it is logical to expect that the hormone changes associated with puberty and pregnancy would produce similar changes in the central nervous system, resulting in changes in personality measures. We do not have the data at present to test this hypothesis.

The origin of personality changes that occur at menopause is obviously complex in nature. As we will see in Chapter 8, changes in the social role of women as mothers commonly occur at this point in the life cycle. In our culture, children become adults at about the same time as their mothers reach menopause. Personality changes, such as depression, have been demonstrated to occur with these sociocultural changes. But the question of interest here is whether or not there exists a physiological component, and the data indicate that there is. We are not attempting to argue that all personality changes at this time in a woman's life are physiologically caused—quite the opposite. We are simply trying to point out that all the changes may not be accounted for by learned factors—that physiological factors are also relevant.

Changes within the Menstrual Cycle

The relationship between the physiological factor of hormone variation over the menstrual cycle and personality change in women has been studied by several people. Judith Bardwick, in particular, has done a great deal of work in this area.

Bardwick (1971) states, without qualification, that "regular, predictable changes occur in the personality of the sexually mature woman, and these changes correlate with changes in the menstrual cycle" (pp. 26–27). Karen Paige (1969, 1971) and Sharon Golub (1976) tested females at regular intervals throughout the menstrual cycle and found that the phase of the cycle had a very significant correlation with the anxiety and hostility levels of the women. These data support the observation often made by women that some personality changes coincide with phases of the menstrual cycle.

The changes that occur just prior to the onset of menstruation and at midcycle have been well documented. The emotional changes that occur in the period just prior to the beginning of menstruation—a period of low levels of both progesterone and estrogens—have been labeled "premenstrual tension." In a study of 150 women, H. Sutherland and I. Stewart (1965) found a general tendency toward depression and irritability. A large proportion of the women who commit suicide or engage in acts of violence have been found to do so in the four days prior to the beginning of menstruation (Dalton, 1964). Further, Dalton reported that 46% of females admitted for psychiatric care, 45% of female industrial employees who report sick, and 49% of females who seek emergency admission do so in the premenstrual or menstrual phases of the cycle, which constitute much less than half of the entire cycle. At the same time, studies of females at midcycle—the ovulation part of the menstrual cycle, when high levels of estrogens and progesterone are present—indicate low levels of anxiety and hostility and, in general, a more positive outlook (Gottschalk, Kaplan, Gleser, & Winget, 1962; Ivey & Bardwick, 1968).

Although these findings indicate a change in behavior within the menstrual cycle, these studies do not test the direct relationship between changes in hormone levels and personality. To test the hypothesis that personality changes are associated with hormone levels, Karen Paige (1969) tested females on two types of oral contraceptive pills—a sequential type (some pills contain only estrogens and some contain estrogens and progesterone) and a combination type (all pills contain both estrogens and progesterone). If hormones affect the changes in personality, it would be expected that normally menstruating women and those on sequential pills would exhibit similar behavior because the hormone changes in females on the sequential pills parallel those in the normally cycling female. Paige found that changes in levels of anxiety for females on the sequential pills did follow the same pattern as those of normally menstruating females. As would also be predicted on the basis of hormone levels, those females on the combination pills, who

Figure 6-1. Many people who are opposed to equal rights for women believe that the hormonal changes to which women are subject make women unfit for high-stress or executive positions. (Photo by Mark Chester.)

were receiving high levels of estrogens and progesterone throughout the entire cycle, did not show any cyclical variation in personality (Bardwick, 1971, pp. 35–37).[1]

The evidence suggests that, for personality changes within the menstrual cycle as well as at menopause, hormone variation is likely to be one of the causal factors.

Summary

Of what importance and magnitude is the role of hormonal variation on the personality changes found in females? Clearly, hormonal variations are not the sole source of control of any aspect of personality. There is always an interaction with learned factors such as cultural stereotypes and role expectations. At the same time, even the small

---

[1] Paige's conclusions about the findings of her study do not completely agree with those of Bardwick, her graduate advisor. A summary of Paige's can be found in Tavris and Offir (1977, pp. 111–118) or in her own words (Paige, 1971).

amount of evidence presently available indicates that physiological factors can play a significant role in some aspects of personality changes. These data do not indicate that hormone levels determine the general scope of personality, but rather that they affect some aspects of the individual's total personality.

The research findings reported here have demonstrated that measures of self-assessment vary directly with changes in hormonal levels within a menstrual cycle. These findings correspond to the phenomenon, often reported by women in informal interaction, of feeling depressed or nervous just before the beginning of a period and feeling very good near the middle of the cycle.

Personality changes have also been found in the life cycle. During menopause, personality changes such as depression, as well as physical symptoms such as "hot flashes," have been shown to be affected by doses of sex hormones. The consistent finding that such symptoms are changed by administering estrogens indicates that there is a physiological component underlying the observed personality changes.

Conclusion

Having now considered a large amount of information in several areas of psychology, we need to answer two questions: (1) Are there overall trends or relationships that tie together these findings from the separate areas of psychology? (2) How does the information presented in this section help us understand and explain the findings presented in subsequent sections of this book? Let us deal with each question in turn.

Are there overall trends? A common component seems to recur in the physiological explanations for most of the findings considered in this section. The sex hormones—estrogens and progesterone for females and androgens, especially testosterone, for males—apparently contribute to many of the observed sex differences. In the developmental chapter, we found that they are likely to control the rate of prenatal growth and to affect levels of aggression in human children and other mammals. In the chapter on sensation, we found that hearing thresholds, sensitivity to light, and temperature adaptation in women vary as the levels of estrogens and progesterone vary during the menstrual cycle. For learning, no data showing a clear relationship between hormonal levels and specific aspects of learning have been presented, although Broverman et al. have proposed that differences in learning are enhanced by the difference in levels of male and female sex hormones. In the personality chapter, data were presented that show a relationship between variations in personality and levels of estrogens and progesterone in normally menstruating females. Changes in the level of female sex hormones at menopause, too, have been shown to affect several personality factors.

All in all, a broad scope of sex-hormone influence on psychological functioning has now been demonstrated. But we may still want to inquire into the origins of this relationship.

Sex hormones have the basic functions of differentiating the organism as male or female and making reproductive behavior possible. Reproduction is a primary survival need of any species. During the course of evolution, selective processes have operated so that those animals who have produced a number of viable offspring are better represented in later generations. The differences in sex-hormone production that are important for reproduction can have other effects as well. Although we do not understand the total impact of hormones, we do know that they are transported via the blood stream throughout the body and are, therefore, available to affect directly many parts of the body. It is likely that the sex hormones affect the various behaviors discussed in this section through centers in the brain that control most types of behavior.

The sex differences observed may have developed because they have survival value, or they may be by-products unrelated to survival. A sex difference that clearly has survival value in some other species is aggression. Higher levels of aggression have been shown to be associated with higher levels of male sex hormones. Aggressive males are more likely to survive and to reproduce, thereby contributing to an increase in the overall aggression and male sex-hormone level of the group. In many species, aggression among males is the direct method used to form the hierarchies that determine who reproduces. For females, dominance patterns are not clearly linked to aggression patterns. Sex differences in temperature adaptation, on the other hand, may be merely by-products without intrinsic survival value.

Whatever the specific evolutionary value of any particular difference between the sexes, it appears clear that a major source of sex differences in behavior is the difference in levels of sex hormones found in males and females and the changing levels of hormones that occur during the menstrual cycle of females.

Does our awareness of physiological influences on behavior help us understand findings in other areas? Many aspects of female behavior will be considered in the subsequent sections of this book. Learning—or, more specifically, socialization—accounts for many of these differences. But the sex differences observed in political, economic, and social behavior are not exclusively the product of learning. Physiological differences play a role, too. Behaviors that we witness every day, in such areas as working, voting, and marrying, have as underlying components the simpler forms of behavior discussed in this section.

Although we do not have enough information to know the total contribution of the physiological factors, there are areas in which we know enough to see a strong indication of the physiological contribution. For example, physical aggression is not a dominant factor in establishing roles in most adult groups. Still, the patterns developed in childhood can be important in affecting adult behavior, and data suggest there is an unlearned component to sex differences in childhood aggression. Therefore, there is the real possibility of an indirect physiological contribution to sex differences in adult patterns of aggression.

To generalize, then, the importance of the physiological contribution to adult sex differences is not properly measured by considering the direct impact alone. It is the sum of the direct effects plus the indirect effects of the physiological contribution that must be considered. A general assessment of the total physiological contribution awaits data not yet collected. At this time, we can agree with Maccoby and Jacklin who conclude that *biology is not destiny*—but we would add that *destiny does have a physiological contribution carried by each of us.*

Points to Ponder

Take a position agreeing or disagreeing with each of the following statements (adapted from Mason, 1975). Support your stand using information from this section or other sources. Be careful to use information to support your stand. An opinion is only as good as your ability to support your conclusions with information. An opinion is not supported because you want it to be true or feel it should be true.

    A. If a woman is not satisfied being a wife or mother, it is a sign she has emotional difficulties. (How would you feel if the statement read: If a man is not satisfied being a husband and father, it is a sign he has emotional difficulties.)

    B. English is a better major for a college woman than mathematics.

    C. Women are less aggressive than men.

D. Men are better able to reason logically than women.
E. Women are as intelligent as men.
F. Women are better equipped to be mothers than men are to be fathers.
G. Women should not compete for the very best grades in school.

Rate women as low, medium, or high on the following items:

Moodiness
Social Competitiveness
Sensuality
Talkativeness
Independence
Complexity
Intelligence

Now estimate the physiological contribution to each of these characteristics, in terms of percentages (from 0% to 100%). Indicate the reasons for your conclusions.

Now try repeating the same process for men.

References

Sources of particular interest to the reader are marked with an asterisk.

Abt, I. A., Adler, H. A., & Bartelme, P. The relationship between the onset of speech and intelligence. *Journal of American Medical Association*, 93, 1351–1355.

Acheson, R. M. Maturation of the skeleton. In F. Falkner (Ed.), *Human development*. Philadelphia: Saunders, 1966.

Alpern, M. Research on vision physiology, reflective errors, and related ocular abnormalities. In *Vision and its disorders*. NINDB Monograph No. 4. Washington, D.C.: U.S. Department of Health, Education, and Welfare, National Institute of Neurological Diseases and Blindness, 1967.

*Anastasi, A. *Differential psychology: Individual and group differences in behavior*. New York: Macmillan, 1958.

Baker, M. A., & Weiler, E. Sex of listener and hormonal correlates of auditory thresholds. *British Journal of Audiology*, 1977, 11, 65–68.

*Bardwick, J. M. *Psychology of women: A study of biocultural conflicts*. New York: Harper & Row, 1971.

Bayer, L. M., & Bayley, N. *Growth diagnosis: Selected method for interpreting and predicting physical growth*. Chicago: University of Chicago Press, 1959.

Bayley, N. Growth curves of height and weight by age for boys and girls, scaled according to physical maturity. *Journal of Pediatrics*, 1956, 48, 187–194. (a)

Bayley, N. Individual patterns of development. *Child Development*, 1956, 27, 45–74. (b)

Beal, V. A. Dietary intake of individuals followed through infancy and childhood. *American Journal of Public Health*, 1961, 51, 1109–1118.

Bennett, G. K., Seashore, H. G., & Wesman, A. G. *Differential aptitude tests*. New York: Psychological Corp., 1959.

Bleier, R. Myths of the biological inferiority of women: An exploration of the sociology of biological research. *The University of Michigan Papers in Women's Studies*, 1976, *2*, 39–63.

Braun, C. *The efficacy of selected stimulus modalities in learning and retention of sex-typed sexual responses of kindergarten children*. Unpublished doctoral dissertation, University of Minnesota, 1967.

Broverman, D. M., Klaiber, E. L., Kobayashi, Y., & Vogel, W. Roles of activation and inhibition in sex differences in cognitive abilities. *Psychological Review*, 1968, *75*, 23–50.

Buffery, A. W. H., & Gray, J. A. Sex differences in the development of spatial and linguistic skills. In C. Ounsted & D. D. Taylor (Eds.), *Gender differences: Their ontogeny and significance*. Edinburgh, Scotland: Churchill Livingstone, 1972.

Cohen, J. *Personality dynamics*. Chicago: Rand McNally, 1969.

Corso, J. F. Age and sex differences in pure-tone thresholds: Survey of hearing levels from 18 to 65 years. *Archives of Otolaryngology*, 1963, *77*, 385–405.

Dalton, K. *The premenstrual syndrome*. Springfield, Ill.: Charles C Thomas, 1964.

Darley, F. L., & Winitz, H. Age of first word: Review of research. *Journal of Speech and Hearing Disorders*, 1961, *26*, 272–290.

Diamond, M., Diamond, A. L., & Mast, M. Visual sensitivity and sexual arousal levels during the menstrual cycle. *Journal of Nervous and Mental Disease*, 1972, *155*, 170–176.

Ernest, C. H., & Paivio, A. Imagery and sex differences in incidental recall. *British Journal of Psychology*, 1971, *62*, 67–72.

Garai, J. E., & Scheinfeld, A. Sex differences in mental and behavioral traits. *Genetic Psychology Monographs*, 1968, *77*, 169–299.

Gardner, W. I., & Kaufman, M. E. Verbal conditioning in noninstitutional mildly retarded adolescents as a function of sex of subject and sex of experimenter. *Psychological Reports*, 1968, *23*, 207–212.

Geblewiczowa, M. Motor learning on the rotary pursuit. *Studia Psychologica*, 1969, *4*, 300–306.

Glorig, A., & Nixon, J. Distribution of hearing loss in various populations. *Annals of Otology, Rhinology and Laryngology*, 1960, *69*, 497–516.

Gold, D. P. Effect of the experimenter in human eyelid conditioning. *Psychonomic Science*, 1969, *17*, 232–233.

Goldberg, M. Medical management of the menopause. *Modern Medical Monographs*. New York: Crane & Stratton, 1959.

Golub, S. The magnitude of premenstrual anxiety and depression. *Psychosomatic Medicine*, 1976, *38*, 4–12.

Gottschalk, L. A., Kaplan, S., Gleser, G. D., & Winget, C. M. Variations in magnitude of emotion: A method applied to anxiety and hostility during phases of the menstrual cycle. *Psychosomatic Medicine*, 1962, *24*, 300–311.

Gray, J. A. Sex differences in emotional behavior in mammals including man: Endocrine bases. *Acta Psychologica*, 1971, *35*, 29–46.

Greenblatt, R. Metabolic and psychosomatic disorders in menopausal women. *Geriatrics*, 1955, *10*, 165.

Hansen, R. & Langer, W. Über Geschmacksveränderungen in der Schwangerschaft. *Klinische Wochenschrift*, 1935, *14*, 1173–1176.

Hirsch, M. J. The changes in refraction between the ages of 5 and 14—Theoretical and practical considerations. *American Journal of Optometry and Archives of American Academy of Optometry*, 1952, *29*, 445–459.

Hirsch, M. J. The refraction of children. In M. J. Hirsch & R. E. Wick (Eds.), *Vision in children.* New York: Chilton Books, 1963.

Hoffman, L. R., & Maier, N. R. F. Social factors influencing problem solving in women. In R. K. Unger & F. L. Denmark (Eds.), *Woman: Dependent or independent variable?* New York: Psychological Dimensions, 1978.

Horner, M. S. Femininity and successful achievement: A basic inconsistency. In J. M. Bardwick, E. Douvan, M. S. Horner, & D. Gotmann (Eds.), *Feminine personality and conflict.* Monterey, Calif.: Brooks/Cole, 1970.

*Hutt, C. *Males and females.* Harmondsworth, England: Penguin, 1972.

Irwin, O. C., & Chen, H. P. Development of speech during infancy: Curve of phonemic types. *Journal of Experimental Psychology,* 1946, 36, 431–436.

Ivey, M. E., & Bardwick, J. M. Patterns of affective fluctuation in the menstrual cycle. *Psychosomatic Medicine,* 1968, 30, 336–345.

Jost, A. Problems of fetal endocrinology: The gonadal and hypophyseal hormones. *Recent Progress in Hormone Research,* 1953, 8, 379–418.

Kantor, H. I., Michael, C. M., Boulas, S. H., Shore, H., & Ludvigson, H. W. The administration of estrogens to older women: A psychometric evaluation. *Seventh International Congress of Gerontology Proceedings,* June 1966.

Kenshalo, D. R. The temperature sensitivity. In W. D. Neff (Ed.), *Contributions to sensory physiology* (Vol. 14). New York: Academic Press, 1970.

Klein, R. F., Hale, G. A., Miller, L. K., & Stevenson, H. W. Children's paired associate learning of verbal and pictorial material. *Psychonomic Science,* 1967, 9, 203–204.

Knox, C., & Kimura, D. Cerebral processing of nonverbal sounds in boys and girls. *Neuropsychologia,* 1970, 8, 227–237.

Kroll, N. E. A. *The learning of several simultaneous probability-learning problems as a function of overall event probability and prior knowledge.* Unpublished doctoral dissertation, University of California at Davis, 1968.

Kumari, K. Sensory-motor learning in high and low anxious male and female undergraduates. *MANAS,* 1970, 17, 29–34.

Kunce, J., Rankin, L. S., & Clement, E. Maze performance and personal, social, and economic adjustment of Alaskan natives. *Journal of Social Psychology,* 1967, 73, 37–45.

Levinson, B. M. Comparative study of verbal and performance ability of monolingual and bilingual native-born Jewish children of traditional parentage. *Journal of Genetic Psychology,* 1960, 97, 93–112.

Littig, L. W., & Waddell, C. M. Sex and experimenter interaction in serial learning. *Journal of Verbal Learning and Verbal Behavior,* 1967, 6, 676–678.

*Maccoby, E. E., & Jacklin, C. N. *The psychology of sex differences.* Stanford, Calif.: Stanford University Press, 1974.

Maier, N. R. F., & Casselman, G. G. The SAT as a measure of problem-solving ability in males and females. *Psychological Reports,* 1970, 26, 927–939.

Mason, K. O. *Sex-role attitude: Items and scales from U.S. sample surveys.* Washington, D.C.: National Institute of Mental Health, 1975.

McCarthy, D. Language development in children. In L. Carmichael (Ed.), *Manual of child psychology.* New York: Wiley, 1954.

Mead, C. D. The age of walking and talking in relation to general intelligence. *Pedagogical Seminary,* 1913, 20, 460–484.

Meinke, D. L. Stimulus properties, sex of subjects, and their effects upon incidental and intentional learning. *Proceedings, 77th Annual Convention, APA,* 1969.

Meiselman, H. L., & Dzendolet, E. Variability in gustatory quality identification. *Perception and Psychophysics,* 1967, *2,* 496–498.

*Money, J., & Ehrhardt, A. A. *Man and woman: Boy and girl.* Baltimore: Johns Hopkins Press, 1972.

Moore, T. Language and intelligence: A longitudinal study of the first eight years. Part I. Patterns of development in boys and girls. *Human Development,* 1967, *10,* 88–106.

Morley, M. E. *The development and disorders of speech in childhood.* London: Livingstone, 1957.

Moss, H. A. Sex, age, and state as determinants of mother-infant interaction. *Merrill-Palmer Quarterly,* 1967, *13,* 19–36.

Nicholson, A. B., & Hanley, C. Indices of physiological maturity: Derivation and interrelationships. *Child Development,* 1953, *24,* 3–38.

Noble, C. E. Acquisition of pursuit tracking skill under extended training as a joint function of sex and initial ability. *Journal of Experimental Psychology,* 1970, *86,* 360–373.

*Ounsted, C., & Taylor, D. C. The Y chromosome message: A point of view. In C. Ounsted & D. C. Taylor (Eds.), *Gender differences: Their ontogeny and significance.* Edinburgh: Churchill Livingstone, 1972.

Ounsted, M. Gender and intrauterine growth. In C. Ounsted & D. C. Taylor (Eds.), *Gender differences: Their ontogeny and significance.* Edinburgh: Churchill Livingstone, 1972.

Paige, K. E. *The effects of oral contraceptives on affective fluctuations associated with the menstrual cycle.* Unpublished doctoral dissertation, University of Michigan, 1969.

Paige, K. E. Effects of oral contraceptives on affective fluctuations associated with the menstrual cycle. *Psychosomatic Medicine,* 1971, *33,* 515–537.

Paletz, M. D. Prior reinforcement history as an explanation for the effects of sex of subject and experimenter in social reinforcement paradigms. *Journal of Genetic Psychology,* 1970, *117,* 227–238.

Pangborn, R. M. Influence of hunger on sweetness preference and taste thresholds. *American Journal of Clinical Nutrition,* 1959, *7,* 280–287.

Parlee, M. B. Comments on D. M. Broverman, E. L. Klaiber, Y. Kobayashi, and W. Vogel: Roles of activation and inhibition in sex differences in cognitive abilities. *Psychological Review,* 1972, *79,* 180–184.

Pecan, E., & Schvaneveldt, R. W. Probability learning as a function of age, sex, and type of constraint. *Developmental Psychology,* 1970, *2,* 384–388.

Quandagno, D. M., Briscoe, R., & Quandagno, J. S. Effect of perinatal gonadal hormones on selected nonsexual behavior patterns: A critical assessment of the nonhuman and human literature. *Psychological Bulletin,* 1977, *84,* 62–80.

Rebelsky, F., & Hanks, C. Fathers' verbal interaction with infants in the first three months of life. *Child Development,* 1971, *42,* 63–68.

Reich, J. W., & Alexander, R. A. Stimulus property mediation of paired-associates learning. *Journal of General Psychology,* 1970, *83,* 213–225.

Rohles, F. H. *Thermal sensation of sedentary man in moderate temperatures.* Special Report, Institute for Environmental Research, Kansas State University, 1970.

Rubin, E. The sex ratio at birth. *American Statistician,* 1967, *21,* 45–48.

Sheldon, M. H. The relationship between familiarity and two measures of the activity of rats in an elevated maze. *Animal Behavior,* 1969, *17,* 537–539.

*Sherman, J. A. *On the psychology of women: A survey of empirical studies.* Springfield, Ill.: Charles C Thomas, 1971.

Sherman, J. A. Problem of sex differences in space perception and aspects of intellectual functioning. In R. K. Unger & F. L. Denmark (Eds.), *Woman: Dependent or independent variable?* New York: Psychological Dimensions, 1978.

Smith, M. E. Development of the sentence in children. *Journal of Genetic Psychology,* 1935, 46, 182–212.

Sutherland, H., & Stewart, I. A critical analysis of the premenstrual syndrome. *Lancet,* 1965, 1, 1180–1183.

Tavris, C., & Offir, C. *The longest war: Sex differences in perspective.* New York: Harcourt Brace Jovanovich, 1977.

Todd, W. B., & Kessler, C. C. *The influence of response mode, sex, reading ability, and level of difficulty on four measures of recall of meaningful written material.* Unpublished master's thesis, University of Nebraska at Omaha, 1973.

Tyron, R. C. Studies in individual differences in maze ability. II. The determination of individual differences by age, weight, sex, and pigmentation. *Journal of Comparative Psychology,* 1931, 12, 1–22.

Unger, R. K., & Denmark, F. L. (Eds.). *Woman: Dependent or independent variable?* New York: Psychological Dimensions, 1978.

Valenstein, E. S., Cox, V. C., & Kakolewski, J. W. Further studies of sex differences in taste preference with sweet solutions. *Psychological Reports,* 1967, 20, 1231–1234.

Wade, G. N., & Zucker, I. Hormonal and developmental influences on rat saccharin preferences. *Journal of Comparative and Physiological Psychology,* 1969, 69, 291–300.

Williams, J. H. *Psychology of women: Behavior in a biosocial context.* New York: Norton, 1977.

Wilson, J. D. Sexual differentiation. *Annual Review of Psychology,* 1978, 40, 279–306.

Wilson, R., & Wilson, T. The non-treated postmenopausal woman. *American Geriatrics Society,* 1963, 11, 347.

Wittig, M. A. Sex differences in intellectual functioning: How much of a difference do genes make? *Sex Roles,* 1976, 2, 63–74.

Zucker, I. Hormonal determinants of sex differences in saccharin preference, food intake, and body weight. *Physiological Behavior,* 1969, 4, 595–602.

SECTION
THREE

ROLES
AND
OPTIONS
FOR WOMEN

Marcia Texler Segal

The three chapters in this section deal with the sociology of women. Sociologists begin with the assumption that people are shaped and molded by the societies in which they live. Human beings have vast potential. They are born with the ability to learn, the flexibility to change, and access to the accumulated knowledge—and the mistakes—of the generations preceding them. Sociologists investigate the ways in which people learn to fit into their societies, the ways those societies and their needs mold people, and the ways people make impacts on each other and on their societies.

The behavior that sociologists look at occurs primarily in group settings, ranging from small, intimate groups—such as a pair of lovers—to large, impersonal groups—such as a university. The factors that sociologists see as influencing behavior include attitudes and beliefs that are learned and shared in society. They also include aspects of social structure, such as how one group—say, the family—relates to another—say, the community; who has the final authority in what situation; and how the size of a group affects communication among its members. Sociologists offer explanations on the group, or aggregate, level; they do not try to account for the behavior of particular individuals. For example, we would be interested in knowing why the birth rate in the United States is declining, rather than why a particular woman decides not to have another child. In order to account for the declining birth rate, we would consider, among other factors, the effects on fertility of attitudes toward children and toward the use of birth control, and the increased participation of women under 45 in the labor market.

In the three chapters of this section, the focus is on aspects of social life that have frequently been ignored, misunderstood, or misinterpreted by sociologists. There are a number of reasons why the behavior studied and the influencing factors and explanations proposed by sociologists have slighted over half the members of society. One reason is that the assumption is often made that everyone in a given social setting—for example, a family, an office, or a community—views that setting the same way. Generalizations are made on the basis of research conducted among wives, executives, or community leaders, without recognizing that husbands, secretaries, or poor people may have a different view of the situation, or take different factors into account when making a decision.

Moreover, to the extent that sociologists focus on "public, official, visible, and/or dramatic role players" (Millman & Kanter, 1975, p. x), the private, supportive roles women often play as assistants, companions, and sounding boards are ignored. A related issue is that research does not routinely consider gender as a possible factor influencing behavior where that behavior does not appear, on the surface, to be related to being female or male. For example, students may react to male teachers differently than to female teachers, or employees may be more or less productive depending on the ratio of males to females in the work group (Ruble & Higgins, 1976, provide numerous examples).

The sociology of women, then, focuses on the behavior of women, and the groups and situations that contribute to shaping that behavior. It asks if male behavior patterns

Section opening photo: New roles and options are opening for women. You don't have to be a man to operate the controls in a waste-water treatment plant. (Photo © by The Courier Journal and Louisville Times Co.)

and male roles have been used in framing sociological explanations of behavior or have been generalized to the total population, and it asks if there is anything about the way we study social life that has produced a biased view of society, or of the roles of women and men within society.

There are some gaps in the findings. For example, a picture of the process by which females develop attitudes about the female role is difficult to draw because we have data about preschool girls and college women, and very little about the age range in between. There are also contradictions. For example, it is impossible to write a clear-cut statement about women's attitudes toward success because each new study raises questions about both the methods and the substantive findings of the previous ones. However, progress is being made. Needed research data are being collected and new concepts and explanations developed. It is becoming possible to write realistically about the sociology of women.

Chapter 7, "Becoming One of the Girls," is devoted largely to the concept of sex role. The traditional image of women in our society is discussed, along with when and how children learn sex roles. The relevant biological factors were discussed in Chapter 3; in Chapter 7, some questions regarding the relationships between biology and socially defined roles are discussed.

Chapters 8 and 9 focus more on institutional and structural factors. Sociologists study the behavior of individuals in the context of groups. The topics discussed in Chapter 8, "Home Sweet Home," include marriage, motherhood, and employment. Chapter 9, "Joining the Club," deals with various community activities and problems. The material presented in these chapters sheds light on some questions raised in Sections IV and V. Women's political participation, for example, is placed in the broader context of participation in a range of activities inside and outside the home. Women's labor force participation is discussed in terms of family needs, education, and personal goals. Looking, as Chapter 9 does, at the position of women in the stratification system or status hierarchy of our society provides a context within which to understand their participation in all spheres of social life.

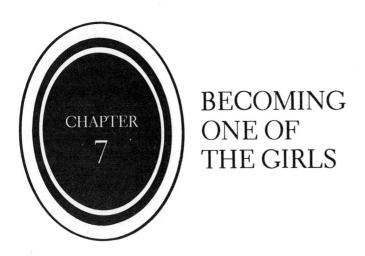

BECOMING ONE OF THE GIRLS

CHAPTER 7

The Culturally Shared Image

Individual women and men differ from each other in many respects. However, our culture provides us with a shared set of expectations or assumptions regarding the behavior, attitudes, and feelings of persons of each gender. The contents of the male and female sex-role images are well known. In a recent study (Williams & Bennett, 1975), male and female college students were asked to pick from a list of 300 those adjectives that best described women and those that best described men. Most of the students picked the same adjectives. Those most often thought to characterize men included: adventurous, aggressive, ambitious, confident, rational, stable, and unemotional; also crude, disorderly, dominant, and loud. Those chosen to describe women included: charming, emotional, gentle, sentimental, and sophisticated; also complaining, dependent, frivolous, rattle-brained, and submissive.

Students are probably not surprised by these results. The images of women as weak, whining, excitable creatures, and men as logical, tough, and boastful beings have a long history in Western culture (Hunter, 1976). These cultural assumptions seem so natural to us that we do not usually wonder how we came to believe them, or if they are really true. In fact, few women or men fit the stereotypes closely. Nevertheless, these images frequently influence our lives.

The woman who behaves in an unexpected way is likely to be labeled "unfeminine," or "unladylike." The label, or the threat of being so labeled, discourages some people from behaving as they otherwise might. In addition, society has standard ways of treating people who violate expectations. One of the most frequent is exclusion. The girl who does not behave like other girls in her class is not included in a peer group. The woman who does not behave as a woman is expected to behave is not invited to join the prestigious organization through which she can—not incidentally—benefit her husband's career.

Susan Darley (1976) discusses the familiar situation in which a woman finds she cannot live up to the stereotyped expectations of two roles, though she probably can do the actual tasks associated with them. The traits thought to be associated with success in business or a profession are very different from those that are supposed to go along with being a good mother. If a woman is known to be successful at her work, she must, popular reasoning goes, be a poor mother. If she is a good mother, she is thought unlikely to be well suited to a position in business or the professions. Such faulty reasoning, supported by stereotypes, undermines the confidence of the woman in her ability to be successful on the job and as a parent. It also makes it less likely that a personnel manager will offer her the job. The same forces can be seen at work in the choice of leadership in organizations that raise funds for social causes and allocate community resources, and in the choice of candidates for political office at the local, state, and national levels.

The shared images of females and males that our culture provides are one component of what social scientists call female and male sex (or gender)[1] roles. The process by which these roles are learned, the parts played by families, friends, and schools in teaching them, and their effects on the self-images and goals of girls and women are examined in the pages that follow.

Sex-Role Socialization

Meaning and Significance of the Concept of Role

Sociologists use the concept *role* to refer to socially defined ways of behaving associated with particular positions in social groups or in society at large. These ways of behaving include rights, duties, and obligations, as well as expected behavior patterns. Some roles include an extensive set of characteristics that the role player is expected to possess; others are less elaborated. An individual usually has several roles at any given point in her life. Examples of social roles are: teacher, soldier, customer, friend, committee chairperson, and woman. In studying roles and role learning, sociologists look at the sources of variation in role behavior, as well as the ways in which players of a given role resemble one another.

The Process of Socialization

The qualities that make a person eligible to play a given role may be physiological or learned. In order to actually play a role, attitudes and behavior associated with it must be learned. Some aspects of role behavior are consciously taught to the players. Other aspects are learned by personal experience, imitation, and trial and error. Some of the behavior associated with roles and regarded as socially appropriate is produced by setting up situa-

---

[1] Some writers use the term *sex roles* when they speak of biological functions (such as having babies) or characteristics (such as breast development) and the term *gender roles* when they mean behavior that is learned and can actually be acted out by persons of either biological sex (such as being emotional or being erotically attracted to men). Other writers use the terms interchangeably, or use *sex roles* to refer to both biological and social behavior. *Sex* and *gender* are used interchangeably here, both because there is no consensus among social scientists and because this practice conforms to popular usage.

tions so that there are limited alternatives, as when the only toys girls have to choose from are dolls. Sociologists call the total process by which roles are acquired *socialization*.

The dynamics of socialization are not fully known. Some of the agents of socialization can be readily identified. Among them are family members, peers, and other significant people in the individual's life, schools, the mass media, and real and imagined experiences. In addition, social scientists have proposed several models of how such learning takes place. The research evidence leads to the conclusion that each model touches on some important aspects of socialization, but that no model completely accounts for socialization (Rosenberg & Sutton-Smith, 1972). A brief outline of the basic premises of some important models will serve to highlight the dynamics of sex-role socialization. The reader should also consult Chapter 5.

The *psychoanalytic* approach developed by Freud and his students sees sex-role learning as fundamental to personality development. In this view, sex-role learning is different from the learning of other roles and aspects of culture. The biological fact of being male or female is seen as far more important than cultural or situational factors. The young child must come to terms with being male or female by resolving the conflict between emotional attachment to a nurturing mother, fear of a powerful father, and the knowledge of which parent she or he resembles physically. If this conflict is successfully resolved, the specific actions and attitudes associated with being male or female follow more or less automatically.

Social-learning and cognitive-development theorists hold that sex roles are learned in the same way as any other role or behavior pattern. *Learning theories* generally focus on overt behavior and on the mechanisms through which learning takes place. They suggest that parents respond to the behavior of children, rewarding some actions and punishing or ignoring others. At first, a baby cannot plan its behavior, but soon actions that achieve gratifying results are repeated. Both very young and older children imitate specific actions. As they mature, they also identify with family members and others and attempt to behave the way they believe the other person would behave or would want them to behave in specific situations. Here, too, parents and others exert influence on the learning process through the use of rewards and punishments.

Cognitive-development theorists do not rule out the effects of reward and punishment, but they insist, like the psychoanalytic theorists, that learning occurs in relatively fixed stages. A 3-year-old not only learns different things, but learns in a different way, from an 8-year-old. Unlike the Freudians, however, theorists such as Kohlberg (1966) hold that the stages involve reasoning processes, not solutions to conflicts between the biological predispositions of children and social constraints represented by parents. Thus, cognitive-development theorists do not maintain that sex roles are learned differently from any other socially prescribed behavior.

According to cognitive-development theorists, during the preschool years children learn to place people and things, including themselves, into categories such as age and gender, and to understand that some categories, such as gender, are permanent. These categories then provide a framework within which the child can organize information and behavior. Certain activities are valued and the skills to enact them learned because they are associated with the child's own gender. Others are rejected because they are characteristic of the other gender. As the reader will see in the following discussion of sex-role socialization, the process is a complex one which can be better understood by keeping each of these models in mind.

Assigning and Responding to Gender

A new member of society is generally assigned to a sex category at birth on the basis of superficial examination of external genitalia. In cases where these anatomical structures do not provide clear guidance, chromosomes, internal organs, and hormonal secretions may be examined. The findings on prenatal development indicate that the sex of the child is not determined solely by the chromosomes, but can be altered by the types of hormones present. Thus, it is possible for a genetically male individual to have female characteristics. (For a further discussion of this topic, see Chapter 3.)

In ambiguous cases, where the decision is made in the first weeks or months of life, the physiological basis on which it is made is less crucial than the certainty with which it is presented to the child and to the world. The very young will usually learn to think of themselves in terms of the label they are given. Outsiders will have little reason to question the family's word. Those who have worked with people whose sex assignment is problematic find it difficult to change a child's feelings about sexual identity when the child is older than 3 (Money & Ehrhardt, 1972). After this age, they advise surgically changing anatomy rather than trying to make a child who sees himself as a boy believe he is really a girl, or vice versa.

This information is important to the sociologist because it indicates how early in life sexual identity is formed, and because it supports the view that learned patterns can override innate characteristics. It does *not* support the assumption that sex-role learning is completed in the toddler period, *nor* does it imply that socialization typically overrides biology.

It is a common observation that many adults respond differently to very young girls and boys. Are these adults responding to differences in the actual behavior of the children? There is evidence that adults' responses are functions of their own gender, their frequency of contact with young children, and the extent to which they believe boys and girls are, or should be, different.

By presenting tape recordings or films of children who were selected so that their voice quality and appearance contained no clues as to gender, researchers (Rothbart & Maccoby, 1966; Meyer & Sobieszek, 1972) were able to show large numbers of adults the same children doing the same things. Some of the adults were told a particular child was male, some that the same child was female. None of the adults questioned the researchers' identifications of the children.

In the Rothbart and Maccoby study, all the adults were parents. They heard a tape recording of a 4-year-old making statements about feelings and requests for help and attention. They were asked how they would respond to those statements and requests if the child were theirs. In the Meyer and Sobieszek study, the extent of contact with small children varied among the adults who viewed the film. They were asked to rate the 18-month-old children seen in terms of a variety of personal characteristics, some associated with the stereotyped views of males and females, some not associated with sex-role images.

As they relate to the question of whether small girls and boys are treated differently by adults, the results of these studies are similar. The greater the believed or desired differences between males and females, the greater is the difference in responses to the male and female children. Adults who had limited contact with children tended to rely more on stereotypes in making judgments. In addition, the adults studied tended to evaluate more completely and have less permissive attitudes toward a child of their own gender than toward a child of the other gender.

These studies deal with a limited range of behavior and a narrow age range. They do not reflect the basis on which adults select or reject such objects as clothes or toys, or encourage or discourage specific interests or activities in children over time and at various ages. These studies are described because they have some bearing on the question of whether treating boys and girls differently stems from characteristics of adults or of children. They also alert us to the fact that sex-role socialization is not a simple process in which certain actions are rigidly reinforced in boys and others equally rigidly reinforced in girls. This should be kept in mind as the discussion proceeds through research on the responses of children and on the environment for sex-role learning in the family, the school, and the peer group.

Sex-Role Orientations and Preferences

Sex-role orientation involves identifying oneself correctly (in terms of assigned sex) and consistently as male or female. It is difficult for an adult to see this as a major problem. However, in a study reported by Walter Emmerich (1972), over 1000 4-year-olds were asked if dolls called "Johnny" and "Janie" could change gender by changing actions, motives, or hairstyles. Most of the children thought that Johnny could become a girl if he had longer hair, or Janie a boy if she wore other clothes. Four-year-olds are generally not certain that gender is a permanent and unchanging attribute. If a fictional child can change, they may believe, fear, or hope, that they, or a sibling, might change. It is not obvious to a young child that the hoped-for baby sister is now, and forever, a baby brother, or that the reason the cat cannot have kittens is not because it is called "Sam" instead of "Flora." Neither is it clear to the child of this age that genitals are less likely to change, or more important in assigning gender, than hairstyle or clothing. The latter are, after all, more readily observable and thereby far more useful to the child trying to determine who is a boy and who is a girl.

Similar studies indicate that 3- and 4-year-old children identify themselves with the same-sex doll consistently, and 5- and 6-year-olds are fairly certain whether they want to grow up to be mothers or fathers. Children 6 to 7 years old generally draw a figure of their own gender when asked to "draw a person." Boys tend to be a few months ahead of girls in identifying themselves by sex with certainty and consistency. For more detailed summaries of representative studies, the reader should consult Biller (1971) and Lynn (1974).

Not only do preschool children learn that they are girls or boys and not likely to change, they also become aware of social expectations for male and female interests and behavior. According to Vener and Weese (1965), children ages 2½ to 5 agree closely with older children and with adults about which household and grooming items are used by mothers and which by fathers. Within this narrow age range, the older children make fewer errors than the younger ones, suggesting that learning is taking place over time. Items associated with the female role are correctly classified more often than those associated with the male role. There are at least two factors involved in explaining this finding: small children generally have more contact with females, and females are more likely to share male-role-related items such as hammers than males are to use lipstick or dishmops. These factors may be added to the fact that girls are learning their own role by learning the female role to provide an explanation for the finding that girls make fewer errors in classifying items than boys.

Numerous studies have been carried out to see when and how knowledge of sex-role expectations is translated into behavior by children and teenagers. Studies of children choosing toys suggest that boys make sex-typed choices earlier, by age 3 or 4, and more consistently, than do girls. Girls occasionally pick toys commonly thought of as boys' toys as late as age 10. There are also social class[2] differences. Middle-class girls show a stable pattern of sex-related toy choices later than boys and working-class girls. The classic toy-preference studies are reviewed in several places, including Kagan (1964), Mussen (1969), and Biller (1971).

The fact that children do choose toys that adults would consider appropriate for their sex reflects their growing knowledge of what is expected of them, and their desire to conform to expectations. The differences between girls and boys, and between middle- and working-class children, are more difficult to explain.

Lynn (1974) points out that middle-class parents are usually less concerned about sex-role differences than working-class parents. Perhaps they make less effort to impress their children with the need to conform in this regard. Lenore Weitzman (1975) suggests that boys' toys are more attractive to both boys and girls because they encourage greater activity and creativity. In choosing the appropriate toy, a boy has only to pick the one he likes; a girl has to learn to make the choice in terms of sex roles rather than attractiveness. Another possibility is that parents and others put more social pressure on boys to shun dolls and other girls' toys than on girls to confine their play to these items. Charlotte Zolotow (1972) poignantly illustrates the nature and sources of such pressures in her children's book about a boy who wants a doll.

It is not meaningful to study toy preferences among preadolescents and adolescents,

---

[2] Social class, or socioeconomic status, is frequently used as an independent variable in this and other chapters. Some of the problems associated with assigning individuals and families to socioeconomic categories are discussed in Chapter 9. Different ways of measuring status are employed in the various studies cited. As a general guideline, *working class* means that the principal wage earner does skilled or unskilled manual labor, neither parent has had formal education beyond high school, and total family income is low to moderate; *middle class* means that the principal wage earner has a white-collar job, both parents are at least high school graduates, and family income is moderate to high. Interestingly, girls develop awareness of social class differences earlier than boys do (Tudor, 1971).

but it is meaningful to study the relationship between society's sex-role expectations and attitudes and decisions. Our society expects females to be more concerned with feelings, their own and those of others, than males. O'Neill, Fein, Velit, and Frank (1976) found that preadolescent girls and boys were equally willing to talk about themselves to others, but that the girls talked about more personal things, including their fears and anxieties. In another study, Rosenberg and Simmons (1975) found that preteen and teenage girls were more concerned about and vulnerable to the feelings of others than were boys of the same ages. Both of these studies suggest that even before they get to high school, girls and boys have begun to shape their behavior to the accepted social conventions that females are interested in and able to express feelings, and males are not.

Teenagers' interests and preferences in the mass media have been studied. Like the toy preferences of younger children, media interests are consistent with sex-role expectations. The finding of Dowse and Hughes (1971) that teenage boys are more likely than teenage girls to watch TV programs with political content, and to watch or listen to broadcast news, is discussed in Chapter 13 in the context of political socialization. Boys and girls also pay attention to different aspects of the same media presentation. In films, girls pay more attention to romantic scenes and to the principal female character, boys to fight scenes and other aggressive content associated with the central male character (Maccoby & Wilson, 1957; Maccoby, Wilson, & Burton, 1958).

The kinds of research presented in the preceding discussion have led sociologists to the conclusion that much sex-role learning takes place during the preschool and early school years, and that both younger and older children make choices that can be plausibly explained in terms of conforming to sex-role expectations.

Sex-role learning takes place within those social groups that are central to a child's life—the family, the peer group, and the school. The contribution of each of these groups will be assessed briefly.

Family Influences on Sex-Role Development

Parents.   Until recently, most socialization research has focused on mothers and children because mothers generally have more contact with children. Ironically, one stimulus for the study of father/child relations has been the current interest in women's roles. Once social scientists began to look at women outside of the family context, we also began to look at men within the family (see especially Biller, 1971, and Lynn, 1974). Once father/child relations came under study, it was found that fathers are more concerned about sex-role differences than mothers.

Evelyn Goodenough (1957) and Leonard Lansky (1967) asked parents of preschool and kindergarten children how they felt about the kinds of opposite-sex-typed behavior in which young children sometimes engage (for example, boys wanting to play with dolls or use nail polish, or girls wanting to play with toy guns). This sort of thing bothered fathers more than mothers.

The average father may be more interested in sex-role differences than the average mother, but a wide range of individual and social class variation exists. In a study of first-graders and their parents (Mussen & Rutherford, 1963), fathers who were most likely to encourage feminine behavior in their daughters were more apt to describe themselves as very masculine. Studies of middle- and working-class families (Kohn & Carroll, 1960; Rubin, 1976) show that sex roles are more sharply differentiated in working-class homes, and that working-class fathers are more concerned about differences in sex-role behavior. Working-class fathers interact less frequently and less intensely with their daughters than with their sons.

Lynn (1974) suggests that fathers are more concerned with sex roles because they are concerned with preparing their children for life in the wider society, while mothers are concerned with getting from one day to the next. Because of this concern, mothers must frequently focus on individual differences among children rather than on male/female differences. This explanation makes sense out of the findings, but Lynn does not offer evidence that parents really do define their responsibilities in this way. An alternative explanation is that males have more to lose if traditional roles are not carefully passed on to the next generation. A third possible explanation is that males—even fathers—have less experience with children than females. As in the Meyer and Sobieszek (1972) study of the children on film, this may lead them to rely more on stereotypes and socially defined role expectations. This is an issue that needs further study.

Studies that compare the attitudes of fathers and mothers are bolstered by the findings of studies of mothers alone. These studies indicate that there are few differences in the ways mothers treat, or advocate treating, girls and boys. Maccoby and Jacklin (1972) describe an experiment in which 4-year-old children were observed playing a game. Girl/girl pairs tended to cooperate; boy/boy pairs tended to compete; girl/boy pairs cooperated less than girls, but more than boys. When the same children played the same game with their mothers, mothers urged boys and girls alike to cooperate. This suggests two things: that different ways of acting toward others can be observed in preschool girls and boys, and that mothers do not appear to encourage these differences. The range of situations to which these generalizations apply has yet to be established.

A survey of 120,000 *Redbook* magazine readers (Tavris & Jayaratne, 1972) provides some information on the opinions of younger (most of them in their 20s and 30s), relatively well-educated (most of them at least high school graduates) women. They advocate similar treatment of children of both sexes. Fewer than 10% said they would encourage aggression in boys and not in girls. More than 94% believed both should be kissed and cuddled after age 5, and virtually all would teach boys and girls to care for younger siblings. More than nine out of ten believed that both should help with household chores; a very few did distinguish between boys' chores and girls' chores.

Children's Views of Parents.   How do children see parents? Do they think parents prefer boys to girls or vice versa? These questions are important because how others evaluate a child is a component of that child's self-evaluation, and because childhood experiences will affect the images that children form of the parent component of male and female adult roles.

Research summarized by Lynn (1974) shows that children do see mothers and fathers differently. Mothers are seen as more affectionate, less powerful, less strict, and more likely to control by means other than physical punishment than fathers. The images of parents vary with the kinds of questions asked in particular studies, and with the age of the child responding. Consistent with the prevailing stereotype, mothers are generally viewed as more nurturant, while children look to fathers for help and protection. For instance, 6- to 8-year-olds say they would run to father if they were being chased by a large dog. Both favorable and unfavorable qualities are associated with each parent. For example, 14- and 15-year-olds say their fathers check up on them less, but also that their mothers are more helpful in solving problems.

Children seem to be aware that male roles and tasks are more highly valued by our society (Hartley, 1960). However, they do not believe that parents in general, or their own parents, prefer boy children (Hartley, 1969). Hartley asked 5- to 8-year-olds in four U.S. and New Zealand subcultural groups whether their family, or any family, adopting a baby would choose a girl or a boy. Within this age range, the younger children tended to select their own gender, the older children showed no pattern of responses. Hartley and her associates report similar findings for other groups of children.

Siblings.   The typical American family has two or three children. This means that most children grow up in homes with at least one other child. In order to obtain a more complete picture of the impact of the family on sex-role socialization, the part played by brothers and sisters must be examined.

Presumably children with siblings of the other gender have a wider variety of potential role models. Also, they have a chance to test commonly held views about male and female behavior against reality. Orville Brim (1958) found that 5- and 6-year-old girls with brothers were more likely to have personality traits associated with boys than were girls with sisters only. This was true regardless of who was older, but the younger children were more likely to be influenced by the older ones.

More recently, Karen Vroegh (1971) studied middle-class suburban children from preschool through grade eight. Although friends and teachers of her subjects did say some children were more feminine or masculine than others, the differences were not explained by whether the child in question had brothers or sisters, or was the oldest, middle, or youngest child in the family. It is hard to explain the seemingly opposite findings of the Vroegh and Brim studies. The findings may reflect actual differences in the children studied, or the time gap between the studies, or differences in the methods of study.

Studying college women, Kenneth Kammeyer (1967) found no relation between having a traditional or a modern orientation toward the female role and having a brother. He did find that college women with older brothers were most likely to deny the existence of great inherent differences between males and females. These findings are consistent with both studies of younger children. The question of the extent to which brothers and sisters influence sex-role socialization is still open.

The studies cited above show that parents do influence the development of sex roles, and that fathers are more likely to be concerned about sex-role learning. The studies also show that children see male and female parents differently, and that having brothers and sisters probably leads children to view female and male roles less rigidly.

The family is not the only influence on sex-role development, even among very young children. As the trend toward nursery schools, day-care centers, and Headstart programs grows, children come under the influence of peers and teachers as well as parents and siblings sooner. Virtually all children ages 6 and older, and an increasing number of those under 6, spend a significant portion of their lives in school or with friends. The peer group and the school as agents of sex-role socialization will be considered next.

Peers and Sex-Role Socialization

The peer group is instrumental in the process of growing up. Friends provide a reference group outside the family to which a child or adolescent can look for standards of behavior and rewards for conforming to those standards. Douvan and Adelson (1966) report that in adolescence both girls and boys look to their peer groups for support, but that girls are better able to discuss the meaning of friendship and their expectations of friends with interviewers than are boys. This seems to reflect the emphasis on interpersonal relationships that is characteristic of adolescent and adult females. It may be part of the reason that adults of both genders find it easier to make friends with women (P. Stein, 1976). Women are more skilled in making friends.

The peer group would seem to have a unique opportunity to teach and reinforce sex roles because the typical friendship unit for children from preschool through early adolescence is the same-sex pair or trio. By age 16 or 17, friendship groups are restructured as groups of couples, but the stable ties within such groups are same-sex friends who bring their current boyfriends or girlfriends into the group (see Broderick, 1966, and Hill & Aldous, 1969).

Actually, there has been relatively little research on precisely how peer groups teach and reinforce sex roles. Janet Lever's (1976) research on play groups and patterns among fifth-graders provides some clues. Boys played in larger groups and groups that included wider age ranges. They were more likely to play outdoors, at competitive games that lasted longer than girls' games, and were more likely to have fixed rules. When girls and boys played together, they played boys' games by boys' rules. Team sports were typical of boys' games; jacks and jump rope, which emphasize turn-taking rather than teamwork and comparison with a norm or standard rather than direct competition, were typical of girls' games. Not only do play patterns among these children seem to reflect adult activity patterns, they also seem to provide training for participation in those adult patterns. Girls receive less training in teamwork, in interaction in heterogeneous groups, and in making sustained efforts in order to achieve a collective goal.

Joyce Ladner (1972) provides some insight into the process by which preteen and teenage girls help each other to enact sex roles. The girls she worked with expected their close friends to give candid opinions about appearance and behavior, and to lend the clothes and jewelry needed for effective role performance. The young people with whom Ladner worked were urban Blacks from relatively poor families. Research is needed to determine how closely their behavior reflects that of girls their age from other ethnic and economic groups.

Schools and Sex-Role Socialization

Schools influence the lives of children in areas not touched by family and peers, and contribute to the world view of children through the factual material presented.

Books.　The male bias of school teaching and testing materials and of literature for children has been well documented (Saario, Jacklin, & Tittle, 1973). Weitzman and Rizzo (1974) surveyed the most popular elementary texts in all major subject areas. Only 31% of the people in the illustrations in these books are female. This percentage declines steadily by grade level to a low of 20% in sixth-grade texts. The books studied show women as mothers, wicked witches, teachers, librarians, sales clerks, and nurses. Men are shown in more than 150 occupational roles. The books portray girls as passive, interested in domestic activities and personal grooming, and as having a wide range of emotions. Boys are shown as active, adventuresome, skillful, but constrained to fit the strong and silent image. Other differences in how girls and boys are depicted are cited in Chapter 14.

Researchers who study sex-role images in children's books assume that the girls identify with female characters and, in doing so, learn to think of themselves and their options as limited. This assumption is supported by several studies (for example, O'Hara, 1962; Looft, 1971; Papalia & Tennent, 1975) which show that the majority of grade school girls choose one of four occupations—nurse, teacher, secretary, or mother—when asked what they would like to be, or anticipate being, as adults. Interestingly, girls often mention mother as an alternative to other occupations; boys rarely mention father as an occupational choice. Boys' choices include many more possibilities; some, like circus performer or cowboy, are far less realistic than the choices of girls. The occupations mentioned by girls are, in fact, among the few that women do enter in large numbers (see Chapter 11). School books do not cause the occupational distribution. But, by encouraging girls to think of themselves only in ways that fit the current expectations for women in our society, they fail to provide a basis for change in the distribution.

Teachers.　Moving from people in school books to real people in schools, both the sex of the child and the sex of the teacher influence what goes on in the classroom and contribute to sex-role socialization. Studies (see Lee & Gropper, 1974, for a review of the literature) indicate that teachers tend to prefer the kind of behavior that fits the female sex-role expectations of society. It is easier, then, for girls to be well liked if they conform to expectations. Girls are also more concerned about the opinions of others and are more likely to be influenced by their teachers, whether male or female (Forslund & Hull, 1972). The classroom situation seems to reinforce the socially defined female role and to highlight the male role by creating in boys a conflict between classroom and wider society expectations. Although classroom standards are generally more consistent with the female role, achievement is valued, and males may be permitted greater freedom to deviate from the standards (Levitin & Chananie, 1972).

The adults encountered in school serve as role models for the students, showing them possible directions for career and personal development. Consider these facts: The majority of elementary school teachers (85%) are female. The majority of principals (79%) are male. Over half the secondary school teachers are male; 80% of college and university faculty members are male, with the proportion of males rising sharply at each rank (*Time*, 1972; Ziegler, 1971). Similar data are presented in Chapter 11, with some discussion of their broader implications. The implication that is most relevant here is that girls and boys do not have the opportunity to see women as administrators and experts, even in a social setting in which they are numerically dominant. Moreover, they have little opportunity to observe men in day-to-day interaction with children.

From the evidence available to us, it can be concluded that peers and schools do teach and reinforce sex roles. There is evidence to suggest that girls look to friends for support in playing sex roles. There is also evidence that learning materials present a biased picture of female roles and options. An interesting finding is that girls are more likely to identify with adults, and that they do so regardless of the gender of the adults. Whether this leads them to imitate respected male teachers, or to do what those teachers wish— which may be to have the girls behave in female-sex-typed ways—is not clear. Female teachers, like mothers, appear to encourage the same things in both girls and boys. Perhaps male teachers, like fathers, enhance traditional femininity in girls to whom they are warm and nurturant (see Johnson, 1963, and Nuzum, 1970, who provide support for the proposition that warm father/daughter relations are associated with traditional femininity in young women).

Influence on Adult Goal Decisions

The previous discussion has indicated the ways in which family, friends, and school situations can influence girls growing up in our society in the direction of conformity to shared cultural expectations for females. In each case, what has been shown is that fathers or friends or textbooks can have a certain effect, not that they must have that effect. It has also been shown that mothers or siblings or teachers have the potential to influence varied outcomes.

In some of the studies reviewed, children were asked to make choices from a very limited pool of alternatives, such as two or three toys. In life, too, people are asked to choose from limited alternatives, limited in two ways: (1) the range of jobs, mates, leisure activities, and so forth in any given place at any given time is only a fraction of those in existence; and (2) the individual making the choice brings to that choice a concept of herself and her needs and abilities that serves to eliminate some options and narrow the field from which she will choose. The influences on the educational and occupational choices of young women of sex-role socialization and the ways in which our society limits the alternatives open to women are discussed in this section.

Figure 7-1. In Grandmother's day, girls typically had few choices in childhood and made no adult goal decisions. (Photo © by The Courier Journal and Louisville Times Co.)

There is little in the sociological literature about the goal decisions of those who do not attend college or prepare for professional or high-level technical employment. The impression one receives from Rubin's (1976) intensive study of 50 White working-class couples in the San Francisco Bay area is that few of the women (all under 40) ever seriously considered anything but marriage and motherhood as a career. Over half of them have outside jobs, some of which—beautician, secretary—required training after high school. However, as they recall them, their childhood dreams were about marrying "Mr. Right," not about a career. There is no question but that the decision to marry within a year or two after high school is partly a product of sex-role socialization. It is also partly a product of limited alternatives available to girls from families with limited resources, many of whom live in homes that are so unpleasant that marriage at 18, often under pressure of pregnancy, seems a welcome relief.

Whether and When to Attend College

During the 1977–78 academic year, 46% of the full-time and 52% of the part-time students in U.S. colleges and universities were female. This follows a long-term trend in higher education: 30 years ago, fewer than 30% of college students were women; 20 years ago, the figure was 35%; 10 years ago, it was 40%. Among young adults (age 21 and under), a higher proportion of women than of men have completed at least one year of college. The number of females attending college continues to rise, while the number of males has leveled off, so that women now account for virtually all of the increase in college enrollments (Magarrell, 1978, p. 1).

One factor that helps account for the increased enrollment of women in college is the growth of community colleges and regional campuses. Such schools lower the cost of attending college and make it easier to go to school part-time (Bishop, cited by Magarrell, 1978).

Many samples of high school and college students have been studied in an attempt to pinpoint all the factors associated with attending, or planning to attend, college (Sewell & Shah, 1967 and 1968, are representative studies). Ability, family income, and parental encouragement all have measurable effects on college plans for males and females, but their relative impact differs by gender. For males, academic ability, as measured by grades or standardized test scores, and family income carry equal weight; for females, family income and parental encouragement carry more weight than grades in determining college plans.

The female college population today includes a large number of women who have been out of school for several years (Young, 1973). By the time the typical contemporary woman reaches her late 20s or early 30s, she has completed the childbearing phase of her life and is ready to begin a new phase that may include school, a paid job, or both.

At present, we do not know what effect factors such as academic ability and family encouragement have on women who begin or return to college some years after high school. Pamela Roby (1975) suggests that standardized tests used to screen applicants to colleges and graduate and professional schools favor the person who has recently completed the preceding phase of education. These tests stress knowledge acquired in high school and lower-division college courses. She also cites studies of small samples that indicate that women returning to college do better than they did before dropping out. It is possible that the way a woman feels about her intellectual ability is more closely related to the chances that she will attend college at some point in her life than is any particular objective test.

Research by Naomi Katz and her associates (Katz, Myers, Lisker, & Peterson, 1974) among mature women in college suggests that the decision to go to college is comparable to the decision to enter the labor force. Approval and cooperation of husbands and other family members is appreciated. However, family support is not always seen by the woman as a necessary condition for attending college.

Occupational Goals

The term *career* is frequently employed by social scientists to refer to professional and managerial occupations that require a relatively high level of training and commitment, in which the incumbent expects to systematically climb a series of steps leading to positions of greater reward and prestige. In studies that identify girls or women as career-oriented, the emphasis is generally on a high level of commitment to any sort of paid employment outside the home. Frequently, no specific occupation is mentioned. The expectation that one will be regularly employed and will derive some satisfaction from that employment would not be remarkable enough to require a label or analysis among boys or men. Virtually all men in our society are career-oriented in this sense. This is an example of the development of concepts that are not equally applicable to studies of the behavior of men and women.

Douvan and Adelson (1966) found that wanting a career was not necessarily related to planning to attend college. Nearly half of the preteen and teenage girls surveyed selected helping professions such as nurse or social worker. About four in ten chose white-collar fields, such as secretary or bookkeeper, in which the proportion of women has traditionally been high and which do not necessarily require higher education. One in ten chose a glamour field such as modeling. Only 2% mentioned manual labor.

Lenore Harmon (1971) asked 1188 female first-year college students to indicate which occupations, out of a list of 135 titles including housewife, they had ever considered. A majority of the women did not recall ever having considered jobs that could not be characterized as traditionally feminine. Interest in jobs requiring unusual talents or long periods of training was recalled as only a passing interest. Fields that would be classified as business or clerical—fields in which large numbers of women are in fact employed—were chosen least often in this study, but it is important to remember that all those responding were already enrolled in college.

Shirley Angrist's work (Almquist & Angrist, 1971; Angrist, 1972) is also based on a college sample. The students sampled were characterized according to their orientation (toward family *and* career or toward family *only*) and the consistency of that orientation during their college years. The data were gathered over a 4-year period. Career-oriented women were likely to be the daughters of working mothers. Career-oriented women already had some work experience and identified faculty members and people they knew in particular occupations, as well as their mothers, as role models. Those who were consistently career-oriented throughout their college years were most likely to plan to enter male-dominated fields.

Peggy Hawley (1972) compared women majoring in math and science (male-sex-typed major) with those majoring in teaching (traditionally female-typed) and counseling (a helping field but not strongly female-typed). The women were asked to respond to statements about women's roles in terms of what they thought significant men in their lives thought. This may not tell us what those men really thought. However, to the extent that what women think men think about women influences women's choices, these data are useful.

Hawley found that women in math and science and those in counseling believe that men see few sex-role distinctions. Education majors believe that men make relatively sharp sex-role distinctions. From her findings, she infers that women in the less traditionally feminine fields do not see themselves as violating the female role image because they have adopted a flexible definition of that image. If Hawley's inference is correct, the implication of her findings is that, within limits, women are able to adjust their concepts of sex-appropriate behavior so that they can engage in nontraditional activities without violating what they believe to be sex-role expectations.

What men really think is a separate question from what women believe men think. The general conclusion from recent studies (for example, Kelley & Suelzle, 1971; Komarovsky, 1973) is that college men are fairly open-minded about women's roles when speaking in generalities, but somewhat more traditional when asked to respond to statements phrased in terms of "my wife" or "my family."

Such easily measured factors as family income and grades, and such intangible ones as what women think men think about women's roles, have been considered as variables in the college and career decisions of young women. Another variable that has received considerable attention in the recent literature is attitude toward success. This factor will be examined next.

Gender and Success

Females and males of all ages have different ideas about the factors that control success and failure, and about their chances of succeeding in a given situation. In a variety of situations, females tend to underestimate, and males to overestimate, their abilities (Stein & Bailey, 1973).

Rosenberg and Simmons (1975) studied the self-concepts, interests, and goals of a representative sample of students from the Baltimore school system (grades 3–12). Consistent with previous research, which the authors cite, they find that adolescent girls are interested in being well-liked, whereas adolescent boys are interested in being successful at work. Asked how good they wanted to be at their jobs, many more boys than girls aspired to be "at the very top." A substantial number of the girls said "about in the middle" or "below the middle." A higher proportion of the boys aspired to occupational success at each age level (roughly, grade school, junior high, and high school). Although being well-liked was still a goal of more girls than boys over the age of 15, older girls were more oriented toward job success than younger ones.

It is possible that girls underestimate their chances of occupational success and channel their energies and aspirations toward social goals, which they feel more confident of reaching. An alternative explanation is offered by Matina Horner (1969). She suggests that females are afraid of success.

Horner asked college students to write a story about Anne/John who found her/himself at the top of her/his class in medical school. Students were asked to respond to the success of the person of their own gender only. Horner assumed that in thinking about Anne/John, the students would reveal something about their own reactions to success. One thing she looked for was evidence that success was expected to have undesirable consequences. In fact, 64% of the female students were negative about Anne. Many predicted that she would be unhappy, or that her achievements as a medical student would make her less successful as a woman. Others pictured her as unattractive or unlikable. Only 10% of the male students expressed similar thoughts about John and the consequences of his performance.

Social scientists and others interested in understanding women initially accepted Horner's findings because they made sense. They were consistent with both personal experience and long-standing scientific findings, which showed that women experience conflicting pressures. Women believe they should succeed intellectually and athletically, but they also believe they should not compete with the men with whom they work and go to school (Komarovsky, 1946).

Recently, however, several researchers (Baruch, 1975; Caballero, Giles, & Shaver, 1975; A. Levine & Crumrine, 1975; O'Leary & Hammack, 1975; R. Levine, Reis, Turner, & Turner, 1976; and others) have cast doubt on the idea that women are motivated to fail because they fear success. Their studies suggest that the generalization is too broad. First, it does not hold for all age levels. Second, girls and women typically do aspire to success in some areas. These areas include not only interpersonal relationships (being well-liked) but also traditionally feminine endeavors (such as nursing school or the presidency of a garden club). Further, concern about the consequences of succeeding in competition with men may be realistically based on the experiences of some women. Some researchers find more fear of success among males than Horner reports, and some find that men have more negative reactions to a story about a successful woman than women do to success stories about either men or women, a possibility Horner did not investigate.

It seems fair to say that, given current sex-role expectations, both women and men will have mixed feelings and mixed predictions about the long-range impact on a woman of her success in a traditionally male-dominated field. It also seems fair to say that this ambivalence may be one of the factors influencing the adult goal decisions of young women.

Summary

In this chapter we have defined *sex role* or *gender role* as a set of socially defined expectations associated with being female or male in a particular society, and *sex-role socialization* as the process by which sex roles are learned.

Although there is no commonly accepted theory that accounts for the total process of sex-role socialization, accumulated evidence shows that adults hold different expectations for girls and boys even in infancy. During the preschool years, children learn to think of themselves as female or male, discover that being a boy or girl is a permanent characteristic, and learn many ways of acting that are associated by society with one gender or the other. Parents and siblings are important in early socialization.

During the school years, boys and girls play differently and learn different skills in their play. They may receive different messages from their textbooks, teachers, and the mass media. The classroom, for example, is a more congenial place for the typical girl than for the typical boy, but the books used in the classroom suggest that the society has more to offer males.

Current college enrollment figures reflect a gradual change in the adult goal decisions of girls, but, overall, those decisions clearly reflect earlier sex-role socialization. Female high school and college students are less career-oriented than their male classmates and aspire to a limited number of traditionally female jobs. Young men and women feel differently about a variety of things from TV news to telling secrets. However, initially accepted findings that females fear success have not been sustained by more recent research, which leads to the conclusion that both females and males have mixed feelings about success, possibly for different, sex-role-related reasons.

HOME
SWEET
HOME

CHAPTER
8

Family life is a central part of the lives of most American women. The roles of wife and mother are the ones girls expect to assume. Some quantitative data on the composition of households and trends in marriage, divorce, and motherhood are presented first to provide a frame of reference for the discussion.

The trends described reflect the relationships among three basic factors. The first consists of technological changes ranging from improved birth control methods to reductions in the amount of physical effort required to perform certain household and labor force tasks. The second factor is a change in socially shared ideas about what women can and should do; legislative changes in rights and protections guaranteed to women constitute the third factor. The discussion of the rise of the contemporary women's movement (Chapter 2) has identified some of the variables involved; the discussion of why women have entered the labor force in larger numbers in recent years (Chapter 11) will deal with others. It is not always possible to say which factors are causes and which effects because the trends identified have not run their courses, and because some of the influences, such as smaller families and working outside the home, can be either cause or effect. Topics considered in this chapter include the distribution of power and the division of labor within households, family planning, and the effects of children on the lives of women. This leads to a discussion of wives and mothers who are also members of the labor force.

It would be desirable to end this chapter with a detailed discussion of the lives of women who are not married or who do not live in family contexts. As the initial statistical presentation will demonstrate, the proportion is relatively low, but it is growing. Not marrying or not having children are indeed options for many women today. Not enough research has been done to provide many details, but some information about single women and unmarried mothers is presented.

Quantitative Data on Marriage and Motherhood

More than 95% of American women marry; the majority of married women have children; the majority of divorced women remarry; the majority of households are composed of a wife, a husband, and their children under 18. Recent trends, however, indicate that some changes are in progress.

U.S. Census data show that from 1890 through 1940 half the women marrying for the first time were 21 or older. From 1950 to 1962, the median dropped to 20.3 years of age. By 1974, however, half those marrying for the first time were again over 21 (Ross & Sawhill, 1975, p. 196). In the 1970s, as in the 1950s, fewer than two in ten American women between 25 and 44 years of age were unmarried. Among White women, there has been very little change in the proportion over 25 who are married, but the proportion between 18 and 24 who are married has declined steadily since 1959. Fewer than 23% of 18- and 19-year-olds, and fewer than 60% of 20- to 24-year-olds, were married in 1970. Except in the 18-to-19 age group, the proportion of non-White women who are married is substantially lower than the proportion of White women. For example, in 1970, more than 87% of White women age 30 to 44 were married, as compared to more than 76% of non-White women. Trends over time are not so clear-cut among non-White women (U.S. Census Bureau data as presented by R. Simon, 1975, p. 20, table 3.1).

The number of children each woman is likely to have is decreasing. During the peak baby-boom years of the late 1950s, there were about 118 babies born for every 1000 women aged 15 to 44 in the United States; in 1973, there were about 69 births for every 1000 women in this age group (census data cited in Ross & Sawhill, 1975, p. 199). Even in a brief period, changes in family size are apparent. In 1970, the average number of children per family (including adopted children and adult children who have never married) was 2.29; in 1975, it was 2.14 (Waldman, 1975, p. 66). In 1972, about 4% of American wives expected to remain childless, and about 8% expected to have only one child (Russo, 1976, pp. 149–150).

Divorce now accounts for a much greater proportion of marriages that end. During the last 100 years, the annual rate of marital dissolution has been around 30 per 1000 marriages. In earlier years, almost all marriages ended with the death of one of the spouses. For example, in 1870–74, about 95% of the marriages that ended, ended because of death. In 1970, 44% of the marriages that ended, ended in divorce. In the period immediately prior to World War II (1935–39), there were just over 8 divorces for every 1000 existing marriages. After the war, the figure rose to nearly 14 per 1000. The figure declined, and then rose again: in 1955–59, the divorce rate was about 9 per 1000; in 1970, it was more than 15 per 1000. In the latter year, about 715,000 marriages ended in divorce (U.S. Census data, cited in Ross & Sawhill, 1975, p. 195). In 1951–53, 16 of every 1000 women age 14 to 44 were divorced; in 1969–71, the comparable figure was 26 per 1000. Until 1966–68, except for the period immediately after World War II (1945–47), the divorce rate for this age group was fewer than 20 per 1000 (Ross & Sawhill, 1975,

p. 196). This age group is most interesting because it includes women who are still young enough to have children and because it represents an age range in which divorce, not death of a spouse, is the major cause of marriage dissolution.

Partly as a result of these changes, household size and composition are changing. In 1940, more than 90% of households were occupied by families, rather than by a single individual or two or more unrelated persons. In 1950, the figure was just about 90%; in 1960, it was 85%; in 1970, it was 81%; by 1975, the proportion of U.S. households occupied by families had dropped to 78%. The average household size in 1975 was 2.9 persons; the average family living together had 3.4 members (U.S. Bureau of the Census, 1975, pp. 1, 4–5).

Family Structures

All societies have some basic family unit in which most people live and in which most children are born and raised. That unit is expected to provide food, clothing, shelter, emotional support, sexual satisfaction, and a position within the wider society for each of its members. The basic family unit is never all of an individual's known relatives, but a specific group whose size and composition vary from one society to another and from group to group within larger societies like our own. In our society at the present time, the typical unit is the nuclear family, consisting of two parents and their young children. This group usually lives in a separate household and functions somewhat independently of other relatives. In 1975, more than 84% of all U.S. families had both husband and wife present, and 98% of husband/wife families had their own households (U.S. Bureau of the Census, 1975, p. 5). This does not mean that families with only one adult, or families that include other relatives, cannot function as well as or better than more typical families. The statistically most frequent arrangement is not necessarily the only or the most desirable alternative.

Nuclear families differ in terms of power distribution, division of labor, emotional closeness and dependency of members, and size. Some of these differences are explained by the relative positions of men and women in society. In turn, differences in the way family members relate to each other help to explain certain differences among women. In some families, husbands and wives share activities and make decisions together. In other families, the lives of wives and husbands are more separate.

Power

Power is the ability to make and carry out decisions. In most American families, husbands have more power than wives (and parents have more than children). Power is based on tradition and control of resources. Tradition accords more power to males (and adults) than to females (and children). The traditional power of men is a reflection of their higher status in society. Men (and adults) also have more access to and control over resources than women (and children). Men are generally stronger than women, they frequently have more knowledge and experience in nonhousehold matters, and they usually provide a greater share of the family income. There are many homes in which these generalizations about resources are not wholly or even partly true. However, our shared sex-role images, which are grounded in tradition, say that they should be true. Where they are not, in fact, true, men often cling to the traditional stereotypes. They insist that their families act as if they were true, or they emphasize the parts, such as greater strength, that are true.

In terms of real families in real situations, this means that in middle-class homes, couples talk of equality and shared decisions, but wives allow themselves to be pressured by husbands who really do have greater resources. In working-class homes, wives say, with resentment or resignation, "he won't let me" (Rubin, 1976, p. 96). Husbands say "a wife's got to learn to be number two" (Rubin, 1976, p. 183; see Rubin, 1976; Scanzoni & Scanzoni, 1976, and Cromwell & Olson, 1975, for discussions of marital power).

An alternative pattern of family power may be seen in the Black community (Ladner, 1972). The stable, hard-working Black woman who makes a substantial economic contribution to her family (see Chapter 12) and is prepared to assume full responsibility for that family, if necessary, is well known in fact and well rooted in tradition. Looking at Black families shows that there are alternative ways of distributing power within families. Recognizing this pattern helps in understanding the reactions of White people to Black families, and the reactions of Black people to the contemporary women's movement.

In thinking about power in families, the factors to be considered as influences must include not only the personal characteristics of the members, but also their ideas about the roles of husband and wife in decision making, and the impact of the wider society on the families within it.

Household Division of Labor

In most homes, women take major responsibility for cooking, cleaning, child care, shopping, and the flowers—but not the grass—in the yard. Ludwig Geismar (1973) found that four out of ten wives perform tasks, such as repairs, usually stereotyped as men's work. In the young urban families he studied, over half the husbands do some of the routine housework, but only in about 5% of the homes is such work shared equally. Most aid by husbands and children is given in emergency situations, when they take over a wide range of activities (also see Berheide, Berk, & Berk, 1976; Lopata, 1971b). These findings of sociologists are consistent with time-budget studies done by economists (see Chapter 10).

Most fathers do share in child care. However, disciplining children appears to be primarily mother's job, especially when children are young, and more exclusively in Black homes than in White (Geismar, 1973).

Focusing on situations in which the wife/mother is totally absent highlights her usual role. When wives die, husbands take over those of their duties that are not seen as requiring special skills, such as laundry. They seek help from relatives, or hire someone, to do those tasks that are stereotyped feminine and require time or skill, such as ironing or cleaning (Bedell, 1972).

Most women see room for improvement in the household division of labor. In a recent survey (Tavris & Jayaratne, 1972, p. 21), about one-fourth of the respondents were "relatively" or "very" dissatisfied with the way household tasks were currently divided; about one-fourth were "very" satisfied. In another survey (Mason & Bumpass, 1975, p. 1214), 52% of the White and 71% of the Black women responding agreed that men should share work around the house.

This brief look at the way families are structured and labor is divided within families shows that families vary in the degree to which husbands and wives share decision making, interests, activities, and responsibilities. Some sharing of housework and household planning is more characteristic of middle-class families than of working-class families. However, in virtually all homes, wives do most of the actual child-care and housekeeping tasks. The fact that leisure activities and decisions are often shared, but work is done by wives, is a potential source of conflict. Both the belief that sharing is an

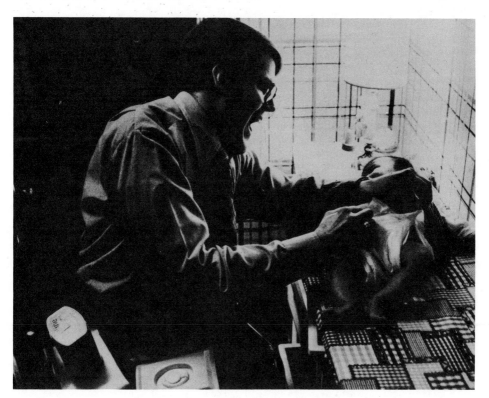

Figure 8-1. A growing number of fathers are assuming active roles in child care today. (Photo © by The Courier Journal and Louisville Times Co.)

important part of marriage and the orientation toward interests outside of the family context are more common in homes where both husband and wife are well educated and where both are employed outside the home.

Motherhood

Planning Motherhood

The trend toward smaller families, noted previously, is probably a result of two kinds of factors: those that predispose people to want fewer children, and those that make it possible for people to control fertility. Medical advances improving the probability of each child's survival, and the shift from children as an economic advantage in a predominantly agricultural economy to children as an economic liability in an urban industrial environment, have both contributed to the desire to have relatively small families. The control of fertility involves the use of contraceptives, abortion, and voluntary sterilization, all of which have improved in quality and gained wider acceptance in the last two decades.

Abortion. It is estimated that the legalization of abortion accounts for about one-fourth of the recent decline in the birth rate (Tietze, Jaffe, Weinstock, & Dryfoos, 1975, p. 86, Appendix). The available data on abortion come from surveys of agencies that provide advice or abortion services rather than from the experiences and plans of individuals. Existing studies of individual experiences (such as Henslin, 1971) investigate the decision to have an *illegal* abortion. About 850,000 legal abortions were performed in 1975. Most abortions were performed during the first 12 weeks of pregnancy. According to statistics published by the Center for Disease Control, a U.S. government agency, about two-thirds of the women who had legal abortions in 1975 were White, about one-third were teenagers, and just over one-fourth were married (*Louisville Times*, 1977).

The legal abortion rate has increased each year since 1973, the year following the U.S. Supreme Court ruling that, in effect, invalidated most state laws regulating abortions in the early weeks of pregnancy. In 1973, the aggregate legal-abortion rate was 16.2 abortions for every 1000 women ages 15–44, or about 238 abortions for every 1000 live births (Tietze et al., 1975, pp. 7–8). In 1974, the rate was 242 per 1000 live births; in 1975, it was 272 per 1000 live births (*Louisville Times*, 1977). It is too soon to tell whether the trend will continue. The yearly increase in legal-abortion rates may not represent an increased number of abortions, but a decrease in illegal and self-induced abortions as medically safe, legal facilities become more readily available to women desiring this service.

Birth Control. According to Tietze (Tietze et al., 1975, p. 86, Appendix), more effective contraceptives and more widespread use of them account for the major part of the declining birth rate. Westoff and Ryder (1969) provide evidence of the increased acceptance of contraception. They compare families of different racial and religious backgrounds in relatively large (2000 to 3000) national samples of families taken over a period of ten years and including a wide range of education and income levels (see Table 12 in Westoff &Ryder, 1969, p. 408). The proportion of White couples who have used, or expect to use, contraceptive measures was 79% in 1955, 87% in 1960, and 90% in 1965. The difference between Protestant and Catholic couples decreased sharply during this time. In 1955, 67% of the Catholic and 87% of the Protestant couples surveyed used or planned to use some means of family planning. By 1965, the percentages were 87% for Catholics and 91% for Protestants. In 1960, 76% of the Black couples surveyed were limiting family size; that figure increased 10% by 1965. Judah Matras (1975) suggests that, as the educational levels of Black and White women converge and as more Black families move from rural to urban areas, the difference in average number of children between Blacks and Whites will disappear.

In the studies reported by Westoff and Ryder, a substantial proportion of the couples expected to use birth control measures at some future date. In the Tavris and Jayaratne (1972) survey, equal proportions of women said that they had planned "all," "some," or "none" of their previous pregnancies. Approximately 20% of first children born to married women are conceived prior to marriage (Wachtel, 1972). These represent only a portion of all unplanned first births, which in turn represent only a portion of all unplanned babies.

These kinds of data point up the fact that a planned family can mean many things. One woman may seek to delay her first pregnancy until a specific goal (completion of her education, for example) can be reached; another may want to prevent additional conceptions once she has as many children as she wants; a third may try to space children at given intervals but not to limit the total number. Beginning to practice birth control after the desired number of children has been reached appears to be a working-class pattern; attempting to space births as well as to determine the total number of children is more common in the middle class (Rainwater, 1965).

Wanting a smaller-than-average or average-sized family as opposed to a large family is not the same thing as planning or not planning one's family. Personality traits, educational levels, and interests of women are related to their ideas about family size. Those who focus their lives on a career or other outside interests, or on being a companion to their husbands, are likely to want smaller families. Those whose lives revolve around home and children are likely to want more children (Rainwater, 1965; Hoffman, 1974b). A recent study suggests that, regardless of the number of children they want, women with more children are more alienated—that is, they feel isolated, powerless, and as if many aspects of life lack meaning. The study suggests that women who tend to be alienated have more children. Women who scored high on alienation in 1963 had more children between 1963 and 1971 than women who were less alienated. They also continued to be more alienated (Neal & Groat, 1975).

Effects of Motherhood

Although most women want to be mothers, motherhood appears to have some negative consequences. Rollins and Feldman (1970) report that women are most likely to be dissatisfied with their marriages in the childbearing and rearing stages of the family life cycle. Men, in contrast, are most likely to be dissatisfied later, as retirement nears. Hoffman (1974c) quotes from her earlier interviews with 217 Detroit mothers. When asked how having children changed their lives, the first response of 40% was that children tied one down; only half of the respondents had anything positive to say in answer to the question.

One aspect of the impact of motherhood is suggested in Chapter 13. Overall, married women have fairly high voter turnout rates. However, mothers of young children have fairly low rates. It is difficult to vote, shop, or do many adult things with a baby, and it is harder to concentrate on the wider world when one is occupied with the care and feeding of a toddler.

The lives of working-class couples tend to revolve around separate activities and interests. Many working-class women find that children provide a common focus of interest for them and their husbands. On the other hand, many wives of all socioeconomic backgrounds complain that the time devoted to children results in less sharing and companionship and less spontaneity in the marital relationship (Lopata, 1971b; Rubin, 1976).

Women are more likely to leave their paid employment, at least temporarily, when they become mothers, than when they become wives. The impact of motherhood on employment and other activities is discussed below. Before considering those issues, the discussion turns to the growing number of women who choose motherhood outside of marriage.

Motherhood outside Marriage

There are almost 7 million families in the United States headed by women. About two-thirds of these families include children. This means that about 15% of all children under 18 live in female-headed households. Divorces and separations among families with children are increasing. The majority of female-headed households are created by this process, a decreasing number through widowhood, and an increasing number through out-of-wedlock births (Ross & Sawhill, 1975, pp. 12–13).

In 1975, more than 14% of the babies born were born to women who were not married; in 1961, out-of-wedlock births represented fewer than 6% of all births (U.S. Department of Health, Education, and Welfare statistics, cited in *Louisville Courier-Journal*, 1977). Among the options open to a woman who is pregnant and unmarried are abortion, continuing the pregnancy and releasing the baby for adoption, marriage, and single motherhood. Over half of those who continue their premarital pregnancies marry before the baby is born. White women are more likely to marry than others. They are also more likely to choose abortion or adoption over single motherhood (Wachtel, 1972; *Louisville Times*, 1977).

Geismar (1973) compares married and single mothers in his study of Newark families whose first child was born in 1964 or early 1965. The principal reasons for not marrying given by those in his sample who chose to remain single are: they, or their parents, felt they were too young to marry; the man did not wish to marry; or they did not like the man well enough or did not feel he would be a good father. Ladner (1972) reports comparable reasons for not marrying based on discussions with poor, Black teenagers in St. Louis. In Geismar's sample, four out of five women who chose to have their babies outside of marriage remained single five years after the birth. These women were slightly less likely than their married peers to have had a second child during this time. More than one-third were receiving financial aid from the child's father. Virtually all had lived with their own parents for a time after childbirth, but after five years, half had established their own homes.

Summary

It is difficult to separate pressures exerted by society from the voluntary choices of women who grow up in that society, but at present most women do elect to become mothers (see Bernard, 1975, for perspectives on this subject). Currently, most women also choose when to become mothers and how many children to have. Women who want, or who have, larger-than-average families appear to be more oriented toward their homes and their children than toward their husbands or the world outside their homes, and more alienated from life and people in general. These differences cut across education and income levels and religions.

Most women choose motherhood. Most women also choose employment and other activities outside the home for all or part of their adult lives. How employment is combined with marriage and motherhood is discussed in the following sections. The combinations are not unworkable, but attitudes toward work and family- and job-related demands and pressures often create dilemmas. Society resolves these dilemmas for men by stressing work above family in male roles. No simple solutions are available for women.

Combining Marriage and Employment

Why Married Women Work

In 1975, 44% of married women who lived with their husbands were in the labor force. The structural and technological factors that have increased the demand for women workers and increased the availability of married women for work are discussed in Chapter 12. In this section, factors that influence the decisions of individual women to seek paid employment and some characteristics of married women who are currently employed or who plan to seek employment in the future are explored.

When women are asked why they work, the most frequent answer is "for the money." Carl Rosenfeld and Vera Perrella (1965) present data from interviews with a national sample of women who started or stopped working in 1963. Among married women, nearly 42% gave financial need as their reason for starting, and an additional 17% gave extra money as their reason. Need was a more important reason for women whose husbands' incomes were relatively low, those with limited educations, and those with preschool-age children.

Without discounting the fact that many women, married or not, choose work as an alternative to welfare or inadequate food, clothing, and shelter, financial need should be seen as a starting point for an investigation, not a final explanation of why women work. Need is a socially acceptable reason for leaving home and family. The woman who works outside the home because she "has to" can be seen as fulfilling family responsibilities. Her outside job is an extension of the wife/mother role. Moreover, economic need is relative. Beyond the basics, people do make choices about how much money they need and how they want to live. For some, the need may be for a down payment on a house or Christmas presents for the kids; for others, the need may be for money that they can feel free to use at their own discretion.

It is noteworthy that even among those who give need as their reason for working, most say that they would not stop working if they did not need the money. The more work experience a woman has, the more likely it is that she will advocate a woman's right to choose a paid job, full-time homemaking, or a combination of the two, regardless of need (Ferree, 1976; Rosenfeld & Perrella, 1965).

Work may be a source of personal satisfaction, a means of feeling useful and important, and an opportunity to interact with other people. The more education and training a woman has, the more likely she is to give personal satisfaction rather than need as her reason for being employed. Lotte Bailyn (1970) found that 30% of a sample of women who were graduated from British universities in 1960 ranked career first or second as a source of satisfaction in their lives. Typically, it was ranked second, with family ranked first. However, Ferree (1976) found that even among women who did not finish high school, those who are employed are more satisfied with their lives and their marriages than those who are full-time homemakers.

It may be that negative feelings about full-time homemaking rather than the positive attractions of work draw women into the labor force. Those women in Ferree's sample who said that they liked housework and were good homemakers saw little value—beyond money—in employment. However, they constituted only one-fourth of the sample. The rest were like the nearly three-fourths of the *Redbook* (Tavris & Jayaratne, 1972) respondents who agreed to some extent that "raising a child provides many rewards, but as a full-time job it cannot keep most women satisfied." Only 40% of the large national sample in the Mason and Bumpass study (1975) believed that women are happier if they stay at home. Many (42%) of the highly educated full-time homemakers in an unpublished study by Judith Birnbaum reported that their lives lacked "challenge and creative involvement" (cited in Nye, 1974, p. 223).

The relationship between husband's attitude and wife's employment is complex. The working-class women interviewed by Ferree (1976) saw a husband's attitudes toward his wife's employment as an issue over which a marriage could break up. Need was seen by many as a justification for working, regardless of a husband's feelings. In fact, some wives used their husband's lack of a job as an excuse to seek one themselves. Where it is not a question of need, most of these wives would advise a woman not to get a job over her husband's objections, but one-third of them would tell her to go ahead if she really wants to do so. As will be seen in Chapter 12, if a woman's mother was employed or wished she had been, it is more likely that the woman will be a working wife. In addition, husbands of working women are likely to be sons of working women (Schooler, 1972).

Is labor force participation related to ideology? It is quite reasonable to think that it might be, and for some women it is. However, not all women in the labor force think women should be employed, and not all who stay home do so by choice or on principle.

The more than 6000 women in the Mason and Bumpass study (1975) were all under 45, and all were presently or previously married. More than three-fourths of the women questioned, including a substantial number of employed women, agreed that "it is much better for everyone involved if the man is the achiever outside the home and the woman takes care of the home and family." When Mason and Bumpass constructed an "equal opportunity scale" out of the reactions to various items such as equal pay for equal work, they found that most women agreed on most issues. They also found that whether a woman was employed did not help predict how she would score on the scale. Rapoport and Rapoport (1971b) report that a substantial proportion (22%) of a sample of 1960 British university graduates planned to return to work despite the fact that they neither favored careers for women nor found much personal satisfaction in their own work.

Why do women who are not in financial need, do not fully approve of working outside the home, and do not derive much satisfaction from their jobs, join the labor force? Both Rapoport and Rapoport (1971b) and Hoffman (1974b) point out that our culture places high value on both paid work and education, and low value on idleness. They suggest that owing to these values, under certain circumstances—such as among highly educated women or women with no small children—a return to work is now the social standard.

There are a number of circumstantial factors that affect employment decisions. For example, farm wives are less likely to be in the labor force than nonfarm wives (Hayghe, 1975, A19–20, Tables H, I). Apart from the additional tasks that may fall to a homemaker on a farm, distance from possible places of employment and lack of child-care alternatives in rural areas contribute to this difference. No one accepts a position just because it happens to be offered, but some women (10% in the Rosenfeld & Perrella study, 1965) cite the offer of a job as a primary factor in their decision to enter the labor force at a particular time. The creation and advertisement of new employment possibilities, and the acquisition of marketable skills not necessarily acquired with a view toward work, are examples of circumstantial factors that might affect the labor market participation of particular women. These have not been systematically investigated.

Two-Job Families

There are several fairly detailed studies of families in which both husband and wife are employed in high-level positions, including college faculty, lawyers, top administrators, architects, and researchers (Holmstrom, 1972; Epstein, 1971; Rapoport & Rapoport, 1971a; among others). There are comparable data on families with similar educational backgrounds in which the husband has an executive or professional position and the wife is not employed (Papanek, 1973; Pahl & Pahl, 1972; and a group of families included for contrast in Holmstrom, 1972). Studies such as Rubin's (1976) involve more typical families—couples in which, for example, a switchboard operator and a factory worker are married to each other—but there are fewer details because the focus is not really on the family members as workers. Some of the studies are from England. The most important difference between the British and American situations is that American corporations make greater demands upon the wives of their management staff (Pahl & Pahl, 1972).

The employed wives in these executive and professional families are efficient and organized at home and on the job. These families generally appear to love children and to be devoted to theirs, but they have fewer than the average family. Those with high-ranking jobs and relatively high combined incomes can use them to purchase child care and to save time and effort—for example, by buying a second car or entertaining in restaurants.

Epstein (1971) has studied female lawyers in the New York City area who are in practice with their husbands. Many of them are from minority or immigrant families, and families that were also working partnerships—for example, co-owners of small retail stores. These lawyers see their roles as supportive of their husbands' careers, even though they have comparable qualifications. They do much of the repetitive routine legal work for the firm, and they place great emphasis on their domestic skills. Epstein says, for example, that they frequently offered her home-baked treats when she went to interview them.

Evidence from interviews (especially Holmstrom's work) suggests that some feelings of competition and jealousy lie beneath the surface in all families in which both husband and wife have highly demanding jobs. These feelings are controlled by emphasis on the ways in which each one's interests enhance the other's life, and by avoiding situations that have proved touchy. For example, if joint authorship has led to arguments that were not confined to the topic being written about, the couple rarely collaborates again.

Working-class women frequently complain that they have two full-time jobs because they receive little or no help from their husbands. In Rubin's (1976) interviews with working-class couples, employed wives frequently bemoan the fact that they come home from office, plant, or shop to make dinner and do housework, while their husbands have a beer in the living room or at a bar with "the boys." Professional women—including women in politics, as discussed in Chapter 15—report that their husbands are generally supportive of their work and facilitate their achievements. Yet even in these families, there is evidence that a dual system of accounting is employed. All costs—whether in time, money, or feelings—incurred by the family are deducted from the benefits of the wife's job. For example, if both have to attend work-related meetings at night, *she* arranges for the babysitter, and the expense is viewed as related to *her* work. Further, decisions about job-related travel, moving to a new community, and who stays home with a sick child are generally resolved in the husband's favor (Holmstrom, 1972).

What about the full-time homemaker wife of a man in a high-level position? She probably held a white-collar position prior to the birth of her first child. Typically, she places high priority on companionship and supportive functions, such as being an accomplished hostess. She participates in those civic and social activities that will enhance her husband's career. Her husband, in turn, acknowledges his dependence on her. She may also serve as an unpaid assistant or collaborator in his work, or be expected by his employer to take on certain tasks. Papanek (1973) calls the situation where both husband and wife are oriented toward the husband's career a two-person career. Holmstrom's research indicates that, depending on the personalities involved, such families can also be highly competitive—over civic contributions, for example. She feels that competition is no more or less likely to be a problem where both partners in a marriage are career-oriented.

Birnbaum's dissertation (cited by Nye, 1974) provides some insights into the lives of women who train for professional careers but do not pursue them. She looked at how highly educated women felt about themselves. She compared those who were married (regardless of employment status) with those who were single, and those who were employed (regardless of marital status) with those who were full-time homemakers. The women rated themselves on self-esteem, social skills, mental and emotional health, and certainty about self. Employed women, whether married or single, gave themselves higher ratings than homemakers gave themselves. The impact of work on the self-images of less well-educated women is probably less dramatic. Women who do not train for professional careers are likely to marry sooner and to see marriage, not employment, as the defining characteristic of adulthood. On the other hand, there are many women like Karen, quoted at the beginning of this volume, who feels truly herself only when she goes to meetings of an organization she joined when she was an office worker.

The problems of marriage and employment are complicated further when there are children. In addition, working mothers have problems stemming from their work and parent roles, regardless of whether they are married. The joys and the strains of combining employment and motherhood are discussed next.

Combining Motherhood and Employment

In March 1974, almost 27 million children under 18 had mothers in the labor force. This figure represents about 42% of all children under 18 and includes 6.1 million preschoolers. More than half the mothers of school-age children work, and more than one-third of the mothers of preschoolers work. Most working mothers (69%) work full-time. Black mothers are even more likely to work than White mothers; this is true regardless of the presence or employment status of fathers. In 1973, the mothers of 58% of Black children and 40% of White children whose fathers had jobs were also employed. Black families tend to be a little larger than White families, which contributes to the statistical difference. Black families also tend to have lower incomes than White families, regardless of how many parents work, and this contributes to the motivation to work of Black mothers. The growing divorce rate is a contributor to the increases in numbers of working mothers. More than two-thirds of White divorced mothers of children under 18 are employed. Divorce is not so likely to alter the employment status of Black mothers, who are already more likely to be employed than White mothers (Waldman, 1975).

Survey data provide some insights into the feelings women have about combining paid work with motherhood. Mason and Bumpass (1975) report those feelings are ambivalent. More than seven out of ten White respondents and six out of ten Black respondents felt that "a preschool child is likely to suffer if his mother works." Yet about half of the women also agreed that "a working mother can establish just as warm and secure a relationship with her children as a mother who does not work," and only four out of ten White women and five out of ten Black women believed that "women are happier if they stay at home and take care of their children." Women who were employed at the time of the survey were somewhat less likely to endorse statements favoring remaining at home than were women not in the labor force. Women who had once been employed did not differ from those who had never held a paying job. Attitudes toward combining paid work and motherhood do not seem to grow out of the experience of trying to do so. If the attitudes were based on experience, we would expect those who had children to feel differently from those who did not, and those who had many children to feel differently from those who had only one or two. This is not the case.

Child Care

The principal problem faced by mothers of preschoolers who want to work is child care. This is also a problem with younger school-age children who require after-school care. Emlen and Perry (1974) estimate that about 90% of children under 6 are cared for in their own homes or someone else's home while their mothers are at work. This estimate is probably too high. It is based on combined data from three surveys, the most recent of which included low- and moderate-income families only. Such families generally prefer to leave their children with relatives or friends because they do not feel comfortable leaving them in day-care centers. This is not only because good day care is expensive, but also because they worry about trusting their children to strangers who may not share their values (Rubin, 1976).

About half the preschool-age children of working mothers are cared for in their own homes, frequently by their fathers or other relatives. Other homes in which children are cared for are as likely to be those of relatives as of nonrelatives. As to school-age children (age 6 to 14, depending on the study), many mothers work only during school hours, some children are left on their own after school, some go to someone else's home, and a very few go to after-school centers. Most children (two-thirds or more) are cared for at home, usually by some family member, after school hours (Emlen & Perry, 1974).

Perry's (1963) study of mothers and paid caretakers in Spokane is especially informative and is consistent with later findings of Emlen and his associates in Portland (summarized in Emlen & Perry, 1974). Mothers have fairly definite ideas about substitutes. They focus on desired qualities, such as fondness for children and dependability, rather than on formal preparation for the job. Caretakers are generally hired through an interpersonal network: someone hears that someone else is looking for child-care help, or for this type of work, and passes the word along. Apart from the fact that 82% had children of their own, the helpers in the sample had little preparation or relevant experience. Although they were fond of children, 40% would have preferred other employment but found this was not possible for various reasons.

Women hired to care for children tend to be homemaker substitutes as well. More than one-third who worked in the child's home were assigned light housekeeping duties; more than one-fourth had some heavy housework to do. Many of those who were not assigned additional duties assumed them anyway.

Effects on Children

As might be expected, the fact that a mother works outside the home does have an impact on the images children have of the roles of woman, wife, and mother. Daughters of employed women, studied in childhood (Hartley, 1960) or in young adulthood (Vogel, Broverman, Broverman, Clarkson, & Rosenkrantz, 1970; Baruch, 1972), do have less traditional views of the female role. How maternal employment affects the sex-role views of sons cannot be clearly stated on the basis of currently available data.

What about other effects of maternal employment? Lois W. Hoffman has reviewed the literature twice (1963, 1974a). In the second article, she observes that there have been few changes in the findings over the 11-year time span. Both what we know and what we do not know are essentially the same as they were earlier.

Broadly speaking, maternal employment appears to have little psychological effect on children. Studies cited by Hoffman (1963) indicate no systematic differences in dependence, anxiety, psychosomatic symptoms, or antisocial behavior between preschool children of employed mothers and those whose mothers are full-time homemakers. Studies of the 9-to-12 age group show no differences related to maternal employment in need for relationship with others or for power. Studies of teenagers show that those whose mothers are employed are no different in terms of a variety of personality traits from those whose mothers are not employed. Teenage children of working mothers do not feel less accepted by their mothers, or more lonely.

Many people worry about the effects of not having a full-time mother figure to relate to during the infant and toddler periods. In fact, there has been very little systematic research on very young children who are cared for part of the day by persons other than their mothers. However, the studies of child-care arrangements cited above indicate that most young children are cared for at home or in homelike settings. More institutional child-care centers are governed by state and local laws, which generally require very low ratios of children to caretakers for young children. Kentucky, for example, requires one adult for every six children under 2, one for every eight children between 2 and 3 years old, and one for every ten children between 3 and 4 years old (Kentucky Department of Human Resources, n.d.).

Unless one assumes—with no available data to support the assumption—that only the biological mother can properly care for a young child, or that caretakers are very different from mothers in ways that matter to the child, fears about the development of babies and toddlers whose mothers are employed seem exaggerated. These fears are often based on reports of children who are deprived of attention and stimulation for long periods of time. Such conditions can occur among children who are hospitalized or institutionalized. There is no evidence that spending about 40 hours a week being cared for in a day-care center or someone's home is comparable to spending months or years in a foundling home or hospital.

Women Who Are Not Married

Some information on women who choose not to marry when they find they are about to become mothers was presented in the context of motherhood. Here, we turn more directly to a discussion of the roles and options for unmarried women, whether formerly married or never married.

Divorce

In the United States in 1974, there were 3.4 million women who were divorced and not remarried, constituting about 4.5% of all women 16 and over.

In the 1960s and 1970s, divorce rates have risen far more rapidly than marriage rates. Remarriage rates are also high, suggesting that people are becoming disillusioned with particular partnerships, not with marriage as such. Characteristics associated with greater divorce proneness include limited income and education; urban residence; marriage while still in teens; an engagement of less than six months; dissimilar educational, financial, and ethnic backgrounds; disapproval of family and friends; and different conceptions of the roles of husband and wife. Divorce rates are higher in the Black community than the White (Goode, 1956, 1962; Scanzoni & Scanzoni, 1976).

The problems that lead some couples to divorce are not essentially different from those mentioned by couples who plan to continue their marriages. Some families avoid pressing issues to the point where open conflict takes place; others, for a variety of reasons, do not. The reasons may include feelings about divorce, the relative importance placed on individual and family needs, and the way in which available alternatives are evaluated.

Regardless of whether they are planning to stay married or planning to divorce, men and women feel differently about marriage and its problems. Women are more likely to be unhappy and to see problems as having started earlier in the marriage and having lasted longer. They focus on interpersonal aspects of the relationship, with complaints about qualities such as coldness. Women are about twice as likely to seek professional help, or to wish they had done so. Men focus on sex and money as sources of problems. Although differences in background (religion, education) and problems with in-laws are frequently complicating factors, neither they, nor children, are usually cited by individuals as major sources of their own marital problems. (See Scanzoni & Scanzoni, 1976, for general discussion; DeBurger, 1967, and Rollins & Feldman, 1970, for data from several major studies.)

The ties between former spouses do not end with divorce. Men are especially apt to feel emotionally bound by guilt or pity. More than 60% of divorced women remain bound to their ex-husbands by children, an additional number by support payments. Those who are neutral toward each other are less likely to quarrel about child rearing after divorce than those who still have feelings, whether positive or negative, toward their former spouse (Hunt, 1966).

Widowhood

Because women tend to marry men older than themselves and have longer life expectancies than men, most women face the prospect of widowhood. In 1974, there were 9.8 million widowed women in the United States—about 12% of all women 16 years of age and over (Hayghe, 1975, Table A). Widowed women are more likely than widowed men to continue participating in various civic and social activities (Booth, 1972), but less likely than widowed men to be employed (Hayghe, 1975, Table 1). Although six out of ten say that widows sometimes feel like a "fifth wheel," according to Lopata's (1971a) study of a representative sample of Chicago area widows, most want to maintain ties with family and friends.

Lopata found that the majority of widows live alone, or with one other person, most often an unmarried child. Her finding is consistent with census data showing that half of all women who do not live with any relative are age 65 or over. Of course, some of these are never-married or divorced women, but most are widows (U.S. Bureau of the Census, 1975). Seven out of ten who do live alone enjoy doing so. Many who live with others would prefer another arrangement.

Widows prefer to live alone for several reasons. They fear loss of freedom, loss of status, and loss of contact with their neighbors and neighborhood. They anticipate conflict over family decisions with those with whom they live. A substantial proportion fear they will be exploited as well. Some feel other children and siblings will abandon them entirely if they go to live with one child or sibling. After a period of bereavement, complicated by the fact that many women are unprepared to maintain a home and a meaningful life alone, most widows adjust, and report that they value their independence.

Never-Married Women

According to recent census figures, there are about 14.4 million single women. About 18% of American women age 16 and over, and about 25% of American men age 16 and over, are single. About 4% of women and 6% of men ages 45–54 have never been married. In the population as a whole, women outnumber men at every age level. However, among single people, women outnumber men only among people age 55 and over (Hayghe, 1975, Tables 1 and B; Dixon, 1976, p. 24).

There has been almost no research on the life-styles of single adults. The work of Peter Stein (1976) is an exception. His samples (college students studied by survey methods, and 40 others living in two East Coast urban communities who were interviewed in depth) are not representative of all single people. They include people who have been married previously and exclude those who are seeing one person only. However, his work provides a basis for further research. He found that fear of loneliness is the major problem in the lives of single people. Having an active social life without a mate is more of a challenge to single women who have to fight sex-role stereotypes before they can fight loneliness. He notes that our society does not provide a basis for relating to others over a long period of time outside of the traditional family context.

Most single women between the ages of 20 and 64 are employed. There is a popular image of the successful career woman who has sacrificed marriage and family to achieve other goals. Among women age 35 and over, single women are indeed more likely than married or formerly married women to be in white-collar positions—particularly the higher-paying, higher-prestige technical and professional fields—and less likely to be manual laborers or service workers. Among women ages 16 to 34, the proportions in each marital status who are clerical workers is about the same; married women are most likely to be professional or technical workers; and formerly married women are most likely to be blue-collar workers (Hayghe, 1975, Table E).

The data do provide some support for the hypothesis that women with the skills to secure better-paying, more prestigious jobs are more likely to remain single than those who do manual labor. An alternative hypothesis is that those who remain single upgrade their skills in order to provide a more satisfying life for themselves. The higher proportion of formerly married women who are in blue-collar positions may reflect the higher divorce and separation rates in the working class, the fact that formerly married women often have families to support and cannot as readily choose to stay home or seek additional training rather than accept an unappealing job, or both.

Lesbian Women

Lesbians constitute an important segment of the female population about which we know relatively little. Lesbian, or homosexual, women are erotically attracted to women and prefer to share all or part of their sex lives with women (Lyon & Martin, 1973). Many regard themselves as married to their lovers, despite the fact that society does not consider such marriages legal (Jensen, 1974). Others are, or formerly were, married to men. In one recent study, 14% of the sample had been heterosexually married at some point in their lives (Hedblom, 1973).

Until recently, research on homosexuality viewed lesbian women and gay men as problematic, sick, or deviant (Hooker, 1978; Morin, 1978). The sociological literature focused on homosexual relationships among women in atypical groups, such as inmates in women's prisons (Giallombardo, 1966; Tittle, 1969) or striptease performers (McCaghy & Skipper, 1969). Work like that of British psychiatrist Charlotte Wolff (1972), using survey techniques and studying the activities and attitudes of women who were not patients, was unusual.

Many gay people, female and male, who formerly concealed their sexual preferences are now living openly homosexual life-styles. This has created greater awareness of homosexuality and acted as a stimulus to new kinds of research. Current investigators are trying to expand our understanding of intimate relationships by asking comparable questions about homosexual and heterosexual women and men (Hooker, 1978; Morin, 1978).

In many respects, lesbian women are more like heterosexual women than like homosexual men (Simon & Gagnon, 1967). They tend to be integrated into the wider community, rather than becoming part of a homosexual community. They are more likely than homosexual men to maintain ties with friends and relatives who are heterosexual. Whether they are more likely than gay men to regard parenthood and a stable, long-term relationship with a loved one as important goals is a matter of debate. Mileski and Black (1972) believe that the fact that gay women have fewer short-term, casual relationships than gay men is a product of their more limited participation in the homosexual community, rather than a factor limiting that participation. Letitia Anne Peplau and her associates (1978) found that, of the 61% of the women in their sample who were emotionally involved with someone, most expected that relationship to continue for six months or more. More than a quarter were certain that their relationship would last at least five years. Recalling past relationships, the women in the Peplau study reported their longest relationships as lasting anywhere from one month to 25 years. The median length of the relationships reported was two and a half years.

Some women have adopted a lesbian life-style as part of a feminist stance. They see relating to women as a sensible alternative to relating to men who do not regard them as equals (for example, Shelley, 1970). Others (for example, Simpson, 1977) argue that to be a lesbian is not necessarily to be a feminist, and they point out that feminists do not always make common cause with homosexuals (see Chapter 2 for a fuller discussion of gay rights as an issue within the women's movement).

Peplau and her associates (1978) looked at the relationships among sex-role traditionalism, feminist involvement, and lesbian activism within their predominantly White, middle-class lesbian sample. Most of the women questioned held relatively nontraditional sex-role attitudes. However, those who placed a high value on security and permanence in a relationship were more traditional than those who sought autonomy and equality. Over half the women in the sample were, at the time of the study, involved in at least one feminist group. Those women who were active in lesbian politics and organizations described themselves with such terms as *radical lesbian* and *lesbian feminist*.

More information is needed before any meaningful conclusions can be drawn about women who are not married or about women who prefer to relate sexually and emotionally to women rather than to men. In order to obtain that information, former and present marital statuses and erotic preferences will have to be included routinely along with such variables as age, race, and occupation in studies of the entire range of women's attitudes and behavior. Studies that ask the same questions of all women will enrich our understanding of majority and minority life-styles and show how individual and social factors produce and shape each alternative way of life.

Summary

In this chapter on home and family, we have noted that the family as an institution and the roles of women within it are changing. Families are smaller; more of them include only younger women and children; and a growing number are composed of older women living by themselves. On the whole, today's women are marrying later and having fewer children than their mothers did. While some married women are choosing not to be mothers, a small but growing number are choosing motherhood outside of marriage.

Traditionally, men are accorded more power within the family than women, but well-educated income-earning women are beginning to exert pressure for a reallocation of power. Most would like a reallocation of responsibilities as well, since women who are employed outside the home also carry much of the work load inside the home.

Women choose to combine paid work with motherhood and marriage for a variety of reasons. Economic need figures into the thinking of most women, but need is sometimes the excuse rather than the reason. There is some evidence that, at least for women who are well educated and have no small children, society's expectations are changing; such women are now expected by many to seek employment.

The mother who does choose to work outside the home can obtain some reassurance from the fact that research does not reveal any serious problems associated with being the child of a working mother. There is, of course, the problem of arranging satisfactory child care. The majority of young children are currently cared for in homes—their own or the caretaker's—often by relatives. The number of child-care centers is growing. These are not equally favored by or available to people in all locations and economic brackets.

Although the vast majority of people do marry, the number of single people in our population is substantial and increasing. The life-styles of women who are not married have not been thoroughly investigated. Their numbers include divorced, widowed, and separated women, and women who have never married. Each of these categories, as well as that of currently married women, includes both heterosexual and homosexual women.

The family lives of women are changing. A growing proportion of American women are electing to delay marriage, remain single, or leave marriage. However, apart from official statistics, the available information about the unmarried segment of the population is scant. We know very little about their attitudes, their daily lives, or their living arrangements.

JOINING THE CLUB

CHAPTER 9

Women in the Community

A community is sometimes pictured by sociologists (1) as a pyramid of layers, or strata, each composed of people with similar life-styles, (2) as a network of groups concerned with solving the problems of everyday life, or (3) as a network of interpersonal relationships. All three of these ways of viewing communities and the place of women within them will be considered in this chapter.

In looking at the community as a pyramid of ranked strata, some questions will be raised about how to determine to which stratum a woman belongs and how to determine when she has changed her position. In viewing the community as a network of groups, women's participation in voluntary organizations will be detailed. Next, friendship, kinship, and neighboring patterns—the informal networks that bind community members—will be examined, with emphasis on the ways in which women are bound into such networks. We will conclude with a brief discussion of some problems faced by individual women, the causes and effects of which have important implications for the community as a whole. (See Lofland, 1975, for a discussion of how and why women have been neglected in traditional community studies.)

Women and Status in the Community

Socioeconomic status, or social class position, is a major explanatory variable in sociology. Social class position shapes life chances and opportunities. The amount, stability, and source of income available to be shared by a household limits the neighborhoods in which it can reside, the material possessions it can obtain, the educational opportunities of its members, and the kinds of services it can afford. Directly and indirectly, these factors, together with the amount of prestige the unit's members have in the community, tend to limit the people with whom they will interact, the opinions to which they will be exposed, and the way in which they will define their self-interest.

There are many indicators of status. Occupation, income, and amount of formal education, singly or in combination, are most frequently used because they are easy to determine and to rank. For males especially, these measures are correlated with each other and tend to predict other indicators of status with fair accuracy.

It is generally assumed that all members of a household share the same position in the status hierarchy. Clearly, they share the income of the unit and those things directly dependent upon income. Whether the less tangible aspects of stratification, such as prestige and class identification, are also shared is less clear. About half the college students in one survey (Kelley & Suelzle, 1971) believed a professionally employed woman had more prestige than the wife of a similarly employed man. Another study (Ritter & Hargens, 1975) examined data on 566 working women who identified themselves as "middle class" in surveys conducted by the Survey Research Center. The results of their statistical analysis lend support to the view that the women's own occupational status, as well as that of their husbands, contributed to their self-identification as middle class.

Given traditional expectations, and recalling the discussion in the preceding chapter of power resources in the family, one would predict problems in families in which the wife has claim to higher social status than the husband. U.S. Department of Labor statistics suggest that status inconsistency within families is fairly widespread (Hayghe, 1975, Table Q, p. 24). For example, nearly 55% of the wives of carpenters—a highly ranked blue-collar occupation—are employed in white-collar jobs, and more than 11% are in positions of higher status than clerical and sales positions. Of the working wives of factory operatives—a less-skilled blue-collar category—almost 44% are white-collar employees, and 10.5% are in positions above the clerical and sales level. Two kinds of questions are raised by such findings. The first is of practical interest: do such apparent inconsistencies really cause problems for individuals and families? The second is of interest to social scientists who want to use social class as an explanatory variable: how can we accurately measure family status so that the impact of wives' and husbands' positions are taken into account?

Social Mobility Patterns

In the words of one recent article, studies of mobility—the movement up or down or across status levels within an individual's adult lifetime, or in comparison to the parental generation—have been largely "man-centric" (Glenn, Ross, & Tully, 1974, p. 683). Studies of mobility patterns of women are needed to fill gaps in our knowledge of women and of our society. As Glenn and his co-authors point out, mobility data are the principal means of assessing the extent to which, consistent with our beliefs, people can and do achieve positions in this society by their own efforts. We have some idea how open the system is for men, but men are only half the members of the system.

The traditional approach to measuring the mobility of women has been to compare a married woman's husband's status or occupation with that of her father. This approach assumes that only men's positions are important, but it can be argued that it does include a larger proportion of women than would be studied if women's paid jobs were considered.

In one recent study (Glenn et al., 1974), it was found that women are more apt to move both up and down in the status hierarchy through marriage than men are by attaining occupational positions different from those of their fathers. Richard Udry (1977) has recently settled a persistent question: do good looks help a woman marry into a higher class than the one in which she was raised? There are some minor differences in the answer depending on whether the woman is Black or White and on how well educated she is. Overall, however, the answer is: no, beauty is not a ticket to higher status.

Since 1971, a number of studies have appeared that seek to determine how much occupational mobility women do experience. Some of the studies (all of the major ones are reviewed by Rachel Rosenfeld, 1978) also attempt to compare women's occupational mobility with men's, or occupational mobility with marriage mobility. As with the research on women and success reported in Chapter 7, the results are inconsistent. Several of the studies analyze the same data, but there is no agreement on just how to perform the analysis.

Rosenfeld does not have any conclusions to offer about how great the opportunities are for women to move up or down in the stratification system. She does present evidence that, if one is going to look at women's occupational mobility, mothers' as well as fathers' occupations have to be considered in establishing the starting point for mobility. She also argues that it would be more accurate to look at job categories than to look, as some studies do, at occupational prestige. In American society, the jobs at which most women are employed have low prestige partly because they are the jobs most open to women.

Community Institutions and Groups

Voluntary Organizations

Looking at women's participation in community civic and social groups tells us something about the position and influence of women in the community. The participation of women in groups seeking to influence political decisions will be discussed in Chapter 14; participation in women's movement organizations was a major focus of Section I. The focus here is more general, giving equal attention to organizations that seek to influence public policy and those that do not.

In addition to responsibilities at home and on the job, women, especially well-educated middle- and upper-class women, participate in a wide variety of civic and social activities. Lopata reports that 64% of her Chicago-area sample of married women belong to at least one organization (1971b). Women devote approximately the same number of hours to community activity regardless of health, age, or marital status. For men, youth, good health, and being married are all associated with higher rates of participation (Booth, 1972). Only the presence of preschool-age children significantly decreases women's levels of participation in activities outside the home (Angrist, 1967).

Women are more likely than men to belong to organizations oriented toward recreational, charitable, and religious activities, and equally likely to belong to civic and

Figure 9-1. Women traditionally have volunteered their time and energy to work toward improving community conditions. (Photo by Wide World Photos.)

political groups. The groups to which women belong are often less prestigious than the ones to which men belong. The pattern observed by Babchuk and Booth (1969) in church-related organizations is instructive. Men are likely to be recruited to church governing boards whose members are invited or elected to join for limited time periods. Women join church groups with broad, continuous membership, such as mission societies and sisterhoods. These latter groups may make major contributions to the church and the community, but they are not influence-wielding, decision-making bodies. This pattern has been noted in political and economic organizations as well: men sit on governing boards and assume leadership roles more often than do women (Booth, 1972).

Except for occupationally focused groups, such as professional associations and unions, women join civic and social organizations earlier in their lives than men do (Babchuk & Booth, 1969). Among teenagers, girls are more likely than boys to belong to organized groups such as church youth groups, Scouts, and high school sororities (unpublished data from Survey Research Center, cited by Hyman & Wright, 1971, p. 201n). Apart from union membership, whether men or women are more organizationally active depends on which social stratum one examines, and whether numbers of organizations or numbers of hours are counted. For example, in Booth's (1972) Nebraska sample, working-class men and women belonged, on the average, to about the same number of organizations (males, 1.3; females, 1.1), but men devoted more time to the organizations (6.8 versus 5.4 hours per month). Among people in higher status categories, men belonged to more organizations (3.1 versus 2.2), but women devoted more hours (11.2 versus 13.5 per month) to organizational activities (p. 187).

Education and income appear to be less important in determining participation among Black women than among White women. This is especially true of Black women with very modest levels of formal education, who are far more likely than comparably educated White women to participate in organizations based in their neighborhood or church (Lopata, 1971b).

Organizations for Women Only

Focusing on organizations with exclusively female membership, Mhyra Minnis (1953) found that they reflected the social cleavages of New Haven as a community. At the time of her research, there were eight separate organizations modeled on the Junior League. Each one drew its members from the elite of a distinctive racial, ethnic, or religious segment of the community. The groups varied in prestige according to the overall community prestige of their membership. The most highly regarded, the New Haven Junior League, represented the traditional upper-class, old Yankee families. In addition, there were the Catholic Charity League, a predominantly Irish-American organization; separate leagues for Italian and Polish Catholic women; leagues for Swedish and Danish women who were White and Protestant; and leagues for Jewish and Black women.

Racial, religious, and ethnic cleavages were just as frequent among groups drawing their membership from less prestigious ranks of the community. Of the 371 women's organizations for which Minnis had demographic information, 335 were exclusively White, 22 exclusively Black, and 14 integrated. Racial duplication existed in all types of groups, from clubs for working women to the auxiliaries of fraternal orders. In more than three-fourths of the organizations, the members were all of the same religion, despite the fact that most of them had no particular religious purpose.

Existing organizations with all-female membership could provide a common focus of interest and a basis for unity among women from varied backgrounds. Instead, in New Haven and elsewhere, they appear to reinforce the existing divisions of the community. About three out of ten women who responded to the *Redbook* questionnaire (Tavris & Jayaratne, 1972, p. 27) belonged to women's organizations.

Explaining Gender Differences in Participation

Women's organizations reflect the existing structure of the community, and women in organizations reflect the existing position of women in the community. The functions women perform are supportive, and the organizations with which they are involved strive primarily to improve conditions and enhance opportunities, rather than to make or change social policy.

Socialization is a key factor in explaining the differences in organizational behavior characteristic of women and men. Women are socialized to be interested in certain issues and activities, and men are socialized to look to women for contributions in these areas.

Rosabeth Kanter's (1976) analysis of the position and behavior of women in business and industry points up another key factor that can be applied to civic and social organizations as well. Her thesis is that women's behavior in organizations is typical of minority-group behavior. In organizational settings, members of social minorities are not treated as individuals. They have limited prospects for advancement, lack power to change the organization, and, when they do achieve positions of power or status, they are uncomfortably obvious—they stand out. Under such circumstances, people from minority backgrounds often have limited aspirations. They are likely to focus on rewards that come from relationships with people, rather than those that come from achieving material goals, such as high salaries and plush offices. Often they are overly polite and cautious in relationships with others in the organization. Kanter points out that studies of men in dead-end, low-status jobs reveal that they, too, lower their aspirations and focus on goals that are not job-related.

Women who devote their organizational energies to groups and goals that reflect sex-role expectations are likely to be treated as individuals, to advance to leadership positions, and to have power within the organization. Moreover, their presence does not threaten to detract from the ability of a group to function as a unit. The current state of affairs reflects both socialized expectations and typical minority-group response patterns. The two are mutually reinforcing; which came first is a moot point.

Informal Relationships in the Community

Whereas employment and participation in community organizations frequently bring together people from different segments of the community, informal relationships tend to be established among people in comparable positions. There are both gender and class differences in relationships with friends, neighbors, and kin.

The residential neighborhood occupies a central place in the lives of working-class and poor women. First, they are more likely than middle-class women to limit their friendships to neighbors and relatives (Goldthorpe, Lockwood, Bechhofer, & Platt, 1972; Lopata, 1971b). In addition, neighboring among less affluent women frequently involves exchanges of goods (such as food and tools) and services (such as babysitting), thus easing the strains of family life on limited resources. Among those with above-average educations and incomes, socializing among neighbors is more likely to be planned around fixed activities (such as playing bridge). It is also more likely to be inside people's homes, rather than outdoors or in public places such as coin laundries.

Gender and class differences overlap. Informal gatherings are more likely to include both men and women in middle-class neighborhoods. Men in white-collar positions report a larger number of friends than do women of similar status. However, friendships among women of all social-class backgrounds are more intimate (sharing confidences) and more spontaneous (doing things together on the spur of the moment) than those among men. Men are more likely than women to claim friendships with members of the other sex (Booth, 1972; P. Stein, 1976).

Lopata (1971b) looks at how the Chicago-area women she interviewed met the couples with whom they maintain friendships, and whether the husband or the wife introduced a given couple into their circle. The responses reflect the interconnections among various parts of the community. About one-fourth of the couples seen most often were childhood friends of one member of the couple, most often the wife. About one-fourth are, or formerly were, neighbors. Work is the third most frequent source of couples who become friends, followed by contacts made through voluntary associations and friendships that developed among relatives.

More than half of the friends made through work were made through the husband's job. However, this may reflect only the circumstances of some women during particular phases of the family life cycle. Among currently employed women, 70% of the friendships that originated at work stem from the wife's job. Only among urban couples in which the wife is a full-time homemaker, and among suburban couples in which the wife is a full-time homemaker under 40, are the majority of work-related friendships a product of the husband's work.

Women tend to have more extensive ties with relatives. They generally maintain strong ties with the family in which they grew up—parents, grandparents, aunts, uncles, siblings, and cousins, all people about their own age or older. Men tend to focus on the family begun at marriage—wives, children, and later grandchildren. Because of this, men maintain the same types and intensities of relationships with relatives throughout their adult lives. As women grow older, many of the relatives who are important to them grow older too, and many with whom they are close die, leaving them with fewer relatives to relate to in later years (Booth, 1972).

Some Problem Areas

A personal problem becomes a community problem when it affects an appreciable number of people, or when its causes or its effects are rooted not in the individual, but in her social environment. Many topics discussed in other chapters of this section and in other sections of this volume could be included in this discussion—for example, discrimination against women in employment (Chapter 12) and the availability of abortion services (Chapter 8). The topics discussed here are both important and interesting but do not fit neatly into the broad topic headings elsewhere in this volume. The use and abuse of alcohol and other drugs, mental and physical illness, and rape are all experienced by women as personal problems, although sociological analysis indicates that their forms, causes, and effects are frequently rooted not within the individual woman, but in her community and society.

Drugs

Alcohol.   Sociologists distinguish between alcohol use and alcoholism—that is, physical or psychological dependence upon alcohol. There are people who drink heavily for whom alcohol is not a problem. There are also people who drink moderately who would experience great distress if they were unable to drink.

Women are more likely than men to be nondrinkers. In one study, slightly more than two out of ten men reported that they never drink, compared with nearly four out of ten women who called themselves nondrinkers. Those women who do drink, drink less, and less frequently, than men. Whether social or problem drinkers, women tend to prefer wine or hard liquor; they are not so likely to drink beer as men (data cited by Segal, 1973).

After studying information gathered over several years, on the same large sample, Mary Cover Jones (1971) concludes that women who abstain completely and women who are problem drinkers have some personality traits in common. Compared with social drinkers, they tend to be more withdrawn, guilty, and anxious. Women who drink only infrequently tend to be more controlled and less able to express emotion than women who drink more often. Personality differences among men do not seem to be as closely related to drinking habits as they are among women.

Estimating sex differences in the incidence of problem drinking is difficult and depends both on the source of the data and on the definition of "problem" drinking. If "problem" means being arrested for drunkenness or drunken driving, such offenses account for about 32% of all arrests of males and fewer than 14% of all arrests of females (R. Simon, 1975, p. 47). About three times as many men as women seek help from private physicians for drinking problems, and about six times as many men are hospitalized for such problems (Jones, 1971, p. 62).

At least among middle-class people, women are more likely than men to have progressed rapidly from little or no drinking to the problem point as a result of a shock or life crisis. This is especially true of those whose self-image is built around the wife or mother role and who lose that role through death, divorce, or marriage of a child. There is some evidence that alcoholism typically begins later in life among women than among men (Curlee, 1967, 1969; Wanberg & Horn, 1970).

Whether in community groups such as Alcoholics Anonymous, in hospital settings, or in outpatient therapy, women are more difficult to treat and have less favorable prospects of recovery than men (Curlee, 1967; Pemberton, 1967). One reason may be that women are more secretive about drinking than men. They drink at home, alone, and are less willing to discuss their drinking with others. This reluctance may stem from a knowledge that heavy drinking is inconsistent with sex-role expectations for women and that the stereotype of the alcoholic woman is a very negative one that includes moral looseness and degradation.

It is useful to look at the situation of married alcoholic women in a sex-role context. Husbands of alcoholic women are less cooperative in dealing with problem drinking than the wives of alcoholic men. In our society, wives are expected to adjust their activities and goals to conform to the needs and desires of their husbands, not vice versa. Both women and men resent the failure of alcoholic spouses to meet their family obligations. However, in such situations, wives are more likely to define their husbands as needful of additional support, whereas husbands are more likely to define their wives as unworthy of support. (See studies cited in Health Communications, Inc., 1977, and studies cited above.)

Other Drugs. Current data indicate that fewer women than men use alcohol to excess. However, women are more likely than men to use and abuse psychoactive drugs, especially those obtained legally by prescription. A large-scale study of a national cross section of adults indicates that 13% of the men and 29% of the women sampled had used psychoactive drugs between late 1970 and spring 1971 (cited in Consumers Union, 1974, p. 256). Data cited in an earlier Consumers Union publication (Brecher, 1972, p. 484) indicate that in 1967 women accounted for 60% to 80% of the prescriptions written for all mood-altering drugs, from sleeping pills to pep pills.

The contemporary drug use of women should be seen in historical perspective. Prior to the passage of restrictive legislation in 1914, during the time of the suffrage and temperance movements, women were more likely than men to be addicted to the opiate-laced medicines then available over the counter (Brecher, 1972). Thus, the use of legally available mood-affecting drugs among American women is not a new pattern; only the drugs of choice are new.

Drug use among adult women appears to have an impact on their children. Teen-agers of both genders whose mothers use tranquilizers are more likely to use every type of drug—legal and illegal, addictive and nonaddictive—than those whose mothers do not use tranquilizers (data cited by Segal, 1973). Whether these young people have been taught an accepting attitude toward drug use by their mothers, or whether a more subtle and more complex process is involved, is not clear.

Women and Illness

The drug-use patterns described above probably reflect both a higher volume of requests for psychoactive drugs on the part of women and the fact that women are more likely than men to be treated for mental or emotional illness. One significant pattern is severe depression, often leading to hospitalization, among middle-aged women with no previous history of such problems. Hormonal changes, especially rapid loss of estrogen associated with menopause, provide one possible explanation for such depression (see Chapter 6 for a more complete explanation and references). Another line of reasoning, supported by current sociological research (Bart, 1970), is that changes in family responsibilities—such as children leaving home, widowhood, or divorce—may precipi-tate depression among women who have made the family their main focus and source of fulfillment.

One explanation for sex differences in mental-illness rates is that women are more likely than men to seek professional advice for personal problems. What is on record is the number who seek help, not the number who have a particular problem. In addition, women from cosmopolitan environments—for example, urban women, women of higher socioeconomic status, and Jewish women—are likely to define the causes of their problems as psychological, even if the symptoms are basically physical. Women of lower socioeconomic status usually experience their symptoms as physical and define them as such, but physicians believe they are emotional in origin unless a physical cause is immediately apparent. In short, even the woman with physical symptoms is more likely than a man in similar circumstances to receive a psychological diagnosis and treatment that includes psychoactive drugs (Bart, 1968; Schwab, Brown, Holzer, & Sokolof, 1968).

The extent to which the apparently higher rates of mental illness among women are purely products of differences in reporting and diagnosing, rather than differences in actual occurrence, is not clear at present. Walter Gove and his associates (see, for example, Clancy & Gove, 1974) argue that the differences are real because they occur even after a large number of extraneous factors, such as whether the symptoms are seen as undesirable, are taken into account.

Generally, married people enjoy better mental and physical health than single people. They are also less likely to be victims of fatal accidents or murder or to commit suicide than single people. However, marriage has a greater positive effect on the health and well-being of men than of women (Gove, 1973).

The social stigma attached to illness may not be so discrediting as that attached to being a failure. Being an unsuccessful wife and mother, or being dependent upon society, are conditions defined as failure by some women. Cole and Lejeune (1972) studied self-reported ill health. Working-class women who were satisfied with their performance in the family were not so likely to report ill health as those who were not satisfied. Welfare mothers who had preschool children, were interested in finding paid work, or who defined welfare aid as a basic human right, were not so likely to report ill health as those who had no small children (children being a socially acceptable reason for dependence) or who saw being on welfare as a sign of personal failure.

To suggest that some women prefer to be defined as ill rather than as failures does not mean that all women who experience physical or psychological symptoms are failures in their own eyes, or in the judgment of society. Neither does it mean that their symptoms are feigned. However, in an achievement-oriented society, where people are expected to perform at a certain level and many cannot do so, they seek explanations. Being ill may seem to some the least negative of available alternatives.

Some Relationships Among Health, Drugs, and Women's Roles

Not all aspects of drug and health problems among women can be related to women's roles, but there is a pattern in the information presented here. Adequate performance of the roles of wife and mother are expected of women in our society. Devotion of one's entire adult life to these roles is socially acceptable, if not demanded. Many women cannot live up to the family role standards they and others around them have set. Sometimes this is because of individual limitations such as ill health, sometimes because of social conditions such as poverty, and sometimes because the appropriate role partners—husbands and children—are no longer present. Moreover, those women who do allow their lives to revolve around the family have no other criteria, such as income or prestige earned through service to the community, by which to evaluate themselves. If, in their own eyes, they fail as homemakers, wives, or mothers, they have failed in life. If their children leave home or their spouse leaves or dies, they may see themselves as having no important work at all.

Being left without an important role is almost inevitable for family-centered women because children do leave home, and more women outlive their husbands than vice versa. The problem is aggravated by the fact that such crises frequently occur at about the same time that changes in hormone balance associated with menopause occur. Mental and physical symptoms with no clear cause and drug and alcohol abuse are possible products of such crises. Where these phenomena are not products of inability, for whatever reason, to perform family roles that have previously given meaning to life, they frequently interfere with a woman's ability to perform such roles and to meet the needs of family members who depend upon her. Differences in the responses of wives and husbands of alcoholics have been mentioned. Similar differences are predictable in families where the wife is chronically ill or physically disabled.

Rape

Rape is a topic that ties, directly or indirectly, into most of the other topics discussed in this chapter on women in the community. Rape is a personal, medical, and social problem reflecting sex-role assumptions and involving women in interaction with various groups and institutions within the community.

Official statistics underestimate, perhaps by as much as half, the number of rapes because victims are embarrassed or afraid to report being sexually assaulted (Thacker, 1975). Current interest in rape, the introduction in many states of legislation to protect the private lives of alleged victims from disclosure in the courtroom, and the growth of rape counseling services can be traced, at least in part, to the women's movement, which has made rape a focus of attention. In 1972, throughout the United States, arrests were made in nearly six out of ten reported rape cases (R. Simon, 1975, p. 36), but unless there has been a drastic change in trends since 1965, only about one-third of those arrested were convicted of rape, another one-third were convicted of lesser offenses or remanded to juvenile court, and the rest were acquitted (MacNamara, 1968).

Rape victims come from all age and economic categories. In more than nine out of ten cases, rapists and their victims come from the same racial group (Amir, 1971). According to a County Crime Commission study in one metropolitan area (Louisville, Kentucky), about half of all reported rapes take place indoors, fewer than two out of ten rapes occur on the street, and about one in three rape victims is acquainted with her assailant (Thacker, 1975).

Recent discussions of rape (for example, Holmstrom & Burgess, 1975, and sources cited by these authors) have sought to analyze this crime in terms of sex-role socialization and the relative positions of males and females in our society. They suggest that the weakness and passivity associated with being female, and the strength and aggressiveness associated with being male, "prepare" women and men for their roles in the drama of rape. They do not imply that sex-role socialization causes rape. Rather, they indicate that the act of sexual assault and its meaning for the participants and the society can be better understood if we take into account the socialization of males and females. Further, they suggest that rape serves to control the behavior of women in two ways: the fear of rape restricts freedom of movement in the community, and the censure and suspicion that victims incur serve to remind women that if they are not ladylike, they will be punished—it will be their own fault. (Susan Brownmiller, 1975, provides a perspective on rape that is both feminist and historical.)

A Note on Minority Communities in a Pluralistic Society

Throughout this section, indeed throughout this book, the subject of discussion has been presented as "women" or "American women." Occasional references have been made to age, educational attainment, and other individual differences that are related to differences in behavior. Occasional references have also been made to the racial, religious, or ethnic backgrounds of the women described. Most frequently, whether stated explicitly or not, the subjects of research are White, Protestant women living in cities or suburbs because most American women are White and Protestant and live in cities or suburbs.

There are two potential dangers involved in basing a discussion of American women on research conducted primarily among the largest segment of the population. The reader who is familiar only with this way of life may assume that the patterns described are characteristic of all American women. The reader who knows that other ways of life exist in our society may assume that the majority pattern is being presented as the proper or better way. Ours is a society made up of people from many racial, religious, and ethnic backgrounds. Each group has its own traditions and values, some of which differ from those of the majority and might, if more widely known, be seen as workable alternatives for women from other groups. An idea of the richness and variety of American life-styles can be gained by reading about the various groups represented in *Ethnic Families in America* (Mindel & Habenstein, 1976).

Summary

Social class, or socioeconomic status, is a key variable in sociology. However, only in the present decade have sociologists begun to address themselves seriously to questions concerning the status of women as individuals and the impact of women's status on family status. Researchers in this area have demonstrated that the positions of wives and of their mothers before them can be measured, but accurate measurement has not yet been undertaken.

The participation of women in the community is not so well documented as that of men, but it is, in fact, as great or greater than that of men. Women are active in a wide variety of organizations, both those for women only and those in which both men and women participate. Women tend to play sustaining and supporting roles in organizations, while men tend to play the decision-making parts. Women also participate in a variety of informal activities.

There are gender differences in patterns and rates of mental and physical illness and in patterns of drug use and abuse. For instance, women are more likely to be diagnosed as having emotional problems and men as having physical ones, even when the presenting complaint is the same. Women are more likely to misuse drugs obtainable by prescription; men are more likely to abuse alcohol and illegal drugs. Men also show signs of emotional stress and develop patterns of drug abuse more gradually than women do. Consideration of sex-role expectations and differences adds a new dimension to the understanding of these and other health-related issues.

In this chapter, the ways that men and women are brought up and the ways in which they relate to each other have been used to increase understanding of subjects as diverse as rape and organizational behavior. Indeed, the influence of gender is pervasive.

Conclusion

The research reviewed in this section should make us hesitant to generalize about the behavior of women. There are many gaps in our knowledge, and what we do know reflects the richness and variety of American women and their lives. Findings that seem both clearly supported by data and consistent with our own experiences are often refuted by further study, or the passage of time. Explanations in which we once had great confidence sometimes turn out to rest on assumptions about males that are less valid for the female half of the population. Nevertheless, a few general statements about the behavior of women and the factors that explain it do seem appropriate at this point.

Sex-role learning begins in the preschool years and continues throughout childhood. The precepts learned are not always consciously taught, and they often have implications for roles that, logically, have little to do with gender. The effects of sex-role socialization are observable in the lives of individuals and in the structure of communities. The culture in which we live, parents, siblings, peers, and schools all have measurable impacts on the attitudes and choices of girls and young women.

Though marriage occurs later and is often less permanent than in the past, most women do marry and have children. But most do not define their roles and their lives exclusively in terms of the family. Employment, voluntary organizations, cultural and athletic events, kinship, and friendship groups are all part of the everyday lives of women.

In most families, men have more power than women, and women do more of the home- and family-related work. Attitudes favoring equality contribute to the distribution of power and division of labor. However, tradition and the greater share of resources that society assists men in bringing to most marriages are also factors here.

Being a mother is central to the self-image of a majority of women. Motherhood is a major turning point in women's lives. When children leave home and motherhood can no longer be the focus of those lives, a few women find the change unbearable.

The roles of women in the family and the community are not so readily separable in life as they are in textbooks. Carrying out day-to-day family responsibilities brings women into contact with many individuals and institutions. Family responsibilities are more limiting for some women than for others. However, the trend toward smaller, more consciously planned families makes it possible for women to consider new options after the childbearing phase of family life. Women would have additional options if the household division of labor were more even and if child-care alternatives were better.

The evidence suggests that both men and women make traditional assumptions about gender roles, and that their attitudes limit options for women. Men are open to equal pay for equal work and the liberation of other men's wives, but not to assuming a greater role in the home so that their own wives can seek options. Women are dissatisfied with the division of labor in their households and are not convinced that homemaking and child care constitute a satisfying full-time job; at the same time, they worry about the safety and emotional security of children who do not have full-time homemaker mothers.

Studies of Black family life and of women educated for careers indicate clearly that strong, capable women are not necessarily dominant or domineering women; that competitive marriage partners will find something to compete over even if the wife willingly assumes the role of unpaid assistant to her husband; and that being professional partners is no guarantee of equality.

From the data in this section, and from the data of sociology in general, it appears as if women's options are limited to family—with or without paid work. Clearly, this does not exhaust the possibilities, but it does exhaust the data. We know very little about the life-styles and attitudes of single women, or about the motivations and accomplishments of women who devote large portions of their lives to unpaid service to the community or to creative endeavors.

The sociology of sex roles is a new specialty within the discipline. Greater interest in roles and options for women has already produced greater interest in the roles and options for men, and greater interest in the contributions that knowledge about women can make to descriptions and explanations of our society. Many of the gaps identified in this section are even now being filled.

Points to Ponder

Beyond the ways women are expected to act and the ways they learn those expectations, beyond the institutions that shape their options, is a more abstract question: why are there sex-related roles and options at all? Here are two views: Heidi Hartmann argues that when jobs are segregated by sex, women and men have different roles and options in all social institutions, but especially in the family. Alice S. Rossi takes a biosocial position, arguing that persistent social patterns associated with gender are innate, though not immutable.

Job segregation by sex . . . is the primary mechanism in capitalist society that maintains the superiority of men over women, because it enforces lower wages for women in the labor market. Low wages keep women dependent on men because they encourage women to marry. Married women must perform domestic chores for their husbands. Men benefit, then, from both higher wages and the domestic division of labor. This domestic division of labor, in turn, acts to weaken women's position in the labor market. Thus, the hierarchical domestic division of labor is perpetuated by the labor market, and vice versa. This process is the present outcome of the continuing interaction of two interlocking systems, capitalism and patriarchy. Patriarchy, far from being vanquished by capitalism, is still very virile; it shapes the form modern capitalism takes, just as the development of capitalism has transformed patriarchal institutions. The resulting mutual accommodation between patriarchy and capitalism has created a vicious circle for women [Hartmann, 1976, p. 139].[1]

Women in all cultures are likely to care for the newborn and to prepare food for household consumption. Men can learn such skills, but as a group they are less apt to show ease in infant handling and food preparation than women are. We know from the Soviet

[1]From "Capitalism, Patriarchy, and Job Segregation," by H. Hartmann, *Signs: Journal of Women in Culture and Society*, 1976, *1*, 137–169. Copyright 1976 by The University of Chicago Press. Reprinted by permission.

experience in training women cosmonauts and the Israeli experience in training women soldiers that specialized training of women is necessary to compensate for male advantage in large musculature. A similar compensatory training may become necessary if more men are to care for young infants. This is an important point to realize in an era when egalitarian ideology argues against innate sex differences and assumes that a unisex education will suffice to remove whatever sex differences currently exist. . . . Since evolutionary changes take place at an infinitely slow pace through long stretches of time, each generation of males and females would require compensatory training. For many generations to come, any slackening of institutional effort directed to compensatory training of the sexes will quickly be followed by a return to sex differentiation as a consequence of the ease with which certain skills are learned by one sex and not by the other [Rossi, 1977, pp. 4–5].[2]

References

Sources of particular interest to the reader are marked with an asterisk.

Almquist, E. M., & Angrist, S. S. Role model influence on college women's career aspirations. *Merrill-Palmer Quarterly*, 1971, *17*, 263–279.

Amir, M. *Patterns of forcible rape*. Chicago: University of Chicago Press, 1971.

Angrist, S. S. Role constellation as a variable in women's leisure activities. *Social Forces*, 1967, *45*, 423–431.

Angrist, S. S. Variations in women's adult aspirations during college. *Journal of Marriage and the Family*, 1972, *34*, 465–468.

Babchuk, N., & Booth, A. Voluntary association membership: A longitudinal analysis. *American Sociological Review*, 1969, *34*, 31–45.

Bailyn, L. Career and family orientation of husbands and wives in relation to marital happiness. *Human Relations*, 1970, *23*, 97–113.

*Bart, P. B. Social structure and vocabularies of discomfort: What happened to female hysteria? *Journal of Health and Social Behavior*, 1968, *9*, 188–193.

Bart, P. B. Mother Portnoy's complaints. *Transaction*, 1970, *8*, 69–74.

Baruch, G. K. Maternal influences upon college women's attitudes toward women and work. *Developmental Psychology*, 1972, *6*, 32–37.

Baruch, G. K. Sex-role stereotyping, the motive to avoid success, and parental identification: A comparison of preadolescent and adolescent girls. *Sex Roles*, 1975, *1*, 303–310.

Bedell, J. W. Role reorganization in the one-parent family: Mother absent due to death. *Sociological Focus*, 1972, *5*, 84–100.

Berheide, C. W., Berk, S. F., & Berk, R. A. Household work in the suburbs: The job and its participants. *Pacific Sociological Review*, 1976, *19*, 491–518.

*Bernard, J. *The future of motherhood*. New York: Penguin, 1975.

Biller, H. B. *Father, child and sex role*. Lexington, Mass.: Heath Lexington, 1971.

Birnbaum, J. A. *Life patterns, personality style and self-esteem in gifted family oriented and career committed women*. Unpublished doctoral dissertation. University of Michigan, 1971.

[2]From "A Biosocial Perspective on Parenting," by A. S. Rossi, *Daedalus*, Spring 1977, *106*(2), 1–31. Copyright 1977 by the American Academy of Arts and Sciences. Reprinted by permission.

*Booth, A. Sex and social participation. *American Sociological Review*, 1972, 37, 183–192.

Brecher, E. M. *Licit and illicit drugs*. Mount Vernon, N.Y.: Consumers Union, 1972.

Brim, O. G., Jr. Family structure and sex role learning by children: A further analysis of Helen Koch's data. *Sociometry*, 1958, 21, 1–16.

Broderick, C. B. Sexual behavior among preadolescents. *Journal of Social Issues*, 1966, 22, 6–21.

Brownmiller, S. *Against our will: Men, women and rape*. New York: Simon and Schuster, 1975.

Caballero, C. M., Giles, P., & Shaver, P. Sex-role traditionalism and fear of success. *Sex Roles*, 1975, 1, 319–326.

Clancy, K., & Gove, W. Sex differences in mental illness: An analysis of response bias in self-reports. *American Journal of Sociology*, 1974, 80, 205–216.

Cole, S., & Lejeune, R. Illness and the legitimation of failure. *American Sociological Review*, 1972, 37, 347–356.

Consumers Union. *The medicine show* (Rev. ed.). Mount Vernon, N.Y.: 1974.

*Cromwell, R. E., & Olson, D. H. (Eds.). *Power in families*. New York: Halsted, 1975.

Curlee, J. Alcoholic women: Some considerations for further research. *Bulletin of the Menninger Clinic*, 1967, 31, 154–163.

Curlee, J. Alcoholism and the "empty nest." *Bulletin of the Menninger Clinic*, 1969, 33, 165–171.

Darley, S. Big-time careers for the little woman: A dual-role dilemma. *Journal of Social Issues*, 1976, 32, 85–98.

DeBurger, J. E. Marital problems, help-seeking, and emotional orientation as revealed in help-request letters. *Journal of Marriage and the Family*, 1967, 29, 712–721.

Dixon, R. B. Measuring equality between the sexes. *Journal of Social Issues*, 1976, 32, 19–32.

Douvan, E. M., & Adelson, J. *The adolescent experience*. New York: Wiley, 1966.

Dowse, R. E., & Hughes, J. A. Girls, boys and politics. *British Journal of Sociology*, 1971, 22, 53–67.

Emlen, A. C., & Perry, J. B., Jr. Childcare arrangements. In L. W. Hoffman & F. I. Nye (Eds.), *Working mothers*. San Francisco: Jossey-Bass, 1974.

Emmerich, W. *Continuity and change in sex role development*. Paper presented at the meeting of the American Association for the Advancement of Science, Washington, D.C., December 1972.

Epstein, C. F. Law partners and marital partners: Strains and solutions in the dual career family enterprise. *Human Relations*, 1971, 24, 549–564.

*Ferree, M. M. Working class jobs: Housework and paid work as sources of satisfaction. *Social Problems*, 1976, 23, 431–441.

Forslund, M. A., & Hull, R. E. Sex role identification and achievement at preadolescence. *Rocky Mountain Social Science Journal*, 1972, 9, 105–110.

Geismar, L. L. *555 families: A socio-psychological study of young families in transition*. New Brunswick, N.J.: Transaction Books, 1973.

Giallombardo, R. *Society of women: A study of a women's prison*. New York: Wiley, 1966.

Glenn, N. D., Ross, A. A., & Tully, J. C. Patterns of intergenerational mobility of females through marriage. *American Sociological Review*, 1974, 39, 683–699.

Goldthorpe, J. H., Lockwood, D., Bechhofer, F., & Platt, J. The affluent worker and the thesis of *embourgeoisement:* Some preliminary research findings. In P. Blumberg (Ed.), *The impact of social class*. New York: Crowell, 1972.

Goode, W. J. *After divorce*. Glencoe, Ill.: Free Press, 1956.

Goode, W. J. Marital satisfaction and instability: A cross cultural analysis of divorce. *International Social Science Journal*, 1962, 14, 507–526.

Goodenough, E. W. Interest in persons as an aspect of sex difference in the early years. *Genetic Psychology Monographs*, 1957, *55*, 287–323.

Gove, W. R. Sex, marital status and mortality. *American Journal of Sociology*, 1973, *79*, 45–67.

Harmon, L. W. The childhood and adolescent career plans of college women. *Journal of Vocational Behavior*, 1971, *1*, 45–56.

Hartley, R. E. Children's concepts of male and female roles. *Merrill-Palmer Quarterly*, 1960, *6*, 83–91.

Hartley, R. E. Children's perceptions of sex preferences in four cultural groups. *Journal of Marriage and the Family*, 1969, *31*, 380–387.

Hartmann, H. Capitalism, patriarchy, and job segregation. *Signs: Journal of Women in Culture and Society*, 1976, *1*, 137–169.

Hawley, P. Perceptions of male models of femininity related to career choice. *Journal of Counseling Psychology*, 1972, *19*, 308–313.

*Hayghe, H. *Marital and family characteristics of the labor force* (March 1974). U.S. Department of Labor, Special Labor Force Report 173. Washington, D.C.: Bureau of Labor Statistics, 1975.

Health Communications, Inc. *An emerging issue: The female alcoholic*. Miami: 1977.

Hedblom, J. H. Dimensions of lesbian sexual experience. *Archives of Sexual Behavior*, 1973, *2*, 329–341.

Henslin, J. M. Criminal abortion: Making the decision and neutralizing the act. In J. M. Henslin (Ed.), *Studies in the sociology of sex*. New York: Appleton-Century-Crofts, 1971.

Hill, R., & Aldous, J. Socialization for marriage and parenthood. In D. A. Goslin (Ed.), *Handbook of socialization theory and research*. Chicago: Rand McNally, 1969.

Hoffman, L. W. Effects on children: Summary and discussion. In F. I. Nye & L. W. Hoffman (Eds.), *The employed mother in America*. Chicago: Rand McNally, 1963.

Hoffman, L. W. Effects on child. In L. W. Hoffman & F. I. Nye (Eds.), *Working mothers*. San Francisco: Jossey-Bass, 1974. (a)

Hoffman, L. W. Employment of women and fertility. In L. W. Hoffman & F. I. Nye (Eds.), *Working mothers*. San Francisco: Jossey-Bass, 1974. (b)

*Hoffman, L. W. Psychological factors. In L. W. Hoffman & F. I. Nye (Eds.), *Working mothers*. San Francisco: Jossey-Bass, 1974. (c)

*Holmstrom, L. L. *The two career family*. Cambridge, Mass.: Schenkman, 1972.

*Holmstrom, L. L., & Burgess, A. W. *Rape reconsidered: The victim's view*. Remarks prepared for round table discussion at the meeting of the American Sociological Association, San Francisco, August 1975.

Hooker, E. Epilogue. *Journal of Social Issues*, 1978, *34*(3), 131–135.

Horner, M. S. Women's will to fail. *Psychology Today*, June 1969, pp. 36–38.

Hunt, M. M. *The world of the formerly married*. New York: McGraw-Hill, 1966.

Hunter, J. E. Images of woman. *Journal of Social Issues*, 1976, *32*(3), 7–18.

Hyman, H. H., & Wright, C. R. Trends in voluntary association memberships of American adults: Replication based on secondary analysis of national sample surveys. *American Sociological Review*, 1971, *36*, 191–206.

Jensen, M. S. Role differentiation in female homosexual quasi-marital unions. *Journal of Marriage and the Family*, 1974, *36*, 360–367.

Johnson, M. M. Sex role learning in the nuclear family. *Child Development*, 1963, *34*, 319–333.

*Jones, M. C. Personality antecedents and correlates of drinking patterns in women. *Journal of Consulting and Clinical Psychology*, 1971, *36*, 61–69.

Kagan, J. Acquisition of sex role identity. In M. L. Hoffman & L. W. Hoffman (Eds.), *Review of child development research* (Vol. 1). New York: Russell Sage Foundation, 1964.

Kammeyer, K. Sibling position and the feminine role. *Journal of Marriage and the Family*, 1967, 29, 494–499.

Kanter, R. M. The impact of hierarchical structures on the work behavior of women and men. *Social Problems*, 1976, 23, 415–430.

Katz, N., Myers, M., Lisker, R., & Peterson, B. *The subject as object: A study of the returning woman student*. Paper presented at the meeting of the American Anthropological Association, Mexico City, November 1974.

Kelley, J., & Suelzle, M. *Family, career and political ideology: A preliminary account*. Unpublished manuscript, Columbia University, 1971.

Kentucky Department of Human Resources. *Standards for all facilities: Relates to KRS 199.892– 199.896 pursuant to KRS 13.082 and 194.050*. Frankfort, Ky.: n.d.

*Kohlberg, L. A cognitive-developmental analysis of children's sex-role concepts and attitudes. In E. E. Maccoby (Ed.), *The development of sex differences*. Stanford, Calif.: Stanford University Press, 1966.

Kohn, M. L., & Carroll, E. E. Social class and the allocation of parental responsibilities. *Sociometry*, 1960, 23, 372–392.

Komarovsky, M. Cultural contradictions and sex roles. *American Journal of Sociology*, 1946, 52, 182–189.

Komarovsky, M. Cultural contradictions and sex roles: The masculine case. *American Journal of Sociology*, 1973, 78, 873–884.

*Ladner, J. A. *Tomorrow's tomorrow: The Black woman*. Garden City, N.Y.: Anchor, 1972.

Lansky, L. M. The family structure also affects the model: Sex-role attitudes in parents of preschool children. *Merrill-Palmer Quarterly*, 1967, 13, 139–150.

*Lee, P., & Gropper, N. B. Sex-role culture and educational practice. *Harvard Educational Review*, 1974, 44, 369–410.

Lever, J. Sex differences in the games children play. *Social Problems*, 1976, 23, 479–488.

Levine, A., & Crumrine, J. Women and fear of success: A problem in replication. *American Journal of Sociology*, 1975, 80, 964–974.

Levine, R., Reis, H. T., Turner, E. S., & Turner, G. Fear of failure in males: A more salient factor than fear of success in females? *Sex Roles*, 1976, 2, 389–398.

Levitin, T. A., & Chananie, J. D. Responses of female primary school teachers to sex-typed behaviors in male and female children. *Child Development*, 1972, 43, 1309–1316.

Lofland, L. H. The "thereness" of women: A selective review of urban sociology. In M. Millman & R. M. Kanter (Eds.), *Another voice: Feminist perspectives on social life and social science*. Garden City, N.Y.: Anchor, 1975.

Looft, W. R. Sex differences in the expression of vocational aspirations by elementary school children. *Developmental Psychology*, 1971, 5, 366.

Lopata, H. Z. Living arrangements of American urban widows. *Sociological Focus*, 1971, 5, 41–61. (a)

*Lopata, H. Z. *Occupation: Housewife*. London: Oxford University Press, 1971. (b)

Louisville Courier-Journal, June 14, 1977, pp. A1; A10.

Louisville Times, July 30, 1977, p. A2.

*Lynn, D. B. *The father: His role in child development*. Monterey, Calif.: Brooks/Cole, 1974.

Lyon, P., & Martin, D. The realities of lesbianism. In E. S. Morrison & V. Borosage (Eds.), *Human sexuality: Contemporary perspectives*. Palo Alto, Calif.: National Press, 1973.

Maccoby, E. E., & Jacklin, C. N. Comments on the etiology of behavioral sex differences. *Science,* 1972, *178,* 887.

Maccoby, E. E., & Wilson, W. C. Identification and observational learning from films. *Journal of Abnormal and Social Psychology,* 1957, *55,* 76–87.

Maccoby, E. E., Wilson, W. C., & Burton, R. V. Differential movie-viewing behavior of male and female viewers. *Journal of Personality,* 1958, *26,* 259–267.

MacNamara, D. E. J. Sex offenses and sex offenders. *Annals of the American Academy of Political and Social Science,* 1968, *376,* 148–155.

Magarrell, J. Women account for 93 pct. enrollment gain. *Chronicle of Higher Education,* January 9, 1978, pp. 1; 11.

Mason, K. O., & Bumpass, L. L. U.S. women's sex role ideology, 1970. *American Journal of Sociology,* 1975, *80,* 1212–1219.

Matras, J. *Social inequality, stratification and mobility.* Englewood Cliffs, N.J.: Prentice-Hall, 1975.

McCaghy, C. A., & Skipper, J. R., Jr. Lesbian behavior as an adaptation to the occupation of stripping. *Social Problems,* 1969, *17,* 262–270.

Meyer, J. W., & Sobieszek, B. I. Effect of a child's sex on adult interpretations of its behavior. *Developmental Psychology,* 1972, *6,* 42–48.

Mileski, M., & Black, D. The social organization of homosexuality. *Urban Life and Culture,* 1972, *1,* 187–199.

*Millman, M., & Kanter, R. M. Editorial introduction to M. Millman & R. M. Kanter (Eds.), *Another voice: Feminist perspectives on social life and social science.* Garden City, N.Y.: Anchor, 1975.

Mindel, C. H., & Habenstein, R. W. (Eds.). *Ethnic families in America: Patterns and variations.* New York: Elsevier North-Holland, 1976.

Minnis, M. S. Cleavage in women's organizations: A reflection of the social structure of a city. *American Sociological Review,* 1953, *18,* 47–53.

Money, J., & Ehrhardt, A. A. *Man and woman, boy and girl: The differentiation and dimorphism of gender identity from conception to maturity.* Baltimore: Johns Hopkins University Press, 1972.

Morin, S. F. Psychology and the gay community: An overview. *Journal of Social Issues,* 1978, *34*(3), 7–27.

Mussen, P. H. Early sex-role development. In D. A. Goslin (Ed.), *Handbook of socialization theory and research.* Chicago: Rand McNally, 1969.

Mussen, P. H., & Rutherford, E. E. Parent-child relations and parental personality in relation to young children's sex role preferences. *Child Development,* 1963, *34,* 589–607.

Neal, A. G., & Groat, H. T. Alienation—Predictors of differential fertility: A longitudinal study. *American Journal of Sociology,* 1975, *80,* 1220–1226.

Nuzum, R. E. Inferred parental identification and perceived parental relationship as related to career- and homemaking-orientation in above-average ability college women. *Dissertation Abstracts International,* 1970, *31*(6-A), 2689–2690.

Nye, F. I. Husband-wife relationship. In L. W. Hoffman & F. I. Nye (Eds.), *Working mothers.* San Francisco: Jossey-Bass, 1974.

O'Hara, R. P. The roots of careers. *Elementary School Journal,* 1962, *62,* 277–280.

O'Leary, V. E., & Hammack, B. Sex-orientation and achievement context as determinants of the motive to avoid success. *Sex Roles,* 1975, *1,* 225–234.

O'Neill, S., Fein, D., Velit, K. M., & Frank, C. Sex differences in preadolescent self-disclosure. *Sex Roles*, 1976, 2, 85–88.

Pahl, J. M., & Pahl, R. E. *Managers and their wives: A study of career and family relations in the middle class.* Harmondsworth, Middlesex, England: Pelican, 1972.

Papalia, D. E., & Tennent, S. S. Vocational aspirations in preschoolers: A manifestation of early sex role stereotyping. *Sex Roles*, 1975, 1, 197–200.

Papanek, H. Men, women and work: Reflections on the two person career. *American Journal of Sociology*, 1973, 74, 852–872.

Pemberton, D. A. A comparison of the outcome of treatment in female and male alcoholics. *British Journal of Psychiatry*, 1967, 113, 367–373.

Peplau, L. A., Cochran, S., Rook, K., & Padesky, C. Loving women: Attachment and autonomy in lesbian relationships. *Journal of Social Issues*, 1978, 34(3), 7–27.

Perry, J. B., Jr. Mother substitutes. In F. I. Nye & L. W. Hoffman (Eds.), *The employed mother in America.* Chicago: Rand McNally, 1963.

Rainwater, L. *Family design: Marital sexuality, family size, and contraception.* Chicago: Aldine, 1965.

Rapoport, R., & Rapoport, R. N. *Dual career families.* Harmondsworth, Middlesex, England: Penguin, 1971. (a)

Rapoport, R., & Rapoport, R. N. Early and late experiences as determinants of adult behavior: Married women's family and career patterns. *British Journal of Sociology*, 1971, 22, 17–27. (b)

Ritter, K. V., & Hargens, L. L. Occupational positions and class identifications of married working women: A test of the asymmetry hypothesis. *American Journal of Sociology*, 1975, 80, 934–948.

Roby, P. Structural and internalized barriers to women in higher education. In J. Freeman (Ed.), *Women: A feminist perspective.* Palo Alto, Calif.: Mayfield, 1975.

Rollins, B. C., & Feldman, H. Marital satisfaction over the family life cycle. *Journal of Marriage and the Family*, 1970, 32, 20–28.

Rosenberg, B. G., & Sutton-Smith, B. *Sex and identity.* New York: Holt, Rinehart & Winston, 1972.

*Rosenberg, F. R., & Simmons, R. G. Sex differences in the self-concept in adolescence. *Sex Roles*, 1975, 1, 147–160.

Rosenfeld, C., & Perrella, V. C. Why women start and stop working: A study in mobility. *Monthly Labor Review*, 1965, 88, 1077–1082.

*Rosenfeld, R. A. Women's intergenerational occupational mobility. *American Sociological Review*, 1978, 43, 36–46.

*Ross, H. L., & Sawhill, I. V. *Time of transition: The growth of families headed by women.* Washington, D.C.: Urban Institute, 1975.

Rossi, A. S. A biosocial perspective on parenting. *Daedalus*, 1977, 106(2), 1–31.

Rothbart, M. K., & Maccoby, E. E. Parents' differential reactions to sons and daughters. *Journal of Personality and Social Psychology*, 1966, 4, 237–243.

*Rubin, L. B. *Worlds of pain: Life in the working-class family.* New York: Basic Books, 1976.

Ruble, D. N., & Higgins, E. T. Effects of group sex composition on self-presentation and sex-typing. *Journal of Social Issues*, 1976, 32, 125–132.

Russo, N. F. The motherhood mandate. *Journal of Social Issues*, 1976, 32, 143–154.

Saario, T. N., Jacklin, C. N., & Tittle, C. K. Sex role stereotyping in the public schools. *Harvard Educational Review*, 1973, 43, 386–416.

Scanzoni, L., & Scanzoni, J. *Men, women and change: A sociology of marriage and family.* New York: McGraw-Hill, 1976.

Schooler, C. Childhood family structure and adult characteristics. *Sociometry*, 1972, *35*, 255–269.

Schwab, J. J., Brown, J. M., Holzer, C. E., & Sokolof, M. Current concepts of depression: The sociocultural. *International Journal of Social Psychiatry*, 1968, *14*, 226–234.

Segal, M. W. *Drug use by females.* Unpublished paper prepared for use in public presentations. Washington, D.C., 1973.

Sewell, W., & Shah, V. P. Socioeconomic status, intelligence, and the attainment of higher education. *Sociology of Education*, 1967, *40*, 1–23.

Sewell, W., & Shah, V. P. Social class, parental encouragement and educational aspirations. *American Journal of Sociology*, 1968, *73*, 559–572.

Shelley, M. Notes of a radical lesbian. In R. Morgan (Ed.), *Sisterhood is powerful.* New York: Random House, 1970.

*Simon, R. J. *The contemporary woman and crime.* National Institute of Mental Health, DHEW Publication No. (ADM) 75-161. Washington, D.C.: U.S. Government Printing Office, 1975.

Simon, W., & Gagnon, J. H. The lesbians: A preliminary overview. In J. H. Gagnon & W. Simon (Eds.), *Sexual deviance.* New York: Harper & Row, 1967.

Simpson, R. *From the closet to the courts.* New York: Penguin, 1977.

Stein, A. H., & Bailey, M. M. The socialization of achievement orientation in females. *Psychological Bulletin*, 1973, *80*, 345–366.

Stein, P. J. *Single.* Englewood Cliffs, N.J.: Prentice-Hall, 1976.

Tavris, C., & Jayaratne, T. *How do you feel about being a woman: The results of a Redbook questionnaire.* New York: Redbook, 1972.

Thacker, P. Presentation by director of Rape Relief Center, Louisville, Kentucky, to Social Problems Classes, Indiana University Southeast, New Albany, Indiana, October 23, 1975.

Tietze, C., Jaffe, F. S., Weinstock, E., & Dryfoos, J. *Provisional estimates of abortion need and services in the year following the 1973 Supreme Court decision: United States, each state and metropolitan area.* New York: Alan Guttmacher Institute, 1975.

Time. Special Issue: *The American Woman.* March 20, 1972.

Tittle, C. R. Inmate organization: Sex differentiation and the influence of criminal subcultures. *American Sociological Review*, 1969, *34*, 492–505.

Tudor, J. F. Development of class awareness in children. *Social Forces*, 1971, *49*, 470–476.

Udry, J. R. The importance of being beautiful: A reexamination and racial comparison. *American Journal of Sociology*, 1977, *83*, 154–160.

U.S. Bureau of the Census. *Households and families by type* (March 1975). Current Population Reports, Series P-20, No. 282. Washington, D.C.: U.S. Government Printing Office, 1975.

Vener, A. M., & Weese, A. The preschool child's perceptions of adult sex-linked cultural objects. *Journal of Home Economics*, 1965, *57*, 49–54.

Vogel, S. R., Broverman, I. K., Broverman, D. M., Clarkson, F. E., & Rosenkrantz, P. S. Maternal employment and perception of sex roles among college students. *Journal of Developmental Psychology*, 1970, *3*, 384–391.

Vroegh, K. The relationship of birth order and sex of siblings to gender role identity. *Developmental Psychology*, 1971, *4*, 407–411.

Wachtel, D. D. Options of the single pregnant woman. *Review of Radical Political Economics*, 1972, *4*, 86–106.

Waldman, E. *Children of working mothers* (March 1974). U.S. Department of Labor, Special Labor Force Report 174. Washington, D.C.: Bureau of Labor Statistics, 1975.

Wanberg, K. W., & Horn, J. L. Alcoholism symptom patterns of men and women. *Quarterly Journal of Studies on Alcohol*, 1970, 31, 40–61.

Weitzman, L. J. Sex role socialization. In J. Freeman (Ed.), *Women: A feminist perspective*. Palo Alto, Calif.: Mayfield, 1975.

Weitzman, L. J., & Rizzo, D. *Biased textbooks*. Washington, D.C.: Resource Center on Sex Roles in Education, National Foundation for the Improvement of Education, 1974.

Westoff, C. H., & Ryder, N. B. Practice of contraception in the U.S.A. In S. J. Behrman, L. Corsa, Jr., & R. Freedman (Eds.), *Fertility and family planning*. Ann Arbor, Michigan: University of Michigan Press, 1969.

Williams, J. E., & Bennett, S. M. The definition of sex stereotypes via the Adjective Check List. *Sex Roles*, 1975, 1, 327–338.

Wolff, C. *Love between women*. New York: Harper Colophon, 1972.

Young, A. M. *Going back to school at 35*. U.S. Department of Labor, Special Labor Force Report 159. Washington, D.C.: Bureau of Labor Statistics, 1973.

Ziegler, H. Male and female: Differing perceptions of the teaching experience. In A. Theodore (Ed.), *The professional woman*. Cambridge, Mass.: Schenkman, 1971.

Zolotow, C. *William's doll*. New York: Harper & Row, 1972.

SECTION
FOUR

THE
ECONOMICS
OF
WOMAN'S
PLACE

Fay Ross Greckel

Until quite recently, televised news reports about the economy were likely to feature a Congressman discussing taxes, or a businessman explaining corporate problems or policies, or male auto workers "manning" an assembly line, or an unemployed family man dealing with the challenges of an indefinite layoff. When women appeared in the economic news, it was nearly always as shoppers—a homemaker, for example, struggling to provide adequate meals for her family in the face of escalating supermarket prices—or occasionally as welfare recipients.

It is gradually being recognized that women play a major role as producers and wage earners, as well as shoppers and dependents. Women account for about 40% of the U.S. work force. The majority of these women still work in teaching, retail sales, nursing, clerical occupations, and other traditionally "female" jobs. However, women are increasingly entering such "male" job areas as engineering, law, accounting, bus driving, police work, and carpentry.

Nearly half of all American working women are either self-supporting or the head of a household, and thus highly dependent on their paychecks. In addition, the earnings of many married women help raise their families' income above the poverty line or make it possible to send a daughter to college or to attain other important family goals. And though no paychecks are received, the daily work of full-time homemakers also affects the standard of living of their families.

The activities and situations just cited are all concerns of economics, which examines how a society provides for its material needs. This includes the study of the decisions a society makes in producing its goods and services, and the study of the distribution of income, which determines who consumes those goods and services.

The next three chapters focus on women as producers and as wage earners. Chapter 10 looks at the economic output of women within the home. Chapter 11 discusses women in the labor force, covering such matters as trends in female employment, the tendency of women (and men) to concentrate in certain types of jobs, and the impact of unemployment on women. Chapter 12 examines the gap between men's and women's earnings and the importance of women's earnings to their families' economic standing.

Among the questions dealt with in these chapters are the following: In what ways do women participate in the United States' economy? To what extent do homemakers contribute to the economic well-being of their families and the nation? What trends can be seen in women's employment, and what factors explain these trends? Why have there traditionally been "men's jobs" and "women's jobs," and what causes these distinctions? Does unemployment differ between women and men? How much lower are women's wages than men's—and why?

Analysis of women's economic roles has never attracted extensive interest among economists, most of whom are men. A few interesting studies were written by female economists in the early years of this century (for example, Abbott, 1910), but very little research was done in this area from about 1930 until about 1960. An increasing number of studies have been published since then, especially in the last five or ten years. However,

Section opening photo: The design for the new Susan B. Anthony coin, which was issued in July of 1979. (Photo by Wide World Photos.)

the coverage is still very uneven. For example, there are a number of good studies of female participation in the work force, but relatively little has been published on the economics of homemaking, on women in clerical or blue-collar jobs, or on women in the labor union movement.

The information presented in these chapters is based on economists' published research about female workers and the economic status of women. Some historical trends will be discussed and a few early studies cited, but most of the information concerns the economic position of women during the past 20 years or so. However, as we turn now to a consideration of the economic contribution of the homemaker, we will attempt briefly to place the current economic role of the homemaker in historical perspective.

CHAPTER
10

KEEPING THE HOME FIRES BURNING

In any one year approximately half of the adult female population in the United States are full-time homemakers. It seems appropriate, therefore, to open this section with a look at the economics of the homemaker. We begin with a brief historical sketch and follow with an analysis of household production, estimates of the dollar value of the work of unpaid homemakers, and a discussion of the homemaker's economic position.

"Women's Work" in Perspective

Throughout most of human history, economic activity involved hunting and fishing, farming, the fashioning of tools, the provision of clothing and shelter, and local or regional trade. Although societies usually distinguished between men's work and women's work, it was generally expected that adults of both sexes would work and that in this way they would all contribute to their family's economic well-being. The economic importance of both sexes was particularly noticeable in low-income agricultural societies. There the work of each family member made a difference to the survival of all, and economic activity was directed at meeting the family's basic needs. This was evident not only in primitive societies, but also in the early North American colonies and among the pioneer families of the 18th and 19th centuries.

Most societies did—and still do—apportion tasks along sex lines, but what was considered men's work in one society would frequently be women's work in another. And men's work has not always been the hardest or the most productive. In many parts of Africa, for example, it was long customary for women to do most or all of the farming (Boserup, 1970). Even when goods are produced for the market, it is not always the man who brings home the money. Among the Navajos, weaving rugs for sale has been an exclusively female prerogative, and in much of Africa and Southeast Asia "market women" dominate the local wholesale and retail trade.

Three broad historical developments—urbanization (the growth of cities), industrialization (the factory system that began around 1800), and affluence (higher average incomes)—have played a major role in reducing the apparent economic importance of women's work. Both urbanization and industrialization meant that the typical family could no longer produce its own necessities. Working for pay became the primary source of income, and this usually required working away from the home. Since large families kept all but the poorest married urban women of childbearing age close to home, the paid labor force came to consist very largely of men and young single women.

In their homes women continued to provide goods and services to meet their families' consumption needs, but the urban family's dependence on the market for many necessities and most luxuries gave much higher status to the husband's paycheck. And since nearly all women were either married or anticipating eventual marriage, paid employment came to be considered primarily men's work and unpaid household production women's work.

Industrial technology and the resulting expansion of marketed goods and services also affected work in the home. The market economy gradually offered a wide range of goods and services—from candles, baked goods, and frozen dinners to dry cleaning and child care—that formerly had to be provided within the home. Other manufactured products, such as vacuum cleaners, electric mixers, and permanent-press fabrics, reduced the homemaker's physical labor. At the same time, these machines and aids created a general impression that most of women's household tasks were neither demanding nor essential. This thinking reinforced the declining significance of the homemaker's economic contribution.

In one way the growing affluence of the average family also reduced women's relative economic position. As Thorstein Veblen noted in 1899 in his *Theory of the Leisure Class*, one of the ways wealthy men emphasized their wealth was through their wives' idleness. A rich family could afford to hire others to do the wife's work. The wife could then give further evidence of the family's affluence by spending money and being very obviously idle.

Of course, the less wealthy would gain status by copying, so far as possible, the life-style of the very wealthy. Thus, the less a woman was required to contribute to her family's economic needs, the higher the family was likely to rise in social status. For many decades, this tended both to stop "respectable" women from seeking paying jobs and to further downgrade women's work in the home—whether paid or unpaid.

These developments help explain the mixed position of the modern homemaker: honored after a fashion, yet given little economic significance; wooed as a consumer, but not taken seriously as a producer. Advertisers bid eagerly for the homemaker's dollars; but if she is accidentally killed, the courts award her widower little money.

What is the real economic contribution of the homemaker today? The next two sections attempt to answer that question.

The Economics of Household Production

When economists analyze household behavior, they most frequently focus on consumption—the buying of goods and services from the business sector. The household is also studied extensively as the owner and supplier of productive resources, such as labor and land. The resulting family incomes also receive much attention. The economist is thus concerned with interactions between the household (supplier of inputs and purchaser of outputs) and the market economy (transformer of inputs into outputs, for profit). In these interactions money changes hands, in exchange for goods or for resources.

In addition to supplying inputs to the market economy and buying outputs from it, however, households provide goods and services directly for their own benefit. Most of this work, such as cooking, gardening, and child care, is done by women. Economists have paid very little attention to this production, probably because it was separate from the market economy, which has always been their center of interest, and because it does not involve monetary exchanges.

In the early part of this century there were a few economic studies of home production, the best probably being Margaret Reid's comprehensive *Economics of Household Production* (1934). Then, for about 30 years, economists virtually ignored the subject. During the past decade, professional interest in household production has revived somewhat (for example, Zaretsky, 1977; Kreps & Leaper, 1976; Leibowitz, 1974, 1975; Becker, 1965). However, most of this research is just getting underway, and little of it has yet been published. The following analysis of the economic role of women in the home is based on the rather limited but interesting studies currently available in this area.

While household production is far from being an all-female activity, there is no doubt that women do most of the work. Homemaking is the full-time occupation of nearly 50% of U.S. women, and the majority of these career homemakers are married. In the following pages, therefore, the typical homemaker is assumed to be a married female who may or may not be employed outside the home. However, the analysis could also apply to unmarried women or to male homemakers.

The Household as a Producing Unit

To put the homemaker's job in perspective, it is useful to contrast today's household with that of a farming family in earlier years. The farm family used its available resources—land, labor, and tools—to produce directly the goods and services that it needed. The utilization of its resources determined the family's real income, or level of living. The goods and services produced included food, shelter, clothing, child care, and entertainment.

Today's households use their available resources to obtain similar goods and services, but more of the activity now occurs away from the home. One or more members of the household work for dollars, which in turn are traded for goods and services desired by that household. But there is still much productive activity that occurs in the home and does not involve dollar transactions. These activities include child care, maintenance of purchased goods (housecleaning, laundry, home repairs), and final processing of semifinished goods (meal preparation, sewing). Both the worker at home and the paid worker, then, are engaged in productive activities that determine the household's level of consumption and real income. The output of the homemaker, like that of the earlier farm family, is directly consumable. The wage earner receives money, and the money must then be traded for consumable goods and services.

Awareness that the homemaker is a producer leads to other questions. How efficient is the typical homemaker? What factors influence the amount of work she does? How important is the homemaker's economic contribution? There has not yet been sufficient research to give a satisfactory answer to the first question, but existing studies do shed some light on the others. We will look first at the economic factors that influence the amount of work the homemaker does.

Studies of Homemakers' Work Time

A number of studies, often done by home economists, have related the time spent on household tasks to different economic variables. One method used to gather these data is interviews with a selected sample of homemakers. Another method requires the homemakers themselves to keep diaries—for example, noting the use of each 15-minute time segment over a 2-day period. There are obvious questions about the complete accuracy of data based on such a self-evaluation of the use of one's time. Also, the studies vary in sample size, type of households included (rural or urban, working wives or not), time period covered, variables considered, and factors held constant. This makes it somewhat difficult to compare the findings of different studies or to draw broad conclusions from them.

The findings summarized below should be viewed as simply a sample of the kinds of information available. The findings are grouped on the basis of the variables to which the homemakers' work time is related.

The Use of Equipment (Home Appliances).   Home appliances can raise efficiency by reducing the time and effort needed for a given task. Interestingly, research indicates that they do not always reduce the homemaker's total work time. One study (Gage, 1960) showed that full-time homemakers with no children under 6 and with a rather large number of modern appliances spent an average of 18 minutes less per day on meal preparation and 12 minutes *more* per day on laundry work than did similar homemakers who had fewer modern appliances. The study indicated that owning certain appliances, such as a washer and dryer, reduced the household help of other family members rather than the work time of the homemaker. Frequently, the ownership of these appliances also raised the expected standards for household services. For example, clothes are washed more often nowadays. These findings are consistent with Joann Vanek's survey (1973) of numerous time-use studies, which showed that the time homemakers spent on laundry work actually increased between 1926 and 1968. In fact, Vanek found that the total time devoted to household work increased during that period.

Education and Household Work.   Vanek's study (1973) revealed that the average time spent on housekeeping has declined over the past 50 years, but this reduction has been more than offset by the additional hours women now devote to child care. Some of the decline in housekeeping time is due to the increased use of appliances and convenience foods. It appears that the rising level of education has also played a part in reducing

Figure 10-1. Many women today hold a full-time paying job in addition to the full-time nonpaying job of homemaking. (Photos by Creative Associates.)

housework. Using data from the Cornell study discussed below, Arleen Leibowitz (1974, 1975) found, for example, that the more educated the woman, the less time she spends on laundry work.

By contrast, Leibowitz found that the more educated the woman, the more time she spends on child care. More educated mothers are also likely to have fewer children and to space their children closer together. Leibowitz suggested that fewer and more closely spaced children may be related to the educated woman's greater interest in paid employment. A better education usually makes possible a better job. Therefore the cost (the income given up) of staying home with the children is greater for the educated mother. Looking at national data, Mullineaux (1976) and Gronau (1973) also linked declining birth rates in part to better education and higher earnings for women. (Chapter 8 raises some questions about whether these changes in childbearing were the result of conscious decisions.)

Employment Status of the Wife.   As expected, employed wives spend less time on household work than full-time homemakers. In interviews with 2200 families in the mid-1960s, a study by the University of Michigan's Survey Research Center (SRC) revealed that employed wives averaged 26 hours per week on household work, while nonemployed wives averaged 56 hours (Vanek, 1973). A Cornell University study (Walker & Gauger, 1973) found the drop in household work time was less dramatic if family size was taken into consideration. According to the Cornell study, working wives (employed at least 15 hours per week) averaged 28 to 56 hours per week in household tasks, depending on family size and children's ages. Full-time homemakers with similar families averaged 35 to 77 hours per week.

Both studies showed that most husbands spent only a few hours per week on household tasks. Those hours did not ordinarily increase when wives were employed. This raises familiar concerns about the unequal sharing of family workloads and about practical barriers to wives' holding demanding jobs outside the home. (Chapter 8 presents some additional information on husbands assisting in the home.)

It is worth noting that the SRC data showed a difference between the household work effort of single women and single men very similar to that between employed wives and employed husbands. Single men reported an average of 8 hours per week on household work; single women averaged 20 hours per week (Sirageldin, 1969, p. 79).

Family Income.   A few studies examined the relation between household work and income (see Sirageldin, 1969; Shamseddine, 1968). Both full-time homemakers and families in general spend less time on household work as family income rises (even when the number of children is held constant). With higher incomes, families can buy more home equipment and convenience products, eat more meals out, and pay others to do more of the household tasks.

How Much Is a Homemaker Worth?

A few pages ago we asked this question: how important is the homemaker's economic contribution? Individual families sometimes confront this question, as when a widower finds it necessary to hire someone to care for his house and his children. Or a full-time homemaker may be killed or disabled in an accident, and the husband may sue for compensation. Usually the amount awarded in such a suit will be rather small, because the wife would have contributed very few dollars to the family's income.[1] Homemakers are not paid wages; therefore their economic contribution is not fully appreciated.

From time to time economists have made estimates of the economic value of the homemaker. These studies were not a response to family problems, such as those just mentioned. Instead, the economists were usually trying to improve the measurement of the nation's total annual output, or Gross National Product (GNP). GNP generally includes all goods and services produced for sale, from oranges and doctors' services to automobiles and new factories. It is equal to the total dollar value of the year's output and is one of the most frequently quoted indicators of a nation's economic health.

---

[1] "Statistics on U.S. court cases in recent years indicate that the highest probable award to compensate for the accidental death of a full-time housewife would be about $35,000 for the services lost to the family—including loss of consortium" (*Changing Times*, April 1973, p. 13). Consortium refers to companionship, including sex. Apparently only the husband has a legal claim to that; in most states, a wife cannot sue for loss of consortium.

The Homemaker and the GNP

Since no money is paid for their work, homemakers' production is not included in the GNP. This gives rise to a paradox noted in most economics texts. It was probably first pointed out by the eminent economist A. C. Pigou (1946):

> If a number of bachelors who were employing housekeepers in the customary manner of exchanging services for money, decided to marry these housekeepers, then the national [product] would be diminished! Obviously the housekeeper, when assuming the role of a wife, regardless of any additional services she assumed by virtue of her marriage, continued to perform those services which she, as a housekeeper, had been performing previously. In other words, the services continued but the value disappeared!

There are always problems involved in placing an accurate dollar value on items that are not bought and sold. The economic contribution of the homemaker is no exception. Should all unpaid household work be included in the computation—or only the work of full-time homemakers? What type of data would be most useful in estimating the value of household work? Are such data obtainable? These and related problems led to an early decision not to include the value of household production in the GNP.

In recent years some economists have questioned that decision (see, for example, Shamseddine, 1968). Over the years several estimates of the dollar value of household production have been made. Not all questions have been resolved, but these studies do give us some idea of the homemaker's economic contribution.

Estimates of Homemakers' Economic Contribution

Most of these estimates begin with the number of homemakers in the nation and the number of hours typically spent on various homemaking tasks each year. Economists next find what hourly wages were earned by workers doing fairly similar jobs for pay. The homemakers' total work hours are then multiplied by these wages.

The economists' actual calculations varied in their complexity (how finely the homemakers' tasks were broken down). Still, they generally agreed that the value of the homemakers' output ranged from about 25% to 30% of Gross National Product—a substantial contribution (Kuznets, 1941; Reid, 1947; Shamseddine, 1968; Gauger, 1973; for estimates based on other methods, see Clark, 1958; Sirageldin, 1969; Kreps, 1971). The 1976 GNP for the United States totaled about $1700 billion. Therefore we can estimate that in 1976 U.S. homemakers produced about $470 billion worth of goods and services.

A study by Kathryn Walker and William Gauger (1973) gives us an idea of what this production means to an individual family. If the wife was employed at least 15 hours per week, the estimated value of her annual household work ranged from $2600 in a young family without children to $5900 in a family with three young children. For full-time homemakers, the range was from $3900 for the young couple to $8100 in families with five to six children, including an infant. (The value of the husband's contribution ranged from $700 to $1700.)

Recently, the U.S. Social Security Administration (U.S. Department of Health, Education, and Welfare, 1975) calculated the typical homemaker's economic value at different stages of her life. Interestingly, this study estimated that in 1972 a full-time homemaker aged 20 to 24 (with young children) was "worth" $6061—exceeding the $5884 earned by the average employed woman of the same age.

These estimates may all be too low. The studies do not credit the homemaker with earnings for work that requires more than simple skills—for example, as a nutritionist, bookkeeper, interior decorator, or child psychologist. Instead, the wages are usually for such jobs as cook and "child-care worker." We do not yet have a complete estimate of the homemaker's economic worth.

Summary and Observations

We have seen that women's production of goods and services within the home parallels the production of goods and services in the market economy. Indeed, virtually all of the goods and services produced in the home can be purchased in the market.

We have also noted some effects of appliance ownership, better education for women, and income levels on the homemaker's workday. Generally, these factors have changed the nature of household production more than they have reduced the homemaker's work time. While housekeeping time has declined somewhat, time spent on child care has increased—despite a trend toward smaller families.

The major difference between home production and market production is the lack of pay for the former. In a capitalist society, where status is linked so closely to earnings, this tends to lower the homemaker's standing in society. For example, the full-time homemaker's status is far more dependent on her husband's income and occupation than on her own accomplishments.

The lack of pay for home production also makes it more difficult for both families and society as a whole to evaluate accurately the real economic contribution of the homemaker. As a result, homemakers may seriously undervalue their home work and make less rational decisions about their use of time and about seeking paid employment. Courts frequently underpay for the loss of a homemaker's services. And GNP-watchers are likely to overestimate the gain in economic well-being that results when increasing numbers of homemakers enter the labor force.

The United States government has given a clear, if startling, picture of the homemaker's present economic stature. The Department of Labor ranks jobs on the basis of skills needed, pay, and complexity of the work done. "Homemaker" is in the lowest ranking, along with such jobs as parking-lot attendant and mud-mixer helper—and below the ranking for dog trainer (Howe, 1977).

Efforts to measure the homemaker's economic contribution should make more accurate evaluations possible. Although these calculations are still in a developing stage, they are nevertheless helpful. Most studies indicate that homemakers' services are equal in value to about one-fourth of our total Gross National Product. Walker and Gauger (1973) also estimated that full-time homemakers in 1971 individually contributed from $4000 to $8000 (depending on family size) to their families' real income.

Full-time homemakers constitute the largest single occupational group in the nation. For that reason alone they deserve (and are beginning to attract) more serious study.

WORKING IN THE "REAL WORLD"

CHAPTER 11

In the previous chapter, we examined the unpaid work of the homemaker. This chapter is devoted to women who are paid workers. In 1978, 42 million women in the United States were working for wages or seeking such work—a total of 42% of the labor force.

In contrast to the limited data on economic aspects of household work, considerable material is available on women in paid employment. Both the federal government and academic economists have collected and analyzed large amounts of data on female workers. Although quite a few studies date from the first half of this century, the bulk of the analyses have been done during the last 20 years. In 1972, for the first time, the program of the annual meeting of the American Economic Association included a session on women in the economy. The January 1973 *Economic Report of the President* (U.S. President, Council of Economic Advisors, 1973), also for the first time, included a chapter on "The Economic Role of Women." (It may have been more than coincidence that the President's Council of Economic Advisors, whose annual report constitutes all but a few pages of the *Economic Report of the President,* for the first time included a female economist, Marina V. N. Whitman.)

Most of the published research on women in the labor force deals with a few areas. There are, for example, numerous explanations for the increasing percentage of women, particularly married women, working for pay; studies of the interrelationships between the number of female job seekers and unemployment rates; analyses of occupational sex-segregation—the tendency for many jobs to become typed as a "man's job" or a "woman's job"; and studies of the gap between men's and women's earnings.

Which women are most likely to be in the labor force? What jobs do they hold? What changes have occurred in women's labor force participation, and what accounts for these changes? How do women's experiences in employment and unemployment compare with men's? These are some of the questions to which this chapter is addressed.

We begin by examining some statistics on working women, to get some idea of which women work. This is followed by a discussion of historical trends, explanations of women's increased labor force participation, some comparisons of male and female employment and unemployment experience, discussion of occupational sex-typing, and studies of a few specific occupations.

A Statistical Portrait of Women in the Labor Force

In 1978, 59% of all U.S. women between the ages of 18 and 64 were in the labor force—that is, they were either gainfully employed, part time or full time, or seeking employment. (The U.S. labor force is usually defined to include all persons 16 years and older who are employed or seeking jobs; however, the 18-to-64 age span gives a clearer picture of the interest that working-age women have in employment.)

A related term we will be using a great deal is the *labor force participation rate*. This rate tells what percentage of a stated group of adults is in the labor force. Thus we can say that in 1978 the labor force participation rate for U.S. women between 18 and 64 years of age was 59%.

Which Women Are Most Likely to Be Working?

Such factors as marriage, children, race, education, and income help determine whether or not a woman joins the labor force. The relation between these factors and female labor force participation is outlined below and summarized in Figure 11-1. Readers may find it interesting to compare the way these factors affect women's political participation, as discussed in Chapters 13 and 15, and to note the sociologist's treatment of these factors in Chapter 8. (The data below are from U.S. Department of Labor, Women's Bureau, 1976b, unless otherwise indicated.)

Marital Status. Women who are single, divorced, or separated are understandably most likely to be working. Almost 63% of all such women 16 years of age and older were working in 1978. Of women who were married, with husbands present, 48%—nearly one out of every two wives—were in the labor force. Only 22% of widows were working women. That small percentage is explained by the fact that most widows are over age 60 (U.S. Department of Labor, Women's Bureau, 1979).

Children in the Home. Predictably, women with preschool children are least likely to be at work. Even so, 5.8 million mothers with children under 6 years old were employed in 1978, and another 10.3 million female workers had children between 6 and 18 years of age. Primarily because of their greater economic problems, a larger proportion of non-White mothers worked. In 1974, 52% of non-White mothers with children under 6, but only 34% of the corresponding White mothers, were in the labor force. That same year, 61% of non-White mothers with school-age children, compared with 52% of the

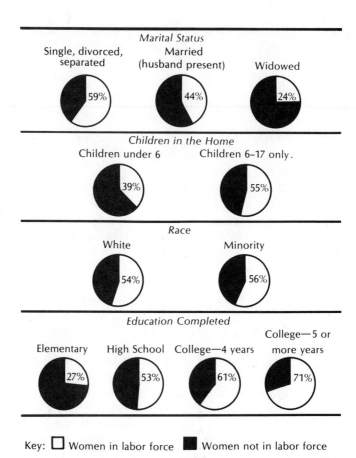

Key: ☐ Women in labor force ■ Women not in labor force

Figure 11-1. Women in the labor force. Data on race refer to women between the ages of 18 and 64. All other data refer to women 16 years and over. Data are for 1975. (Data from U.S. Department of Labor, Women's Bureau, Women Workers Today. *Washington, D.C., 1976.)*

corresponding White mothers, were in the labor force (U.S. Department of Labor, Women's Bureau, 1974, 1976b, 1979).

Education. The greater her educational attainment, the more likely it is that a woman will be working outside the home. Only 27% of women with no more than an elementary school education are in the labor force—compared with 53% of those completing high school, 61% of those completing four years of college, and 71% of those with five or more years of college.

Husband's Income. Studies in earlier decades showed that the higher the husband's income, the less likely it was that the wife would be working. This is only partially true today. In 1969, for example, married women's labor force participation increased as their husbands' income rose, up to an income range of $5000 to $6999; above that level, as income increased, wives' labor force participation declined (Kreps, 1971). A similar pattern has been found in succeeding years. In 1975, peak labor force participation for wives occurred when their husbands earned between $7000 and $10,000.

Composition of the Female Labor Force

So far, we have discussed which groups of women are more likely to be in the labor force. This does not provide an accurate picture of the actual makeup of the female labor force, however, because some of the groups are much larger than others. Married women, for example, far outnumber single, divorced, and separated women in the total adult population.

If a member of the female labor force were selected at random, she would most likely be married, have no children under 18, have a high school education, and be working full time (see Figure 11-2). In 1978, married women with husband present

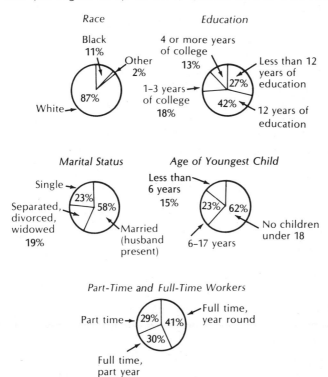

Figure 11-2. Composition of the female labor force in 1975. (Data from U.S. Department of Labor, Women's Bureau, Women Workers Today. Washington, D.C., 1976.)

accounted for 56% of the female labor force, and 61% of female workers either had no children or had children over 18 only. More than 40% of female workers held full-time jobs the year round. About half of the remainder had full-time jobs for part of the year, and the rest had part-time jobs. One out of ten working women was the head of a family (U.S. Department of Labor, Women's Bureau, 1979).

Trends in Female Labor Force Participation

Increasing Percentage of Women Working

The past 35 years have seen a dramatic rise in female labor force participation. Prior to World War II, one out of every four adult women held a job. By 1975, approximately one out of every two adult women was in the labor force.

Table 11-1 shows the percentage of women in the labor force from 1900 to 1975, based on national census data. It is apparent from the table that female labor force participation increased very slowly from 1900 to 1940 (with an unusual peak in 1910) and then rose rapidly thereafter. Looking at the pre-1940 period, some analysts pointed out that instructions to census workers were different in 1910. This could have resulted in an "overcount" of female workers. However, others argued that 1910 was the only census prior to 1940 that made a special effort not to overlook female workers, particularly unpaid female farm laborers. In that case, the 1910 figure would be more accurate than those for 1900, 1920, and 1930. Therefore, the percentage of women in the labor force may have remained at about 25% from 1900 to 1940 (Smuts, 1960; Oppenheimer, 1970, pp. 2–5).

In any event, all sources agree that there has been a large, continuing movement of women into paid employment since World War II. The number of women in the labor force increased by 35% between 1950 and 1960, and by 37% during the following ten years. In the 1970s, women are entering the labor force at a rate that will yield a 39% increase by 1980. (During the same three decades, the male labor force grew by 7%, 9%, and—for the 1970s—by 17%.) Economists have tried to explain why the female labor force grew so rapidly. Before considering such explanations, however, let us look at the underlying patterns of change.

Changing Composition of the Female Labor Force

From 1900 to 1940, the female labor force consisted primarily of single, widowed, or divorced women of all ages and young wives who had not yet borne a child. In 1940, for example, 70% of all female workers were single, widowed, divorced, or married with husbands absent; 59% were under 35 years of age. By far the highest participation rate was for the 20-to-29 age bracket. From age 30 on, there was a continuous and often sharp decline in the percentage of women working (Oppenheimer, 1970).

By 1975, three out of every five working women were married and living with their husbands, and two out of five had children under 18. This trend has been accompanied

Table 11-1. Percentage of Adult Women in the Labor Force, 1900–1978

Year	Percent[a]
1900	20.4
1910	25.2
1920	23.3
1930	24.3
1940	25.4
1950	33.9
1960	37.8
1970	43.4
1975	46.3
1976	47.3
1977	48.4
1978	50.0[b]

[a] Percentages refer to women 14 years and older for 1900–1940, and 16 years and older for 1950–1978.
[b] For women 18 to 64 years of age, this percentage was 58.7.
Data from Oppenheimer, 1970, p. 3; U.S. President, Council of Economic Advisers, 1973, p. 91; U.S. Department of Labor, Women's Bureau, 1976b, p. 2; U.S. Department of Labor, Women's Bureau, 1979.

by an increase in the average age of female workers, with half now being at least 35 years of age (U.S. Department of Labor, Women's Bureau, 1976b).

These developments have changed the composition of the female labor force drastically, from one of mostly young and/or unmarried women to one spanning fairly evenly all age groups and marital situations. Figure 11-3 traces these changes, in terms of age groups, from 1940 to 1975. The change in the life-cycle pattern is striking. The tendency to leave the labor force during the prime childbearing years has weakened, and the tendency to reenter and remain in the labor force after age 35 has become much stronger.

Explanations of Labor Force Trends

It is fairly easy to explain the pattern of female labor force participation during any one year. For example, there are obvious reasons why a large percentage of single women hold jobs—and why a much smaller percentage of women with preschool children do so. It is much harder to explain the steady increase in female labor force participation since 1940. Many economists have studied this development, attempting to pin down the causes.

For a study of this sort, an economist might look first at the factors that make women more likely to enter the labor force today. For example, highly educated women today are very likely to be employed. The economist would then look for data showing how these influencing factors have changed over the last two or three decades. Using statistical

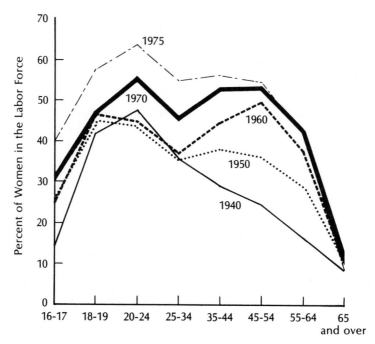

Figure 11-3. Labor force participation rates of women by age, 1940–1975. (Adapted from Sex in the Marketplace: American Women at Work, *by J. M. Kreps. Copyright © 1971 by Johns Hopkins University Press. Based on data from "Women Workers Today,"* Monthly Labor Review, *June 1970, U.S. Department of Labor, Bureau of Labor Statistics. Reprinted by permission.)*

techniques, the researcher would then see how closely the changes in the factors under study, such as female education, matched the changes in female labor force participation. If the match, or correlation, is quite close, then we can conclude that those factors very probably did help to encourage increasing numbers of women to seek jobs.

Using this approach, economists usually work with variables (influencing factors) for which numerical data are available. They also depend on data that relate to very large numbers of women. For both reasons, they generally rely on census data and other government data sources, rather than on the detailed interviews of relatively small numbers of women favored by sociologists and other social scientists. A sociologist might ask women directly why they work or what their career goals are. An economist is likely to feel that individual women may not be fully aware of all the variables influencing them to be in or out of the labor force. And individual women cannot really say why so many more of them hold jobs today than in 1940. So the economist looks for a different type of information.

Keep in mind, then, that the discussions in this chapter and in Chapter 8 of why women work relate to somewhat different questions. The sociologists in Chapter 8 are trying to find out why some women work and others do not, or which factors women themselves feel are important in their decision to enter or leave the labor force. In the present chapter we are primarily interested in why so many more women hold jobs today than in 1940 or 1950. The answers to these questions are related, but they are by no means identical.

The factors discussed below are divided into two groups. The first group includes variables that may have affected the *supply* of women workers. Supply refers to the availability of women for work, or to their willingness to enter the labor force. The second group includes variables that may have affected the *demand* for women workers. Demand refers to the opportunities facing women, or to the availability of jobs for them. In other words, supply variables influence the number of women who want paying jobs; demand variables influence the number of job openings for women. Keep in mind, as we consider the supply and demand factors, that we are looking for explanations of why the percentage of women holding paying jobs has been going up (and why the percentage of women who are full-time homemakers has been going down).

Supply Factors

Demographic Changes. Demographic changes (changes in the size or makeup of the population) *could* lead to an increase in the female labor supply. Let's consider one way in which this might occur. As noted earlier, the great majority of the 1940 female labor force consisted of young and/or unmarried women. Marriage and motherhood caused women to leave the labor force. Therefore, *if* the percentage of women who were married had fallen during the following two decades, that would have helped to explain why so many more women were in the labor force.

Quite the opposite actually occurred. By 1960 there was a marked increase in the percentage of women who were married and had children under 5 years old. Despite this, the percentage of women who were in the labor force rose. Obviously, we have to look at some other variables to explain why this occurred.

Husband's Income. For many years both theory and fact supported the idea that as the husband's income increased, the wife would be less likely to work. According to the theory, this "income effect" should occur for two reasons. First, the family has less need for additional income in order to achieve a given standard of living. Second, at higher income levels there is likely to be a desire for increased leisure in which to enjoy the use of that income. Until fairly recently, census data and economists' studies supported this hypothesis (Long, 1958). In any one year, families in which the husband's income was low were more likely to include working wives than families in which the husband's income was high.

However, wives' labor force behavior over the years was not consistent with the single-year findings. Husbands' real incomes (incomes adjusted to hold the purchasing power of a dollar constant) have increased greatly since World War II, yet wives' labor force participation has also risen sharply. In fact, "the most substantial post-war increases in labor force participation of married women have been among those whose husbands' income is above the average" (Perrella, 1968, p. 5).

How can this apparently contradictory evidence be reconciled? One possibility is that the husband's rising income does not affect the behavior of a family if the family's relative income position remains about the same. In other words, if everyone else's income rises too, this family may still feel relatively deprived. The wife will therefore choose to work, in spite of her husband's higher income.

There is also evidence that other variables are dulling the impact of husbands' rising incomes and are having a major influence on wives' job decisions. Women's wages and women's education are two such variables.

Wife's Wages.   During the decades after 1940, wages for women, as well as for men, increased. That meant that the wife's decision to work only at home resulted in an increasingly large sacrifice of income. As real wages rose, more and more married women responded to this strong incentive to take paying jobs (Mincer, 1962; Cain, 1966; Fair, 1971).

Higher wages were much more effective in bringing women into the labor force (or increasing their time on the job) than was true for men. This is not surprising, since most women face not simply a choice between work and leisure, but a more complex division of time among paid employment, unpaid household work, and leisure.

However, most studies have focused on married women (with husbands present). It is likely that the response of unmarried women to rising wages will more closely resemble that of men. Like most men, most single women have relatively little choice about whether to seek paid employment.

Education.   We saw earlier that there is a strong positive relationship between women's level of education and their labor force participation rate. "Highly educated women are likely to work for pay, whether or not they are married" (Kreps, 1971, p. 24).

The rising educational level of women since 1940 is certainly consistent with their increasing entry into the labor force. It is likely, however, that their increased education has been both a cause and an effect of women's growing interest in paid employment. That is, additional education has made women more interested in employment—but in addition, more women have become interested in employment and then sought more education to achieve their work goals. This latter point is especially relevant for the last two decades, when minimum educational requirements for many jobs have been rising.

Studies of the female labor supply have raised some related questions. Was it education itself that increased female labor force participation, by changing women's attitudes toward work? Or was it the higher wages and more attractive working conditions made available by their better education that drew more women into the labor force? Both effects probably occurred. Economic data, however, provide more information about the second effect. Economists have found a strong enough correlation between greater education and higher wages to give educational levels a key place in several studies.

Readers may want to compare the influence of education on women's labor force participation with its impact on their political participation (Chapter 13).

Taxes. How taxes affect working women is an interesting subject in itself. It is also relevant to the present discussion, since higher taxes are equivalent to lower wages. How have taxes affected women's desire to work?

The current income tax rate structure should tend to discourage many married women from working, since their after-tax earnings are most seriously affected. For example, a single woman (or man) earning $10,000 in 1978 would have paid $1216 in federal income tax.[1] Thus, her after-tax earnings would have been $8984. Now compare this situation with that of a married woman who decided to take a job paying $10,000 in 1978. Assume that her husband has also earned $10,000 that year. As a result of the progressive tax rates and of reforms a few years earlier that benefitted single taxpayers, the after-tax earnings of the married woman would have been only $7858. If her husband's job paid $30,000 that year, the wife's earnings would have amounted to only $6083 after taxes.[2]

This tax effect provides one more explanation of why wives with high-income husbands are less likely to seek paying jobs. Furthermore, the fact that only money income is ordinarily subject to the tax gives all wives another incentive to remain at home. Any increase in the family's well-being that results from the wife's concentration on household work is tax free.

The social security tax also works to the disadvantage of working wives or, rather, to the advantage of nonworking wives. All women married to working men are entitled to spouse's benefits (equal in amount to one-half the husband's benefits).[3] If a wife takes a job, she will pay social security taxes on her earnings, just as a man or a single woman would. Upon retirement, she will receive *either* her own earned benefits or the benefits she is entitled to as the wife of a retired worker. She will, in effect, be receiving very little in additional benefits for her tax dollars. (See Griffiths, 1976, for some tax reform suggestions in this area.)

All of this should have discouraged labor force participation by wives. As Michael Boskin (1974) points out, it should have particularly discouraged wives from reentering the labor force after their children were grown. That is when the husband's earnings—and thus the income tax on the wife's earnings—would be highest. Yet that is the very time in their life cycle that most wives reenter the labor force.

As discussed earlier, in any one year, married women in general, and especially those with high-income husbands, are less likely to work than are other women. It is very possible that the tax structure contributes to this behavioral pattern. Nevertheless, over the

[1] Computations are based on the tax rates, personal exemptions, and standard deduction (zero bracket amount) in effect for 1978. For some working couples, deductible child-care expenses will reduce the tax differentials indicated here.

[2] CBS's 60 *Minutes*, in a segment broadcast March 7, 1976, documented an interesting protest to this tax treatment. One working couple saved about $2500 by divorcing in late December 1975—thereby qualifying to file their 1975 tax returns as two single persons—and then remarrying in January 1976. Other couples divorced secretly, but continued to live together—and still others, for tax reasons alone, chose to live together unwed. After 1976 the IRS successfully opposed tax reductions based on a temporary divorce.

[3] However, women who are divorced after less than 20 years of marriage lose all right to spouse benefits. (This rule changed to "less than ten years" in February 1979.)

past 30 years the labor force participation of wives, including those with high-income husbands, has increased at well above the average rate.

Thus the *actual* effect of taxes on wives' employment decisions is not clear. Would more wives have worked if the tax rates had been lower? Was the pull of rising wages and better education so strong that the taxes did little to discourage wives from entering the work force? Or was the tax impact simply ignored? No real answers are available yet in published studies.

Wife's Occupation.   In their extensive study of labor force participation, William Bowen and T. Aldrich Finegan (1969) looked at the relationship between a wife's occupation and her labor force participation.

The 1960 census asked women what they considered their occupation to be (even if they were not working at that time); the same census also showed the woman's current job, if any. Comparing these two sets of data, Bowen and Finegan found three broad types of occupation in which married women were most likely to continue working: (1) occupations with rather high earning opportunities, such as professional jobs; (2) occupations that are difficult to reenter after temporary periods of withdrawal, such as managerial work; and (3) jobs in which flexible hours or part-time work are fairly common, such as clerical work. In other words, women's attachment to the labor force increased when working arrangements were fairly convenient or when the cost of leaving an occupation was rather high.

Between 1950 and 1970 there was a definite shift of female employment toward occupations that Bowen and Finegan found to have high continuing participation. This means that more and more married women were working in occupations with fairly low "dropout" rates. This greater percentage of wives continuing in their jobs would help to raise the average participation rate for women.

Attitudes.   To what extent is the increase in female labor force participation attributable to more favorable attitudes of women and men toward women working outside the home? Economists prefer to use variables that can be quantified; they usually leave this type of question for sociologists to answer (see Chapter 8). However, a few economic studies have included an attitude variable.

One study of more than 2000 White and non-White wives found that the husband's attitude toward his wife's working was both statistically significant and important in explaining wives' current labor force status (Morgan, David, Cohen, & Brazier, 1962). In this study, the husband's attitude was more important than the general level of unemployment, the frequency of the husband's unemployment, or the husband's income in determining the likelihood of the wife's working. The attitude factor was found to be much less important, however, than the age, education, or race of the wife, or the age of her children.

Another study (Mahoney, 1961) found a statistically significant relationship between the wife's attitude and her labor force participation. However, neither of these studies showed whether the favorable attitude actually preceded the wife's decision to work (see Cain, 1966, p. 39).

Valerie Oppenheimer (1970) discusses the question of attitude changes over time, summarizing a number of public-opinion polls and studies from various disciplines. She found that the attitudes toward wives' working outside the home changed a little more slowly than the actual increase in wives' labor force participation. Thus it does not appear that more favorable public attitudes caused the increase in female labor force participation. In fact, the limited evidence suggests that the opposite may have occurred. That is, the presence of so many more wives in the labor force may have led to greater acceptance of wives' holding paying jobs.

Still, it is difficult to reach a firm conclusion as to the role played by attitude changes. The various polls and studies are often inconsistent in the questions used and in the groups questioned. Attitude changes are usually complex and subtle, making them difficult to measure accurately.

Studies by sociologists underscore the complexity of attitudinal factors. For example, they note that a husband's positive attitude toward his wife's working is more likely to encourage her to work than a negative attitude on his part is likely to prevent it (see Chapter 8).

In summary, there has been a gradual shift in the attitudes of both husbands and wives toward greater approval of wives' working. However, this more favorable attitude may have followed, rather than preceded, wives' greater labor force participation. Regardless of which came first, the gradual shift of opinion toward acceptance of female employment surely has made it easier for some women to decide to look for a job, or to stay in the labor force. And a favorable attitude on the part of a husband and wife would have helped determine *which* women entered the labor force in a particular period.

Mother's Work Experience. One additional variable, considered more often by sociologists than economists, is the employment experience of the woman's mother (see Chapter 8). Various studies have noted that women whose mothers worked, even for a relatively brief period, are more likely to have a positive attitude about female employment and to be in the labor force themselves (Eyde, 1962, pp. 47–48; Baruch, 1972).

The women in these rather small samples usually come from middle- or upper-middle-class families, with parents in white-collar or professional occupations. Thus they may not be typical of the female population as a whole. But if this is a valid finding for most women, it could provide an important explanation of the fairly steady increase in female labor force participation during recent decades. The World War II work experiences, discussed below, would become especially significant. Let us now consider that experience and other changes in the demand for women workers.

The Demand for Women Workers

Up to now, we have been looking at supply factors—variables that affect the number of women who want to work. Now we will look at demand—at factors that explain why more jobs have become available to women.

A number of changes between 1940 and 1970 increased the demand for female labor. Rising incomes, for example, resulted in a rapidly increasing demand for consumer goods and services. While this meant a greater demand for nearly all workers, women were particularly affected. Women's educational levels and work skills also increased during this period, making women more valuable as employees. For example, training in typing, shorthand, and sometimes office machines became widely available in high schools at no cost to the student or the employer. More recently, the influx of women into keypunch-operator jobs has given many of them both useful experience and the opportunity to move into the rapidly growing computer programming field.

The demand for female workers has received less thorough attention from economists than has the supply. However, some aspects of demand have been studied, and the findings are discussed below.

Education.   Education affects both labor supply and demand. On the supply side, better-educated women are more likely to seek employment. Also, since education makes workers more productive, the demand for female workers will rise as their education improves. As indicated earlier, female educational levels have risen noticeably since 1940. This by itself would have affected demand. In addition, changes in production methods and the rapid growth in demand for services (such as health care and education) have caused a strong increase in the demand for workers with a high school or college education.

Trends in Predominantly Female Occupations.   It is possible to speak of the demand for female workers—rather than simply the demand for workers—only because of the high concentration of women in a few occupations. As Janice Hedges (1970) observed:

> Although more than 250 distinct occupations are listed in Bureau of the Census tabulation, half of all women workers were employed in only 21 of them in 1969. About a fourth of all employed women were in five occupations—secretary-stenographer, household worker, bookkeeper, elementary school teacher, and waitress. . . . Male workers were much more widely dispersed than women, with 50 per cent in 65 occupations [p. 19].

The concentration of women within this narrow range of jobs means that there are several occupations in which nearly all the workers are female. In 1970, for example, 47 occupations, including the five listed above, had at least 70% female membership. A total of 57% of the female labor force worked in these 47 occupations (Greckel, 1978). This list of female-intensive occupations was not too different in 1950. Thus, we can reasonably conclude that during the postwar period rising demand for, say, secretaries, nurses, waitresses, or elementary teachers has meant an increased demand for female workers. (We will look more closely at these female-intensive occupations later in this chapter.)

Many female-intensive occupations have enjoyed unusually rapid growth during the past 20 to 30 years. For example, between 1950 and 1970, the number of jobs in the service sector—which is predominantly female—increased by 77%, while jobs in the industrial sector—which is predominantly male—rose by only 26%. (The industrial sector refers mostly to factory work; the service sector includes such job areas as food service, health services, and the professions.) Between 1950 and 1960 alone, employment in the 70%-female occupations increased by nearly 40%. This growth was much more rapid than in the labor force as a whole (Kreps & Leaper, 1976, p. 64; Kreps, 1971, pp. 33–40).

This strong demand for female labor—the knowledge that there are "suitable" jobs available—has played an important part in attracting a large number of additional women into the labor force. The increase in clerical and sales jobs seems particularly important because it has increased the availability of part-time employment, which is more acceptable than full-time work to many women with children.

Employment of Women during World War II.   World War II brought women into the labor force in previously unheard-of numbers—showing how willingly they would respond to a sharply increased demand for female labor. The National Manpower Council study, *Womanpower* (1957), noted the "strenuous efforts" made to recruit additional female workers, particularly married women, from 1943 to 1945. A typical government-sponsored billboard advertisement from those war years illustrates that recruiting effort:

Mothers in Overalls

"What Job is mine on the Victory Line?"
If you've sewed on buttons, or made buttonholes, on a machine,
you can learn to do spot welding on airplane parts.
If you've used an electric mixer in your kitchen,
you can learn to run a drill press.
If you've followed recipes exactly in making cakes,
you can learn to load shell.
[Lapin, 1943; quoted in Baxandall, Gordon, & Reverby, 1976, p. 284]

Women responded impressively to this mushrooming demand. As Table 11-2 shows, the female labor force jumped from fewer than 14 million women (27% of the female population) in 1940 and 1941 to nearly 20 million (37%) in 1945. Chapter 15 notes a parallel, but less dramatic, increase in the number of women holding elective office during wartime.

The World War II work experience demonstrated that women could perform very well many "men's jobs," from assembly of small articles to riveting, welding, and blueprint reading. Women worked on drill presses, milling machines, lathes, and other machine tools. By shifting to mass-production techniques, the shipbuilding industry opened 200 new types of jobs, including repair work, to women. Prior to this time very few women had worked on aircraft, but during the war "they were to be found in practically every job in the aircraft industry" (National Manpower Council, 1957, p. 159). Special efforts were made to keep women in the wartime labor force. Even child care was sometimes provided.

But the demand for female employees was a temporary phenomenon. With the end of the war, over 2 million women were laid off; many others were transferred to clerical

Table 11-2.   The Female Labor Force, 1940–1956

Year	Number (Thousands) of Women	Percentage of Women Aged 14 and Over	Percentage of All Workers
1940	13,840	27.6	25.4
1941	13,930	27.4	25.3
1942	15,460	30.1	27.7
1943	18,100	34.9	33.0
1944	18,450	35.2	34.0
1945	19,570	37.0	36.1
1946	16,590	30.9	29.4
1947	16,320	30.0	27.6
1948	17,155	31.2	28.3
1949	17,167	30.9	28.2
1950	18,063	32.1	29.0
1954	19,726	33.4	31.2
1956	21,194	35.1	31.8

From *Womanpower*, by H. David for The National Manpower Council, 1957, p. 112. Published by Columbia University Press. Reprinted by permission.

jobs with lower pay, and another propaganda campaign urged women to get back into their "beloved kitchens." The returning men were given back "their" jobs. Yet various surveys showed that a large majority of women in the labor force wanted to continue working, and most of those working in factories wanted to stay in "mechanical work" (Trey, 1972; Baxandall, Gordon, & Reverby, 1976, p. 310).

The jobs were simply not available—at least not for women. The female labor force declined by over 3 million women from 1945 to 1947. Nevertheless, it remained above the 1942 level. After 1947 the trend was again upward, with the wartime employment records surpassed by the early 1950s.

The National Manpower Council (1957) concluded that the war had a positive influence on female employment. It affected both the inclinations of women (supply) and attitudes of employers (demand). The Council's observations included the following:

> [The war] helped to alter the traditional approach of women, particularly married women, toward paid employment. . . . Many were now reassured about their ability to handle a job. . . . Not to be underestimated was the satisfaction that many found in bringing home a sizable paycheck every week. . . . [Employers] discovered that introducing women in considerable numbers . . . [was not] a prelude to a breakdown in either factory discipline or sexual morality. Employers also discovered that for certain types of work women were more productive than men. . . . Each of these developments helped to break down powerful traditions concerning the employment of women [pp. 162–163].

There is little doubt that the wartime demand for women workers had some lasting impact on female employment. However, no one has been able to assess to what extent the postwar increases in the supply of women workers were caused by the experiences of the war years. Many of the women who left the labor force in 1946 and 1947 returned to work in later years. Daughters' interest in paid employment may also have been heightened by their mothers' wartime work experience.

Summary

We have seen that women's rising labor force participation during the last 30 years has resulted from increases in both the demand for women workers and the supply of women workers. On the demand side, the most important factors have been the growth of demand for all types of labor as the economy expanded, and the particularly rapid growth of employment in many traditionally female occupations. Thus, many more women entered the labor force because they were aware of improved employment opportunities.

On the supply side, rising educational levels stimulated women's interest in paid employment, while at the same time increasing their earning potential. The temporary jump in demand for female workers during World War II encouraged their later return to the labor force. It probably also strengthened their daughters' interest in working for pay. In addition, the female labor supply was increased somewhat by a modest shift in female employment toward (a) jobs in which the costs of dropping out of the labor force were relatively high and (b) jobs with convenient working hours, making it easier to remain in the labor force.

Employment and Unemployment

We turn next to a number of topics dealing with employment or unemployment. The topics all relate in some way to entering or leaving the labor force, or to seeking, losing, or leaving jobs. In most cases we will be comparing the experiences of men and women.

Women Have Not Displaced Men

Between 1950 and 1976, the labor force participation rate of women (the percentage of adult women who are working) increased from 34% to 47%, while that of men declined from 86% to 76% (U.S. Department of Labor, Bureau of Labor Statistics, 1975b, p. 3; O'Riley, 1976). This trend has led some observers to argue that women have been displacing men at various jobs, but that has not been the case. The decline in male labor force participation has been mostly in the 16-to-24 and 45-and-over age brackets. The younger men are postponing their labor force entry in order to begin or remain in college. The lower participation rate of older men reflects primarily the move toward earlier retirement. Neither change is closely related to the entry of women workers. Also, as noted earlier, most women do not enter the same occupations that men do.

Another result of these same trends is that for most men there has been a reduction in the time spent in paid work over their life spans, while for the average woman there has been an increase. However, men are far more likely than women to remain continuously in the labor force once they have completed their education.

Unemployment Rates Are Higher among Women

Up to now, we have been interested in the decisions of men and women to enter the labor force. But the labor force consists not only of workers but also of the unemployed—those who want a job but do not have one. In this regard, women have been consistently worse off than men. In the 1961–1971 decade, for example, the unemployment rate for males over age 20 ranged from a low of 2.1% to a high of 5.7%. During the same period, the unemployment rate for females over age 20 ranged from 3.7% to 6.3% and was always higher than for males. The gap continues. The unemployment rates in early 1977, for example, were 7.5% for adult men and 8.5% for adult women (U.S. Department of Labor, Bureau of Labor Statistics, 1975a; Michelotti, 1977).

In most years women are somewhat more likely than men to leave their jobs voluntarily (often temporarily dropping out of the labor force). Men are more likely than women to lose their jobs. The average length of unemployment is shorter for women than for men. This is because, among both males and females, those who voluntarily change jobs or enter the labor force find work more readily than those who have lost their jobs (U.S. President, Council of Economic Advisors, 1973, pp. 96–97).

Are Women More Likely to Quit Their Jobs?

It is a common belief among employers that a woman is more likely to leave a job than a man is. Very few studies have actually compared male and female quit rates—the percentage of workers leaving their jobs during any given month. Among the existing studies, the typical approach has been to look at male and female behavior across a wide range of jobs, without separating the results into different job categories. The data generated by this approach show women having higher quit rates than men (U.S. Department of Labor, Women's Bureau, 1969b, pp. 76–77).

This finding is very misleading. Regardless of gender, workers in dull, dead-end, poorly paid jobs are much more likely to quit than workers who have more rewarding jobs. Studies comparing men and women in similar job situations have found little or no difference in behavior. For example, a study among large chemical and pharmaceutical laboratories found men's and women's quit rates to be about the same when the employees were grouped by "type of degree required for the grade of work to be performed." People working at the higher job levels had the lowest quit rates.

Thus when we find that, on the average, women have higher quit rates than men, what we are looking at is not really a difference in the way women and men behave when they have jobs. Instead, it is largely a reflection of the different kinds of jobs most women and men hold. Women are more likely to hold the unfulfilling jobs that both men and women tend to leave frequently, whereas men are more likely to be employed in the kinds of jobs that reward those who stay on. (See our Chapter 15; also U.S. Department of Labor, Women's Bureau, 1969a, 1969b.)

One important difference does remain. Many of the women who quit jobs also leave the labor force, at least temporarily. Most of the men under age 45 who quit jobs remain in the labor force.

The Sex-Segregation of Occupations

As observed earlier, most women work in a few female-intensive occupations. (Female-intensive occupations are those in which a high percentage—frequently defined as 70%—of the employees are women.) Has this pattern of sex-segregated jobs changed much over the years? What causes jobs to be sex-typed—that is, to be viewed as "men's jobs" or "women's jobs"?

Trends in the Sex-Segregation of Occupations

At the beginning of this century women were even more concentrated in a handful of occupations. As Table 11-3 shows, in 1900 nearly 29% of all female workers were "private household workers" (private cooks, housekeepers, and so forth). More than half of

Table 11-3. History of Occupations in Which Women were Predominant in 1900

Occupations with at Least 70% Female Membership in 1900	1900		1950		1970	
	Women in Each Occupation as a Percentage of:					
	All Workers in Occupation	*Female Labor Force*	*All Workers in Occupation*	*Female Labor Force*	*All Workers in Occupation*	*Female Labor Force*
Dressmakers/seamstresses	100%	7.8%	97%	0.9%	95%	0.3%
Private household workers	97%	28.7%	95%	8.6%	97%	3.6%
Nurses	94%	0.2%	98%	2.9%	97%	2.7%
Health service workers	89%	1.8%	74%	1.6%	88%	3.5%
Telephone operators	80%	0.3%	96%	2.1%	94%	1.3%
Teachers	75%	6.1%	75%	5.2%	70%	6.4%
Librarians	72%	0.0%	89%	0.3%	82%	0.3%
Secretaries/typists/stenographers	72%	1.8%	94%	9.3%	97%	12.4%
Factory workers in apparel/textile products	70%	3.3%	66%	1.7%	76%	0.2%
Seven other occupations	86%	4.4%	68%	1.9%	64%	1.7%

Data from Greckel, 1978; Oppenheimer, 1970, pp. 79–80.

the female labor force worked in one of about 20 occupations that had a 70% or greater female membership at that time. In all but three of these occupations, women still accounted for at least 70% of the workers in 1970. By that year, however, there were about 30 more female-intensive occupations to choose among. As in 1900, over half of the female labor force was employed in these female-intensive occupations. The number of these occupations increased again in the 1970s, and women continue to crowd into these predominantly female fields. By 1977 nearly two out of every three employed women worked in one of the 50 or more occupations that had at least 70% female membership (Greckel, 1978; Oppenheimer, 1970).

The range of male-intensive occupations has always been much broader.[4] How might we identify a male-intensive occupation? Men accounted for about 62% of the total labor force in 1970. If all occupations were equally open and equally attractive to both sexes, we would then expect to find about 38% of the workers in each occupation to be

Figure 11-4. Garment making has always been a female-intensive occupation. (Photo courtesy of the University of Louisville, Canfield and Shook Collection.)

[4]This helps explain why political scientists have found that women in the federal civil service come from fewer occupations than do their male counterparts. See Chapter 15.

women, and about 62% men. Thus we might consider any occupation in which more than 80% of the workers were men to be a male-intensive occupation. The 1970 census listed about 400 different occupations. Nearly 200 of these met our male-intensive criterion. These occupations employed two out of every three male workers and one out of every 12 female workers.

Women have made some slight inroads into this male job territory in recent years. More than 20 of the occupations that had at least 80% male employees in 1960 were off that male-intensive list by 1977. Indeed, in six of these jobs—baker, bill collector, bartender, bus driver, insurance adjuster, and asbestos or insulation worker—women now account for 40% or more of the employees. Among the other occupations whose male membership fell below 80% by 1977 were such diverse jobs as accountant, advertising agent, postal clerk, bank official, newsboy, upholsterer, and stock clerk (see Greckel, 1978).

Between 1960 and 1970, women entered many other "male" occupations in impressive numbers, although women still held only a small minority of the jobs. In the skilled trades, for example, while the number of male carpenters increased by 6000, female carpenters increased by 8000, raising the female share from 0.4% to 1.3%. The number of female electricians increased from 2500 to 8700. Comparable increases occurred among female plumbers, auto mechanics, tool and die makers, machinists, and typesetters.

In the business world, the number of female branch-bank managers jumped from 2100 to 54,400 during the 1960s. The number of women with jobs as nonretail sales managers grew from 100 to 8700. Women also made substantial gains as insurance agents and brokers, real estate agents, and stock and bond sales agents.

In the professions, female engineers increased from 7000 to 19,600, female lawyers from 5000 to over 12,000, female doctors from 16,000 to 26,000, and female dentists from 1900 to 3100 (U.S. Department of Labor, Women's Bureau, 1975a, pp. 92–94). Although these professions still remained more than 90% male in 1970, current graduate school enrollments promise that the proportion of women in these professions will continue to grow. Meanwhile, more men have entered such traditionally female occupations as nurse or stenographer.

Despite these encouraging trends, the total picture has not changed very much. To provide an overall measure of changes in occupational sex-segregation, the Council of Economic Advisors (U.S. President, 1973, p. 158) constructed an "occupational dissimilarity index" for 1960 and 1970. This numerical index can range from 0 (meaning women and men were proportionally represented in each occupation) to 1 (meaning "men and women were completely occupationally segregated, so that they were never in the same occupation"). The Council's calculations showed a slight movement away from sex-segregation: the index declined from .629 in 1960 to .598 in 1970.

Thus, all findings agree that there is somewhat less extreme job segregation by sex today than there was 10, 20, or 70 years ago. However, a very substantial number of occupations still appear to be considered either "men's work" or "women's work."

Why Is Occupational Sex-Segregation So Persistent?

The division of work along sex lines has been the standard practice in just about all societies down through the ages. Despite this common practice, the specific jobs assigned to each sex have varied greatly. Once tasks are sex-typed, the socialization process helps perpetuate that division of labor. (As explained in Chapter 7, the socialization process refers to the way in which boys and girls—and adults—are conditioned to adopt socially approved male and female roles.)

We can see the influence of socialization on the sex-segregation of jobs today. Many traditionally female occupations, such as teacher, waitress, or garment worker, are related to childbearing or homemaking tasks. Others, such as secretary or nurse, center around such socially approved feminine roles as nurturing, serving, or assisting others.

Socialization also ensures the continuation of this sex-typing. Childhood and adult experiences transmit the information that secretaries, nurses, bank tellers, and telephone operators are females, whereas business executives, doctors, car salesmen, and electricians are males. These impressions are reinforced from early childhood on, by the attitudes of parents, teachers, counselors, and peers, by the messages conveyed by textbooks, comic strips, and television, and even by the selection of "appropriate" toys for boys and girls. As a result, most young men avoid the "female" occupations, and most young women avoid the "male" occupations. Guidance counselors, employment agencies, and employers operate on the basis of similar impressions about the type (gender) of worker that is suitable for a specific job.

Earnings opportunities further cement the existing occupational distribution. "Women's jobs" tend to be lower paid than "men's jobs." This gives men an additional reason to seek work outside the female-dominated occupations, and most men find that they have more attractive alternatives.

What about women's alternatives? As suggested above, most women do not view these "men's jobs" as *really* open to them. In addition, discriminatory practices kept women out of a number of occupations, such as medicine and coal mining. Therefore, women continued to crowd into the more open traditional occupations. As a result of this crowding, wages in these "female" jobs remained low, and men continued to seek their fortunes elsewhere.

Physical differences between men and women play some part in occupational sex-typing. Because men are, on the average, larger and (partly as a result of socially approved differences in exercise) physically stronger than women, it is understandable that jobs requiring a great deal of physical exertion have come to be viewed as men's work. Of course, there are numerous examples, as in farming, of women routinely doing heavy work—and of women who are stronger than men. Thus there is no legitimate reason to shut out women from these jobs. Also, modern technology has greatly reduced the amount of "muscle" required for many jobs.

Furthermore, sex-typing is often inconsistent with the physical abilities we associate with one sex or the other. For example, women are frequently praised for their superior manual dexterity. Yet, as Janice Hedges (1970) has observed, "finger and hand dexterity and eye-hand coordination" are basic requirements for most of the male-dominated skilled crafts. She further notes:

> The particular combination of aptitudes required for a number of crafts, including office machine repairman, radio and television repairman, automobile mechanic, aircraft mechanic, and household appliance repairman are found as frequently among female as male students, according to aptitude tests of students in the 11th grade. Yet only 3 percent of the craftsmen in 1968 were women [p. 26].

It appears, therefore, that sex-segregation of occupations generally owes more to our views of appropriate male and female roles than to actual differences in ability.

The reader interested in pursuing the subjects of occupational sex-typing and occupational choice will find additional information elsewhere in this book. Chapter 7 contains a detailed account of the socialization process and its impact on work decisions. Readers may be surprised to find out at how young an age strong sex-role identification develops. The discussion of intelligence in Chapter 3 provides some additional insights— for example, why men are more likely than women to choose careers in math and science. Chapter 5 discusses sex differences in learning and in motor skills. Chapter 15 offers some explanations for the prevalence of men in politics. And the next section of this chapter includes an account of how teaching has changed from a male-intensive to a female-intensive profession. (See also Blaxall & Reagan, 1976.)

Studies of Specific Occupations

Some of the recent research on women in the economy looks at various white-collar or professional occupations. (Comparable economic studies of other types of women's jobs—such as secretary, factory worker, or waitress—are few, and mainly from a sociologist's perspective. See, however, Baxandall, Gordon, & Reverby, 1976, and Stromberg & Harkess, 1978, for interesting and informative accounts of women's experiences in clerical, blue-collar, and service occupations.)

One predictable theme runs through all of these studies: the higher the position within a field, the less likely it is that a woman will be filling it. This holds true whether women are a minority or a majority within that occupation. Chapter 15 illustrates this situation among women in the federal bureaucracy. Women's status within organized labor is no better than in business, government, or the professions. Although more than 20% of union members are women, in 1973 they accounted for less than 7% of the positions on union governing boards (U.S. Department of Labor, Women's Bureau, 1975a, pp. 77–78).

We turn now to some of the findings of the occupational studies. We will look at the employment of women in three areas: the banking industry, business management, and the teaching profession.

Women in Banking

Commercial banking as an industry is quite open to women, but primarily at lower-level jobs. Two-thirds of the 970,000 bank employees in 1971 were women. In a study of 18 large commercial banks in six major cities, Rodney Alexander and Elisabeth Sapery (1973) found that female employees were "heavily concentrated in low-level, poorly paid positions where the outlook for advancement is bleak" (p. 7). Women constituted about 73% of office and clerical personnel, 24% of technical and sales personnel, and only 15% of official and managerial personnel.

Even that last figure of 15% greatly overstates women's managerial influence in banking. Of the 8000 female bank officers who were members of the National Association of Bank Women (NABW), more than 3000 were assistant cashiers, the lowest-level officer position. At the upper end of the executive ladder, only 18 were senior vice-presidents, 30 were executive vice-presidents, and 41 were bank presidents (see Kropf, 1969).

Alexander and Sapery found little reason to expect the situation to change greatly in the near future. In 1970, of all first-time promotions to officer positions, from zero to 12.5% (depending on the bank) went to White women. None went to minority women. Female executives are excluded "almost completely from commercial lending, the most prestigious and best-paid aspect of commercial banking and the commonest route to the top rungs on the executive ladder. . . . Instead, female executives are most often found in personnel departments or in branch banking, where the lending activity is retail-oriented and the size of the loans comparatively small" (Alexander & Sapery, 1973, pp. 49, 160). In an earlier section of this chapter, we noted that a substantial number of women became branch-bank officers around 1970. It remains to be seen how many of them will have real advancement opportunities.

The First Women's Bank, which opened in 1975 in New York City under female management, suggests an alternative route up the executive ladder. That much publicized bank has not had completely smooth sailing. However, a few other all-female banks exist and are doing well. For example, the West Point Bank, in Hardin County, Kentucky, has been run exclusively by women since 1941. The usual position of men and women in banking is well illustrated by the following remark made by the president of the West Point Bank: "We've had men apply, but they always wanted to be officers in charge" ("All-Woman Hardin Bank," 1977).

As the next section shows, women managers have fared even less well in many other industries.

Women in Management

The Council of Economic Advisors found women occupying about 17% of all nonfarm managerial and administrative positions in 1970. This was slightly better than their 14% share in 1950. However, most of these women were in middle-management positions in retail trade or lower-level positions in banks and insurance companies, or were postmasters, administrators in local government, or managers of small retail or service establishments. Among executives earning at least $10,000 in 1960, only about 2% were women. Since then, the situation has improved very little (Bowman, Worthy, & Greyser, 1965; U.S. President, Council of Economic Advisors, 1973, p. 156; Wallace, 1973, p. 79).

One survey of 300 male and female executives has provided a profile of women managers in a number of industries. This survey, by Douglas Basil (1972), also yields extensive information about attitudes toward women executives. Basil's survey indicated that, in about 70% of the responding companies, women held more than 3% of the managerial positions. This probably overstated the prevalence of women in management. About 1700 firms did not return the questionnaire, and it is likely that the responding firms had better-than-average records on female employment.

Among the firms Basil studied, women fared best in government, banking, and merchandising. They had little or no managerial opportunities in insurance, transportation, or utilities companies. Firms located in the Midwest were far less likely to employ women as managers than were firms in other regions. In all industries covered, the greatest number of managerial positions for women were in office management or personnel management. Two-thirds of the firms employed no women in positions calling for "policy and major decision-making responsibilities." Three-fourths employed no women in production or marketing supervision.

Responses from the highest-level male and female executives in each firm showed that the men were more than twice as likely to be married as the women. The men were also far more likely to have college or graduate degrees. This educational difference should gradually narrow, since the younger women were better educated than the older women. These results are consistent with other studies of female managers (see Business and Professional Women's Association, 1970).

Among the reasons given by both men and women for the greater number of male executives were the following: (1) women candidates' more limited educational background and business experience; (2) the belief that women lack the necessary drive and motivation; (3) the reluctance of many married women to take a job that requires traveling or moving to a different city; and (4) the greater risk perceived in admitting women into training programs. This "risk" was apparently based on the belief that females have higher turnover rates than males for the same job—a belief that we showed earlier to be incorrect.

Most respondents felt that both men and women preferred to work for a man. Men who had worked for or with women, however, reacted much more favorably to that arrangement. Surprisingly, a survey of male college students cited by Basil found them even more opposed to female executives than were the male executives.

Basil concludes that the scarcity of female executives results both from prejudice and from legitimate reasons. He suggests that a change in the situation will require not only that prejudice be reduced, but also that more women obtain formal business training—particularly the MBA (Master of Business Administration) degree. He identifies other needs as well. For example, myths about women's lesser ability, emotional instability, and higher turnover rate need to be exposed. Firms need to consider more women for training programs and educational benefits—and encourage their promising female employees to participate. And women themselves need to demonstrate greater motivation and career commitment.

Women in Elementary and Secondary Education

Today the words "elementary teacher" would generally bring to mind a female image—perhaps a young woman just out of college or a mature, motherly woman who had dedicated her life, despite a relatively low salary, to the education of her young charges. But teaching was not originally a female profession in the United States. In the first half of the 19th century, as public education spread across the country, most teachers were men. Then, as public schools multiplied, and as economic growth provided better earning opportunities in other jobs, local townships found it more and more difficult to locate enough men willing to teach for the low salaries offered.

Thus, around the middle of the 19th century, despite a preference for male teachers, schools began to rely more on women. Once it was recognized that women could provide a plentiful and inexpensive supply of teachers (female teachers were usually paid about half the males' salary), attitudes toward women became much more favorable. Written articles began to suggest that women, with their traditional patience and gentleness, were better suited for teaching than were men. Although teaching salaries were low, women had few attractive employment alternatives. By 1890, two-thirds of the nation's public school teachers were women. Their share increased to more than four-fifths by 1920 (Abbott, 1910, p. 119; Woody, 1966, pp. 492–499).

The past 20 years or so have witnessed a moderate reversal of this trend. Male elementary teachers increased from 9% in 1950 to 15% in 1960 and 17% in 1973. Why have men shown this renewed interest in teaching? On the demand side, the postwar "baby boom" caused the demand for new teachers to multiply more rapidly than the female teacher supply, leading to an increase in salaries. On the supply side, the number of male college graduates increased faster than did suitable jobs outside of teaching. Also, many men viewed teaching jobs as a stepping-stone to better-paying and more "masculine" administrative positions.

Advancement opportunities for men have thus far proven bright. Even in this "female" profession, men fill the overwhelming majority of the higher-paid, more prestigious, authoritative positions—such as principal or school system superintendent. For example, in Indiana during the 1977–1978 school year, 89% of the elementary school principals, 98% of the junior high school principals, 99.5% of the high school principals, and 99.7% of the school superintendents were men. Nationwide, women account for about 20% of all school principals, mostly at the elementary level. There are only a few female superintendents, almost all in remote rural school districts.

Some Observations on the Occupational Studies

"The higher the fewer" describes women's position in any occupation—not merely in the fields just discussed. Why are women so consistently found at the bottom of each occupational hierarchy? Discrimination plays a part. Women have often had little or no access to the best graduate schools, to equal employment opportunities, to valuable on-the-job training programs, and to important channels for advancement. Moreover, there are ample cases that can be cited of more promising or better-qualified women being passed over at promotion time in favor of men.

But such overt discrimination is not the whole answer. There is also evidence that women are often less inclined to seek advancement opportunities. Why is this so? Part of the answer lies in the socialization process. Socialization encourages males to be assertive, ambitious, and independent—to "take charge"—while encouraging women to be submissive, self-denying, cooperative, and helpful.

Women are given fewer opportunities to develop leadership and decision-making skills (see Chapter 7). Men logically expect to gain status and social approval by moving up the administrative or professional ladder. Many women, however, fear that such advancement will bring them considerable disapproval. They worry that others will view them as less feminine and that relations with men (including husbands) may become somewhat strained. (See Chapter 14 for a discussion of the development of male and female self-confidence, and Chapter 7 for research on women's "fear of success." Also see Epstein, 1970.)

Women also have more practical reasons for hesitating to seek advancement— namely, their roles in home and family life. So long as the responsibility for homemaking and child rearing falls primarily on wives' shoulders, many women who are married or who expect someday to be married will avoid the additional responsibilities of administrative positions. This does not mean that women are basically less ambitious than men. It does mean that women realize that, given the traditional division of family roles, most women who pursue the more demanding careers must pay a higher price for achievement than most men.

For these and related reasons, both the demand for women and the supply of women in the upper levels of most occupations will remain far smaller than they would be in a world free of discrimination and of sex-role stereotyping—at home as well as on the job.

Women in the Labor Force: Summary

In this review of women in the labor force, we have noted the impressive increase in female labor force participation during the past 30 years. Educational gains for women, rapidly growing employment opportunities in many traditionally female occupations, and rising wages are important explanations for this trend. During any one year, a woman's marital status, age, children, occupation, education, and (if married) her husband's attitude help determine whether she will be among the many women in the labor force.

Women have higher unemployment rates than do men. Unlike men, married women in particular have a pattern of leaving and reentering the labor force, in response to changing family demands or to changing employment opportunities. But if similar jobs are considered, women are no more likely to leave a specific job than are men—although they may have different reasons for leaving.

Studies have detailed the extent and persistence of occupational sex-segregation. The majority of women in the labor force are still crowded into female-intensive occupations. At the same time, there has been a trend of increasing female participation in some of the male-intensive occupations. But in all occupations, whether or not men are in the majority, women are seldom found in higher-level positions.

The occupational distribution of working women and their failure to occupy high-level positions greatly affect female earnings. That is the main subject of the next chapter.

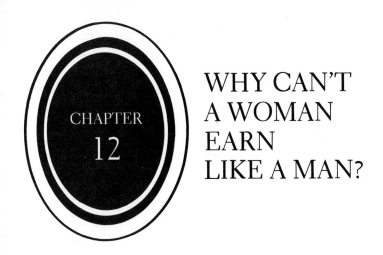

WHY CAN'T A WOMAN EARN LIKE A MAN?

CHAPTER
12

In the previous two chapters, we have looked at women as producers in the home and in the working world. In this chapter, we will consider the incomes women receive. We will be paying particular attention to the gap between male and female earnings and the reasons for this gap. We will also look at the incomes of households headed by women and the contribution women's earnings make to the well-being of their families.

The Male/Female Earnings Gap

It is widely recognized that women's earnings average much less than those of men. Among full-time year-round workers in 1976, the median earnings for men were $13,455 and for women, $8099—60% of male earnings. (When part-time as well as full-time workers are included, women earn only about 40% as much as men—because so many more women work only part time or part of the year.) As Table 12-1 shows, the earnings ratio has remained close to 60% for many years.

Instead of steadily improving, women's relative earnings deteriorated between 1955 and 1967, recovered somewhat, then fell again, reaching a low of 57% of men's earnings in 1973. Despite three years of improvement—some of it due to lawsuits or affirmative action programs (see Chapter 2)—women's earnings were farther behind men's in 1976 than in 1969. The continuing wide earnings gap is very evident in Figure 12-1. (Unless otherwise indicated, data in this section are from U.S. Department of Labor, Women's Bureau, 1976a.)

Minority women and single women have gained relative to other female groups during most of the postwar period. Orley Ashenfelter (1970) found that the earnings gap

Table 12-1.   Median Earnings of Full-Time Year-Round Workers, By Sex, 1955–1976

| Year | Median Earnings | | Women's Median Earnings as Percentage of Men's |
	Women	Men	
1955	$2719	$4252	63.9
1956	2827	4466	63.3
1957	3008	4713	63.8
1958	3102	4927	63.0
1959	3193	5209	61.3
1960	3293	5417	60.8
1961	3351	5644	59.4
1962	3446	5794	59.5
1963	3561	5978	59.6
1964	3690	6195	59.6
1965	3823	6375	60.0
1966	3973	6848	58.0
1967	4150	7182	57.8
1968	4457	7664	58.2
1969	4977	8227	60.5
1970	5323	8966	59.4
1971	5593	9399	59.5
1972	5903	10,202	57.9
1973	6335	11,186	56.6
1974	6772	11,835	57.2
1975	7504	12,758	58.8
1976	8099	13,455	60.2

Note: Data for 1967–1974 are not strictly comparable with those for prior years, which are for wage and salary income only and do not include earnings of self-employed persons.
    Data from U.S. Department of Labor, Women's Bureau, 1976a, p. 6.

between Black women and White women narrowed steadily between 1950 and 1966. This gap has continued to narrow. In 1960 minority women earned, on the average, 70% as much as White women. By 1974 minority women's earnings were 94% as high as the earnings of White women. The earnings of minority women also drew closer to minority men's earnings during this period, rising from 63% of the men's earnings in 1960 to 73% in 1973.

The earnings of single women are closer to those of single men, and the difference narrowed during the 1960s. In 1959 White women who had never married earned 81% as much as men of comparable age, schooling, and marital status. By 1969 this ratio had increased to 86%. A major reason for this comparatively high female/male wage ratio is that males who have never married earn considerably less, on the average, than other males (Fuchs, 1974).

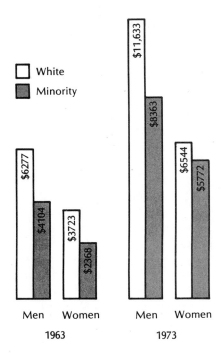

Figure 12-1. In the United States, fully employed women continue to earn less than fully employed men of either White or minority races. ("Minority" includes all races other than White.) (From U.S. Department of Labor, Women's Bureau, 1974.)

Explanations for the Earnings Gap

Economic Theories

Not surprisingly, the earnings gap has attracted considerable attention among economists. Empirical studies have dealt with various aspects of the wage differentials. There have also been efforts to develop a comprehensive theoretical explanation for the higher male earnings. Most of the theoretical approaches can be grouped into a few general categories, outlined briefly below. (For a more thorough discussion of the various theories, and references to the major studies, see Blau & Jusenius, 1976; Stevenson, 1978.)

Lower Productivity. In general, the more productive a worker is, the more valuable he or she is to an employer and to society. If a market system operates efficiently, more productive workers earn more. Economists stressing productivity differences point out that one way workers can increase their productivity is by "investing" in their own "human capital"—through acquiring special job skills, more education, or valuable on-the-job experience. On the average, men in the labor force have built up a higher stock of human capital than women.

Occupational Crowding.   This theory is based on the fact, discussed in Chapter 11, that most women continue to seek jobs in the traditionally female occupations. In many of these occupations the demand for workers has not kept pace with the influx of new jobseekers. The effect of this excess supply is to keep wages from rising as fast as in other, less crowded occupations. Male workers may benefit from these conditions. Since women are *not* crowding into traditionally male job areas, wages in those fields are more likely to rise.

Dual Labor Markets.   This approach, used at first to explain racial wage gaps, also begins with occupations divided into two different categories. It assumes that there is limited access to "primary" jobs (managerial jobs, for example), and such jobs are typified by high wages and good advancement opportunities. "Secondary" jobs (such as clerical work) have much more open access—but also much lower wages and limited advancement opportunities. Secondary jobs contain a higher proportion of women (and minorities) than do primary jobs. One reason given for this is that employers are reluctant to hire women for primary jobs because they believe that women are less likely to stay with the firm for many years. (Chapter 11 pointed out the inaccuracy of this belief.) Radical economists see such segmented labor markets as means by which employers maintain their own superior positions and limit the aspirations and solidarity of workers.

Figure 12-2.The woman on the left is one of the few female U.S. astronauts; the woman on the right is one of the few female carpenters in the United States. Male-intensive professions such as these pay far more than most female-intensive occupations. (Left photo courtesy of Stanford University; right photo © by The Courier Journal and Louisville Times Co.)

Discrimination.   Hiring the most productive workers, regardless of sex (or race), should increase a firm's profit. Thus, economists have felt the need to explain why there is substantial evidence of employment discrimination in our profit-oriented economy. One theory suggests that men often gain psychic satisfaction from maintaining economic or social superiority over women. Therefore, even if women are equally productive, an employer (or personnel director or male co-workers) may feel a loss of prestige or other satisfaction when women are employed in any but subservient positions. In such a situation women will tend to be hired only for the subservient positions (which carry lower wages), or they may be hired in the more advanced positions but paid lower wages than men, to compensate for the psychic costs they are inflicting on the firm or its personnel. An alternative theory suggests that firms may pay all women workers lower wages than men because they believe that the average woman is a less stable employee.

Economists are far from agreement on any of these theoretical approaches to the earnings gap. There is some empirical evidence to support each, but no single theory has been able to account for the whole difference between the earnings of men and of women. In some ways, the approaches complement each other. For example, inadequate education or training (which may be due to discriminatory treatment) may not only lower the productivity of women but also leave them few alternatives except to crowd into the traditional female occupations. Similarly, the dual labor market analysis includes discriminatory hiring and promotion practices.

The theoretical approaches identify various factors that help account for women's lower earnings. These include wage discrimination, productivity differences, and occupational differences. Let us look at each of these factors.

Wage Discrimination

Wage discrimination can be defined as "the payment of higher wages to men than to equally qualified women, holding (or performing) the same job" (Cohen, 1971, p. 435). Individual case histories and court settlements show that wage discrimination does occur. Studies suggest that one-quarter or more of the earnings gap may result from such discrimination (U.S. President, Council of Economic Advisors, 1973, p. 106; Bergmann & Adelman, 1973; Sanborn, 1964).

As noted earlier, discrimination sometimes plays a part in other earnings-gap factors as well. For example, state laws limiting the number of hours women may work have kept many women from earning overtime pay. There is also ample evidence that sex biases have barred women from many jobs and training programs and limited their advancement opportunities. Nevertheless, discrimination is still only part of the wage-gap story. Let us turn now to some other explanatory factors.

Productivity Factors

As noted earlier, workers' wages reflect, in part, their productivity. A member of the labor force becomes more productive by working longer, harder, or more efficiently; by combining his or her labor with highly productive machinery; by having better training or education; or by acquiring on-the-job expertise that increases the worker's value to an employer. Among the productivity factors relevant to women's lower wages are the hours worked by men and women, differences in their work experience, and differences in the educational attainments of men and women.

Differences in Hours Worked.   Among year-round full-time workers, women work about 10% fewer hours than men do. This difference reflects a combination of elements. Personal choice plays a part. So do laws and practices limiting working hours for women, but not for men. Perhaps most important is the fact that men are much more likely to hold the jobs that provide overtime work.

Working more hours ordinarily results in higher earnings. It has been estimated that this accounts for about six percentage points in the earnings gap (U.S. President, Council of Economic Advisors, 1973, p. 103). In other words, if men and women had worked for the same number of hours in 1976, that year's female/male earnings ratio would have been 66%, instead of 60%.

Differences in Work Experience.   One major difference in typical male and female work experience is in their work continuity. After leaving school, most men remain continually in the labor force until retirement. A very large percentage of working women withdraw from the labor force for brief or extended periods. Thus, at any given age men will have built up more work experience than women.

This lack of continuity works to the disadvantage of women in several ways. For one, women will tend to be promoted later in life; therefore they will have fewer remaining work years in which to receive a relatively high income. Women who work for several years, leave the labor force to raise a family, and then reenter after an absence of perhaps 15 years will ordinarily find their earlier labor force experience discounted by employers. They will also have lost their seniority standing. Work skills and knowledge of the field usually suffer as well. All of these developments tend to reduce women's earning power.

Obviously, a temporary departure from the labor force will be more costly to women in some jobs than in others. The Council of Economic Advisors' (CEA) 1973 report gives some indication of the dollar effect. The Labor Department had been studying a group of working women over a period of several years. The CEA focused on the women in this group who worked full time year round in 1966 and who were then between 30 and 44 years old. Nearly 50% of these women had worked fewer than half of the years since leaving school, and their median 1966 income was $3655. Women who had been in the labor force continuously had median earnings of $5618 that year. Men in the same age group working full time had median earnings of $7529 (U.S. President, Council of Economic Advisors, 1973, pp. 104–105).

The lower earnings pattern of the first group of women resulted from more than their interrupted work experience. Women who leave the labor force are in lower-salaried occupations, on the whole. Women in better-paid occupations or in occupations affording real opportunities for advancement tend to be more reluctant to leave the labor force.

Many of them would consider the loss of earnings and opportunities to be greater than the benefits of staying home for several years.

Women who expect their work life to be interrupted for child rearing almost inevitably wind up in low-paying jobs. As Solomon Polachek (1975) notes, they are not likely to invest time, money, and effort to acquire the skills, education, and experience necessary to prepare them for jobs that will, in turn, be costly to interrupt. As a result, the jobs they do enter, and later return to, pay rather poorly. Thus, so long as society views child rearing as primarily the mother's responsibility, women's average earnings will tend to remain low.

Although many married women will continue to interrupt their labor force participation, these interruptions are becoming shorter and less common. Figure 11-3 showed that today a larger proportion of women than in earlier decades remain in the labor force during their child-rearing years. Along the same line, a recent government study compared the past experience of mothers now 40 to 44 years of age with that of mothers in the 30-to-40-year age bracket. The younger generation tended to return to the labor force more quickly following the birth of their first child (U.S. Department of Labor, Women's Bureau, 1975a, p. 60).

Differences in Education.   The education level of both male and female workers has been increasing for decades, but at different rates. Throughout the 1940s and 1950s the typical female worker had considerably more schooling than the typical male worker. In 1940 the average working woman had finished 11 years of school, compared to 8.6 years for men. In that year 51% of working women and 36% of working men had a high school education or better. During the 1960s this educational difference decreased. It finally disappeared in 1970, when 12.4 years was the average education level for both female and male workers (Deutermann, 1970, 1972). By 1977 the average had risen to 12.6 for both males and females in the labor force.

In 1940 a higher percentage of female than male workers had completed either high school or college. In 1977 female workers still were more likely to have completed high school, but a higher percentage of male workers had received college degrees. These trends reflect the steady gain in male educational levels. They are also due to the influx of women of all educational backgrounds into the labor force. Women's share of college and graduate degrees has been rising. As a result, among younger members of the labor force, women are almost as likely as men to have completed four years of college or more.

When we look at individual occupations, educational differences increase. In lower-status jobs, women tend to be as well educated or even better educated than their male counterparts. However, in many higher-status occupations this is not the case. For example, Oppenheimer (1970) found that men in elementary and secondary teaching, and male professionals in general, averaged about one-half year more of schooling than the women. Surveying women in management, Basil (1972) found that male managers were nearly twice as likely to have earned bachelor's or graduate degrees.

A number of sources, including Basil, indicate that these educational differences contribute significantly to the lower job levels and earnings of women in the business world. Salaries are more nearly equal when educations are similar. Richard Mancke (1971), for example, compared starting salaries of men and women receiving master's degrees in business administration from the University of Chicago in 1970 (a small and not necessarily representative sample). He found that the women's starting salaries averaged 90% or 94% of the men's, depending on marital status. This is a much smaller salary difference than we find for managers as a whole.

A college education does raise a woman's earning power, but on the average only to about the level of a male high school graduate. Figure 12-3 illustrates the relative "return on education" for men and women who were full-time, year-round workers in 1971— that is, the average earnings associated with different levels of education. The "return on education," in dollars earned, is clearly much higher for men. One reason is that a college-educated woman is likely to wind up in a less well paid occupation than a college-educated man.

Occupational Differences

Differences between Occupations.   We have already established that over half of all women workers are employed in predominantly female occupations. We need only compare a list of female-intensive occupations—secretary, nurse, waitress, teacher, tele-

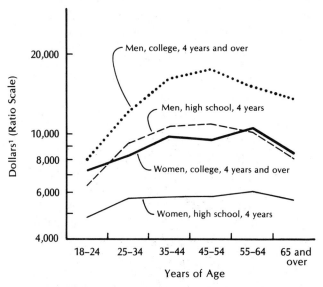

[1]Median income of full-time, year-round workers, 1971.

Figure 12-3.   Annual income, by age, for male and female high school and college graduates. (From U.S. President, Council of Economic Advisors, 1973, p. 105.)

phone operator—with a list of male-intensive occupations—doctor, engineer, business manager, steelworker, electrician—to see that the types of occupations in which most women work help explain their lower incomes.

Oppenheimer (1970, pp. 100–101) provides some interesting evidence of low earnings. She examined 25 professional and clerical occupations in which (a) the majority of the workers were female and (b) the workers had more schooling than the average for the male labor force. In every case, from bookkeepers and stenographers to elementary teachers and dietitians, women's earnings were substantially below the average for the male labor force.

Oppenheimer also found that, in every occupation she examined, the average earnings of women were lower than those of men. Let us look next at these differences within occupations.

Differences within Occupations. Not only are women likely to work in lower-paid occupations, they also earn less than men in the same occupation. In fact, Polachek (1975) has calculated that there are substantially larger male/female wage gaps within occupations than between occupations (p. 118). Different starting salaries for male and female business graduates already have been mentioned. In the study referred to above, Oppenheimer found that male dancers, dietitians, librarians, nurses, social workers, elementary teachers, bank tellers, bookkeepers, file clerks, receptionists, secretaries, typists, telephone operators, and cashiers had higher average incomes than females in the same occupations.

Part of the explanation for the wage gaps, Oppenheimer suggests, lies in the higher-status positions held by men within every occupation. However, even when jobs are examined at a single status level, women tend to earn less. The Women's Bureau found such differences in many nonprofessional jobs. As one example, Table 12-2 shows the lower wages paid to women in the wood furniture industry. Similarly, men working in textile mills and shirt manufacturing plants earned more per hour than women in similar jobs; male insurance underwriters and claim approvers earned substantially more per week (on a straight-time basis) than did their female counterparts; male Class A computer programmers averaged higher weekly salaries than female Class A programmers; waiters earned higher hourly wages than waitresses; and male dishwashers earned more than female dishwashers (U.S. Department of Labor, Women's Bureau, 1969b, p. 155; 1975b, pp. 166–171).

There is, then, ample evidence of women being paid less than men for doing similar work. Some of this wage difference results from discrimination within some individual firms. A greater cause appears to be the concentration of women in low-wage firms. A Bureau of Labor Statistics study (McNulty, 1967) surveyed pay differences for 11 occupations, including payroll clerks, office boys, and elevator operators. The results showed an average 20% male/female wage gap within a job category, but only a 2% wage gap for a given job within the same firm.

Table 12-2.   Number and Average Straight-Time Hourly Earnings[a] of Production Workers in Wood Household Furniture Manufacturing, 1971

| | Metropolitan Areas of United States | | | | Nonmetropolitan Areas | | | |
| | Number of Workers | | Average Hourly Earnings | | Number of Workers | | Average Hourly Earnings | |
Occupation	Women	Men	Women	Men	Women	Men	Women	Men
Assemblers, furniture (except chairs)	1930	4730	$2.32	$2.86	2379	6147	$2.14	$2.35
Assemblers, chairs	177	297	2.06	2.54	194	429	1.85	2.21
Off-bearers, machine	391	1073	2.12	2.22	1047	3398	2.05	2.08
Packers, furniture	475	1134	2.21	2.65	560	1771	2.16	2.19
Rubbers, furniture (hand)	284	229	2.15	2.56	1228	1095	2.03	2.20
Sanders, furniture (hand)	1445	1231	2.25	2.49	2634	1846	2.03	2.21
Sanders, furniture (machine)	500	1812	2.27	2.66	863	3854	2.19	2.35
Sprayers	666	1886	2.50	2.94	918	3433	2.28	2.38

[a] Excludes premium pay for overtime and for work on weekends, holidays, and late shifts.
Data from U.S. Department of Labor, Women's Bureau, 1975b, p. 169.

The Earnings Gap: Some Concluding Comments

At the beginning of this chapter, we observed that women earn 40% less than men do. Estimates suggest that at least one-fourth of this earnings gap is the result of women being paid less than men for the same work. The remainder appears to be due largely to women's concentration in lower-paid occupations and on the lower rungs of professional ladders. Other factors that contribute to the income gap include the greater amount of overtime worked by men, the higher education of men in some professional areas, and the effects of women temporarily leaving the labor force.

As noted above, there are some discriminatory elements in these explanatory factors. Efforts currently being made to reduce this type of discrimination will doubtless help to raise earnings for many women. Nevertheless, a large earnings gap is likely to remain so long as society reinforces traditional views of the female role. Until both the views and the realities of women's roles change, many women will still feel that they have no alternative but to crowd into the traditional occupations and remain in lower-level jobs.

The Importance of Women's Incomes

Female Heads of Families

Nearly half of the women in the labor force today are widowed, divorced, separated, or have never been married. Labor force earnings are the primary source of income for most of these women, many of whom head families.

As of March 1977, about one out of every seven families—including one out of every three minority families—was headed by a woman. This represents nearly 8 million families, two-thirds of them including children under age 18. In fact, one out of every six children now lives in a family headed by a woman (Johnson, 1978). Families headed by women are families in which there is no husband or father. Whenever there is a male relative present, the family is officially classified as male-headed, even if the man is totally disabled and the woman is the sole breadwinner. (The Bureau of Labor Statistics is in the process of eliminating the term "head of family," largely because of this situation.)

The number of families headed by women has been growing very rapidly, primarily as a result of the increasing divorce rate. Most of these families include children. Between 1960 and 1970, the number of female-headed families with children grew ten times as fast as the number of families that included two parents (Sawhill, 1976, p. 201).

Families with female heads are particularly likely to be poor. Their incomes have long averaged less than half that of husband/wife families. The median income for the latter families in 1976 was $16,350; for families headed by women, the median income was $7211. In 1967, 45% of all families headed by women were classified as poor. By 1976, this figure had declined to about 33%, but only 6% of husband/wife families were then below the poverty line. Despite the declining percentages, the number of poverty-level families has been increasing, and virtually the entire numerical increase has been in families with female heads. More than half of all children living in poverty-level families are in families headed by women (Johnson, 1978; Stein, 1970).

More than half of the female family heads work, accounting for 10% of the female labor force. Some of these women certainly have well-paid professional positions. However, by far the majority hold jobs as clerical workers, cleaning women, waitresses, nurses' aides, or garment workers. Therefore, even those female family heads who are in the labor force are likely to have low incomes.

Working Wives and Family Incomes

Working wives contribute substantially to their families' incomes, often making the difference between poverty and lower-middle-class status. In 1971, when the wife did not work, 13% of all families with both husband and wife present had incomes below $4000. Only 4% of husband/wife families with working wives had incomes that low (U.S. Department of Labor, Women's Bureau, 1973).

With both spouses working, many families are better able to satisfy middle-class aspirations. The median 1976 income for husband/wife families with only the husband working was $14,426; with both spouses working, the median rose to $19,080. In 3% of the husband/wife families, the wife was the sole wage earner. The median income for those families was $9296 (Johnson, 1978).

On the average, working wives account for at least one-fourth of their families' income—two-fifths when the wife works full time throughout the year. And 12% of all working wives earn at least half of the family income (U.S. Department of Labor, Women's Bureau, 1976b).

Women's Incomes: Summary

This chapter has documented the relatively low incomes received by women. Largely because of discrimination, weaker labor force attachment, and the types of jobs they hold, women with full-time jobs typically earn only about 60% as much as men do. Still, wage-earning wives make important contributions to their families' income. So, of course, do the millions of women who head families, but their families are still likely to be poor. It continues to be true that the majority of women who live in affluence do so not because they have the opportunity to earn high incomes themselves but because they are wives or daughters of affluent men.

Conclusion

Since 1940, women have joined the labor force in increasing numbers, so that today well over half of those aged 18 to 64 work for at least part of the year. Married women, including those with young children, have made particularly large employment gains. Studies by economists show that higher educational levels, rising wages, and expanding employment opportunities, particularly in traditionally female occupations, are the major factors accounting for this trend.

In addition, the constant increase in the number of working mothers has made marriage plus employment seem a valid adult option for a growing number of daughters. And a combination of social, demographic, and technical changes has made the full-time homemaker's job less satisfying to many women. Economic studies have not included these latter factors, perhaps in part because of the specialist's tendency to concentrate on economic variables, but also because of very real problems in obtaining data that will fit into labor-market studies.

Chapter 11 documented the concentration of working women in a limited number of female-intensive occupations and on the lower rungs of occupational and professional ladders. This, in turn, contributes to women earning, on the average, only 60% as much as men.

The lower earnings and opportunities resulting from the sex-segregation of jobs poses particular problems. This is because, as we have seen, once jobs are sex-labeled they tend to stay that way. As discussed elsewhere in this book, in many subtle ways from early childhood on, the socialization process channels women into the traditional occupations. Elementary teacher, nurse, or secretary are perceived as "normal" career plans for young women. Doctor, engineer, political leader, business manager, or auto mechanic are not. It is likely that the traditionally female occupations seem particularly appropriate to many women because they are consistent with the accepted female sex role. These traditional occupations generally involve helping, nurturing, waiting on others, or extensions of such "womanly" duties as cooking or sewing. An expanding demand for nurses, teachers, and retail and clerical workers has made it easy for women to enter these occupations during most of the postwar period.

Given their socialization and the fact that most women would tend to feel more comfortable and welcome in a "woman's" job, it is hardly surprising that women have responded to this rising demand. Reinforcing these attractions, women have perceived greater barriers to entry into the more financially rewarding "male" occupations. These barriers include discrimination (actual or anticipated), both in the preparatory stages and on the job; the possibility of social disfavor resulting from "unfeminine" ambition; and, in some cases, the need to master subjects in high school, college, or technical school that are believed (particularly by teenagers) to be more appropriate—and easier—for males. Thus, although the potential rewards in many male occupations are higher, the perceived costs or risks tend to be greater for women than for men.

Furthermore, a woman who is married or who expects to marry (and the over-whelming majority of both men and women expect marriage to be part of their lives sooner or later) has to consider the possibility that she will have to fit a full-time homemaker's job into her "leisure" hours, because the division of labor still has not changed much in the typical household. It is also possible that her future career may be interrupted by childbearing demands or by her husband's transfer to a new job location. Such possibilities reduce the potential rewards for women, in comparison with men, since men ordinarily have no need to take account of such factors in their career plans. (The draft has been the only comparable male hazard, and it was usually dealt with before embarking upon a career.)

With perceived costs higher for women and potential rewards possibly lower, the high salaries in the "male" occupations lose a good deal of their luster. Furthermore, some of the traditionally female jobs, such as teaching, part-time clerical work, or dental hygiene, offer hours that combine more readily with family demands or offer greater geographic mobility. Therefore, a very large number of women continue to enter the female occupations. In turn, this large increase in the labor supply helps keep wages in those occupations relatively low.

The same factors have tended to reduce women's upward mobility within most occupations. This is often reinforced by discriminatory advancement procedures and by the socialized tendency for both men and women to expect and accept male leadership. Thus, even in the female-intensive occupations, women are likely to hold lower positions and to earn lower incomes.

What is the outlook for the future? Some changes are already evident. There is increasing feminine awareness of the wide range of vocational options. Equal employment opportunity legislation, executive orders, and judicial decisions are opening career doors that were formerly closed. As a result, a few female coal miners, carpenters, jockeys, and rabbis have been making headlines. Also in the headlines have been the very large back-salary payments that the courts have imposed upon Bell Telephone and other companies found guilty of paying women less than men for similar jobs. Starting salary differentials appear to be narrowing.

Many new elementary school textbooks show women in roles other than mother, teacher, and nurse. There is some evidence that husbands are becoming more supportive of their wives' work and a little more willing to share some housekeeping tasks. And many working wives can now deduct child-care expenses from their federal income taxes.

Although the direction of change is clearly toward greater employment opportunities and equal pay for women, and although there have been impressive individual gains in those areas, nonetheless the overall rate of change appears to be slow. Women are not flooding the medical schools, nor are corporations suddenly promoting scores of women to highly responsible posts. And most working wives still bear the major family responsibility for housekeeping and child care. Institutions and socialization processes seldom change rapidly.

Women entering the labor force in the next several years should have a particularly strong interest in seeing that these changes continue and accelerate. Several of the female-intensive occupations, such as teaching, will be growing more slowly in the years ahead. Therefore, more women than in past years will need to look in other directions for employment. And nine out of ten women will be seeking employment at some time in their lives.

Finally, let us reconsider the economic position of the full-time homemaker. As indicated earlier, only part of a wife's labor force salary represents a clear economic gain to herself and her family. There are obvious costs such as taxes, commuting, and child care. In addition, we must consider the increased outlays for convenience foods and services, any other reductions in household output, and the loss of leisure time. If the quality of family life has become less satisfying, that should also be taken into account. Often, though, there will be an offsetting entry for the wife's greater job satisfaction.

Some such accounting is often done subjectively. Still, more rational labor force decisions would probably result if the economic contribution of the homemaker were more clearly acknowledged. That should also increase the full-time homemaker's satisfaction with her career. In our society, where success is so widely measured in dollars, the lack of pay tends to make a job seem less important, in the eyes of both the jobholder and society in general.

Minor improvements—both practical and symbolic—appear feasible. In some European countries, full-time homemakers have their own social security accounts, and there have been proposals to begin a similar program here. Another European innovation is not counting a wife as a personal exemption on her husband's income tax return. Instead, the wife receives the equivalent amount each year (it would be $750 in the United States) in a "housewife's allowance" check from the government. Including an estimated value of homemakers' annual output of goods and services in our Gross National Product would be another small but significant step toward properly evaluating and rewarding their economic contributions.

Nevertheless, until society is ready to define men's and women's roles more broadly, most women are unlikely to experience substantial improvements in their economic status, either in the home or in the labor force.

Points to Ponder

The following quotations make some thought-provoking points about women's work, at home and in the labor force.

Recently the following want ad appeared in *Ms.* magazine:

HELP WANTED. REQUIREMENTS. Intelligence, good health, energy, patience, sociability. Skills: at least 12 different occupations. HOURS. 99.6 per week. SALARY. None. HOLIDAYS. None (will be required to remain on stand-by 24 hours a day, 7 days a week). OPPORTUNITIES FOR ADVANCEMENT. None (limited transferability of skills acquired on the job). JOB SECURITY. None (trend is toward more layoffs, particularly as employee approaches middle age; severance pay will depend on the discretion of the employer). FRINGE BENEFITS. Food, clothing, and shelter generally provided, but any additional bonuses will depend on financial standing and good nature of the employer. . . .

Absurd? But true. This is a fairly accurate summary of the job of a full-time housewife [Chester & Goodman, 1976, p. 102].

Common parlance uses the term *independent income* quite differently for men than for women. We describe a man's profession or job, and if we refer to his independent income we always mean inherited wealth or property income of some kind. "John Jones can pursue his hobby of collecting eighteenth-century snuff boxes because he enjoys an independent income from his holding of oil stocks." But if we speak about Mrs. John Jones and her independent income we mean that she has money of her own, aside from her husband's support. . . . To be economically independent, for a man, means not to have to work for a living; for a woman, not to need a husband for support [Bell, 1977, p. 34].

While some women are insisting that career patterns of women be made as nearly like those of men as possible, there are others who are asking if this is not actually just one more illustration of sexism? Is this not accepting the male pattern as the standard against which to judge all patterns? [Bernard, 1971, p. 192.]

In speaking of men, the question, "Why do they work?" seems odd indeed. Men work because they must. Women holding blue-collar and service jobs also work because they must [Baker, 1978, pp. 343–344].

The woman who looks about her today, at the increasing divorce rates, at the abandoned wives and children, at the high number of women and children on welfare, at the high rate of inflation gnawing away at incomes and savings, is likely to realize that the most valuable gift she can bestow on her daughters is the gift of career opportunity [Griffiths, 1976, p. 154].

References

Sources of particular interest to the reader are marked with an asterisk.

Abbott, E. *Women in industry.* New York: Appleton, 1910.

Alexander, R., & Sapery, E. *The shortchanged: Minorities and women in banking.* New York: Dunellen, 1973.

All-woman Hardin bank is old news. *Kentucky Business Ledger,* March 1977, p. 1.

Ashenfelter, O. Changes in labor market discrimination over time. *Journal of Human Resources,* 1970, 5, 403–430.

Baker, S. H. Women in blue-collar and service occupations. In A. H. Stromberg & S. Harkess (Eds.), *Women working.* Palo Alto, Calif.: Mayfield, 1978.

Baruch, G. K. Maternal influences upon college women's attitudes toward women and work. *Developmental Psychology,* 1972, 6, 32–37.

*Basil, D. C. *Women in management.* New York: Dunellen, 1972.

*Baxandall, R., Gordon, L., & Reverby, S. (Eds.). *America's working women: A documentary history.* New York: Vintage Books, 1976.

Becker, G. S. A theory of the allocation of time. *Economic Journal,* 1965, *75,* 493–517.

Bell, C. S. Economics, sex, and gender. In N. Glazer & H. Y. Waehrer (Eds.), *Woman in a man-made world* (2nd ed.). Chicago: Rand McNally, 1977.

Bergmann, B. R., & Adelman, I. The economic role of women. *American Economic Review,* 1973, *63,* 509–514.

Bernard, J. *Women and the public interest.* Chicago: Aldine-Atherton, 1971.

Blau, F. D., & Jusenius, C. L. Economists' approaches to sex segregation in the labor market: An appraisal. In M. Blaxall & B. Reagan (Eds.), *Women and the workplace.* Chicago: University of Chicago Press, 1976.

* Blaxall, M., & Reagan, B. (Eds.). *Women and the workplace: The implications of occupational segregation.* Chicago: University of Chicago Press, 1976.

* Boserup, E. *Women's role in economic development.* New York: St. Martin's Press, 1970.

Boskin, M. J. The effects of government expenditures and taxes on female labor. *American Economic Review,* 1974, *64,* 251–256.

* Bowen, W. G., & Finegan, T. A. *The economics of labor force participation.* Princeton, N.J.: Princeton University Press, 1969.

Bowman, G. W., Worthy, N. B., & Greyser, S. A. Are women executives people? *Harvard Business Review,* 1965, *43,* 14–28.

Business and Professional Women's Association. *Women executives: A selected annotated bibliography.* Washington, D.C.: 1970.

Cain, G. *Married women in the labor force.* Chicago: University of Chicago Press, 1966.

Chesler, P., & Goodman, E. J. *Women, money & power.* New York: Morrow, 1976.

Clark, C. The economics of housework. *Bulletin of the Oxford Institute of Statistics,* 1958, *20,* 205–211.

Cohen, M. S. Sex differences in compensation. *Journal of Human Resources,* 1971, *6,* 434–447.

Deutermann, W. Educational attainments of workers, March 1969 and 1970. *Monthly Labor Review,* October 1970, pp. 9–16.

Deutermann, W. Educational attainment of workers, March 1972. *Monthly Labor Review,* November 1972, pp. 38–42.

Durand, J. D. *The labor force in the United States, 1890–1960.* New York: Social Science Research Council, 1948.

* Epstein, C. F. Encountering the male establishment: Sex-status limits on women's careers in the professions. *American Journal of Sociology,* 1970, *75,* 965–982.

Eyde, L. D. *Work values and background factors as predictors of women's desire to work.* Columbus: Ohio State University, Bureau of Business Research, 1962.

Fair, R. C. Labor force participation, wage rates, and money illusion. *Review of Economics and Statistics,* 1971, *53,* 164–168.

Fuchs, V. R. Short-run and long-run prospects for female earnings. *American Economic Review,* 1974, *64,* 236–242.

Gage, M. G. *The work load and its value for 50 homemakers, Tompkins County, New York.* Unpublished doctoral dissertation, Cornell University, Ithaca, N.Y., 1960.

* Gauger, W. Household work: Can we add it to the GNP? *Journal of Home Economics,* 1973, *65,* 12–15.

Greckel, F. R. *Trends in occupational sex-segregation.* Paper presented at the meeting of the Midwest Economics Association, Chicago, April 1978.

* Griffiths, M. W. Requisites for equality. In J. M. Kreps (Ed.), *Women and the American economy.* Englewood Cliffs, N.J.: Prentice-Hall, 1976.

Gronau, R. The effect of children on housewife's value of time. *Journal of Political Economy*, 1973, *81* (Part II), S168–S199.

*Hedges, J. Women workers and manpower demands in the 1970s. *Monthly Labor Review*, June 1970, pp. 19–29.

*Howe, L. K. *Pink collar workers: Inside the world of women's work.* New York: Putnam's, 1977.

*Johnson, B. L. Women who head families, 1970–1977: Their numbers rose, income lagged. *Monthly Labor Review*, February 1978, pp. 32–37.

*Kreps, J. M. *Sex in the marketplace: American women at work.* Baltimore: Johns Hopkins Press, 1971.

*Kreps, J. M., & Leaper, R. J. Home work, market work, and the allocation of time. In J. M. Kreps (Ed.), *Women and the American economy.* Englewood Cliffs, N.J.: Prentice-Hall, 1976.

Kropf, E. Careers for women in banking. *Journal of Business Education*, 1969, *45*, 28.

Kuznets, S. *National income and its composition.* New York: National Bureau of Economic Research, 1941.

Lapin, E. *Mothers in overalls.* New York: Workers Library Publication, 1943.

Leibowitz, A. Education and home production. *American Economic Review*, 1974, *64*, 243–250.

*Leibowitz, A. Women's work in the home. In C. B. Lloyd (Ed.), *Sex, discrimination, and the division of labor.* New York: Columbia University Press, 1975.

Long, C. D. *The labor force under changing income and employment.* National Bureau of Economic Research. Princeton, N.J.: Princeton University Press, 1958.

Mahoney, T. A. Factors determining the labor force participation of married women. *Industrial and Labor Relations Review*, 1961, *14*, 563–577.

Mancke, R. B. Lower pay for women: A case of economic discrimination? *Industrial Relations*, 1971, *10*, 316–326.

McNulty, D. J. Differences in pay between men and women workers. *Monthly Labor Review*, December 1967, pp. 40–43.

Michelotti, K. Educational attainment of workers, March 1977. *Monthly Labor Review*, December 1977, pp. 53–57.

Mincer, J. Labor force participation of married women: A study of labor supply. In National Bureau of Economic Research, *Aspects of labor economics.* Princeton, N.J.: Princeton University Press, 1962.

Morgan, J. N., David, M. H., Cohen, W. J., & Brazier, H. E. *Income and welfare in the United States.* New York: McGraw-Hill, 1962.

Mullineaux, D. J. An economic approach to family size: A new perspective on population growth. Federal Reserve Bank of Philadelphia, *Business Review*, January/February 1976, pp. 3–12.

*National Manpower Council. *Womanpower.* New York: Columbia University Press, 1957.

*Oppenheimer, V. K. *The female labor force in the United States* (Population Monograph Series, No. 5). Berkeley: University of California, Institute of International Studies, 1970.

O'Riley, J. The outlook: Review of current trends in business and finance. *The Wall Street Journal*, September 20, 1976, p. 1.

Perrella, V. C. Women and the labor force. *Monthly Labor Review*, February 1968, pp. 1–12.

Pigou, A. C. *The economics of welfare.* London: Macmillan, 1946.

Polachek, S. W. Discontinuous labor force participation and its effect on women's market earnings. In C. B. Lloyd (Ed.), *Sex, discrimination, and the division of labor.* New York: Columbia University Press, 1975.

Reid, M. *Economics of household production.* New York: Wiley, 1934.

Reid, M. The economic contribution of homemakers. *The Annals of the American Academy of Political and Social Science*, May 1947, pp. 61–69.

Sanborn, H. Pay differences between men and women. *Industrial and Labor Relations Review*, 1964, 17, 534–550.

*Sawhill, I. Discrimination and poverty among women who head families. In M. Blaxall & B. Reagan (Eds.), *Women and the workplace*. Chicago: University of Chicago Press, 1976.

Shamseddine, A. H. *Expansion of imputations in national income and product accounts with a case study on the value of housewives' services in the United States*. Unpublished doctoral dissertation, George Washington University, Washington, D.C., 1968.

Sirageldin, I. A. *Non-market components of national income*. Ann Arbor: University of Michigan, Institute for Social Research, 1969.

Smuts, R. W. The female labor force: A case study in the interpretation of historical statistics. *Journal of the American Statistical Association*, 1960, 55, 71–79.

Stein, R. L. The economic status of families headed by women. *Monthly Labor Review*, December 1970, pp. 3–7.

Stevenson, M. H. Wage differences between men and women. In A. H. Stromberg & S. Harkess (Eds.), *Women working*. Palo Alto, Calif.: Mayfield, 1978.

*Stromberg, A. H., & Harkess, S. *Women working: Theories and facts in perspective*. Palo Alto, Calif.: Mayfield, 1978.

*Trey, J. E. Women in the war economy. *Review of Radical Political Economics*, 1972, 4(3), 40–57.

*U.S. Department of Health, Education, and Welfare, Social Security Administration. Economic value of a housewife. *Research and Statistics Notes*, Publication No. 75-11701, Note No. 9. Washington, D.C.: U.S. Government Printing Office, 1975.

U.S. Department of Labor, Bureau of Labor Statistics. *The employment situation: October 1975*. Mimeo News Release, USDL 75-627, Washington, D.C.: 1975. (a)

U.S. Department of Labor, Bureau of Labor Statistics. *U.S. working women: A chartbook* (Bulletin 1880). Washington, D.C.: U.S. Government Printing Office, 1975. (b)

U.S. Department of Labor, Women's Bureau. *Facts about women's absenteeism and labor turn-over*. Washington, D.C.: U.S. Government Printing Office, 1969. (a)

U.S. Department of Labor, Women's Bureau. *1969 handbook on women workers* (Bulletin 294). Washington, D.C.: U.S. Government Printing Office, 1969. (b)

U.S. Department of Labor, Women's Bureau. *Women workers today*. Washington, D.C.: U.S. Government Printing Office, 1973.

U.S. Department of Labor, Women's Bureau. *Marital status of women in the labor force, March 1973–74* (mimeo tables). Washington, D.C.: 1974.

* U.S. Department of Labor, Women's Bureau. *1975 handbook on women workers* (Bulletin 297). Washington, D.C.: U.S. Government Printing Office, 1975. (a)

U.S. Department of Labor, Women's Bureau. *Why women work*. Washington, D.C.: U.S. Government Printing Office, 1975. (b)

*U.S. Department of Labor, Women's Bureau. *The earnings gap between women and men*. Washington, D.C.: 1976. (a)

* U.S. Department of Labor, Women's Bureau. *Women workers today*. Washington, D.C.: 1976. (b)

U.S. Department of Labor, Women's Bureau. Unpublished data. Washington, D.C., 1979.

* U.S. President, Council of Economic Advisors. *Economic report of the President*. Washington, D.C.: U.S. Government Printing Office, 1973.

*Vanek, J. *Keeping busy: Time spent in housework, United States, 1920–1970.* Unpublished doctoral dissertation, University of Michigan, Ann Arbor, 1973.

Walker, K. E., & Gauger, W. H. *The dollar value of household work* (Information Bulletin 60). Ithaca, N.Y.: Cornell University, New York State College of Human Ecology, 1973.

Wallace, P. Sex discrimination. In E. Ginzberg & A. M. Yohalem (Eds.), *Corporate lib: Women's challenge to management.* Baltimore: Johns Hopkins Press, 1973.

Woody, T. *A history of women's education in the United States* (Vol. 2). New York: Octagon Books, 1966.

*Zaretsky, E. Capitalism, the family, and personal life. In N. Glazer & H. Y. Waehrer (Eds.), *Woman in a man-made world* (2nd ed.). Chicago: Rand McNally, 1977.

SECTION FIVE

THE
POLITICAL ROLES
OF
AMERICAN WOMEN

Linda Carstarphen Gugin

As noted in Section 1, some groups within the women's movement have sought to expand the participation of women in the political process. The women who advocate the goal of increased political participation by women are reacting, in part, to the fact that in all areas of political life women as a group are less active than men. The limited activity by females is especially noticeable in the area of public officeholding. Female officeholders are always the exception, never the rule.

Some people, both men and women, see the limited political role of women as the proper and natural order of things. These individuals accept the traditional assignment of wife, mother, and homemaker roles to women, and they believe that a political role for women conflicts with their more traditional roles. Some are concerned that the stability and moral fiber of our society will be threatened or undermined if women in large numbers "abandon their homes and families" to pursue political careers.

Other groups of people, especially feminists, view limited female participation as a deplorable state of affairs. They advocate an increased role for women in politics for several reasons. Some argue that there is a need for equality between the sexes—that if women make up over half of the population, then they should hold at least half of the official positions of power within society. Another argument concerns equal opportunity—that women ought to have the same access to political power as men do. Advocates of this view maintain that to limit women's chances to exercise power limits not only their political rights, but also their opportunity for personal development and fulfillment. Then there are those individuals who want to see more women in politics because they see women as more virtuous and moral, or less self-serving, than men. Finally, there are those who believe that women would make better public policies. They believe that adequate laws pertaining to women's rights and opportunities will not be passed and implemented until more women hold public office. They also believe that a greater role for women in policymaking will result in more humanistic types of public policy and less emphasis on war and military strength.

This section, devoted to the political roles of U.S. women, does not address itself directly to any of these beliefs and assumptions about the proper roles of women or the consequences that may result if women do or do not increase their political participation. However, it does offer information and ideas that may be relevant to such beliefs and assumptions and that may help the reader draw his or her own conclusions about these matters. The specific purpose of this section is to examine the roles that women do have in American politics and to consider explanations for the particular nature of those roles.

In examining the political roles of women in American politics, this analysis will seek to answer three broad questions:

- In what forms of political participation do women engage, and to what extent?
- What are the characteristics of women who do participate?
- How does their participation compare to that of men in form and degree?

Section opening photo: Bella Abzug, an outspoken political activist, was formerly a Democratic Representative from New York in the U.S. House of Representatives. (Photo © by The Courier Journal and Louisville Times Co.)

This analysis of women's roles in American politics emphasizes official and formal political roles and activities. The chapters in this section deal with participation in three areas: (1) voting and expression of public opinion; (2) political party and interest group involvement; and (3) holding public office. Participation by women is greater, as it is with men, in the functions of voting and expression of public opinion than in party and interest group activity or in holding public office.

In emphasizing such official and formal political activities as voting, expressing public opinions, participating in parties and interest groups, and holding public office, we do not mean to ignore or deny the possibility that women exert political influence in roles, such as wife and mother, that are not explicitly political but that may nonetheless have important implications for political behavior. Readers interested in pursuing the topic of the maternal influence on children's political preferences should consult the following sources: Maccoby, Matthews, and Morton (1953); Nogee and Levin (1959); and Jennings and Langton (1969). Studies of wives' impact on their husbands' political behavior include: March (1953); Campbell, Gurin, and Miller (1954); and Steinem (1972).

This is a study about women in U.S. politics. There are only occasional references to women in politics in other countries. Where appropriate, however, some cross-national comparisons have been made. Also, our concern is more contemporary than historical in nature. Historical information has been included only where it offers direct insight into the current status of women in politics.

The particular approach used in this section is not one with which all political scientists agree. For example, feminists within the discipline object to the narrowness of the traditional view of politics employed here. An explanation of the feminist approach to politics and political analysis is offered here to point out to the reader that there are other ways of looking at political questions.

Mary L. Shanley and Victoria Schuck (1974) are two political scientists who have attacked the traditional assumptions of their discipline. Their criticisms are directed not only at early political scientists, but at contemporary ones as well. Early political scientists focused on the description of formal political institutions, such as Congress, the presidency, and the courts. Contemporary political scientists tend to focus on group and individual behavior and thus are called behavioral scientists. Both early and contemporary political scientists, however, have accepted the same definition of *political*—namely, those things that concern public institutions. Whereas the early focus was on the structure and operations of public institutions, the more recent focus has been on the behavior of people within or aspiring to those same institutions. Shanley and Schuck point out the bias of this approach. "To the extent that 'politics' was thought of as the activity of the political elites, politics would be male-dominated activity" (p. 639). The approach used in this section illustrates that point.

"The consequence of this identification, "Shanley and Schuck continue, "has been to make male behavior the standard for 'political' behavior, and to dismiss female activities as non-political and of no interest to political science" (p. 640). Similarly, Nancy McWilliams (1974) has observed that because of the tendency to define politics as an inherently male domain, those areas dominated by females are considered to be nonpolitical. "Thus, for instance, what Jane Addams did in Chicago was not politics but 'social work,' and Margaret Sanger's crusade was not political but 'educational'" (p. 161). McWilliams argues that unless we broaden our definition of the political to include not only the traditional model of competition for power but also such things as values, emotions, and interpersonal experience, "a great many political trends will continue to escape academic notice until they are already restructuring our institutions and reformulating our public discourse" (p. 167).

Thus, feminists seek to broaden the definition of the "political" to include what has traditionally been considered as the "personal." In suggesting a feminist strategy of analysis, Jane Jaquette (1976) proposes

> the integration of another very important area of research into feminist political analysis—the "politics of everyday life" or the arena of personal interactions. . . . Here I am talking about research such as small group studies of male and female communication styles and how they are perceived by others, nonverbal communication, . . . [research] analyzing roles of women and men in long-term dyadic relationships, and recent research on mixed-sex consciousness raising groups [p. 163].

Jaquette cites examples of each type of research in her article.

One can see how the feminist approach to and definition of *political* differs from that used in this section. The more traditional approach is used here for practical as well as personal-interest reasons. Since the traditional approach is the one that has been applied the longest and the most frequently, much more information is available from those studies. Conversely, because the feminist approach is newly emerging within the discipline, data from these studies are neither so extensive nor so accessible. Many of the studies have been presented at professional meetings, but only a small portion have been published. Citations for some of these studies, both published and unpublished, can be found in Jaquette (1976), Shanley and Schuck (1974), and McWilliams (1974).

TURNING OUT AND SPEAKING UP

CHAPTER·
13

The political participation of most citizens, whether male or female, does not extend beyond the activities of voting and expressing views on public issues. Political scientists have shown a great deal of interest in electoral behavior and public opinion, and there are great quantities of data about these types of political activities. These citizen roles derive their importance from the value we place on democratic government. The theory of democratic government rests on the assumption that citizens will keep informed and participate in elections and thus hold public officials accountable to the people. This assumption has not always proven correct, as citizens often tend to be apathetic and ill informed about political affairs.

Four significant questions can be raised about the nature and extent of participation by women in elections and about the views they hold on public issues:

- Is the level of voting turnout by women substantially different from that of men?
- Do women have marked preferences for a particular political party?
- Do women have a preference for a particular type of candidate?
- Do the attitudes of women about public issues differ from those of men?

These questions will be answered primarily in the context of national rather than state or local elections because electoral studies have focused on national elections far more frequently.

Level of Turnout among Women

The term *turnout* refers to the number of people who vote in any given election. The rate of turnout in the United States is measured according to the number of eligible voters who actually vote in a particular election. Current statistics show women voting at about the same rate as men.

This has not always been the case. In 1920—the year that the 19th Amendment, which prohibited denying the right to vote on the basis of sex, was passed—approximately 43% of the eligible women voted. In 1924, the figure dropped to 35%. By 1940, the percentage of eligible women voting had risen to 49%, compared to 68% for men (Gruberg, 1968). The authors of *The American Voter* (Campbell, Converse, Miller, & Stokes, 1960), a landmark study of the 1952 and 1956 presidential elections, reported that the participation rate of women was approximately 10% below that of men.

Since 1960, when the difference was about 11% (Lansing, 1974), the gap between the sexes has steadily narrowed. According to the U.S. Bureau of the Census, which conducts a survey of voter participation after each national election, the difference between male and female voting was 4.7% in 1964, 3.8% in 1968, 2.1% in 1972, and less than 1% in 1976. The level of turnout was 59.6% for men and 58.8% for women in the 1976 election (U.S. Bureau of the Census, 1965, 1969, 1973, 1977).

The phenomenon of lower turnout for women has been found in other countries as well as the United States. Maurice Duverger's (1955) study of voting patterns in France, Germany, Norway, and Yugoslavia found that a higher proportion of women than men failed to vote. Jean Blondel (1963) found that the same was true of British voters.

Explanations for Lower Turnout among Women

Political scientists have offered several reasons for the historical differences in turnout between men and women. Campbell and his associates (1960) attribute the differences between the participation rates of men and women to such cultural factors as "vestigial sex roles." They argue that in earlier times sex roles in politics were clear-cut, with the men tending to political matters for the family and the women tending to household matters. Although these roles are becoming less distinct today, nonetheless "social roles are deeply ingrained in day-to-day assumptions about behavior in any culture, and these assumptions are not rapidly uprooted" (p. 484).

Robert Lane (1959) has expanded on the theme of sex roles and participation. He notes that our culture does not reinforce a political image for women: "The media, and also the literary heritage reread by every generation, tend to create images of women in domestic, or, perhaps, artistic and literary or dramatic, or even career roles, but not in political roles" (p. 212). Lane also suggests that an additional factor contributing to lesser involvement is the image of the female vote as a "reform" vote:

> We know that the reform vote is a cyclical phenomenon which has to be kicked off periodically in municipal elections by revelations of new and greater corruption. If it is the matrix of "idealism" which is supposed to bind women to politics—at least as the public sees it—there is little wonder that the binding loosens in many areas. . . . The net effect of this moralistic orientation has been not only to provide an ineffective and relatively "ego-distant" tie with political matters but also as Riesman has remarked to limit attention to the superficial and irrelevant aspects of politics [p. 213].

One may not agree with Lane's characterization of reform issues as the "superficial and irrelevant aspects of politics," but we do know from Section 1 that women historically have expressed concerns about moral issues such as abolition and temperance. We will see later in this section that women continue to express concern with moral issues in politics and that female office-seekers are more likely to specify altruistic reasons for aspiring to public office than are men.

Some of the theories of political socialization, which deal with the acquisition of political beliefs and attitudes by children, suggest other reasons for sex differences in political participation. Political socialization is one dimension of the general process of socialization discussed in Chapter 8. Several political-socialization studies point to differences in the political behavior of boys and girls that occur at early ages. For example, Fred Greenstein (1965) found in a sample of fourth- through eighth-graders in New Haven that boys were better informed about political affairs than girls. A similar study of Illinois students (Orum, Cohen, Grasmuch, & Orum, 1974) in grades 4 through 12 found the same thing. These findings coincide with those reported in Chapter 8 about the literature and mass-media preferences of teenagers. Boys are more likely to select programs with political content and watch news programs more frequently than girls. These differences in media attention and political knowledge and interest between males and females are also found in adults. Public opinion polls indicate that women are less interested in and knowledgeable about politics than men are.

Robert Hess and Judith Torney (1967), whose study included students in grades two through eight, found that boys were about one year ahead of girls in the development of political attitudes. Boys demonstrated greater familiarity with and understanding of political concepts such as citizen's duty or political party, were better able to distinguish between the Republican and Democratic parties on the basis of issues, and gave fewer "don't know" responses. In addition, girls exhibited a greater tendency to personalize government. They were more likely to identify with personal symbols of government, such as the President, while boys were more likely to identify with less personal symbols of government, such as Congress. Girls also see authority figures in more positive terms than boys do. Girls view leaders as more responsive and benevolent. These differences in orientations toward authority are reflected in adult political attitudes also. (For example, see Chapter 14 for a discussion of female teachers' attitudes toward officials of teachers' organizations.)

The sex differences that have been found in political socialization studies are usually not very large, but taken as a whole the findings indicate a more rapid political development for males than for females. These findings are particularly interesting when compared to the findings about the development of males and females presented in Chapter 3. There we find that both mentally and physically, girls tend to develop more rapidly than boys. Yet in the development of their political beliefs and attitudes, boys mature more rapidly.

The implications of these early sex differences for adult behavior are seldom made clear in political socialization studies. The implicit assumption of these studies is that early political socialization does affect adult political behavior, but the direct relationship has not been demonstrated. Some investigators (Orum et al., 1974) have suggested that careers, education, child rearing, and other forces probably have greater impact on the political behavior of women than the way in which they were politically socialized in childhood. Now, let us consider the influence of these other factors.

Factors Affecting Turnout of Individual Women

Several factors have a differential effect on the voting participation of women. These factors can be grouped into two very broad categories: (1) social, economic, and demographic variables; and (2) psychological factors. The first six variables discussed below are in the first category; the last variable is psychological. Although many of these variables are closely related, each is independent of the others to some degree.

Race. The level of participation among Black voters, both male and female, has always been less than among White voters. This is the case not only in the South, but in other areas of the country as well. Up through the 1960s, White males were outvoting Black males, and White females were outvoting Black females. Within each race, men outvoted women, but these differences were greater among Blacks than among Whites. More recent data suggest that the situation may be changing. The U.S. Bureau of the Census (1973) reported that in the 1972 election there were virtually no participation differences between Black men and Black women. For both sexes, the turnout rate among Blacks was 52.1%, compared to 65.6% for White males and 63.4% for White females. Although Black females have increased their voter participation to the point where it is comparable to that of Black males, it still lags behind that of White females. However, Lansing (1977) has observed that the rate of increase in voter turnout among Black women has exceeded that of any other sex/race group in the population.

Education. In 1960, Campbell and his associates observed that the "increase in participation with education is steeper for women than men" (p. 485). With increases in education, that is, voter participation increases much more substantially for women than it does for men. Thus, education seems to even things up between the sexes, as far as voting is concerned. In the Campbell et al. studies, college-educated women were found to vote as often as college-educated men. The same is true today. In 1972, with few exceptions, women with a high school diploma or better outvoted men with comparable education, regardless of race (U.S. Bureau of the Census, 1973).

Employment. Using data from nationwide surveys during the 1954, 1960, and 1964 elections, Morris Levitt (1967) found that working experience has a greater effect on political participation than education. He found that women who work outside the home are more politically involved and have a higher level of participation than those who stay at home. Levitt attributed this increase to widened contacts made through employment. He reasoned that employment provides women with the opportunity to discuss events and share views with fellow employees, giving those who work a keener insight into social problems, which leads in turn to higher interest and turnout rates.

The U.S. Bureau of the Census (1969, 1973) postelection data for 1968 and 1972 confirm that women who are employed have a higher rate of participation than women who are either unemployed or not in the labor force. Unemployed women have the lowest rate of participation among females but a higher rate of participation than unemployed males.

The impact of employment on female political participation has been borne out in a study by Kristi Andersen (1975). According to Andersen, the narrowing of sex differences in political participation from 1952 to 1972 can be attributed to women who are employed outside the home. Their rate of political participation equals that of men. Chapter 11 provides a statistical portrait of women in the labor force and indicates that an increasing number of women are participating in the labor force. Women with preschool children are the least likely to be working; women with young children also have a low turnout rate.

The impact of employment on Black female participation is less clear. According to the U.S. Department of Labor (1976), Black women have a slightly higher labor force participation rate (49%) than White women (46%). (Also see discussion in Chapter 11 on labor force participation of non-White mothers.) Despite these employment statistics, however, Black women vote less than White women.

Donald Matthews and James Prothro (1966), who studied political participation among Southern Blacks, attributed the lower participation by Black women to the double barrier that they had to overcome—that is, the bias against Blacks and the bias against women. Matthews and Prothro also pointed to low levels of education. The authors did observe, however, that Black women who were the heads of families and who worked outside the home had higher participation rates than did wives who were employed and wives who stayed at home. Wives who were employed had a slightly higher participation rate than those who stayed at home. These data are consistent with the pattern of working and voter participation in general.

Age.   Generally, voter participation is low among young people, increases among middle-aged voters, and then decreases among older citizens. For women, participation begins to decline around the age of 55 and decreases more sharply at 65. For men, a slight decline in voter participation begins around the age of 65, with a sharper decline appearing around 75. This pattern was evident in the 1964, 1968, and 1972 presidential elections and appears to be a stable phenomenon. Just why the participation rate for women declines at an earlier age is uncertain. Perhaps it can be attributed to the fact, noted in Chapter 11, that the labor force participation of women declines at about the same age. We have already observed that labor force participation is closely related to voter turnout among women; it follows that as women leave the labor force, their voter turnout will decline. It is ironic in a way that at the time when many women are ceasing to participate in elections, other women are just beginning their political careers. The late age at which women enter public life is discussed in Chapter 15, dealing with women in public office.

Region.   Place of residency is another factor related to male/female participation rates. Sex differences in participation are greater in the South than other parts of the country. The greater sex differential in the South has been attributed to the strength of traditional sex roles there (Gruberg, 1968; Campbell et al., 1960). Census data for the 1968 and 1972 elections indicate that regional differences in male/female voting still exist but are declining. In 1972, sex differences in voting had dwindled to 1% in the North and West and less than 4% in the South. The lower rate of participation among White females in the South accounts for the greater differential in that region (U.S. Bureau of the Census, 1969, 1973).

Differences between urban and rural residence are also related to differences in voting. Campbell and his associates (1960) found that outside the South (the Southern portion of their sample was too small to be subdivided) men voted, on the average, 5% more than women in metropolitan areas, 20% more in towns and cities, and 28% more in villages and rural areas. In 1964, the last presidential election for which the Census Bureau gathered data on participation by each sex according to area of residence, sex differences in voting still remained greater in nonmetropolitan areas, but the difference was only 6%. Since the Bureau did not report the same type of statistics for the 1968 and 1972 presidential elections, it is not possible to determine the stability of this trend.

Marital Status and Parenthood.   Married women have a higher turnout rate than unmarried women. In the 1972 elections, married women with spouses present voted more than married women without spouses present in the home, women who were widowed or divorced, or those who had never married. Only married men with spouses present outvoted married women with spouses present. In all other categories, women outvoted men of the same marital status (U.S. Bureau of the Census, 1973). Since married men vote more than married women, and married women vote more than unmarried women, we might conclude that husbands stimulate their wives to vote. If, however, husbands stimulate their wives to vote, rather than the other way around, how can we explain the fact that women without husbands vote more than men without wives? To answer that, we would have to know more about the characteristics of both men and women who are not married. In the absence of additional data, we can merely speculate. Perhaps the higher turnout rate of married people, both male and female, stems from a reinforcing effect that each spouse has on the other, regardless of who has the higher level of interest. Such a reinforcing effect would not be present for the unmarried individual.

Several studies confirm a relationship between the presence of young children in the home and the level of female voter participation. Campbell and his associates (1960) found almost no sex differences in voting among young single voters or married voters without children, but substantial differences in the participation rates of mothers and fathers of young children. Regardless of age or education level, mothers of young children were far less likely to vote than the fathers of young children.

It is not difficult to understand why motherhood has a negative effect on women's political participation. Chapter 8 discusses the general effects of motherhood on women's lives. They leave their jobs, are more interested in the home, and feel tied down by the

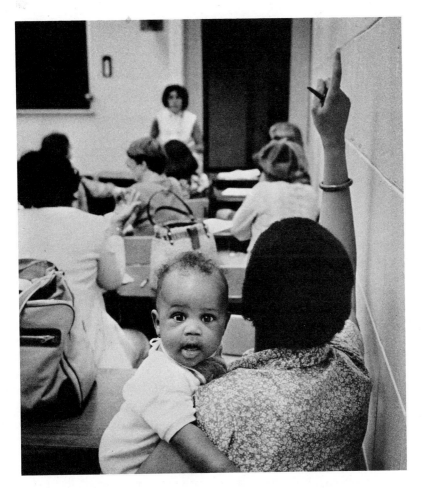

Figure 13-1.   *The primary responsibility for child care accorded to women in our society is one of the greatest obstacles to female political participation. (Photo © by The Courier Journal and Louisville Times Co.)*

responsibilities of child rearing. Certainly, none of these factors would have a positive effect on political participation. Becoming a parent does not affect men's political participation as much as women's because men's participation in the world outside the home is basically unaffected.

Political Efficacy and Civic Responsibility.   In addition to social, economic, and demographic factors, we find that psychological factors have an influence on turnout. In *The American Voter*, Campbell and his associates (1960) note that the stronger the psychological involvement, the more likely the individual will be to vote. Two attitudes that help to determine the voter's psychological involvement are political efficacy and sense of civic responsibility.

The term *political efficacy* refers to the feeling of effectiveness that an individual has in relation to the political system. Those who have a strong sense of political efficacy believe that by participating they can have an influence on governmental affairs. Electoral studies have shown that those who feel effective are more likely to vote. Researchers have found that the sense of political efficacy is stronger among males than among females.

Among women, Levitt (1967) found that both employment and education were related positively to political efficacy, but that work was more important than education in increasing women's sense of efficacy. The presence of young children in the home is associated with a decrease in political efficacy among women. Naomi Lynn and Cornelia Flora (1972) found in a survey of mothers and nonmothers that women without children under the age of 18 had much higher levels of political efficacy than those with young children in the home. This relationship did not seem to be affected by place of residency nor by labor force participation, but it was influenced by socioeconomic status. Women with lower socioeconomic status (SES) had a low sense of political efficacy independent of motherhood. For women of higher SES, who normally have a fairly high level of political efficacy, motherhood decreased this feeling.

In spite of the fact that women feel less effective than men in the political process, they feel almost as strongly as men that they *ought* to vote. Surveys taken during the 1950s found very little difference between male and female attitudes regarding the civic responsibility of voting (Campbell et al., 1960). Levitt (1967) suggests that the problem for women is that they have not been taught to believe that their own participation is worthwhile. They lack the confidence to feel competent. He adds that women who work do not experience this frustration as much as others. Employment increases a woman's sense both of political efficacy and of civic responsibility to vote. For a large number of women, these two psychological forces do not reinforce each other; thus, he concludes, they are less likely to vote.

Summary.   Numerous statistics have been offered regarding the level of political participation among males and females. Such a myriad of statistics may serve as the proverbial trees, blocking a broader view of the forest. A few generalizations may help to bring that view into clearer focus:

1. Women in the aggregate traditionally have had a lower rate of turnout than men.
2. By 1976, however, sex differences in voter participation had decreased to less than 1%.
3. There is considerable variation in the participation rates of different types of women, and in some instances women outvote men in similar categories.

Table 13-1 summarizes and illustrates differences in the voting participation of different groups of women.

We should add that the same factors that seem to increase or decrease voter participation among women *generally* have the same effect on men, although some factors, such as education, may have a stronger impact on women than on men. Two exceptions to this

Table 13-1. Level of Participation among Different Groups of Women

Category	Higher Participation	Lower Participation
Race	White	Black
Education	High school and above	Grade school and below
Employment	Employed in labor force	Unemployed or not in labor force
Age	Under 55	Over 55
Region	North, West, and urban areas	South and nonurban areas
Marital status	Married	Nonmarried (single, divorced, and widowed)
Parenthood	No young children present in home	Young children present in home
Political efficacy	High sense of efficacy	Low sense of efficacy
Civic responsibility	No relationship	No relationship

pattern are worth reiterating: (1) parenthood negatively affects women's participation, but has little observable effect on that of men; and (2) a strong sense of civic responsibility increases turnout among men, but not among women.

Partisan Choices

The term *partisan choices* is used here to refer to the final voting preferences expressed at the ballot box. Three factors directly related to how a person will vote are party identification, candidates, and issues. Of these, party identification is usually the most important determinant of the voter's final choice. The party label provides the voter with cues about the candidates and issues. It becomes a device for simplifying the complex process of evaluating political events and issues. The partisan affiliation of most voters remains fairly stable over a long period of time. Voters on occasion, however, do abandon their party loyalty. These deviations are usually related to either the candidates or the issues or both, but most often to the candidates. In analyzing the voting behavior of women, we will examine in turn three factors that ultimately influence how they vote— their party identification, their candidate preferences, and their attitudes about issues.

Party Identification

Some studies (Lipset, 1960; Blondel, 1963; Duverger, 1955) indicate that women in other countries prefer more conservative parties. This does not seem to be the case with American women. Although Campbell and his associates (1960) did find that women voters were more likely than men to support the more conservative Republican party, by a margin of three to five percentage points, they dismissed these differences as insignificant. The differences are rather small, and they may well be explained by the fact that more affluent women are both more likely to favor the Republicans and more likely to vote.

In a 1972 poll (Harris), women expressed a stronger preference for the Democratic party than men did. Among women, 48% considered themselves to be Democrats, 25% Republicans, and 18% Independents. Nine percent supported some other party or were undecided. By comparison, 44% of the men said they were Democrats, and 25% Republicans. The rest were Independents, supported another party, or were undecided. An interesting aspect of these data is that 73% of the women claim a partisan affiliation, compared to only 69% of the men. Because party label helps simplify the voting decision and because many women are less interested in and knowledgeable about politics than men, perhaps women feel a greater need for party identification.

Candidate Preferences

Candidate preferences do not always reflect party identification. Presidential election results, presented in Table 13-2, show that women preferred the Republican to the Democratic candidate in four of the six elections between 1952 and 1972. If we look *only* at the female vote, it would be easy to conclude that women are decidedly more Republican than Democratic. However, the analysis of the female vote in relation to that of men and the national majority (or plurality in some cases) shows that the voting patterns of women are very similar to those of men. In the 1976 elections, the candidate preferences of men and women were identical. For both sexes, 52% voted for Carter and 48% for Ford (Pomper, 1977).

Only in 1960 and 1968 did women vote in the opposite direction from both men and the national majority. Ironically, both of these elections involved the candidacy of Richard Nixon. In 1960, women supported Nixon over Kennedy, but in 1968, they supported Humphrey over Nixon. Sex differences in candidate preferences have been declining steadily since the 1950s. The one exception to this trend was the 1968 election, in which the third-party candidacy of George Wallace affected the normal two-party patterns. In that election, women supported Humphrey 4% more and Wallace 4% less than men. Both sexes gave virtually equal support to Nixon.

We can only speculate why women voted differently than men did in these two elections. One factor we can probably discount is the liberal/conservative difference between the candidates: in 1960, Kennedy was the more liberal of the two candidates; whereas in 1968, Humphrey was more liberal. Perhaps women in each election were concerned about the changes in the direction of public policy that might result from changing the party in power. Thus, in supporting Nixon, they may have been voting for the continuation of Eisenhower policies, and in supporting Humphrey, they may have been voting for the continuation of Johnson policies. In each instance, more women supported the candidate who represented the least change from current policies.

Attitudes about Specific Issues

Compared to party identification and candidate preferences, issues generally have limited impact on voters' decisions. Numerous studies have shown that voters, both male and female, are unaware and poorly informed about candidates' stands on issues.

Table 13-2.   Vote by Sex in Presidential Elections since 1952 (Based on Gallup Survey Data)

1952	Men	Women	Combined
Stevenson	47%	42%	44.6%
Eisenhower	53%	58%	55.4%
1956			
Stevenson	45%	39%	42.2%
Eisenhower	55%	61%	57.8%
1960			
Kennedy	52%	49%	50.1%
Nixon	48%	51%	49.9%
1964			
Johnson	60%	62%	61.3%
Goldwater	40%	38%	38.7%
1968			
Humphrey	41%	45%	43.0%
Nixon	43%	43%	43.4%
Wallace	16%	12%	13.6%
1972			
McGovern	37%	38%	38%
Nixon	63%	62%	62%

Data from Republican National Committee, 1972 Election Summary, p. 36B.

Campbell, Gurin, and Miller (1954) discovered this to be especially true of women in the 1952 election. They reported that "women were disproportionately low in their concern with issues, contributing only 39 percent of the highly issue-involved people and 75 percent of the uninvolved" (p. 155).

In spite of this finding, there is ample evidence that most women are concerned with and register strong views about a variety of issues. Drawing upon several attitude surveys, especially those conducted by Louis Harris and his associates, it is possible to discuss the attitudes of women in several issue areas. In *The Anguish of Change* (1973), which reviews American public opinion as recorded in surveys from 1960 to 1973, Harris devotes an entire chapter to women's views. In 1971 and 1972, he conducted a survey for the Virginia Slims Company that analyzed in detail the opinions of women (Harris, 1972).

War.   One of the areas in which the attitudes of women are clearly distinguished from those of men is that of war. Women express greater concern about and opposition to war than men do. Harris (1954) suggested that in 1952 "women were among the real prime movers in making the Korean War a major and decisive influence in the final outcome of the election" (p. 111). Initially, women were almost as supportive of the Korean War as men, but by the time of the November election, women were 10% more concerned about the fighting than men. Seven out of every ten women gave priority to ending the war.

Over 20 years later, the attitudes of women toward war had not changed significantly. According to Harris (1973), a majority of women opposed the escalated bombing of North Vietnam in August 1972, while a majority of men favored it. Also, two-thirds of the women became more opposed to the war after witnessing it on television, while less than a majority of men were so affected. A plurality of women were unable to justify the killing of civilians by U.S. soldiers in Vietnam, but a plurality of men could do so.

In 1969, women were supportive of war protesters by a margin of 43% to 40%, while men opposed them by 50% to 35%. In 1972, women were less favorable to defense and defense commitments than men.

The Economy.   Harris (1972) observed that whereas women in 1972 were more concerned about the war than men, men were more troubled about the economy. Harris based his observations on the fact that 9% more women than men cited the war as one of the more urgent problems facing the United States, while 12% more men than women gave top priority to the economy.

Nevertheless, women have expressed strong feelings about economic issues. Harris (1954) concluded that one of the major reasons women supported Eisenhower in 1952 was the issue of high prices and the belief that the Republican party could keep prices in line better than the Democrats. Women's concern with economic issues was exhibited in 1972 when they rated three economic issues—checking inflation, reducing unemployment, and keeping taxes in line—as being among the top ten national problems to be attacked first. Women's concern with these matters, however, continued to be less than that of men. For example, 18% of women, compared with 29% of men, cited inflation as one of the problems that should be attacked first—a difference of 11% (Harris, 1972).

On economic issues, women do not appear to be more conservative than men (Green & Melnick, 1950). They are more likely to favor government intervention in the economy and government ownership and operation of economic enterprises, and they are more supportive of the concept of the service state—a government that provides for many of the basic needs of its citizens. All of these attitudes are associated with the liberal viewpoint in American politics.

Race.   Most studies about racial attitudes have shown women to be more sympathetic to the plight of minorities than men. Perhaps this is because women understand what it is like to be treated as a minority. In a study that measured several citizenship attitudes about government and society among various age groups in all regions of the country (Campbell, Ferris, & Nichols, 1971), females were found to be more willing to mix with other races in a variety of public situations than men were. Males, however, were more aware of racial discrimination.

In general, women have been more favorable to integration in the public schools than men, more likely to believe that discrimination against Blacks was widespread, and more in favor of open housing (Harris, 1973). Men have been slightly more prone to think that Blacks in America were trying to move too fast and that Black demands were not justified (Harris, 1972).

Women in Politics. In 1971, Hazel Erskine wrote that "a woman running for president would get more votes from men than from women" (p. 275). Erskine based her statement on the results of Gallup polls taken since 1937.

Audrey Wells and Eleanor Smeal (1974) have taken issue with the type of survey utilized in the Gallup polls. They note that the question "provided insufficient information regarding the support of women candidates among women because it questioned support only for the highest office, for which women had no role model" (p. 56). Also, Wells and Smeal are critical of the wording of the question, which has varied in important ways over the years.

Wells and Smeal conducted a study of their own to test several hypotheses about women's support for female candidates. Two different groups of women in the Pittsburgh area, one consisting of registered voters and the other of Democratic and Republican committee members, were asked about the support they would give a female candidate for offices ranging from city council member to U.S. president. Of the combined samples, 94.4% said they would be as likely to vote for a woman as for a man for city council, but only 43.4% felt the same about a woman for president. Wells and Smeal concluded that "the Gallup Poll question regarding propensity to vote for a woman for President is the most extreme measure of support for women in politics and, therefore, an imperfect indicator of support among women for women. Such a measure overlooks broad support for lesser offices" (p. 69).

The 1972 Virginia Slims poll (Harris, 1972) shows women to be somewhat ambivalent about women in public office. For example, although 74% of the women surveyed agreed that "women in public office can be equally logical and rational as men," three out of five also expressed the view that men are emotionally better suited for politics than women. Significant pluralities of men and women agreed that women could perform as well as men in dealing with most policy problems, and both sexes agreed that women would do *better* than men in such areas as dealing with family problems, encouraging the arts, and protecting consumer interests. A plurality of women felt they could also do a better job in assisting the poor, but a plurality of men felt that women would only do as good a job as men. On the other hand, both men and women agreed that women probably would not be as effective as men in dealing with big business or the military. It is apparent that views about women's capabilities in public office stem in part from stereotypes of women based on their traditional role assignments.

When asked about women holding specific offices, women were generally more receptive to the idea of supporting female candidates than men, but not overwhelmingly so. A female vice president was more acceptable to both sexes than a female president, and a female Supreme Court justice was even more acceptable.

Nonconformity. In 1954, during the McCarthy era, when anticommunist emotions were strong, an extensive survey was taken to measure attitudes about the threat of a communist conspiracy and about the potential danger to civil liberties posed by strategies to deal with it (Stouffer, 1955). Civil liberties consist of basic individual rights such as freedom of expression, freedom of belief, and freedom of thought.

In the Stouffer study, women as a group were found to be more intolerant than men. They were more willing to limit the civil liberties of socialists, atheists, communists, or even persons whose loyalty had been questioned but who swore they had never been communists.

Controlling for a variety of variables, including education, region, age, and type of community, Stouffer still found women to be less tolerant as a group than men. He suggested that women were less tolerant, in part, because they went to church more frequently than men. In the Stouffer study, churchgoers expressed less tolerance of nonconformity than did nonchurchgoers. Stouffer concluded, however, that differences in church attendance alone were not sufficient to explain the less tolerant attitude of women; even among those not attending church, women were less tolerant than men. He theorized that the lesser tolerance of women stemmed from their restricted social environments as homemakers, which limited their interaction with others unlike themselves. Stouffer reasoned that women who were working outside the home would be exposed to a broader range of ideas and thus become more tolerant of views that did not conform to their own. The logic of that theory did not hold up, however, when Stouffer found that working women were as intolerant as full-time homemakers.

David Riesman (1956) has suggested that working women do not become more tolerant when exposed to the outside world because of the peculiar nature of women's labor force participation. Riesman reasons that women work because of domestic needs rather than occupational commitment, and that they discuss domestic concerns and not politics at work. For Riesman, the key to tolerance is the breadth of a person's orbit—that is, how broad an exposure she or he has to that which is new, or different, or strange. In the past, the orbits of men have been broader than those of women because of differences in education and employment. As these differences between men and women decrease, Riesman predicts, so will the differences in the level of tolerance.

It is our opinion that the higher levels of female intolerance can be attributed, in part, to the nature of their upbringing—the socialization process. Women are encouraged to be more conformist and conventional and less explorative. The effect of their socialization may lead them to place a greater value on conformity and to disapprove, even fear, less conventional ideas and behavior.

One must read and interpret the data on women's political opinions with caution. We have generalized on the basis of survey data about the views of women as a whole and compared these to the views of men. In many cases, we found that attitudinal differences between the sexes do exist, but we must be careful not to overstate the extent of these differences. Often the opinions differ in degree rather than in substance. It is also important to keep in mind that the views of individual women, or particular categories of women, may be quite different from the aggregate views of women. For example, although women as a group are opposed to war, many women actively support military actions. The various factions of the feminist movement described in Chapter 2 give evidence of the lack of uniformity in female opinions.

Summary

In the areas of political behavior examined here, the characteristics of female political activity are remarkably similar to those of males. Women vote almost as frequently as men, and in some instances more often. Their party identifications, like those of men, are a reflection of their socioeconomic status rather than sex, and their votes for presidential candidates have been consistent with those of men and the electoral majority (or plurality) with only two exceptions. Even then, the differences were not great.

The one area in which female behavior is somewhat distinctive from that of men is in their public opinions. In general, women are more opposed to war and violence, not quite so sensitive to economic issues, more sympathetic to the problems of minority groups, but less tolerant of nonconformity and corruption in office. They are becoming more receptive than men to the idea of supporting women for public office. In some ways, women in the aggregate seem more liberal than men; in other ways, they seem more conservative. There is no clear and consistent pattern.

THE ORGANIZATION WOMAN

CHAPTER 14

This chapter is concerned with that level of political activity at which the individual's commitment extends to participating in some type of organized political activity short of holding public office. There are two such types of political organizations—political parties and interest groups. Both are concerned with government and public policies, but there is one chief difference: parties seek to influence government policies by electing their own candidates to office; interest groups seek to influence governmental decisions without running for office. Though interest groups use several techniques for affecting policy, the best-known technique is lobbying.

Women in Political Parties

In this survey of the role of women in political parties, two areas will be emphasized: (1) participation by women at various levels of party organization; and (2) differences between male and female party activists.

Participation at Various Levels of Party Organization

State and Local Level. Although the available data are limited, there is every indication that women are more active in local party organizations than in the state or national parties, and that most of their activities tend to be routine and mundane in nature. Samuel Grafton (1962) suggests that the day-to-day political work of precinct organizations is done mainly by women for two reasons: (1) the extension of civil service coverage, which deprived political parties of patronage positions; and (2) the fact that women seem more willing to do party work for altruistic reasons. Prior to the establishment of civil service systems, most political positions were awarded on the basis of party loyalty. Men worked for the party in the hope of being rewarded with a job or a government contract. Women, it seems, are more willing to work without the promise of substantive or material rewards.

Women do hold leadership positions at the local party level, but since the extent of this officeholding has not been systematically documented, it is impossible to say how many women serve in such positions.

We also know very little about the participation of women in state party organizations. This lack of information may be indicative of limited participation by women at this level of party organization. What information there is on women in state party organizations indicates that women devote more time to party activities but have lower status within the party than men do (Costantini & Craik, 1972; Cotter & Hennessy, 1964).

National Level.   The active role of women in national party politics first began in 1892, when women were seated for the first time at a Republican party convention (Good, 1963). Since that time, women not only have increased their convention representation, but also have participated in other party activities such as national committees, women's divisions, and occasionally party office.

Since 1900, when each party's nominating convention had only one female delegate, the proportion of women delegates has expanded greatly. The greatest increase in participation occurred between 1968 and 1972. In the 1968 presidential nominating conventions, 13% of the Democratic delegates and 17% of the Republican delegates were women. By 1972, the figure had risen to 40% for the Democrats and 30% for the Republicans. At the 1976 nominating conventions, the number of female delegates declined to 34% in the Democratic party and rose to 31% in the Republican party.

The decline in the percentage of women at the Democratic national convention in 1976 was the result of several converging factors. In 1976 the rules had been changed, and the party simply put less emphasis on increasing female representation. Then, too, many women were elected in 1972 because the local party organizations had not anticipated the consequences of the 1972 rules, which made it easier for those who were not party regulars to get elected. Finally, feminist organizations, which had been an important impetus in the 1972 convention, were disillusioned by the convention and the subsequent campaign and election, and some of their members gave up on traditional party politics.

Both parties provide for their national committees to be composed of one committeeman and one committeewoman from each state. Since 1952, however, the Republican national committee has also included certain state chairs. This provision has created an imbalance in favor of men because few women hold state chairs. National committees serve mostly symbolic functions and exercise very little actual power. Hence, the role of women within these organizations, although roughly equal in most respects to that of men, does not accord them much real power in national party affairs.

Ever since the Democratic party established its Women's Bureau in 1916 and the Republicans created their Women's Division in 1918, the national committee of each party has had a special auxiliary unit devoted to women's activities. The women's units seek to increase the number of female voters, to stimulate female participation in party affairs, and to support female candidates for public office. In addition, they gather and present information about women in various party and public affairs.

Until Jean Westwood was named chairperson of the Democratic National Committee by George McGovern in 1972, no woman had ever held that high a position in either national party. Although Westwood was ousted after less than a year, there is no available evidence to indicate that her removal from office was because of her sex. Rather, it appeared to be the result of intraparty conflicts and the need to find a compromise candidate who could unite the badly divided party after the 1972 elections. In September 1974, one of the first appointments made by President Gerald Ford was that of Mary Louise Smith as chairperson of the Republican National Committee, a position she managed to maintain even after heavy Republican losses in the 1974 elections. Although she could not have been blamed for losses occurring so soon after she assumed the post, this might have provided antifeminists within the party with a basis for demanding her resignation.

Differences between Male and Female Party Activists

The term *party activist* is used here to refer to any individual who participates directly in any type of party activity, ranging from serving as a local party official to attending national conventions or serving on national committees. Studies reveal that male and female party activists differ in a number of ways, including their social, economic, political, and geographic backgrounds, as well as in their attitudes about policies.

Age.   As a rule, female party activists tend to be older than male party activists. Kent Jennings and Norman Thomas (1968), in a survey of Michigan delegates to the 1964 Republican and Democratic national conventions, found sharp age differences between men and women. Only 8% of the female delegates were under 40, compared with 26% of the male delegates. Furthermore, 35% of the women, but only 26% of the men, were over 55.

> The most plausible explanation of this phenomenon is that younger women are to a considerable extent occupied with the tasks of raising children and maintaining a home. They do not have as much time or energy to engage in political activity early in life as they do later on. Men, in contrast, have more freedom to move into political activity when they are younger. Not only that, but certain occupations encourage early political participation [p. 476].

Costantini and Craik (1972), who surveyed California party leaders, including convention delegates, suggest that women may be limited by the attitudes of men who have influence in the parties. As an example, they suggest that "for the woman to assume elite status in the parties she may be required to serve a longer period of apprenticeship than the similarly motivated male" (p. 222).

Education.   Sharp differences in education have been found between male and female party activists. Costantini and Craik (1972) report that among the California party leaders, only 51% of the women had a college degree, compared to 72% of the men. Among males, 43% held a graduate or professional degree, compared to only 12% of the females. Similarly, Jennings and Thomas (1968) report substantial educational disparities among the Michigan delegates they surveyed. Jennings and Thomas offer two reasons for this educational disparity between male and female party activists. First, male delegates were in professional or business occupations, which require high academic credentials. Second, the authors suggest that highly educated women tend to prefer nonpartisan to partisan activities, much more so than men at the same educational levels. No data are offered to support this second explanation.

The educational disparity between male and female party activists may be explained in part by the fact that, within the general population, a much higher percentage of men than women hold college and professional degrees. A recent report by the Bureau of Labor Statistics (U.S. Department of Labor, 1975) reveals that 14.5% of the male population has had four years of college or more, compared to only 9.5% for the female population.

Employment. Male party activists tend to hold more prestigious positions of employment. Jennings and Thomas (1968) found among Michigan delegates that a little more than half of the women were full-time homemakers, whereas most of the men were in either business or professional occupations. Among the employed delegates of both sexes, there were three times as many male lawyers and other professionals, while four times as many females held other sorts of white-collar jobs. These differences are consistent with the fact that 54% of the men, but only 29% of the working women, were self-employed. Jennings and Thomas hypothesize that these differences in occupation are the result of different criteria for male and female party elites, in that a high-status occupation is more essential for a man to achieve elite status within the party than for a woman.

Income and Class. In general, male party activists have higher income and class status than females, when these variables are measured in the standard way. (For a discussion of the problems of measuring income and class, see Chapter 8.) Among California party leaders, Costantini and Craik (1972) report 19% of the men and 10% of the women had family incomes of $50,000 per year, while the family incomes of 56% of the women and 37% of the men were $20,000 or under. The median family income for men was $25,000, compared to $18,750 for women. These differences in income hold true for both parties. Jennings and Thomas (1968) theorize that these differences in the class backgrounds of men and women are the result of differences in opportunities between affluent and less affluent women. For less affluent women, party activities are the major vehicle for political involvement; for upper-class women it is only one of several outlets. Affluent women have more opportunities for participation in high-status civic and social organizations.

Regional Differences. Regional differences historically have existed in the percentage of female delegates attending national nominating conventions. These regional differences have not always been consistent between parties, nor have they remained constant over time. At the 1952 conventions, the Western states had the highest percentage of women delegates at both party conventions, but that was the only interparty similarity in the regional origins of delegates. Six Democratic delegations and eight Republican delegations had no female delegates at all (David, Goldman, & Bain, 1960).

At both party conventions in 1972, all regions had substantially higher proportions of female delegates than they had in 1952, but variations still existed in regional distribution. In the Democratic party, the Northeast—which had the smallest female representation in 1952—had the highest in 1972, followed by the West, the Midwest, and the South. In the Republican party, the greatest female representation in 1972 was from the South, followed by the West, the Midwest, and the Northeast.

Political Careers.   Costantini and Craik (1972) found major differences in political careers between male and female party leaders in California. The careers of men were more oriented to public officeholding. Of the men, 48% had held elective office, compared to only 28% of the women. Although women may have limited access to elected public positions, their officeholding within both political parties exceeded that of men. Among Republicans, 56% of the women, compared to 50% of the men, had held party office. There were even greater differences among Democrats, with 77% of the women having held party positions, compared to 55% of the men. The results of other studies are consistent with these findings (Cotter & Hennessy, 1964; Jennings & Thomas, 1968). In a survey of 1976 convention delegates, Jeanne Kirkpatrick (1976) found in both parties that fewer women had held public office. However, she also found that Democratic women had held fewer party offices than Democratic men, while the record of Republican women in holding party office equaled that of Republican men.

Men and women also differ in their motivations for participating in party activities. Costantini and Craik found that both male and female respondents reported being motivated by a concern for public issues and a sense of community obligation, but that they differed sharply in other respects. Women in both parties were less prone than men to be motivated by self-serving reasons, such as a desire to run for public office, to be close to influential people, to achieve power and influence, to make business contacts, or to enhance their prestige. The sex differences in the responses were sharpest in the desire to run for public office and the search for power and influence. Women attached greater importance than men to party loyalty, to the influence of national party leaders, and to the desire to attend national conventions as reasons for party involvement. In general, women seem to be motivated by more altruistic reasons than men, and by factors that are external to themselves. These motivations are consistent with the characteristics associated with the female role. It is "unfeminine" to desire power and influence; it is not unfeminine to want to make the world a better place in which to live. Feminists offer a different interpretation—that women are simply being realistic about their chances for exercising power and influence.

Political Attitudes.   In explaining their reasons for becoming involved in party activity, women tend to focus on helping others, rather than helping themselves. This kind of external orientation is reflected in other attitudes as well. For example, when

Jennings and Thomas (1968) asked the 1964 Michigan delegates to the national nominating conventions what influences ought to shape a delegate's vote, there were sharp sex-related differences. Most men (79%) said that a delegate should rely on his own self-judgment. Fewer than half (45%) of the women agreed with that view. Most women thought that delegates should be guided by public opinion, party leaders, or other external factors—that is, external to themselves. Jennings and Thomas point out that the sex-related attitudes regarding the proper role of a delegate may have been due in part to the large proportion of men in their survey (54%) who were self-employed.

Attitudes regarding delegate roles may also be a reflection of traditional role perceptions, as suggested in *The Psychology of Sex Differences* by Eleanor Maccoby and Carol Jacklin (1974):

> The greater power of the male to control his own destiny is part of the cultural stereotype of maleness, and is inherent in the images of the two sexes portrayed on television and in print. For example, in a recent study of stories in elementary school textbooks, Jacklin and Mischel (1973) found that when good things happened to a male character in a story, they were presented as resulting from his own actions. Good things happening to a female character (of which there were considerably fewer) were at the initiative of others, or simply grew out of the situation in which the girl character found herself. It is not surprising, then, that young women should be externalizers, by reason of cultural shaping if for no other reason. What is surprising is that the sex difference in this scale does not emerge earlier in life [p. 157].[1]

Maccoby and Jacklin go on to cite studies that do, in fact, indicate that males develop a higher sense of self-confidence and sense of potency than females. Men perceive themselves as capable of controlling events more than women do. This difference, which has been observed among grade school students, has also been found among college students.

On policy issues, Jennings and Thomas (1968) found that party differences were greater than sex differences. The attitudes of Republican women were more like those of Republican men than of Democratic women, and the attitudes of Democratic women resembled the attitudes of Democratic men more than those of Republican women. However, intraparty variation between men and women did occur on two major policy issues. Democratic men reflected a more favorable view of expanding economic and military aid to foreign countries than did Democratic women. An even greater difference occurred between Republican men and women over civil rights, with the women substantially more favorable toward a stronger federal role to assure racial equality. These differences, over foreign economic and military aid and over civil rights, seem to be generally consistent with the differences in men's and women's views on these issues reported in Chapter 13.

Wilma McGrath and John Soule (1974) found rather consistent sex differences in the political attitudes of delegates to the 1972 Democratic national convention. On ten

[1] From *The Psychology of Sex Differences,* by Eleanor E. Maccoby and Carol Nagy Jacklin. Copyright 1974 by Stanford University Press. Reprinted by permission.

issue questions—dealing with amnesty, marijuana, abortion, eavesdropping and wiretapping, communism as a threat, busing, protection of radicals, withdrawal from Vietnam, guaranteed minimum income, and federally financed day-care centers—women were "more liberal" on every question than men. (The terms *liberal* and *conservative* were not precisely defined.) When the authors controlled for such factors as race, education, region, and income, they found that the same pattern remained constant in most socioeconomic categories. The exceptions were found among delegates with less than a high school education, and also among delegates under 21 and between the ages of 30 and 40. In these categories, male delegates were more liberal than females.

Kirkpatrick (1976), on the other hand, found virtually no difference between the policy positions of male and female delegates to the 1976 conventions. The only exception concerned military policy. Consistent with previous findings, female delegates tended to adopt a more liberal view on military issues.

Assessing the findings of these three studies of delegate attitudes toward issues, we can conclude that, with some exceptions, male and female delegates do not differ significantly in their views. Women at the 1972 Democratic convention may have been an exception to the rule because of the strong effort put forth by feminists and feminist organizations to stand up and be counted within the party circles.

Summary

In retrospect, we can see that the role of women in the major political parties has been less than that of men, but that it is expanding. Women seem to have a more significant role at the local level than anywhere else. Within each party, they differ from men more in their socioeconomic characteristics and political careers than they do on policy issues, with the exception that Democratic women at the 1972 convention appeared to be more liberal on policy issues than Democratic men. Female party activists seem to be motivated to become politically active more for altruistic reasons, and less for reasons of self-interest, than are men.

Women in Interest Groups

Interest groups consist of people who share common interests and attitudes, and who seek to protect and further their interests by obtaining favorable governmental policies. The group theory of politics holds that the demands made on government by these organized groups provide the chief source of energy for the political system. The demands of one group frequently conflict with the demands of another or several other groups, and it is the function of the political system to regulate group conflict in such a way that the system maintains its stability. The resolution of intergroup conflict is commonly achieved through bargaining, whereby the groups reach an agreement acceptable to each in proportion to their group strength.

We can identify two types of interest groups in which women have been active. First, there are the groups concerned about issues not directly related to gender, such as civil rights, the environment, busing, or social security. These organizations may be composed of members of both sexes, such as the American Civil Liberties Union, or the membership may be predominantly female, as in the League of Women Voters. Second, there are the groups commonly referred to as women's organizations. These are composed primarily of women who are seeking to change the roles and status of women in society. Chapter 2 has examined in depth two types of women's organizations—those that make up the women's rights branch of the movement, and those that comprise the women's liberation segment.

The present focus on interest groups pertains less to the women's liberation type of organization, not because these groups are deemed less important, but rather because their objectives often involve nonpolitical goals and change through other than existing governmental channels. It is important to make this distinction between the two types of women's organizations, not only because they have different goals and tactics, but also because of the strong possibility that there may be important differences in the backgrounds and attitudes of their members.

Very little of the research on women in politics has been devoted to interest group activities. We seem to know little about either the women who participate in women's organizations or those who participate in groups oriented to more general courses. Drawing upon the limited data, we will deal with two very broad questions: (1) the characteristics of women active in groups; and (2) the effectiveness of women's organizations.

Characteristics of Women Active in Interest Groups

Chapter 9 contains a section on participation by women in voluntary organizations. That chapter provides excellent background information for this discussion of women's participation in political organizations because it provides data on male/female differences in participation as well as on the characteristics of women who are likely to be involved in organizational activities.

There are two ways of looking at the characteristics of women involved in interest-group activity. One way is to compare the characteristics of those who are active, often labeled "politicals," to those who are not active, or "apoliticals." A second way is to compare females who are active in group politics to males who are similarly involved. Both types of comparison will be made here.

In a study of citizens of the Tucson, Arizona, area, Bernard Hennessy (1958) compared women active in party politics (party politicals) to those active in pressure group politics (pressure group politicals) and to a group of women who were not politically active (apoliticals). Hennessy discovered that women involved in pressure group politics expressed a lower need to exercise power than either the party politicals or the apoliticals. He attributed this to the fact that female pressure group politicals seemed more concerned with issues and the indirect effect of ideas upon public policy. Pressure group politicals were also more willing to compromise than were party politicals or apoliticals.

On the other hand, party politicals displayed a greater willingness to take risks than either of the two other groups, which may be one of the reasons they were active in parties. They were willing to serve in roles that are nontraditional for females.

Earl Kruschke (1966) also studied personality traits of women active in key issue areas of a local community. He focused on one key variable—level of optimism about the future. The basic hypothesis of the study was that women active in community politics would be more optimistic about the future than politically inactive women. The differences in optimism between the two groups were large enough to confirm the hypothesis. Kruschke suggests that the positive outlook of female politicals explains why these women are willing to assume roles uncharacteristic of females.

These two studies offer some evidence of differences between women who are active and those who are not. There is also evidence of differences between men and women active in pressure group politics. In *The Political Life of American Teachers*, Harmon Zeigler (1967) presents an in-depth analysis of the behavior and attitudes of both men and women in one type of organization—a teachers' association. Like other interest groups, teachers' associations seek to influence public policies favorable to their members. This type of association is unique in that it involves a profession to which males and females have relatively equal access, if not equality of status. (See Chapter 11 for a discussion of the status of women in the teaching profession.)

A representative sample of high school teachers in Oregon provided the basis for the Zeigler study. Within teachers' organizations, women were found to be more active than men. Also, women belonged to more organizations, other than educational ones, than men. The greater participation by women in educational associations may be attributed to differing perceptions about what the organization should do. Teachers' associations traditionally have avoided political involvement beyond school issues, but male and female teachers disagreed about whether this should be the case. Women, especially those with organizational experience, supported involvement in school elections but not general elections; men believed that teachers' organizations should be actively involved in both types of elections. Men were more willing to risk going beyond the limited role of noninvolvement in political affairs and to engage in more controversial activities.

It is not surprising to discover that male teachers were more dissatisfied with the organization than females. Fully 97% of active women agreed with the policies of the organization, compared to 75% of active men. Women were also more trusting of organizational leadership and more likely to attribute greater influence to the organization than were men. Women believed that the leadership responded to the desire of the "average teacher," whereas men tended to believe that the leadership responded more to "influential teachers" and administrators. Earlier, we noted that girls exhibit greater trust toward authority figures than boys; thus, the differences in male and female teachers' attitudes toward leadership may be traceable back to the early political socialization process.

The Zeigler study raises some interesting questions about the role of women in pressure group politics, suggesting that, at least among teachers, women have a different perspective on the proper role of a professional association. Their perspective leads to limited political involvement and the avoidance of conflict where possible. This tendency to avoid conflict is frequently found among women in politics; we would suggest that it is a direct effect of the way in which women are socialized.

The primary focus of research on women in interest groups tends to be on middle-class organizations. In fact, most interest groups do tend to have a middle-class or an upper-class bias; that is, the members of most interest groups come from middle-class or upper-class backgrounds.

There are, of course, other organizations that represent the interests of the poor, the working class, ethnic groups, Blacks, and other minorities. Women are active in all of these organizations. For example, women have been the predominant force in the creation of welfare rights organizations. In fact, the National Welfare Rights Organization (NWRO), which links together local welfare groups into a nationwide organization, began with a walk by a group of Ohio welfare mothers. The continuing influence of women in the NWRO can be seen in the makeup of its executive committee, which is almost exclusively female (National Welfare Rights Organization, n.d.).

There have been few systematic studies of women in interest groups representing the poor, Blacks, ethnic groups, and other minorities. One work that does offer some excellent insights is Nancy Seifer's *Nobody Speaks for Me* (1976), which presents the results of in-depth interviews with ten women who became active in their communities. The range of issues with which these women became involved includes Chicano politics, coal-mining politics, sexism in the workplace, union organizing, blockbusting, neighborhood social-welfare problems, civil rights, and feminism. Seifer believes that these women are representative of many others in their attitudes, perceptions of the world, life-styles, and responses to the problems of daily life. She concludes:

> Whatever the motivation, there is a spirit of communalism that exists among working class women that one finds less frequently among the middle class. They seem not to be infected by that college-bred disease of competition, survival of the fittest. Perhaps it is because middle class people do have more options in life and have less need to depend on one another in exercising them that we tend to be more individualistic and self-interested than communal [p. 37].

Women's Groups: Factors Affecting Their Success

Political organizations dominated by women are not new phenomena. The emphasis here is on organizations of fairly recent origin that have developed out of or in response to the current women's movement. Such organizations are often confronted with conflicts over (1) goals and (2) organizational structure.

In terms of goals, an organization may focus outward and pursue narrow, well-defined political goals, such as electing women to office or achieving ratification of the Equal Rights Amendment (ERA). Alternatively, an organization may adopt an approach that emphasizes self-development and interpersonal relationships and examines the societal factors that contribute to or impede these values. Organizations associated with the women's rights segment of the movement are more prone to pursue politically ori-

Figure 14-1. The National Organization for Women, an interest group that seeks to change the roles and status of women in society, has sponsored rallies to promote the Equal Rights Amendment. (Photo by Creative Associates.)

ented goals, whereas those associated with the women's liberation branch tend to focus more on self-development and interpersonal factors—striving, for example, to eliminate sexism in society. Sometimes women with differing attitudes about goals are part of the same group, and this results in conflicts about what the organization should be doing.

Conflicts over organizational form or structure result primarily from a concern over how power within the group ought to be distributed and exercised. The main issues seem to involve the level of formality in discussing issues and making decisions and the nature and function of leadership roles within the organization.

Julianne Oktay (1972) reported on the conflict within one group, the Howard County (Maryland) Women's Political Caucus. The group was split between those who were oriented toward politics—that is, getting women elected or appointed to office and ratifying the ERA—and those oriented toward broader issues concerning women, such as the need to raise the consciousness of women or to alter the process of sex-role socialization. There was also a conflict over organizational structure. The politically oriented group wanted a more traditional organizational structure, with elected leaders, dues-paying members, and decision making based on majority rule. The other group wanted as little structure as possible, with no leaders, membership based on attendance, and decision making based on consensus.

In the end, the group members opted for a fairly informal structure that included two official leaders, known as chairpeople, a system of rotating officers elected every six months, the making of decisions by consensus rather than majority vote, and membership through participation rather than payment of dues. This organizational form, a compromise between the two factions, proved to be ineffective. Two groups, pursuing divergent goals, each sought to establish an organization that best suited its own purpose. The compromise organization that resulted was ill suited for either purpose.

Many women's movement organizations are primarily political in their goals: they seek legal, policy, and structural changes that will provide equality for women along with men. Chapter 2 discusses several such organizations. Perhaps the best example is the National Women's Political Caucus (NWPC), begun in 1971 for the explicit purpose of increasing the number of women in public office. The early leaders of the organization included such well-known feminists as Betty Freidan and Gloria Steinem and politicians such as Bella Abzug and Shirley Chisholm. The caucus has a national office, as well as branches at the state and local levels. The NWPC is not able to provide female candidates with financial support, but it does provide other forms of support such as publicity, speakers, and political expertise. Susan and Martin Tolchin's *Clout: Woman Power and Politics* (1974) makes several references to the role of the NWPC in various campaigns and elections.

Research by Joan Rothschild (1972) on women's organizations in Massachusetts focuses on the question of how political goals can best be achieved. Rothschild proposes that the essential element of success is a "female constituency," with four main characteristics:

- members' consciousness of being women as a common element and binding force
- a commitment to collective action
- a commitment to political activity
- a broad base of support, transcending issues

Rothschild analyzed the effectiveness of four different types of organizations operating in Massachusetts in terms of their potential for creating a female constituency. The four types were single-issue organizations (such as abortion, ERA, child care); service groups (health care, pregnancy and birth control counseling, rape squads); political and ideological organizations (women's political caucuses, peace and freedom parties); and consciousness-raising groups (those designed to make women aware of themselves, each other, and the common problems of women). Rothschild concluded that few of the organizations possessed the potential for becoming the type of "female constituency" she envisioned, but she did find "that the elements of a female constituency would more readily emerge through mobilizing women around issues rather than ideology, and that a feminist political and ideological commitment can develop through service and issue oriented tasks" (p. 12).

In a follow-up study, Rothschild (1973) examined a newly developed organization in Massachusetts, the Women's Lobby, which, she says, has the potential for providing the elusive "female constituency." This organization emerged out of the need to coordinate the activities of numerous women's organizations that were lobbying for various bills, especially ratification of the ERA. The organization helped diverse groups keep abreast of legislative activities by establishing a communication network and organizing task forces around specific issue areas. One of the chief assets of this organization was that it sought to establish and maintain a broad base of support. The Women's Lobby addressed itself to issues of concern to poor and to lower-middle-class women, and it was flexible enough to allow women to support some of its issues without supporting all of them. Perhaps the most important element of success for the Women's Lobby has been its ability to solve the dilemma of goals and structure. "At this point in the Lobby's development, the central commitment is to women's issues rather than to women. Or, one might say the commitment is to functional feminism, not ideological feminism" (p. 12).

There are literally hundreds of women's organizations that seek to influence policy decisions at the national level, and there is a great diversity among these groups in terms of their goals, resources, and strategies. In a recent work, Irene Murphy (1973) has sought to measure the effectiveness of four types of women's groups that have adopted, in whole or in part, the goals of legal and economic equality for women.

Murphy measured the effectiveness of these groups on the basis of their ability to obtain optimal access to decision makers, which depended on three factors: (1) the acceptance of their goals by both decision makers and the public; (2) their resources such as membership, funds, and organizational structure; and (3) their strategies in terms of getting publicity, electing sympathetic candidates, and maintaining open channels of communication to decision makers as well as other groups. Applying these measures to the various organizations surveyed, Murphy found that none possessed all of the critical factors for success.

Echoing the same theme as Rothschild, Murphy suggests that a critical factor in the success of women's organizations at the national level is coordination. She predicts that the success of feminist goals will depend on the ability of women's organizations to establish firm alliances with each other and thereby establish a broader base of support for such goals. She does not offer any predictions about whether or when such alliances might come about.

Summary

On the whole, we do not seem to have a great deal of information about women's participation in interest groups. Women who become involved in group politics appear to have different personality characteristics from those who remain inactive, but there is not enough evidence to draw any firm conclusions. Little attention has been given to differences between men's and women's interest group participation. The one case study cited here suggests that men and women have differing perceptions about organizational goals, strategies, and tactics.

As for women's groups, a prevalent issue of concern is the extent to which the achievement of organizational goals and objectives should be placed ahead of the needs of individual members. The emphasis that any given organization places on each value is determined by the internal politics of the organization, and the effectiveness of any organization should be judged against the value that it deems to be most important. In general, it seems that women's organizations, like most other organizations, will be more successful in accomplishing their *political* objectives if their goals are specific and not oriented toward broad structural change in the system, if they use a pragmatic rather than an ideological approach, and if they can create and maintain a broad social base of support.

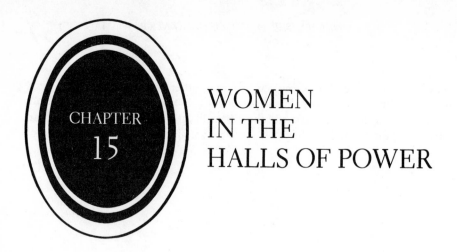

CHAPTER 15

WOMEN IN THE HALLS OF POWER

Since the passage of the 19th Amendment in 1920, women have slowly but steadily expanded their participation in elections, political parties, and pressure groups. Their participation in public office has been far more limited. The fact that such a limited number of public offices are held by women raises two different kinds of questions—one factual, the other theoretical. First, we are interested in knowing what types of women achieve public office, how they behave in public office, and the factors that influence their ability to gain office. A second, and perhaps more critical, question is why there are not more women in public office.

Women in Legislatures

Although the exact number of women serving in the U.S. Congress has fluctuated over the years, the percentage has always remained quite small. As of January 1979, when the 96th Congress began, 88 different women had served in the U.S. House of Representatives. There have been only 14 female senators. Only one woman, Margaret Chase Smith of Maine, has served in both houses. Table 15-1 shows the number of women in each session of Congress since 1953. The total number of women in Congress reached a peak of 19 in 1961–1963 and then declined until 1971. Since then, the number has slowly increased, reaching a total of 19 (out of 535) again in 1978.

At the beginning of the 95th Congress (1977–1978) there were only 17 women in Congress, all in the House of Representatives. Two women senators were added when Muriel Humphrey took over her husband's Senate seat after the death of Hubert Humphrey in January 1978 and when Maryon Allen was appointed to succeed her husband, James B. Allen of Alabama. Senator Humphrey did not run for election to complete the remaining years of the term; she retired. Senator Allen was defeated in a primary election. In the 1978 elections, 17 women were elected to Congress—16 to the House, and 1, Nancy Landon Kassebaum of Kansas, to the Senate.

At the state level, the number of female legislators also has fluctuated over time. The number of women in state legislatures increased gradually from 1921, when there

Table 15-1. Number of Women in the U.S. Congress, 1953–1954 through 1979–1980.

Congress	Senate	House	Total
83rd (1953–1954)	3	12	15
84th (1955–1956)	1	16	17
85th (1957–1958)	1	15	16
86th (1959–1960)	1	16	17
87th (1961–1962)	2	17	19
88th (1963–1964)	2	11	13
89th (1965–1966)	2	10	12
90th (1967–1968)	1	11	12
91st (1969–1970)	1	10	11
92nd (1971–1972)	2	13	15
93rd (1973–1974)[a]	0	16	16
94th (1975–1976)[a]	0	18	18
95th (1977–1978)[a]	2	17	19
96th (1979–1980)[a]	1	16	17

[a]Data for the 93rd, 94th, 95th, and 96th Congresses have been added by the author. They include not only those women elected in the general election but also those chosen in special elections or appointed to office.
Data from *Congressional Quarterly Almanac*, 1972, p. 1035.

were only 31, until 1964, when 351 women were elected. Then the number declined to 323 in 1967, 305 in 1969, and 293 in 1970–1971 (Werner & Bachtold, 1972). This decline in the number of female legislators occurred mostly in the larger industrialized states of the East and the Midwest and the border states of the South. In contrast, the number of women in legislatures in the Western and Southern states increased. The number of women in state legislatures has increased steadily through the years. According to the National Women's Political Caucus, which collects data on women in elected office, there were only 344 female state legislators in 1972. By 1978 that number had almost doubled. There were 441 in 1973; 457 in 1974; 598 in 1975; 611 in 1976; 703 in 1977; and 761 in 1978. Women now constitute 10.2% of all state legislators.

Background Characteristics of Female Legislators[1]

Several studies indicate that women legislators have many characteristics in common, including age, education, marital status, occupation, and political experience.

---

[1] A large number of biographical studies, mostly of Congresswomen, provide a wealth of details about women who have served as legislators. Annabel Paxton's *Women in Congress* (1945) focuses on the 65th through 79th Congresses. In *Few Are Chosen*, Peggy Lamson (1968) provides biographical sketches of four Congresswomen—Frances Bolton (Republican, Ohio), Martha Griffiths (Democrat, Michigan), Patsy Mink (Democrat, Hawaii), and Margaret Heckler (Republican, Massachusetts). Hope Chamberlin's *A Minority of Members* (1973) offers biographical information on all the female members of the U.S. Congress from 1917 through 1972 and describes their congressional activities.

Age.   Women tend to enter legislatures at an older age than men. Among the women in the 88th Congress, the youngest was 49, and the oldest 78 (Werner, 1966). Of all the women who had served in Congress up to that time, only 10% had entered Congress before the age of 40. Nearly 75% had entered between the ages of 40 and 60. Frieda Foote Gehlen's studies (Foote, 1967; Gehlen, 1972) of the 88th and 91st Congresses solidly support Werner's findings. Kirkpatrick's (1974) study of women legislators confirms that women also enter state legislatures at a later age than men.

Two aspects of the age differential between men and women are significant. One is why women wait so late in their lives to seek political office, and the other is the effect of age on their legislative roles. The most obvious reason why women delay their legislative careers is that they wait until their child-rearing responsibilities are over. Most women who pursue public office are mothers, and because women in our society have been assigned primary responsibility for child care, they do not have the freedom to run for political office until these responsibilities have ended. One important effect of this delay in undertaking a legislative career is that it limits the ability to attain leadership positions. Traditionally, such positions have been based on seniority, and women have less time to accumulate the necessary seniority to achieve positions of power.

Education.   The level of education among Congresswomen is generally higher than it is for female state legislators. Gehlen (1972) noted that of the women who had served in Congress through 1964, 80% had more than a high school education, and more than 50% were college graduates. Of the latter, 40% had undertaken some type of postgraduate work, and several had received postgraduate degrees, mostly in law. The level of education is rising among Congresswomen, but it remains lower than for Congressmen. Charles Bullock and Patricia Heys (1972) found that congressional widows—that is, women who gained a seat after the death of their husbands—had less education than women elected on their own. Also, a much higher percentage of regularly elected Congresswomen had received postgraduate education.

Marital Status.   Many people believe that most Congresswomen became legislators upon the death of their husbands. Although the number of "congressional widows" has been large, they do not constitute the majority of Congresswomen. Of the 62 women who had served in Congress through 1964, 28 were "congressional widows," and 34 were not. Of the latter group, 7 were single, 16 were married, 8 were widows of non-Congressmen, and the marital status of 3 is unknown (Foote, 1967).

More recent statistics indicate that fewer and fewer women are entering Congress through the widow's mandate. Of the 13 women serving in the 92nd Congress, only three were congressional widows. Of the 16 women in the 93rd Congress, only two—Corrine (Lindy) Boggs (Democrat, Louisiana) and Cardiss Collins (Democrat, Illinois)—became Representatives *directly* through the death of their husbands. Both won special elections after the death of their husbands. A third widow, Leonor K. Sullivan (Democrat, Missouri), was not nominated by the St. Louis Democratic Central Committee to fill her husband's vacancy after his death, but she ran in the next primary and won on her own.

She ran on the ballot as Mrs. John B. Sullivan, and she attributes her initial victory to his name. Since then, however, she has made a name for herself. She retired in 1976 after serving for 24 years. Both of the women elected for the first time in 1976 were single.

The fact that more married women than single women pursue and attain public office may seem inconsistent at first glance. It would seem that a woman fulfilling the more traditional homemaker role would have less time for and interest in public office. In many instances, however, the fact that a woman is *not* the family breadwinner means that she has the time and the economic flexibility to pursue a legislative career. This is especially true at the state level, where serving in the legislature often takes only a few months out of the year and does not provide a full-time income.

In addition to economic support, the moral support of a spouse is a critical factor. In her interviews with female state legislators, Kirkpatrick (1974) found the married legislators generally had the support of their husbands. Most of them said they would not have run without their husband's approval. The general tendency is for husbands who approve of their wives' careers to do so by acquiescing rather than becoming actively involved. "In essence, the acquiescent husband agrees not to protest (frequently or strenuously) against his wife's prolonged absences, her long hours, her preoccupation with the business of the legislature, her failure to provide many of the services which are usually accorded in this society" (p. 233). The role of the political husband is a far cry from the role society has established for the political wife!

Occupation. The largest single occupational group among Congresswomen has been teachers. According to Emmy Werner (1966), about one-third of all women who served in Congress through 1964 were educators. This is not surprising in view of the fact that education accounts for a large percentage of all working women, and an especially high percentage of all professional women (see Chapter 11). The second most frequent fields were law and public service. In contrast, a substantial majority of Congressmen have a background in the legal profession. Among the female state legislators sampled by Werner in 1964, the predominant occupational background was business and public relations, followed by education (Werner, 1968).

Political Background. Women reach legislative positions by many different routes, but virtually all have had some kind of previous political experience. To this extent, the recruitment pattern for women is similar to that for men. However, it seems that this previous political experience is more critical for women than men. According to Kirkpatrick (1974), there seem to be two different paths to legislative office for women— volunteer community service and party activity. According to Kirkpatrick, these activities are crucial because they provide women an opportunity to acquire the experience, skills, and reputations necessary for public office.

Volunteer service and party activity are so important to women because they seldom have occupational careers that lead to public office. Women who do have such careers— in law, for example—can succeed without a long record of community or party service (Kirkpatrick, 1974, p. 83).

Party activity is especially important for women, not only because of the experience and visibility it offers, but also because a woman is more likely to need the resources of party than a man. By virtue of being the nominee of a party, she automatically picks up the votes of the party loyalists. At the same time, being a party nominee lends legitimacy to her candidacy in the eyes of the voters. It is no coincidence that no woman has ever been elected to Congress as an independent, and that fewer than 5% of female legislators at the state level have been independents.

The fate of women as legislative candidates varies with the fortunes of the party with which they are affiliated. (For a discussion of this point, see the section below on factors affecting the election of women to legislative positions.) Most of the female members of Congress have been Democrats. Of the 11 female Senators prior to 1978, 6 were Democrats and 5 were Republicans. In the House, there have been 56 women who were Democrats and 29 who were Republicans. These figures include the two women who were newly elected in 1976, both of them Democrats. Prior to the Depression, Republican women were the more numerous; since then, the number of Democratic women has steadily increased, reflecting national patterns of party affiliation (Werner, 1966).

At the state level, as of 1964, the predominant party affiliation of female legislators was Republican, a pattern that reflected their geographic distribution. The New England states, which have traditionally been Republican, exceeded all other regions in the proportion of female legislators. After 1964, the number of women in state legislatures began to decline in the Northeast, the Midwest, and the border states, and to increase in the West and South (Werner, 1968).

Women in the Legislative Role

The legislative role, like all other political roles, has been characterized as a masculine one. It has been occupied almost exclusively by male incumbents. The masculine nature attributed to the legislative role raises many questions about how women adjust to it. This section deals with three aspects of women's responses to the legislative role. First, there is the question of how women approach the role in terms of solving conflict between it and their traditional sex roles. Second, there is the question of whether women have a different orientation toward the role of legislator than men have. Do their opinions about what a legislator should be and do differ from those of men? Finally, there are questions about differences between the performances of women and men in the legislative role. Do female legislators vote and act differently from male legislators?

Approaches to the Legislative Role.   An in-depth analysis of female legislators and role conflict is Foote's (1967) study of women in the 88th Congress. Foote was concerned with whether Congresswomen encountered "blockage," or obstacles that adversely affected the fulfilling of their legislative roles. She also wanted to determine how women dealt with these obstacles. Did they resolve the conflict by trying to eliminate the obstacle? Or did they instead limit their role involvement? Foote discovered that of all the potential sources of blockage, informal relationships presented the greatest obstacle, and that most Congresswomen sought to remove the blockage rather than reduce their involvement.

Informal relationships are an extremely important ingredient of legislative success. These relationships include such things as unstructured informal groups and friendship cliques, as well as more structured groups such as classes (all the members first elected in a given year), the Democratic Study Group (a reform-oriented group of liberal legislators), and prayer-breakfast groups. Foote found that the extent to which Congresswomen were affected by these various informal associations differed. The informal friendship groups appeared to be the least permeable by women, but some females were more acceptable than others:

> Those women who were mentioned most frequently as the ones men would accept in the informal political network were the group of women who had won their seats on their own, who had worked with men for years in men's occupations . . . and particularly in state political situations . . . but who were not constantly on guard about being discriminated against [p. 330].

Marie Rosenberg (1972) was also concerned with role conflict. In a study of Representatives Edith Green and Julia Hansen, she focused on the attitudes that women have prior to their legislative service. Certain types of attitudes make it easier to adjust to the legislative role. Rosenberg theorized that "this pre-existing set of attitudes may have greater significance in explaining the differences in Congressional performance than the route through which these women arrive at the legislative body" (p. 3). Representatives Green and Hansen, whom Rosenberg characterizes as effective legislators, both came from family and social backgrounds in which they were exposed to women who had other roles in addition to the traditional ones of wife and mother. They were also taught how to be effective citizens and the importance of economic self-sufficiency. This background provided them with a broad perspective on the role of women and the ability to be adaptable and flexible—characteristics that made their subsequent adjustment to the legislative role easier.

Orientation toward the Legislative Role. It is easy to see a relationship between women's views of the legislative process and their sex-role socialization. (See Chapter 7 for a discussion of this process.) Most of the female legislators interviewed by Kirkpatrick (1974) held a very idealistic view of politics:

> As they see it, conflict is not an important dimension of politics; politics is not a jungle in which each is pitted against all. Nor is it a zero sum game where one person's advantage is another's disadvantage. In fact, there is almost nothing of the "game" model of politics with its teams, alliances, strategies, victories and losses [p. 143].

The tendency for women to deemphasize the conflict in the legislative process shows up in other ways. One way, discussed later in this chapter, is the tendency of women not to oppose openly programs that they cannot support. Another example comes from a study by James Barber (1965) of Connecticut state legislators. Barber found that a substantial number of women in his survey (40%) adopted a legislative role that was more like that of a spectator than an active participant. They did not use their legislative positions to achieve personal goals such as their own notoriety or advancement. Instead, they chose a role of limited involvement which, intentionally or not, entailed less conflict than a more active role.

Kirkpatrick's (1974) assessment of female legislators differs somewhat from Barber's, which was conducted ten years earlier and focused on only one state legislature. Kirkpatrick, who interviewed female legislators in several states, did not find women playing a less active role. Two-thirds of the women in her survey were characterized as "inventors"—those who seek new ways of solving old problems. According to Heinz Eulau, who developed the concept, "the inventor is interested in solving the current problems of his state—public welfare, education, highway construction, the rehabilitation of the mentally ill, and so on" (Wahlke, Eulau, Buchanan, & Ferguson, 1962, p. 255).

What is significant about the high proportion of female legislators playing the inventor role is that this role focuses on the government as an agency for achieving the public good. To this extent, it tends to deemphasize conflict and compromise. Very few of the women legislators interviewed by Kirkpatrick were characterized as "brokers"—those who conceive of politics as an arena in which multiple self-interested groups compete with one another, with the function of the legislator being to resolve these conflicts through bargaining and compromise.

When these various findings are pulled together, we find a certain consistency among them—namely, that women's orientation to the legislative process and the roles they play in that process reflect in some ways the characteristics of the traditional female role. Especially striking is the tendency either to avoid or to deemphasize conflict.

Note that what is suggested here is only a tendency, not an iron rule of behavior. Nor is there the suggestion that female legislators make a deliberate decision to avoid conflict. Rather, what we are suggesting is that women learn responses to situations through the process of sex-role socialization and that these responses affect their orientation to legislative roles, as to other roles in life. The following section suggests, moreover, that the actual role performance of women conforms to their role orientation.

Legislative-Role Performance.   In many ways, the behavior of female legislators is indistinguishable from that of male legislators. In examining the voting records of women in the 91st Congress (1969–1970), for example, Gehlen (1972, 1977) found that, in most instances, women voted similarly to men. She found few differences between men and women in the percentage of roll-call votes answered, in the degree of support for bipartisan measures, or in support for the President's programs. The greatest differences between Congressmen and Congresswomen occurred in the area of opposition to legislation. Women were more reluctant to vote against their own party, against bipartisan measures, or against the President's programs. Gehlen observes that "the most consistent finding of all from the studies is the evident reluctance of women members to oppose openly programs which they cannot support. More so than men, they seem to have a tendency to 'opt out' rather than go on record as opposed" (1972, p. 11). Here we see the influence of the traditional female role on political behavior—the idea that women are supposed to be supportive and avoid conflict.

One of the expectations of legislators in general is that they will specialize in a particular area of legislation. The requirement for specialization lies at the heart of the legislative committee system. Each committee specializes in a certain area of policy, and committee members are expected to develop expertise in the policy area for which their committee is responsible.

One might expect female legislators to specialize in "feminine" issues or issues of general interest to women in order to facilitate their adjustment to a predominantly male environment. Women's issues consist not only of matters directly related to women, such as women's rights, but also matters of a more general nature, such as education, health, and welfare. The Kirkpatrick study (1974) indicates that female legislators at the state level are more likely to specialize in these areas of feminine concern.

In her study of Congresswomen, Foote (1967) did not find sufficient evidence to support the hypothesis that women seek to adjust to the legislative role by specializing in feminine areas. There was some evidence of specialization in that women were more likely than men to introduce legislation in areas that could be categorized as traditionally feminine. Most of the legislation sponsored by women was *not* in these areas, but a greater percentage of the legislation sponsored by women fell into this category than was true for men.

In her more recent study of the 91st Congress, Gehlen (1977) found that the committee assignments of women did reflect a certain specialization. Although there is no evidence that women sought assignment to committees dealing with conservation, consumer affairs, or health, education, and welfare, that is where a disproportionate number of them have been assigned. This sex-related aspect of committee jurisdictions may simply reflect the bias of male legislators responsible for committee assignments.

One area in which one expects to find a difference between men and women is that of tenure. The term *tenure* refers to length of continuous service in the legislative role. Tenure is important because of its relationship to positions of power within the legislative body: it is one of the criteria for achieving leadership roles. If one of the objectives of women is to achieve positions of power within the legislative body, then tenure becomes a critical factor in achieving this goal. The matter of comparing the tenure of men and women, however, is not as simple as it may seem.

Gehlen (1972) makes three observations about the tenure of Congresswomen: (1) the length of tenure varies widely, from 2 months to 35 years; (2) the majority have served three terms or more; and (3) the length of tenure has risen consistently. According to Gehlen, the average tenure of Congresswomen in the 88th Congress (1955–1956) was 6.7 years, and it increased every year thereafter. By the time of the 91st Congress (1969–1970), the average tenure for Congresswomen was around 11 years. A random sample of men in the 91st Congress revealed an average tenure of 9.4 years, much lower than the 11.3 years average for a sample of men in the 88th Congress.

Average tenure, of course, is quite different from individual tenure—and when it comes to individuals, those who have the highest seniority are men. Because women enter legislatures at an older age than men, they simply cannot accumulate the kind of seniority that many men have. This factor is important in explaining women's lack of leadership positions in legislatures.

At the state level, the length of tenure among women legislators has been relatively brief. Among women in the 1963–1964 legislatures, 60% had served 4 years or less, about 32% had served 5 to 10 years, and the remaining 8% had served 15 years or more (Werner, 1968). The relatively brief tenure of these women may be explained, in part, by the fact that most of them served in the lower house of the state legislature, where tenure is generally lower.

The greatest differences between male and female legislators are found in the area of leadership. The most important positions of leadership in Congress are the Speaker of the House, the president pro tempore of the Senate, the majority and minority party floor leader and whips, and the committee chairs. The only positions of power that women have held are committee chairs—and they have held very few of those.

Six women had served as committee or subcommittee heads up through the 92nd Congress (1971–1972) (Van Helden, 1971). In the 93rd Congress (1973–1974), there was only one woman chairing a full committee, Representative Leonor Sullivan (Democrat, Missouri) of the Merchant Marine and Fisheries Committee. Three other Congresswomen chaired subcommittees. No women chair committees in the 96th Congress.

Generally speaking, if women do perform differently from men in legislative roles, it is not easily discernible in their voting records or their areas of legislative specialization. The most noticeable points of differentiation are found in the reluctance of women to vote against legislation they do not support and in the paucity of women in leadership positions.

Factors Affecting the Election of Women to Legislative Positions

Numerous explanations have been offered for the small proportion of women in both federal and state legislatures. These explanations center around three types of factors—stable, fluctuating, and individual.

Stable Factors.   A predominant view is that women are socialized to accept a home-oriented role that is basically passive in nature, and that seeking public office runs counter to this traditional sex role. It has been well documented that many women believe that holding public office is an "improper" role for women (Lee, 1974; Lane, 1959; Campbell et al., 1960). The Virginia Slims poll (Harris, 1972) produced evidence that women believe men to be more capable of running for office. Thus, the effects of socialization on some women, at least, are sufficiently strong to prevent their seeking public office.

The influence of these factors is borne out in a study by Karnig and Walter (1976), who analyzed election contests for city council posts in 774 municipalities with populations of more than 25,000. They found that women stood for council positions in approximately 21% of the races. They won close to 50% of these contests. The result was that women constituted only 10% of all city councillors. Karnig and Walter conclude that what limits women's representation in legislative councils is their failure to become candidates. This failure they attribute to the effects of the socialization process and to women's cultural roles of homemaking and child rearing.

Another constraining factor is that women fear they will be discriminated against in politics. In a survey of women active in local politics in four New York counties, Marcia Lee (1974) found a high proportion of women who believed that women in public office would have problems of being accepted by men. Women also believed they might be discriminated against by voters in general.

Whether women are discriminated against purely because of their sex is open to question. Darcy and Schramm (1977) analyzed elections for the U.S. House of Representatives in 1970, 1972, and 1974. They found that the sex of the candidate had little or no effect on election outcomes. More important than gender is the candidate's party affiliation and whether he or she is an incumbent. In general, Democratic candidates get more votes than Republicans, and incumbents receive more votes than challengers.

The constraining factors of socialization and perceived discrimination are reinforced by the fact that relatively few women have careers in government, law, or business—the occupations that most often lead to legislative careers. A substantial majority of the members of Congress are lawyers, and relatively few women are members of that profession. Chapter 11 provides additional data on the scarcity of women in professional occupations.

Fluctuating Factors. Political scientists have discovered that fluctuations in the number and proportion of women elected to office are related to certain other variables. Certain socioeconomic conditions and political situations are thought to be more favorable to the election of women than others.

In *Understanding Politics*, Louise Young (1950) observed that female candidates for state legislatures did not fare so well during economic crises, such as depression. Young theorized that women stand a better chance when times are good and public confidence high. During wars, on the other hand, Young suggested, female candidates have a better opportunity of being elected, in part because there are not so many males available.

Jean Lipman-Blumen (1973) has argued that the numbers involved are too small to attribute the increase in female legislators during wartime to a lack of available male candidates. Instead, she suggests that in times of uncertainty resulting from crises, the social structure is more flexible, and roles are more open to change. One factor that contributes to role instability during wartime is the increase in women's participation in the labor force (see Chapter 11).

Some political scientists believe that the presence of "morality issues" also enhances opportunities for women candidates. As we have seen, voting studies and public opinion polls have shown women to be more moralistic in their views about politics. Alan Otten (1973) of the *Wall Street Journal*, reflecting on the potential effect of Watergate on incumbent politicians, commented: "The anti-politician mood might also help elect a record number of women candidates. Not only do voters seem to regard ladies as being more "amateur" but polls show the voters tend to see them as more honest, less corruptible" (p. 1). The number of female candidates did increase in the year of the Watergate affair, but there is no clear evidence that morality issues were the cause. In 1974, the number of female candidates was up 24% over 1972, and 74% over 1970 (Witcover, 1974). Although a higher proportion of women were elected to the 1975–1976 state legislatures, the number of women in Congress increased by only two.

Political factors also seem to affect women's chances of success. At both the state and national levels, female candidates seem to be more successful in presidential election years, when voter interest is generally higher and turnout is greater (Werner, 1968).

There is no evidence, however, to support the notion that certain types of constituencies are more likely to elect a female member of Congress than others. In examining the constituencies of Congresswomen, Foote (1967) found a wide range of demographic characteristics in constituencies that elected women. The variables she tested included rate of population growth, percentage of Blacks, percentage of foreign born, median income, and education. In a more recent study, Gehlen (1972) reexamined the question and still found no special pattern in the demographic characteristics of female constituencies.

In local politics, where constituencies are smaller and more homogeneous than congressional constituencies, the socioeconomic makeup of the district may make a difference in the electoral success of female candidates. Bernstein and Polly (1975) examined a city council election in Dallas, Texas, in 1969. Their analysis showed a relationship between the racial and class makeup of a district and the fate of female candidates. Lower-class districts, regardless of race, were significantly less supportive of female candidates than were middle- and upper-class districts. (The discussion in Chapter 7 of working-class families offers some understanding of this voter behavior.) Among lower-class districts, Black districts were more receptive to female candidates than White districts. In middle- and upper-class districts, there were no differences in voting associated with race.

There is some evidence that the geographical location of a constituency makes a difference in the electoral success of female candidates. Gehlen (1972) observed that "no one area of the country has a monopoly on sending members to the House . . . [but the] pattern differs from area to area on one significant point. The women from the South are predominantly the widows of Democratic Congressmen" (p. 6).

Individual Factors.   Certain factors are thought to contribute to the likelihood that any given woman will seek public office. One of the more important factors seems to be whether there are politically active members in the woman's family. Several studies (Werner, 1966; Jennings & Thomas, 1968; Kirkpatrick, 1974) have focused on this factor, and the consistency of the reported findings is impressive. Alfred Fengler (1973) has hypothesized that having a political role model is more important in stimulating women to enter politics than it is for men because politics is an acceptable male occupation.

Kirkpatrick (1974) found that the role model for a large percentage of the women in her study was a politically active mother. She found that 40% of the mothers and 50% of the fathers were politically active. Kirkpatrick stresses that having a politically active mother dispels the view that politics is "men's business." (Parallel influences on women's decisions to seek employment are discussed in Chapter 8.) Daughters of working mothers are likely to become working wives and mothers.

On balance, it seems that we know far more about women who are elected to legislative positions than we do about why they are elected. All that the available evidence indicates is that a variety of factors affect the chances of women in general, and of any given woman in particular. For females to win legislative seats probably requires a combination of factors, but what those factors are remains a matter of conjecture at this point.

Women in the Executive Branch

The executive branch of government consists of those agencies and departments responsible for administering government programs. It includes the ten departments headed by cabinet secretaries, such as the Department of Justice and the Department of Health, Education, and Welfare. It also includes a series of agencies and commissions independent of the departmental structure, such as the Civil Service Commission and the Federal Communications Commission.

The executive branch is as political as the legislative. The political role of bureaucrats, both executives and nonexecutives, stems from two different functions: (1) The executive branch plays a major role in the development of public policy. Most of the legislation considered by Congress, for example, originates in the executive branch. (2) The executive branch implements the policies passed by legislative bodies. In many cases, this involves only routine decisions, but in others it means exercising broad discretion. Thus, bureaucratic decisions can and do have an important impact on the ultimate outcome of any given policy. Anyone in a position to influence policy outcomes is in a political role. Therefore, whether a woman is a political appointee—such as a presidential advisor or cabinet secretary—an executive at the upper levels of the civil service, or a career civil servant at the lower levels of government service, hers is a political role.

The executive positions that are most familiar to the public are those in the President's cabinet. After a presidential candidate has won election and before he is sworn in as President, the press and the public await his decisions about his cabinet appointees. Rarely have these appointees been women. Only five women have ever served as cabinet secretaries, and three of those were appointed between 1975 and 1977. Most other executive positions in the federal government are covered by civil service regulations. That means the appointment is supposed to be based on merit and ability, rather than political ties. We refer to these employees as members of the federal service.

In the last ten years, there have been numerous reports by governmental agencies about women in the federal service. These reports usually present raw data about the number and percentage of women at various grade levels and the departments and agencies in which they serve. There is seldom much analysis in the reports, and political scientists have not made serious efforts to fill that void. A notable exception is a study of female federal executives by Mary Lepper (1972), which will be used extensively here as a source of data about women in the federal service.

The Historical Role of Women in the Federal Service

Until 1883, very few positions in the federal government were open to women. In 1883, the Civil Service Act (Pendleton Act) established the merit system, allowing women to compete in civil service examinations on an equal basis with men, and in 1923, the Classification Act required equal pay for equal work. After 1940, the number of women in federal service increased, but mainly at the lower levels. When President Kennedy appointed the Commission on the Status of Women in 1961 (see Chapter 2 for origins of the commission), 24 women and 2,026 men held "supergrade" (GS 16 and above) positions. This paucity of women in high-level positions is paralleled in the private sector as well. (See Chapter 11.)

Through the commission's efforts, an 1870 law permitting agencies to specify a particular sex for an available position was repealed by Congress. Despite this development, progress toward increasing the status of women was very slow. One of the most significant actions taken to remedy discrimination against female federal employees was the issuance in 1967 by President Johnson of Executive Order 11375, which prohibited sex discrimination in federal employment. In implementing the President's order, the Civil Service Commission established the Federal Women's Program, designed to improve the status of female federal executives.

Two years after the establishment of the Federal Women's Program, President Nixon issued Executive Order 11478, which instructed federal departments and agencies to establish affirmative-action programs to assure all civilian employees and applicants equal employment opportunities. When these programs did not result in any substantial increase in the number of women in high-level positions, President Nixon sent a memorandum to heads of executive departments and agencies in April 1971. The memorandum "called for agency plans to increase the number of women in supergrade (GS 16 and higher) and senior level (GS 13–15) positions, and for an increase in the participation of women on advisory boards and committees" (Markoff, 1972, p. 220). A White House coordinator was appointed to direct the program for recruiting more women for high-level government positions.

The most recent action to improve the status of women in the federal service was the passage of the Equal Employment Opportunity Act of 1972, which extended the equal-employment provisions of the 1964 Civil Rights Act, including the prohibition against sex discrimination, to all federal agencies. The Civil Service Commission was given the responsibility for overseeing federal practices, and the Equal Employment Opportunity Commission for overseeing state and local practices.

The Current Status of Women in the Federal Service

Assessing the impact of these efforts is difficult because of the lack of current data. The annual reports of women in the federal government released by the Civil Service Commission are 10 to 12 months out of date by the time they are issued (Fields, 1972). Nonetheless, the available statistics are useful in providing some measure of the impact of these various women's programs.

There are several ways of approaching the statistical data on women in the federal service. One way is to assess the proportion of women compared to men at each grade level in the total government work force. Figure 15-1 clearly demonstrates the disparity in status between men and women. Women dominate the very lowest grade levels, and their numbers decline sharply at the higher levels. Very few women are found at levels of GS 13 and above.

Another way to examine the position of women is to compare the distribution of grade levels among women to that of men. Such a distribution is found in Figure 15-2. Of those women in the federal work force, nearly three-quarters were below grade level 7, whereas only one-fifth of the men were in such positions. Fewer than 2% of the women were in positions at the level of GS 13 or above, whereas almost 23% of the men were in these higher-level positions.

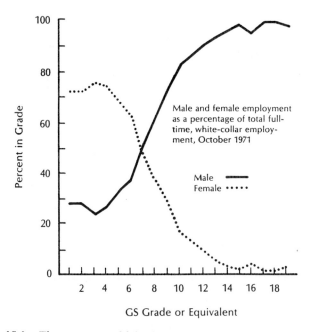

Figure 15-1. The proportion of federal employees of each sex at comparable grade levels. (From The Bureaucrat, *1972, 1, 212. Copyright 1972 by the American Society for Public Instruction. Reprinted by permission.)*

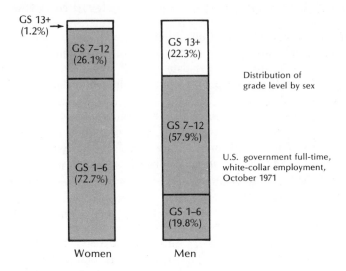

Figure 15-2.   Distribution of the total federal work force by sex and grade level. (From The Bureaucrat, *1972, 1, 213. Copyright 1972 by the American Society for Public Instruction. Reprinted by permission.)*

One of the main objectives of the Federal Women's Program has been to increase the number of women at the senior and supergrade levels. In the four years after the initiation of the program, very little change had occurred. Slight increases were registered in GS 13, 14, 16, and 18, while a slight decrease occurred in GS 15, 17, and all above 18. Overall, the percentage of women at GS 13 and above increased only .2%.

A Profile of Female Federal Executives

In her study of female federal executives, Mary Lepper (1972) compared several socioeconomic characteristics of men and women. She found that men, as a group, came to the federal service with a wider variety of background experiences than women. Three occupational groups—medicine, administration, and social science—accounted for 71% of the female executives. For men, the three chief occupational groups—administration, engineering, and medicine—accounted for only 54% of the executives. These findings are not surprising in light of the employment data on women in Chapter 11. In the private sector, female workers tend to be concentrated in a relatively few occupations. Lepper also found that female executives were better educated than their male counterparts. Of the men, only 25.4% had a Ph.D. or equivalent, compared to 49.3% of the women.

A 1963 study of federal executives (Warner, Van Riper, Martin, & Collins) reported that two of the greatest differences between men and women executives were age and marital status. Above the GS-15 level, female executives were considerably older than male executives, and a much higher proportion were unmarried. Of the female executives, 65.3% were single, compared to fewer than 5% of the men.

Earlier we noted that most women who serve in legislatures are or have been married. This pattern contrasts sharply with the high percentage of single female executives in government. We gain additional insight from the observation in Chapter 11 that female executives in the private sector are far less likely to be married than male executives. The obvious question is why married women are more likely to become legislators than executives. One reason may be that a legislative career does not require the years of continuous experience and building of seniority that are usually necessary to become an executive. It is possible for a woman to be a full-time wife and mother while she is young and to pursue a legislative career when her homemaking responsibilities have declined. To become an executive, however, a woman, like a man, needs career continuity, and women who leave their jobs to become full-time wives and mothers may lose the opportunity for future executive positions.

The career patterns of women in the federal service are characterized by discontinuity. Women generally serve for shorter periods of time. Lepper (1972) found that the modal group of males had 20 to 24 years of service, whereas the modal group of females had only 5 to 9 years of service. The President's Commission on the Status of Women (U.S., 1963) reported on another aspect of women's career patterns—their voluntary leaving. The rate of women voluntarily quitting was 2½ to 3 times greater than that for men. The commission noted that women predominated in younger age groups and low-paid occupations, where turnover rates are higher for both sexes. The most prominent reason given by women for leaving the federal service concerned family responsibilities. One-quarter of the women, compared to one-half of the men, said they left for broader experience, better pay, or dissatisfaction with their working conditions.

We might consider whether these responses of men and women might be different if women were prepared for better-paying jobs and could in fact get them. In an economy where a woman could earn as much if not more money than her husband, we might see more men dropping out of the labor force to care for the children. Women do not always leave their jobs to take care of children as a matter of choice. If the father earns more money than the mother, the logical decision from an economic point of view is for her to assume the responsibility for child care.

Female Executives at the State and Local Levels

State Level.   At the state level, there are a larger number of elective executive positions than at the federal level, where the only elected executives are the President and Vice President and all of the other high-ranking executives, such as cabinet secretaries, are appointed. In many states, not only are governors and lieutenant governors elected, but also many of the department heads are elected, such as the secretary of state, the state treasurer, and other executives such as the superintendent of schools, the commissioner of highways, and the like. In some states, however, governors do pick their own cabinet secretaries.

Whatever the method of selection for office, few women have been chosen to serve in executive positions. In 1968, Gruberg noted that 15 states had no women elected to important executive positions. A 1970 report by Helen Shaffer noted that only 31 women held statewide elective executive positions, 10 fewer than a decade earlier.

The 1974 elections may have been a turning point for women in state executive positions. Three women ran for governor, and one of those, Ella Grasso, a Democrat, won the governorship of Connecticut. She was the first woman elected to governor on her own. In 1976, Dixie Lee Ray was elected governor of Washington. She is single. The three other women who have served as governor all succeeded their husbands. Nellie Taylor Ross became governor of Wyoming in 1925 after the death of her husband; Mariam ("Ma") Ferguson was elected governor of Texas in 1926 after her husband was impeached and disqualified from office; and Lurleen Wallace was elected as Alabama governor when her husband was ineligible to seek another term.

Since 1974, seven states have elected women as lieutenant governors. Six of those are currently in office. They include Evelyn Gandy in Mississippi, Thelma Stovall in Kentucky, Madeline Kunin in Vermont, Nancy Dick in Colorado, Ferdinan (Nancy) Stevenson in South Carolina, and Jean Sedako King in Hawaii. There are also three women who serve as secretary of state in states where there is no lieutenant governor. These women are first in line to succeed the governor. They include Thyra Thompson in Wyoming, Rose Mofford in Arizona, and Norma Paulis in Oregon.

Women have improved their positions in other statewide offices also. As of January 1979 there were 10 female secretaries of state and 6 female state treasurers.

Local Level.   Much less is known about women in local government than about women who serve in the state and national governments. We do know that their participation has always been greater at the local level, although relatively few women achieve executive status. Lee Sigelman (1976) found that among government employees at both the state and local levels, the proportion of women is equal to or greater than their share of the working-age population. However, the number of women in higher level posts is disproportionately low in every state. Even fewer women are selected for the executive positions of mayor or city manager.

A survey taken in 1965 by Norma Flesch indicated that there were 112 female mayors in 31 states, most of them in cities of fewer than 5000. There were only 17 female mayors in cities of more than 10,000 in population, and 7 in cities between 5000 and 10,000. As a group, these female mayors appeared to be successful politicians. A total of 60% were serving in at least their second term, and two of them were serving their sixth term.

The National Women's Political Caucus reported in 1973 that 42 women were serving as mayors in the 1000 largest cities of the United States, comprising 4.2% of the total. There were 27 female mayors in the 750 cities having a population over 30,000,

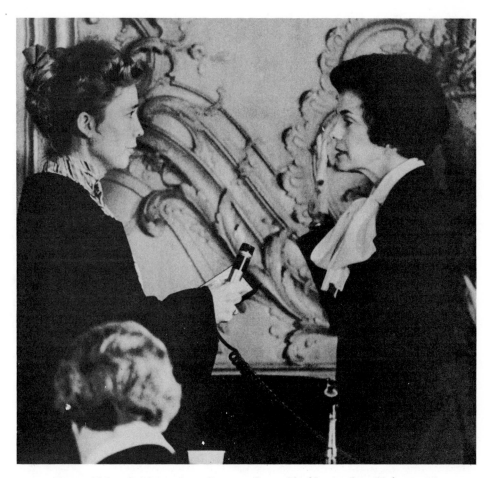

Figure 15-3. California State Supreme Court Chief Justice Rose Bird swears in Dianne Feinstein as San Francisco's first woman mayor, December 1978. (Photo by United Press International.)

representing 3.6% of the total. By 1976, there were 566 women serving as mayors, some of these in such major cities as Phoenix, Arizona, and Cincinnati, Ohio ("Women in Politics," 1976).

There are even fewer female city managers than there are female mayors. A city manager is a person appointed by the city council to take care of administrative responsibilities. In many municipalities, the city manager exercises a great deal of influence over the city councillors and their policy decisions. In other municipalities, the role of the manager is more limited in scope and influence. In 1963, there were 11 municipalities with female city managers, and 6 of those were in Maine (Stewart, 1964). By 1972, out of a total of 2534 municipalities, there were only 15 female managers (Rubin, 1973). Maine still led with 10. The fact that female managers, unlike female mayors, continue to serve only in those jurisdictions with relatively small populations, where their function is more like that of town clerk, can probably be attributed to the lack of education and professional training for the field of management. Some of the factors that contribute to women's failure to obtain the educational and professional background necessary for executive positions are discussed in Chapters 11 and 12.

It is interesting to note that female executives at the local level are more numerous in elective than appointive positions. Regardless of whether the position is an elective or appointive one, however, the fact remains that few women hold public office at the local level. In a recent study of both men and women in local politics, Marcia Lee (1976) discovered some of the main reasons why few women seek local office, despite the fact that they devote considerable time to local political affairs.

Lee conducted a survey of men and women who participated in local politics in four municipalities of Westchester County, New York. Questionnaires were completed by 301 women and men who had been identified as "political participants," defined as "a person who is a *board member* of an ongoing, organized group whose primary objective is to elect people to office or to influence the policies of *local government* in the manner it feels appropriate, or who holds public office by election or appointment" (p. 300).

One of the clearest survey results was that women devoted more time to political activity than men. However, Lee found that the participation of women was limited to certain types of activities, mainly women's organizations or work at low levels of the party hierarchy. Very few women held elected or appointed public office. Three major factors accounted for this small number of women in public office: having children at home, women's perceptions of their proper role and of politics, and fear of sex discrimination.

Having children at home appeared to be an important influence on seeking public office, but it did not affect the amount of time women devoted to political activities in general. Lee reasoned that having children at home affected only the pursuit of public office, and not other types of political activities, because of the peculiar nature of public office.

> It appears that odd working hours and spur-of-the-moment activities are the aspects of public office which discourage women from pursuing such activities. For men, this is apparently less the case. Since they are not the ones primarily responsible for child care, they feel more free to engage in such activities [p. 306].

In addition, Lee discovered that women are inhibited from running for public office because they feel it is not proper for women to do so, and because others might disapprove. Such activities run counter to their traditional sex role. Women also expressed fear that their sex would create problems for them, especially in the form of discrimination by men who would not be willing to accept them. All these attitudinal factors kept women from public office.

Some social scientists have theorized that although women do not hold many local offices, they still exercise a great deal of influence in local politics through voluntary associations. Nicholas Babchuk, Ruth Marsey, and Wayne Gordon (1960) examined the role of women in one community power structure by analyzing the composition of the boards of various civic organizations. These organizations were rated according to the importance of their functions to the welfare of the community, and whether their functions were primarily instrumental, instrumental-expressive, or expressive—qualities which the authors defined as follows:

> Instrumental agencies, as a type, may provide a service, produce a product, or serve as organizations designed to maintain or create some normative condition or change (for example, the Council of Social Agencies or a hospital). Expressive agencies provide a framework within which activity for the participants is immediately gratifying (for example, a settlement house). Instrumental-expressive agencies provide a framework within which both instrumental and expressive activities are self-consciously exercised (for example, the Jewish Home and Infirmary) [p. 401].

Babchuk and his associates discovered that the instrumental agencies were directed by boards composed primarily of men. The few instrumental agencies whose boards included a majority of women were all concerned in one way or another with children. Men also controlled the boards of expressive agencies, but a much larger proportion of board members in these agencies were women than was true for instrumental agencies. Men also dominated the boards of agencies ranked most vital in terms of community function. Nearly 90% of the board members of these vital organizations were men. Among agencies ranked as "least vital," men held only 61% of the board positions. The overall conclusion of this study is that the more instrumental the agency and the more vital its functions, the lower the proportion of women serving as board members.

If the findings of Babchuk and his associates are typical of other communities—and, in the absence of other studies, it is impossible to predict—we can conclude that women's lack of power in local public office is not offset by their influence in key community organizations.

Women in Judicial Positions

The judicial branch of government, at both the state and federal levels, is almost exclusively a male domain.

The federal judicial structure consists of three levels. The lowest tier consists of federal district courts, where virtually all cases in the federal system originate. There are a total of 91 district courts, with over 400 district court judges. Eleven circuit courts of appeals, which hear appeals from the federal district courts within their jurisdiction, make up the second level in the federal system. There are approximately 100 federal circuit court judges. The highest court in the federal system is the Supreme Court, made up of eight associate justices and one chief justice. In addition to these courts, there are also some special federal courts such as the U.S. Court of Claims and the U.S. Court of

Customs and Patent Appeals. All federal judges are appointed by the President, with the advice and consent of the Senate.

In 1964, only 3 of 425 judges on the federal bench were women. By 1974, the number of female judges had increased to 5, while the total number of federal judges had increased to around 500. Four of these five women serve as U.S. district court judges; only one is a judge of a circuit court of appeals. The only other woman ever to serve as a federal circuit court judge was appointed by President Roosevelt in 1934, after she had served as the first female judge of a state supreme court. Circuit court judge is the highest federal judicial post ever held by a woman.

There are numerous judicial positions in the federal system in which no women have ever served, including the Supreme Court. According to Maurine Abernathy (1969), the United States lags behind other countries in this respect. Both France and Germany have named women to their highest courts. Nor have any women ever held positions on the U.S. Court of Claims or the U.S. Court of Customs and Patent Appeals.

That there have not been any more women holding federal judgeships may be explained in part by the scarcity of female lawyers. The legal profession is the background that leads most often to a judicial position. At the federal level, though not always at the state and local level, a law degree is a necessary prerequisite for appointment. Table 15-2 demonstrates that the number and proportion of women in the legal profession is very small. Even though the numbers nearly doubled from 1950 to 1970, the percentage of female lawyers and judges remained quite low.

State and local judicial systems are somewhat more complex than the federal system. In the state court hierarchy, the lowest court is usually the justice of the peace, with .jurisdiction over minor cases. In many states, justices of the peace have been replaced by municipal courts. The major trial courts in the state system are called superior, district, or circuit courts. The most common method of selecting all lower court judges is election. States usually have two higher levels of courts that hear appeals from lower courts. Most of these judges are elected, but in some states they are chosen by the legislature, and in a few states they are appointed by the governor.

It has been difficult to determine how many female judges serve at the state level. *Time* magazine reported in 1965 that out of a total of 8748 judges in the United States, only 300 were women ("Judges," 1965). Since we know that very few of these female

Table 15-2. Female Lawyers and Judges in the Civilian Labor Force—1950, 1960, and 1970

	Total Number of Female Lawyers	Proportion of Female Lawyers and Judges
1950	7000	4.1%
1960	7500	3.5%
1970	13,400	4.9%

Data from U.S. President, *Economic Report of the President*, 1973, p. 155.

judges served at the federal level, this statistic refers primarily to female judges at the state or local level. Gruberg (1968) reports that most female judges do serve at the local level and are commonly found in family and juvenile courts. According to the U.S. Bureau of the Census (1973), there were 12,249 judges employed in the field of public administration in 1970; of this number, 869 were female.

In 1973, there were four female state supreme court judges. In 1974, Susie Sharp of North Carolina became the first woman to be elected chief justice of a state supreme court, and Alabama elected its first female supreme court justice, Janie Shores. Rose Elizabeth Bird became the second female chief justice when she was appointed by Governor Jerry Brown of California.

Women in Public Office: Summary

Women today compose more than half of the U.S. population and cast more than half of the votes in national elections, but they remain an extremely small minority in public office. At the federal level, out of 435 members of the House of Representatives, only 16—fewer than 4%—are women. Of 100 U.S. Senators, only one is a woman. Only five females have ever served as cabinet secretaries, and no woman has served as a U.S. Supreme Court justice, not to mention President or Vice President. At the state level, only five women have held the office of governor, and a very few have held other statewide offices. The number of female mayors and city managers is miniscule, relative to the total.

Those women who have succeeded in holding public office have many things in common. They are usually middle-aged or older, are married or have been married, have had some education beyond high school, and frequently hold a college degree. Many have had family members who were active in politics and thus were exposed to politics at an early age.

A variety of influences determine the number and proportion of women in public office, but the specific factors and precise effects are unclear. It is apparent that current social and economic conditions, cultural norms, and political factors all play a part. In addition, the individual circumstances of each potential candidate are important. Income, education, support of a spouse, and presence of children are some of the factors that seem to influence whether any given woman will seek public office.

Conclusion

In reviewing the information presented in this section, it is apparent that the participation of women in American politics is greater in voluntary situations, where they can participate if they so choose—such as voting and political organizations—than in chosen situations, where they must be selected by others before they can participate—including elective and appointive office. (See Stiehm & Scott, 1974, for a discussion of voluntary and chosen situations.) Why is this the case? As a tentative explanation, we suggest that the situation is related to both structural and socialization factors. In the sex-role structure of our society, women are assigned the primary responsibility for child care. This role assignment affects females not only as adults, when they become mothers, but also as young girls through the process of sex-role socialization.

Girls learn, both by observation and by being taught, that young ladies do not become politicians. They can observe that most of the important political positions are held by men, and they are taught that "politics is a man's business" and "a woman's place is in the home." From an early age, girls, presumably in anticipation of their future roles, demonstrate less interest in and knowledge about political affairs. They do not anticipate becoming politicians. Nor, as we saw in the section on economics, do they anticipate becoming business executives, managers, doctors, or bankers. Rather, they anticipate becoming wives, mothers, teachers, nurses, or secretaries. The educational preparation of females reflects these anticipations in a manner that often limits their subsequent opportunities for political careers.

We can hypothesize that this socialization process influences the adult woman's views about politics in such a way that she lacks the interest, the motivation, and the preparation necessary to pursue politics as a profession. Since socialization is an ongoing process, however, other factors can counteract the influence of earlier socialization. Factors that appear to be the most influential in countering the effects of earlier socialization are those that direct the woman's attention away from the home and toward the "outside world." Particularly important are education, participation in the labor force, and the presence of politically active family members to serve as role models. By the same token, the one factor that seems to create the greatest obstacle to a woman's pursuit of public office is the presence of children. Women who have young children usually must direct their attention toward the home.

Numerous social changes are occurring which, if they continue, should result in increasing the number of women in public life. Among these are the higher levels of education being attained by women, increased labor force participation by women, and the growing tendency for women to have fewer children and to have them at an earlier age. Each of these factors, discussed in Sections 3 and 4, could contribute to increased political roles for women.

We cannot expect rapid change. So long as women continue to bear the primary responsibility for child care, then their participation in public office will be limited. And although views on child care may be changing, they are changing at a snail's pace. Women's participation in public office, therefore, can be expected to increase at a similar rate.

Points to Ponder

The following statements are based on questions used in sample surveys conducted in the United States to measure sex-role attitudes (Mason, 1975). Discuss your response to each statement in light of what you have learned in this and the previous four sections.

1. We need more women in politics.
2. One-half of the delegates to the national nominating conventions should be women, to represent their half of the U.S. population.
3. The U.S. would be governed better if there were more women in Congress and in other government positions.
4. If there were more women in important positions in government, there would be less graft and corruption.
5. Most men are suited better emotionally for politics than are most women.
6. Women are more attentive to detail and therefore can be better administrators in high office than men can.
7. Although women hold few public offices, they work behind the scenes and really have more influence in politics than they're given credit for.
8. When it comes to _____ *(choose items from the list below)*, women in public office could do a better job than men.
   a. strengthening the economy
   b. encouraging the arts
   c. conducting diplomatic relations with other countries
   d. improving the prison system
   e. solving the urban crisis
   f. protecting the environment
   g. working for peace in the world
   h. balancing the federal budget
   i. dealing with big business
   j. protecting the interests of the consumer
   k. dealing with health problems
   l. assisting the poor
   m. improving our educational system

References

Sources of particular interest to the reader are marked with an asterisk.

Abernathy, M. Women judges in United States courts. *Women Lawyers Journal*, 1969, 57, 57–58.
*Andersen, K. Working women and political participation, 1952–1972. *American Journal of Political Science*, 1975, 19, 439–453.
Babchuk, N., Marsey, R., & Gordon, W. Men and women in community agencies: A note on power and prestige. *American Sociological Review*, 1960, 25, 399–403.

Barber, J. *The lawmakers*. New Haven: Yale University Press, 1965.

Bernstein, R. A., & Polly, J. D. Race, class and support for female candidates. *Western Political Quarterly*, 1975, 28, 733–736.

Blondel, J. *Voters, parties and leaders*. Baltimore: Penguin, 1963.

Bullock, C., & Heys, P. Recruitment of women for Congress: A research note. *Western Political Quarterly*, 1972, 25, 416–423.

The Bureaucrat, 1972, 1, 212–213.

Campbell, A., Converse, P., Miller, W., & Stokes, D. *The American voter*. New York: Wiley, 1960.

Campbell, A., Gurin, G., & Miller, W. *The voter decides*. Evanston, Ill.: Row, Peterson, 1954.

Campbell, V., Ferris, M., & Nichols, D. National assessment report 6, 1969–70 citizenship group results for sex, region and size of community. Denver: Education Commission of the States, 1971.

Chamberlin, H. *A minority of members: Women in the U.S. Congress*. New York: Praeger, 1973.

Congressional Quarterly Almanac, 1972, p. 1035.

*Costantini, E., & Craik, K. Women as politicians: The social background, personality, and political careers of female party leaders. *Journal of Social Issues*, 1972, 28, 217–236.

Cotter, C., & Hennessy, B. *Politics without power: The national party committees*. New York: Atherton, 1964.

*Darcy, R., & Schramm, S. S. When women run against men. *Public Opinion Quarterly*, 1977, 41, 1–12.

David, P. T., Goldman, R. M., & Bain, R. C. *The politics of national party conventions*. Washington, D.C.: Brookings Institution, 1960.

*Duverger, M. *The political role of women*. Paris: UNESCO, 1955.

Erskine, H. The polls: Women's role. *Public Opinion Quarterly*, 1971, 35, 275–290.

Fengler, A. *Women in state politics: Why so few?* Unpublished manuscript, Middlebury College, Middlebury, Vt., 1973.

Fields, D. A case of non-feasance. *The Bureaucrat*, 1972, 1, 226–234.

Flesch, N. Her honor, the mayor in 112 cities. *American City*, 1965, 80, 110.

Foote, F. *Role stress and cultural resources: A study of the role of the woman member of Congress*. Unpublished doctoral dissertation, Michigan State University, East Lansing, Mich., 1967.

Gehlen, F. Foote. *Women members of Congress: A distinctive role*. Paper presented at the meeting of the Southwestern Social Science Association, San Antonio, Texas, March 1972.

*Gehlen, F. Foote. Legislative role performance of female legislators. *Sex Roles*, 1977, 3, 1–17.

Good, J. *The history of women in Republican national conventions and women in the Republican National Committee*. Washington, D.C.: Women's Division, Republican National Committee, 1963.

Grafton, S. Women in politics: The coming breakthrough. *McCall's*, September 1962, pp. 102–103; 156; 158; 160.

Green, A., & Melnick, E. What has happened to the feminist movement? In A. Gouldner (Ed.), *Leadership and democratic action*. New York: Harper & Bros., 1950.

Greenstein, F. *Children and politics*. New Haven: Yale University Press, 1965.

*Gruberg, M. *Women in American politics: An assessment and sourcebook*. Oshkosh, Wis.: Academia Press, 1968.

Harris, L. *Is there a Republican majority?* New York: Harper, 1954.

Harris, L. *The 1972 Virginia Slims American women's opinion poll: A survey of the attitudes of women on their roles in politics and the economy*. New York: Louis Harris and Associates, 1972.

Harris, L. *The anguish of change*. New York: Norton, 1973.

Hennessy, B. Politicals and apoliticals. *Midwest Journal of Political Science*, 1958, 3, 336–355.

Hess, R., & Torney, J. *The development of political attitudes in children*. Chicago: Aldine, 1967.

Jacklin, C. N., & Mischel, H. N. As the twig is bent—Sex role stereotyping in early readers. *School Psychology Digest*, 1973, 2, 30–37.

*Jaquette, J. (Ed.). *Women in politics*. New York: Wiley, 1974.

*Jaquette, J. Political science. *Signs: Journal of Women in Culture and Society*, 1976, 2, 147–161.

Jennings, K., & Langton, K. Mothers versus fathers: The formation of political orientations among young Americans. *Journal of Politics*, 1969, 31, 329–357.

*Jennings, K., & Thomas, N. Men and women in party elites. *Midwest Journal of Politics*, 1968, 12, 469–492.

Judges: Her honor takes the bench. *Time*, January 29, 1965, p. 41.

Karnig, A. K., & Walter, O. Elections of women to city councils. *Social Science Quarterly*, 1976, 56, 605–613.

*Kirkpatrick, J. *Political woman*. New York: Basic Books, 1974.

*Kirkpatrick, J. *The new presidential elite: Men and women in national politics*. New York: Russell Sage Foundation and the Twentieth Century Fund, 1976.

Kruschke, E. Level of optimism as related to female political behavior. *Social Sciences*, 1966, 41, 67–75.

Lamson, P. *Few are chosen: American women in political life today*. Boston: Houghton Mifflin, 1968.

Lane, R. *Political life*. Glencoe, Ill.: Free Press, 1959.

*Lansing, M. The American woman: Voter and activist. In J. Jacquette (Ed.), *Women in politics*. New York: Wiley, 1974.

*Lansing, M. The voting patterns of American Black women. In M. Githens & J. Prestage (Eds.), *A portrait of marginality: The political behavior of the American woman*. New York: McKay, 1977.

Lee, M. *Towards understanding of why few women hold public office: Factors affecting the participation of women in local politics*. Paper presented at the meeting of the American Political Science Association, Chicago, September 1974.

*Lee, M. Why few women hold public office: Democracy and sexual roles. *Political Science Quarterly*, 1976, 91, 297–314.

Lepper, M. *Women: Their status, achievements and the future—A view from the federal service*. Paper presented at the meeting of the American Political Science Association, Washington, D.C., September 1972.

*Levitt, M. The political role of American women. *Journal of Human Relations*, 1967, 15, 23–25.

Lipman-Blumen, J. Role de-differentiation as a system response to crisis: Occupational and political roles of women. *Sociological Inquiry*, 1973, 43, 105–129.

Lipset, S. M. The British voter: II. Sex, age and education. *The New Leader*, November 21, 1960, pp. 15–20.

Lynn, N., & Flora, C. Child-bearing and political participation: The changing sense of self. Paper presented at the meeting of the American Political Science Association, Washington, D.C., September 1972.

Maccoby, E., & Jacklin, C. *The psychology of sex differences*. Stanford, Calif.: Stanford University Press, 1974.

Maccoby, E., Matthews, R., & Morton, A. Youth and political change. *Public Opinion Quarterly*, 1953, 18(4), 23–39.

March, J. Husband-wife interaction over political issues. *Public Opinion Quarterly*, 1953, *17*(4), 461–470.

Markoff, H. Signposts of success. *The Bureaucrat*, 1972, *1*, 219–225.

Mason, K. O. *Sex-role attitude items and scales from U.S. sample surveys.* Washington, D.C.: National Institute of Mental Health, 1975.

Matthews, D., & Prothro, J. *Negroes and the new Southern politics.* New York: Harcourt, Brace & World, 1966.

* McGrath, W., & Soule, J. Rocking the cradle or rocking the boat: Women at the 1972 Democratic national convention. *Social Science Quarterly*, 1974, *55*, 141–150.

*McWilliams, N. Contemporary feminism, consciousness-raising and changing views of the political. In J. Jaquette (Ed.), *Women in politics.* New York: Wiley, 1974.

Murphy, I. *The impact of women's groups on national policy on the status of women.* Washington, D.C.: Center for Women Policy Studies, 1973.

National Welfare Rights Organization. *All about NWRO.* (Pamphlet distributed by the NWRO.) n.d.

National Women's Political Caucus. *Women in elected office fact sheet.* Washington, D.C., 1973.

Nogee, P., & Levin, M. Some determinants of political attitudes among college voters. *Public Opinion Quarterly*, 1959, *22*, 449–463.

Oktay, J. *Women in politics or women's politics? The growth of a woman's political caucus in a new town.* Paper presented at the meeting of the Southern Political Science Association, Atlanta, November 1972.

Orum, A., Cohen, R., Grasmuch, S., & Orum, A. Sex, socialization and politics. *American Journal of Sociology*, 1974, *39*, 197–209.

Otten, A. Politics and people. *Wall Street Journal*, August 9, 1973, p. 1.

Paxton, A. *Women in Congress.* Richmond, Va.: Dietz Press, 1945.

Pomper, G., with Baker, R. K., Jacob, C. E., McWilliams, W. C., & Plotkin, H. A. *The election of 1976.* New York: McKay, 1977.

Republican National Committee, Political Research Division. *1972 election summary.* Washington, D.C., n.d.

Riesman, D. Orbits of tolerance: Interviewers and elites. *Public Opinion Quarterly*, 1956, *20*, 49–73.

Rosenberg, M. *Political efficacy and sex role: Case study of Congresswomen Edith Green and Julia Butler Hansen.* Paper presented at the meeting of the American Political Science Association, Washington, D.C., September 1972.

Rothschild, J. *On building a female constituency: The case of Massachusetts.* Boston: Women's Research Center, 1972.

Rothschild, J. *On building a female constituency: Part two. The women's lobby in Massachusetts.* Paper presented at the meeting of the Northeastern Political Science Association, Buck Hills Falls, Pa., November 1973.

Rubin, C. Where are the women in management? *Public Management*, 1973, *55*, 8–9.

Seifer, N. *Nobody speaks for me: Self portraits of American working class women.* New York: Simon and Schuster, 1976.

Shaffer, H. Status of women. *Editorial Research Reports*, 1970, *2*, 565–585.

*Shanley, M. L., & Schuck, V. In search of political woman. *Social Science Quarterly*, 1974, *55*, 632–644.

*Sigelman, L. The curious case of women in state and local government. *Social Science Quarterly*, 1976, *56*, 591–604.

Steinem, G. Women voters can't be trusted. *Ms.*, July 1972, p. 47.

Stewart, A. Feminine city managers. *American City*, 1964, 79, 154–156.

Stiehm, J., & Scott, R. *Female and male voluntary and chosen participation: Sex, SES and participation*. Paper presented at the meeting of the American Political Science Association, Chicago, September 1974.

Stouffer, S. *Communism, conformity and civil liberties: A cross-section of the nation speaks its mind*. New York: Wiley, 1955.

*Tolchin, S., & Tolchin, M. *Clout: Womanpower and politics*. New York: Coward, McCann and Geoghegan, 1974.

U.S. Bureau of the Census. *Voter participation in the national election, November 1964* (Current Population Reports, Series P-20, No. 143). Washington, D.C.: U.S. Government Printing Office, 1965.

U.S. Bureau of the Census. *Voting and registration in the election of November 1968* (Current Population Reports, Series P-20, No. 192). Washington, D.C.: U.S. Government Printing Office, 1969.

U.S. Bureau of the Census. *Census of the population: 1970. Occupation by industry*. Final Report PC(2)—7C. Washington, D.C.: U.S. Government Printing Office, 1972.

U.S. Bureau of the Census. *Voting and registration in the election of November 1972* (Current Population Reports, Series P-20, No. 253). Washington, D.C.: U.S. Government Printing Office, 1973.

U.S. Bureau of the Census. *Voter participation in November 1976* (Current Population Reports, Series P-20, No. 304). Washington, D.C.: U.S. Government Printing Office, 1977.

U.S. Department of Labor, Bureau of Labor Statistics. *Special labor force report* (July 1975). Washington, D.C.: 1975.

U.S. Department of Labor, Women's Bureau. *Women workers today*. Washington, D.C.: 1976.

U.S. President. *Economic report of the President*. Washington, D.C.: U.S. Government Printing Office, 1973.

U.S. President's Commission on the Status of Women. *American women*. Washington, D.C.: U.S. Government Printing Office, 1963.

Van Helden, M. *Women in the United States Congress*. Washington, D.C.: Congressional Research Service, Library of Congress, 1971.

Wahlke, J., Eulau, H., Buchanan, W., & Ferguson, L. *The legislative system: Explorations in legislative behavior*. New York: Wiley, 1962.

Warner, L., Van Riper, P., Martin, N., & Collins, O. *The American federal executive*. New Haven: Yale University Press, 1963.

*Wells, A., & Smeal, E. Women's attitudes toward women in politics: A survey of urban registered voters and party committee women. In J. Jaquette (Ed.), *Women in politics*. New York: Wiley, 1974.

*Werner, E. Women in Congress: 1917–1964. *Western Political Quarterly*, 1966, 19, 16–30.

*Werner, E. Women in the state legislatures. *Western Political Quarterly*, 1968, 21, 40–50.

*Werner, E., & Bachtold, L. *Personality characteristics of women in American politics*. Paper presented at the meeting of the American Political Science Association, Washington, D.C., September 1972.

Witcover, J. 1974 may be the year for women in politics. (Louisville) *Courier-Journal and Times*, June 23, 1974, p. G-10.

Women in politics—They're moving into the front ranks. *U.S. News & World Report*, August 23, 1976, pp. 18–19.

Young, L. *Understanding politics*. New York: Pelligrini and Cadahy, 1950.

Zeigler, H. *The political life of American teachers*. Englewood Cliffs, N.J.: Prentice-Hall, 1967.

SECTION SIX

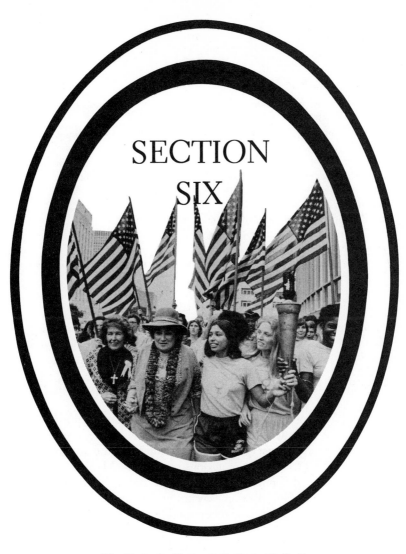

CONCLUSION

Where is it written

That husbands get twenty-five dollar lunches and invitations to South America for think
  conferences while

Wives get Campbell's black bean soup and a trip to the firehouse with the first grade and

Where is it written

That husbands get to meet beautiful lady lawyers and beautiful lady professors of Ancient
  History and beautiful sculptresses and heiresses and poetesses while

Wives get to meet the checker with the acne at the Safeway and

Where is it written

That husbands get a nap and the Super Bowl on Sundays while

Wives get to help color in the coloring book and

Where it is written

That husbands get ego gratification, emotional support, and hot tea in bed for ten days when
  they have the sniffles while

Wives get to give it to them?

And if a wife should finally decide

Let him take the shoes to the shoemaker and the children to the pediatrician and the dog to
  the vet while she takes up something like brain surgery or transcendental meditation,

Where is it written

That she always has to feel

Guilty?[1]

This whimsical poem by Judith Viorst reflects some of the same concerns that this
book does. Where *is* it written that men and women have different needs, dirrerent responsibilities, and different roles? And where *is* it written that the wife in the poem cannot
also be the beautiful lady lawyer or professor in the poem? Many people would say it is
written in the biological differences between females and males, or in the ways they are
raised, or in the structure of society. Some say it is written in the Bible. Some say it is etched
in the irrational prejudices of men who control things. Some say it is not written at all.

These opinions, like the poem, have strong emotional content. And yet, as we have
shown in this book, there is at least some factual basis for each. However, it is important
not to overemphasize any one set of factors or oversimplify what is in reality a complex
situation. It may be reassuring to rely on simple explanations, but they are not adequate.
The findings presented in this book demonstrate the need for explanations that encompass
many factors.

What must be stressed in explaining female behavior is a process of interaction
between the individual and society. We begin with an individual who is biologically a

Section opening photo: The International Women's Year torch began its journey in Seneca Falls, New
York, and ended it in Houston, Texas, on November 17, 1977. Pictured here leading the parade are, from left to
right, Billie Jean King, tennis pro; Susan B. Anthony, grandniece of the suffragist; Bella Abzug, chair of the
International Women's Year convention; Sylvia Ortez, University of Houston track star; and Peggy Kokernot,
marathon runner. (Photo by Wide World Photos.)

[1]From *It's Hard to Be Hip over Thirty and Other Tragedies of Married Life*, by J. Viorst. Copyright ©
1968 by Judith Viorst. Reprinted by permission of W. W. Norton & Co., Inc.

female. This biological being interacts with the society into which she is born. That is, she is affected by the society, and she responds to it. The particular structure of the society—a product of historical, cultural, and technological forces—governs the options available to each individual woman. She responds on the basis of her particular set of learned and biological experiences. Clearly, the pattern of learned and biological factors differ somewhat for each individual. For example, some women are born into middle-class families, and others are born into working-class families. As a result, many of their experiences are different. Some women are tall, and some are short. Tall women may have different options and experiences than short women. In such ways, the interaction of biology, the social learning process, and social structure accounts for both similarities and differences among women.

Obviously, this interactive process also accounts for similarities and differences among men and—more to the point of this book—the similarities and differences between men and women. The structure of society offers different sets of options for women and men. Even where major aspects of the environment are comparable, the learned experiences of men and women differ in important ways. For example, a brother and sister born into a middle-class family will have different experiences than will a brother and sister born into a working-class family. At the same time, the experiences of the sister will differ from those of her brother in both families. Within the family, the school, and other social institutions, there is a different set of expectations, rewards, and penalties for each sex.

We have identified three major aspects of interaction: biology, the social learning process, and social structure. Now let us consider the significance of each of these major factors in greater detail, focusing more specifically on how each affects behavior.

Biology

As we indicated in Section 2, biology is not destiny, but biology does play a role in what each of us is. There are obvious differences in male and female anatomy. These obvious differences do not have to lead to different roles for men and women, even when we consider the most dramatic biological difference—the ability of women to bear children. Nature does not require that the person who bears the children must also raise them. Our society has done that. In other societies, older children, co-wives, servants, and even fathers are assigned the child-rearing role. The different roles of men and women in our society are the result of the way in which our society has responded to and built upon these biological differences.

In the same way, society has responded to other biological differences that are less obvious. When society builds upon biological differences, it becomes very difficult to distinguish the learned influences from the biological ones. This is one reason why social scientists are still unable to assess the separate effects of each type of factor.

What biological factors affect behavior? Certainly there are many, but for our purpose in explaining differences in male and female behavior, some have a more significant effect than others. Apart from the obvious anatomical distinctions, the most important of these biological differences include sex hormones, rate of maturation, and development of the brain.

Section 2 gave many examples of behavioral differences in which sex hormones play a part, though the full scope of their impact on behavior is not yet known. It appears, for example, that hormonal differences contribute to the greater physical aggressiveness of boys. Our society reinforces this tendency by approving of aggressive behavior in boys and frowning upon it in girls.

A number of measures of verbal ability show that females develop this ability more rapidly than do males. Biological factors contribute to this verbal superiority in females. Females mature overall at a faster rate than males and develop dominance of the verbal half of the brain earlier than males. Beginning even in infancy, society reinforces this verbal development in females. However, it is interesting to note that society later fails to make full use of these verbal abilities of females: jobs requiring verbal skills, such as journalist, preacher, newscaster, and political speech writer, are overwhelmingly held by men.

Biological factors have a continuing influence. They are present throughout life, although the importance of any given factor for an individual is likely to change over time. Because social factors also are present through the life cycle, there is continual interaction between biology and society. In terms of society, two factors are critical to the interaction process. One is the social learning process, and the other is the social structure.

The Social Learning Process

The social learning process, or socialization, is a key to understanding the interaction between the individual and society. Socialization is the process by which members of a society learn what is proper in various situations—proper subjects to study in school, proper games to play, proper clothes to wear, proper life goals to pursue. The kinds of studies, interests, and ways of handling situations that our society deems proper for girls and women turn out to be ones that prepare them for their expected roles, rather than leading them to run for mayor or become an electrician. They lead to careers in helping others, to activities that emphasize support and caring, and to goals that amount to being the power behind the person in the front office or driver's seat.

Socialization clearly contributes to an explanation of why most women choose to become wives and mothers and most employed women choose fields such as elementary teaching, nursing, and clerical work. It contributes to an explanation of why women participate in community organizations, vote, and support candidates, but men occupy the majority of elected and appointed decision-making positions. And it contributes to our understanding of why women are more concerned with public issues such as war, violence, and discrimination, and less concerned about economic issues, than men.

Women who want to pursue nontraditional roles and careers find themselves limited by the socially learned attitudes of others—attitudes about what certain jobs require and how certain people behave. The woman who would be governor must overcome beliefs of party officials, campaign donors, and ultimately voters, that women are incapable of good leadership. The woman who applies for a training program for highly skilled craft work, such as tool and die making, or for middle management must overcome the beliefs of employers that women are not suited for such jobs.

Once past the stereotyped ideas of others, women may still be thwarted by customary arrangements stemming from how things have always been done. There may not be female restroom facilities on the shop floor. Policy decisions are frequently made at the athletic club. Studies of women in government and industry have shown that such arrangements make it harder for a woman to do her job once she has the job.

Social Structure

The lives of women in general and the options available to individual women are affected not only by biological factors and socialization, but also by the broad processes and institutions that we call social structure. Economic forces, for example, which are among the components of social structure, affect women's employment options. Thus, employers have historically been more open to the hiring of women in periods when the number of jobs available was growing more rapidly than the supply of male workers.

The way in which roles are distributed is another aspect of social structure and one that is crucial in understanding the lives of women. In Chapter 7, we defined *role* as a set of rights, duties, and expectations associated with a particular position in society. Each person always has several roles. In our society, a woman is generally expected to fulfill such roles as daughter, wife, mother, volunteer, and neighbor.

Some of these roles have a wider impact on the lives of women than do others. For example, we have found that motherhood has a more dramatic effect on the lives of women than does marriage. So long as she has preschool-age children, a woman is likely to withdraw from many time-consuming and formal activities of social life. She votes less often, she is less likely to be employed, and she participates less in community activities. When the children reach school age, she frequently seeks full- or part-time employment or returns to school herself. She is also more likely to resume the round of organizational and recreational activities common to members of her social class.

The impact of motherhood is far-reaching. We have seen, for example, that women elected to Congress for the first time are older, on the average, than their male counterparts. Member of Congress is one of many roles requiring a kind of flexibility that is difficult to achieve if one is also taking primary responsibility for a household with school-age children.

When the children leave home, many women experience what social scientists have labeled the empty-nest syndrome. This decrease in the demands of the motherhood role comes at about the same time as, and may be complicated by, the change in hormones accompanying menopause. Thus, middle age often finds those women who have devoted their lives to home and family without a focus. Although emotional and physical problems need not accompany menopause or seeing one's children leave the nest, there is an increase in problems such as alcoholism and mental depression among some women at this time.

Role expectations are influenced by such factors as economic and technological trends. We have seen how these have affected the roles of women in the home and the marketplace. Work and home are now more separated than they were when most people lived on farms or operated small family-owned businesses. When most families lived above their shops or on farms, women found it easier to combine income-earning and household roles. In urban industrial societies, where stores, offices, and factories are miles away from home, and someone needs to mind the baby or wait for the plumber, it is easier for one family member to assume the wage-earning burdens and the other the home burdens. Thus, the norm for our society has become that men go out to work and women stay home to work. This is no longer the dominant pattern in fact, but large percentages of people who are polled still say that this is a desirable arrangement.

Despite the attitudes reflected in the polls, more women are assuming the role of paid worker, for several reasons. First, the demand for typists, clerks, and first-grade teachers—jobs that men are neither willing to fill nor trained to fill—has increased throughout much of this century. Second, families want to live comfortably, have a few luxuries, and provide college educations for their children. These goals are far more likely to be reached if both husband and wife make financial contributions to the family income. Third, we have the technical knowledge to make family planning a practical reality and to insure the survival of most children who are born. This means that the childbearing and infant-rearing phases of women's lives are much shorter and much less physically demanding today than in the past. More time and energy are available for community and labor force activities. Fourth, as women's educational levels have increased, so has their interest in paid employment. Finally, we have the technology to change the nature of work, both inside and outside the home. Most paid work no longer requires great physical strength, household work is relatively routine, and products that used to take hours to make can now be purchased. All of these developments have contributed to the increased labor force participation of women.

In essence, what we have been describing is the process by which a female becomes a woman and the factors that shape what she becomes. This process reflects the influence of both biology and society.

To take the most obvious example, biology endows women with the capacity to bear children. In some ways, our society places a high value on motherhood. However, mothers are not given the rewards—power, property, and prestige—our society values most. Instead, society assumes that motherhood is the ultimate feminine fulfillment, containing its own intrinsic rewards. In accordance with our society's norms and values, most women do choose to have children. Society then defines what is expected of them as mothers. This emphasis on motherhood affects the options, limitations, and decisions women face in most other areas of their lives. Thus, biology, society, and the individual interact to shape women's lives.

A Look Ahead

The outcome of the interaction we have been describing changes over time. As a result, the status and roles of women in our society are changing. Like most social change, these developments have occurred at a slow but continual pace. As we contemplate the nature of these changes, it seems to us that women are not exchanging one set of role obligations for another. Rather, they are adding more roles to their traditional ones of homemaker and mother. Despite their increased levels of education, labor force participation, and involvement in community and political affairs, women still bear the primary responsibility for housework and child care. Men may be assuming more of these responsibilities, but they have yet to accept primary or even equal responsibility for them. Until there is a change in the division of labor within the family, there will not be a fundamental change in the position of women. The more rewarding economic and political positions make demands that impose too high a cost for most women with substantial household obligations.

We do perceive the forerunners of change in the distribution of power within the family. The resources, such as education and income, that husbands and wives bring to the family are becoming more nearly equal. As this happens, the power of the marriage partners becomes more equal, and this, in turn, has an effect on the division of labor within the home. And as the household responsibilities become more evenly divided, women feel freer to assume demanding roles outside the home.

At the same time, the women's movement and the publicity given to its ideas, as well as the experiences of women in the economic and political spheres, are causing more women to reassess their options and roles. This reassessment leads to increased demand for legal, technological, and structural changes that facilitate wider options for women. The availability of these options, in turn, affects the lives of other women. More equitable credit laws, child-care facilities, scholarships for women returning to school, equal-opportunity legislation, and surer, safer means of family planning are among the broad social changes that increase the options available to women.

We expect women's roles and options to continue to expand and women's economic and political positions to improve. But we expect that, for most women, these changes will come very slowly.

NAME INDEX

SUBJECT INDEX

299